Writing and Reading Connections

D1560962

Also Available

Best Practices in Writing Instruction, Third Edition
Edited by Steve Graham, Charles A. MacArthur, and Michael A. Hebert

Design-Based Research in Education: Theory and Applications
Edited by Zoi A. Philippakos, Emily Howell, and Anthony Pellegrino

Developing Strategic Writers through Genre Instruction:
Resources for Grades 3–5
Zoi A. Philippakos, Charles A. MacArthur, and David L. Coker Jr.

Developing Strategic Young Writers through Genre Instruction:
Resources for Grades K–2
Zoi A. Philippakos and Charles A. MacArthur

Differentiated Literacy Instruction in Grades 4 and 5, Second Edition:
Strategies and Resources
*Sharon Walpole, Michael C. McKenna,
Zoi A. Philippakos, and John Z. Strong*

Handbook of Learning Disabilities, Second Edition
Edited by H. Lee Swanson, Karen R. Harris, and Steve Graham

Handbook of Writing Research, Second Edition
Edited by Charles A. MacArthur, Steve Graham, and Jill Fitzgerald

Writing and Reading Connections

Bridging Research and Practice

edited by
Zoi A. Philippakos
Steve Graham

Foreword by Jill Fitzgerald

THE GUILFORD PRESS
New York   London

Copyright © 2023 The Guilford Press
A Division of Guilford Publications, Inc.
370 Seventh Avenue, Suite 1200, New York, NY 10001
www.guilford.com

Printed in the United States of America

This book is printed on acid-free paper.

Last digit is print number: 9   8   7   6   5   4   3   2   1

Library of Congress Cataloging-in-Publication Data is available from the publisher.

ISBN 978-1-4625-5046-3 (paperback)
ISBN 978-1-4625-5050-0 (hardcover)

For my parents,
who taught me the value of writing and reading,
and for my academic parents,
who inspired my academic path

—Zoi

For Leah—
Pagan princess, Celtic warrior, child of mine—
The úll didn't fall far from the tree.

—Dad (Steve)

About the Editors

Zoi A. Philippakos, PhD, is Associate Professor in the Department of Theory and Practice in Teacher Education at The University of Tennessee, Knoxville. Her research interests include reading and writing instruction in K–12 and postsecondary classrooms, strategy instruction with self-regulation, and teacher professional development. Dr. Philippakos is a recipient of the Faculty Research Excellence Award from the College of Education, Health and Human Sciences (2021) and the Provost Award for Professional Promise in Research and Creative Achievement (2022) from The University of Tennessee, as well as the Early Career Achievement Award from the Literacy Research Association. She chaired the Writing Task Force for the International Literacy Association and coauthored a Research Advisory titled *Teaching Writing to Improve Reading Skills*. Dr. Philippakos is coauthor or coeditor of several books and presents her work at national and international conferences.

Steve Graham, EdD, is a Regents Professor and the Warner Professor in the Division of Leadership and Innovation at Mary Lou Fulton Teachers College, Arizona State University. For more than 40 years, he has studied how writing develops, how to teach it effectively, and how it can be used to support reading and learning. Dr. Graham's research involves typically developing writers and students with special needs in both elementary and secondary schools, with much of this research occurring in classrooms in urban schools. Dr. Graham is a recipient of the Thorndike Career Award from Division 15 of the American Psychological Association, the William S. Gray Citation of Merit from the International Literacy Association, and the Exemplary Research in Teaching and Teacher Education Award from Division K of the American Educational Research Association, among other awards. He is the former editor of several journals, including the *Journal of Writing Research*, and is coauthor or coeditor of several books and three influential Carnegie Corporation reports on writing.

Contributors

Laura K. Allen, PhD, Department of Educational Psychology, University of Minnesota, Minneapolis, Minnesota

Pamela Shanahan Bazis, PhD, Department of Theory and Practice in Teacher Education, The University of Tennessee, Knoxville, Knoxville, Tennessee

Alison Boardman, PhD, School of Education, University of Colorado Boulder, Boulder, Colorado

Sybille Bruun, Department of Human Development, Teachers College, Columbia University, New York, New York

Sandra A. Butvilofsky, PhD, School of Education, University of Colorado Boulder, Boulder, Colorado

Huy Q. Chung, PhD, School of Education, University of California, Irvine, Irvine, California

Scott A. Crossley, PhD, Department of Special Education, Vanderbilt University, Nashville, Tennessee

Paul D. Deane, PhD, Educational Testing Service, Princeton, New Jersey

Nell K. Duke, EdD, Combined Program in Education and Psychology, University of Michigan, Ann Arbor, Michigan

Steve Graham, EdD, Mary Lou Fulton Teachers College, Arizona State University, Tempe, Arizona

Mariel Halpern, PhD candidate, Department of Human Development, Teachers College, Columbia University, New York, New York

Anne-Lise Halvorsen, PhD, Department of Teacher Education, Michigan State University, East Lansing, Michigan

Brian Hand, PhD, College of Education, University of Iowa, Iowa City, Iowa

Karen R. Harris, EdD, Educational Leadership and Innovation, Mary Lou Fulton Teachers College, Arizona State University, Tempe, Arizona

Michael A. Hebert, PhD, School of Education, University of California, Irvine, Irvine, California

Young-Suk Kim, EdD, School of Education, University of California, Irvine, Irvine, California

Jenell Krishnan, PhD, Strategic Literacy Initiative, WestEd, Irvine, California

Deanna Kuhn, PhD, Department of Human Development, Teachers College, Columbia University, New York, New York

Catherine Lammert, PhD, Department of Teacher Education, Texas Tech University, Lubbock, Texas

Charles A. MacArthur, PhD, School of Education, University of Delaware, Newark, Delaware

Linda H. Mason, PhD, Helen A. Kellar Institute for Human DisAbilities, George Mason University, Fairfax, Virginia

Margaret G. McKeown, PhD, School of Education, University of Pittsburgh, Pittsburgh, Pennsylvania

Adiba Nusrat, PhD, Forsyth Technical Community College, Winston-Salem, North Carolina

Carol Booth Olson, PhD, School of Education, University of California, Irvine, Irvine, California

Zoi A. Philippakos, PhD, Department of Theory and Practice in Teacher Education, The University of Tennessee, Knoxville, Knoxville, Tennessee

Sarah R. Powell, PhD, Department of Special Education, University of Texas at Austin, Austin, Texas

Abby Reisman, PhD, Graduate School of Education, University of Pennsylvania, Philadelphia, Pennsylvania

Tanya Santangelo, PhD, School of Education, Arcadia University, Glenside, Pennsylvania

Timothy Shanahan, PhD, College of Education, University of Illinois at Chicago, Chicago, Illinois

Allison N. Sonia, PhD, Department of Psychology, Lyon College, Batesville, Arkansas

Foreword

What a wonderful compendium of work on the topic of writing–reading relationships and instruction for practitioners! As I read the chapters of this book, I was amazed at the depth and breadth of coverage for evidence-based activities. Not only is the book jam-packed with loads of practical applications that can be taken to the classroom tomorrow, but chapters also portray supporting research and theory. Moreover, every chapter is written in reader-friendly fashion. I suppose you could pick and choose chapters to read, but I suspect once you dig in, you won't be able to put this book down.

While I read, I was thinking about how so many of the instructional recommendations actually resonate with my own processes and strategies when I'm reading and writing. For instance, several authors reference the use of "mentor texts" and ways in which reading others' writing on a topic can assist one's learning and stimulate generation of new ideas. I find when I'm at an impasse in my own writing, or when I want to elaborate or confirm some ideas, I tend to seek inspiration by reading other authors' works. As I thought about writing this foreword, after reading all of the chapters, I wound my way back through a collection of antecedent works that focused on models and theories of how reading and writing are related (e.g., Ahmed, Wagner, & Lopez, 2014; Berninger, Abbott, Abbott, Graham, & Richards, 2002; Kim, 2020; Tierney & Pearson, 1983). All of those works and more have been mentor texts for me.

Most of all, as I read through the chapters in this book, I was thinking about how classroom teachers might delve into it. I tried to put myself into my shoes from those former days of teaching in the primary grades and as a reading teacher. In some ways, those days are far from view, but in other ways, I can easily imagine myself considering, "How would I use this book to improve my own instruction?" As I leaned into that question, I realized that I've been thinking a lot about how the chapters might be considered in relation to a sort of framework of writing and reading processes, processes that are at the heart of reading and composing.

I want to talk about that framework, but I have to start by saying that after spending several decades as a teacher and researcher, one thing that I know about myself is that I seek structure in just about everything. I'm a Gestaltist at heart. *Gestalt* is a German word that means "configuration." I find comfort and understanding in knowing the elements of something and how the elements fit together. I make sense of parts by considering the greater whole. Here's an example. As a researcher, early on I was interested in ways in which narratives are organized (e.g., Whaley, 1981a, 1981b; Fitzgerald, 1984; Fitzgerald & Teasley, 1986). I realized that elements in a narrative have interdependencies. For instance, certain kinds of problems occur in some settings but not others, and resolutions in narratives can be dependent on qualities of characters. Those interdependencies mean that understanding the whole of a narrative is something greater than simply summing up the parts. Once I had a decent understanding of narrative organization, I was able to think about how to help students to read and write narratives well.

Let me offer another example. Lately, I've been studying vocabulary meaning not as something "captured" in a word, but as something that sits in whole contexts like networks of words (Fitzgerald, Elmore, & Relyea, 2021; Fitzgerald, Elmore, Relyea, & Stenner, 2020). Vocabulary networks are "wholes" that have elements in them (words and connections between words, semantic overlap). In written and oral discourse, a given word is an element that sits in the context of many other words. Often, a given word's meaning is to some degree determined by the company it keeps (e.g., Firth, 1957; Landauer & Dumais, 1997). Word networks inform individual word meanings. In that sense, a word's meaning is, to some degree, dependent on the meanings that words around it bring to that word. So, a word's meaning is, in a way, distributed in the whole of the context. For example, the word *gravity* has several dictionary definitions. One definition is "the force that causes things to fall towards the earth" (Gravity, n.d.). But if *gravity* appears in a science textbook with the words *Newton*, *acceleration*, *friction*, *weightless*, *astronaut*, *space*, and *orbit*, some of that context likely brings added meaning to *gravity*. I won't bore you with more personal examples. I'll just say that the Gestaltist in me has driven a lot of my own thinking about reading and writing processes and products, their relationships, and instruction.

Here's where the Gestalt perspective fits in when I think about reading and writing. I know that a lot of different processes and knowledge are involved in reading and writing. I categorize a whole kit and kaboodle of processes and knowledge and fit them into a sort of orderly array, a "framework." The framework does simplify what is really a very complex process, but it gives me a sense of organization. By organizing the processes and knowledge, I can try to understand the parts in relation to the whole of the framework. Finally, I can think about the elements in the framework as a catalyst for instructional practices.

Figure F.1 shows the framework for reading and writing that I carry around in my mind. The framework reflects a sense of how reading and composing rely on a set of cognitive and social processes and knowledge. I use the word *process* purposefully to contrast with *products* that are often measured in reading performances and written compositions. For instance, students use cognitive and social processes to create meaning when reading, whereas a comprehension score after reading a passage is a product, a result, that reflects the processes and knowledge that were employed during reading. Students use mental and social processes and knowledge to compose an essay, whereas spelling, word diversity, and overall coherence of a composition are products of the processes and knowledge that were used to create the composition.

Early on, my framework was simpler—"bare bones" really (Fitzgerald, 1990). There was the reader, the writer, the text/composition, and the fundamental cognitive processes, but also a focus on readers' and writers' sentiments. I thought quite a bit about how "mind meeting" happens during reading and writing, about ways in which readers and writers navigate meaning-making. Later, together with Tim Shanahan, we put more flesh on the cognitive features (Fitzgerald & Shanahan, 2000). The version in Figure F.1 is the latest version (Fitzgerald, 2013). As several chapter authors note, of course, there are differences between the acts of reading and composing, but for now, I'm just thinking about this set of processes and knowledge from which both reading and writing emerge.

The framework is a "Transactional Universe of Reading and Writing Processes and Knowledge." The word *transactional* is used to convey the philosophical sense that meaning is in the whole of the experience (Cunningham &

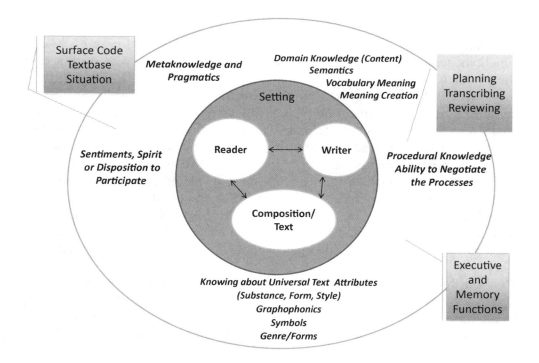

FIGURE F.1. Transactional processes and knowledge in the universe of reading and writing. Reprinted with permission from Fitzgerald (2013). Copyright © 2013 Springer Nature.

Fitzgerald, 1996; Rosenblatt, 1978). The meaning in a reading–writing situation is bound up in the reciprocity among elements in the whole of the experience. Whenever readers read, there is always an author behind the text. Whenever writers write, there is always an imagined reader (though sometimes we do write for ourselves as readers). Readers, writers, and texts together construct knowledge and make meaning and learn. We can take the elements separately and talk about them and teach them, but the meanings that are created during reading and writing arise from the whole experience.

I'll just very briefly describe the elements of the transactional universe. In this book, you'll see classroom activities designed to activate many of the processes and knowledge shown in Figure F.1. I think we are hovering around the same ideas. As I describe elements in the transactional universe, I'll point to some of the overlaps with chapter topics.

Some elements in the transactional universe are cognitive processes and knowledge, and some are social processes and knowledge. I'll start with the cognitive processes and knowledge. The five sets of elements in the outer circle represent mental knowledge that we bring to bear whether we are reading or writing (cf. Fitzgerald & Shanahan, 2000). Metaknowledge and pragmatics include knowledge of functions and purposes of reading and writing, knowledge that authors and readers transact together, and that they use to monitor meaning-making.

Domain knowledge references what someone knows about the content or substance involved in the reading or writing task. Sometimes it is called world knowledge or prior knowledge. For example, McKeown discusses ways in which vocabulary meaning and domain knowledge are central to reading and composing (Chapter 3).

Procedural knowledge means knowing how to access, use, and create knowledge and how to integrate various processes together at once. In Chapter 15, Hebert, Bazis, and Santangelo offer thoughts about procedural knowledge.

To participate in reading and writing, an individual needs to know about the characteristics of texts that would universally be considered to be desirable, for instance, ways in which sounds are commonly meted out in correct spelling patterns, acceptable syntactical arrangements, and how different genres organize elemental information. Several chapters in this book focus on knowledge of universal text attributes. For instance, Kim covers aspects of graphophonics (spelling and word reading) in Chapter 2, and Philippakos addresses genre in Chapter 6.

Last, but not least, spirit or disposition to participate in the universe is a critical element in the universe. Authors such as Olson, Krishnan, and Chung, in Chapter 10, address the issue of motivation. After all, if there is no will to read or write, many of the other knowledge elements are practically unimportant.

The call-out box in the upper left corner of Figure F.1 shows three layers of how meaning and knowledge are mentally represented and activated during reading and writing (Kintsch, 1988): (1) the "surface code" that is the mental representation of the printed words in a text during reading or a composition during composing; (2) a textbase of propositional meanings created in a reader or writer's mind (free of what a printed text looks like); and (3) a mental situation or "microworld" in which propositions are integrated with reader and/or writer knowledge (e.g., domain knowledge or procedural knowledge).

The call-out box in the upper right corner of Figure F.1 references three now well-known procedural "phases" that readers and writers take up during composing—planning (which often involves goal setting and knowledge mobilization in both writing and reading [cf. Tierney & Pearson, 1983]), understanding and generating text, and reviewing and revisioning. Finally, the last call-out box represents other significant cognitive elements that are used during reading and composing, for instance, working memory, self-regulation, executive control over multiple processes, and long-term memory. Several such cognitive elements are touched on in this book. For instance, Harris and Mason discuss self-regulation in Chapter 8.

But that's not all. We readers and writers also use social processes. Social processes in the figure are captured in the setting and two-way arrows. To participate in the universe, readers work to imagine text authors, and writers work to imagine readers as they create compositions. Over 30 years ago, Nystrand (1989) said writers compose on the premises of the reader, and readers read on the premises of the texts' author. "Written communication is a fiduciary act for both writers and readers in which they continuously seek to orient themselves to a projected state of convergence between them" (Nystrand, 1989, p. 75). Also, schools, teachers, and peers can become part of the social fabric of reading and writing because they influence readers and writers. Finally, reading and writing can be considered in relation to ideology and power because schools and classrooms influence ways in which authors and readers are viewed and how teachers teach.

Importantly, the transactional processes and knowledge are deployed whenever an individual reads or writes. So the processes and knowledge are applied during digital reading and writing (which Sonia, Allen, and Crossley discuss in Chapter 9) as well as "hard copy" reading and composing. They are also applied during disciplinary learning. In Chapters 10 through 13, the authors center the reading–composing transactions in language arts, social studies, science, and mathematics. Moreover, the transactional processes and knowledge can be addressed during assessment (Chapter 7) and for specific groups of learners (Chapters 14 through 16).

I might add that with a few exceptions, many, if not most, of the processes and knowledge represented in Figure F.1 likely apply to oral language as well. For instance, "text" and "composition" in the center circle can be oral (without print), and most of the remaining elements apply to oral language as well. Of course, for oracy, knowledge of universal attributes would be free of print, but otherwise the lexical, syntactic, and discourse-level attributes are features of oral language. However, oral language—for example, day-to-day conversation—does not always entail planning, drafting, and/or reviewing. But most of the processes and knowledge in Figure F.1 entail "languaging" processes and knowledge that are meted out in listening, speaking, reading, and writing. In Chapter 4, Kuhn, Halpern, and Bruun address oral dialogic-, discussion-, and debate-oriented instructional practices that would involve many of the elements of the transactional universe.

So, that's my Gestaltist view of the processes and knowledge that are used whether I am reading or composing. When I think about reading and writing instruction, I start with this framework in my mind. I think of the processes and knowledge as sort of modality-free or modality-universal, that is, something that exists with mental representation of some sort that I can nurture through instruction in reading and through instruction in writing. The processes and knowledge are my targets for instruction first, and I then work to figure out instruction that will help students to develop those processes and knowledge during reading and writing.

Clearly, it is very possible to take another approach to instructional practice. Rather than starting with an organizational framework of the transactional processes and knowledge, you might start with assessment of students' products. Perhaps while reading your students' essays, you realize that a group of students could profit from special attention to spelling and to organizational coherence. You know that spelling and organization are factors that enter into students' writing scores on end-of-grade tests. Consequently, you plan spelling and genre instruction in writing. Or, you may notice that some students are having difficulty comprehending grade-level science material. You investigate and perhaps you find that the students are having difficulty reading and understanding multisyllabic words—which may be impeding their comprehension. So, you plan some word-recognition activities during reading lessons for those students. You might or might not integrate some writing into the reading instruction, and you might or might not integrate some reading into the writing instruction.

Thinking about instruction in this way entails a "functional," "utilitarian," "practical" instructional approach. The functional approach is a very reasonable and common one. We teach in reading to improve students' reading. We teach in writing to improve students' writing. Then, as chapter authors in this book point out, what we teach in reading can, and does on average, impact students' writing, and what we teach in writing can, and does on average, impact students' reading. For example, in Chapter 5, Graham and Nusrat offer writing activities that will also promote reading comprehension. Shanahan closes Chapter 1 in favor of integrating writing into reading-focused activity and vice versa.

Some chapter authors address the question "How can what is taught in reading transfer to writing, and how can what is taught in writing transfer to reading?" One conjecture is that it happens because the instructional methods used are actually targeting and nurturing students' mental cognitive and social *processes* and *knowledge* that are in some sense either modality-free or modality-universal. The intention in teaching spelling or genre or comprehension may be primarily focused on the products—better spelling and improved organization in compositions, better reading comprehension. But perhaps what the instruction actually impacts is some element(s) in the transactional universe of processes and knowledge. If that is the case, then the underlying cognitive and social knowledge and processes learned in one modality can be meted out in either reading or composing regardless of which modality was originally used in instruction.

A good friend and I once studied this proposition as she taught first-grade children (Fitzgerald & Ramsbotham, 2004). We found that if she focused on some particular knowledge development first in reading instruction (for instance, the sound–symbol relationships between a particular set of sounds and letters), soon after that instruction, the knowledge was manifested in a child's writing even when it hadn't been taught in writing. But if she taught the knowledge first in writing, soon after it was taught in writing, it was manifested in a child's reading. So it wasn't the special connection to a modality—learning in reading or learning in writing—that mattered so much, but rather it was the actual learning of the modality-free or modality-universal knowledge and processes.

Still, that's just one study, and there is some contrary evidence that suggests the possibility that in the elementary grades some processes and knowledge learned in reading tend to be taken up in writing more so than the reverse case (Ahmed et al., 2014; Kim, Petscher, Wanzek, & Al Otaiba, 2018). I do wonder about the impact of instruction on that finding about directionality—because reading tends to be emphasized more than writing in schooling. Could that common instructional phenomenon influence the directional effect?

I hope that my Gestaltist view of reading and writing processes might in some way serve as a frame for you as you read the chapters in the book and consider new instructional activities for your classroom. Perhaps the transactional universe perspective might serve as a sort of graphic organizer to situate chapter authors' content in relation to the targeted processes and knowledge in Figure F.1. The chapters are replete with theory- and evidence-based activities. I suspect that when you complete the book, you will figure out how to scope and sequence the many practices you will choose to implement in your own classroom. I wonder which of the practices you will use first, then second, and so on. I guess my Gestaltist compulsion is taking over again.

JILL FITZGERALD, PhD
University of North Carolina at Chapel Hill

REFERENCES

Ahmed, Y., Wagner, R. K., & Lopez, D. (2014). Developmental relations between reading and writing at the word, sentence, and text levels: A latent change score analysis. *Journal of Educational Psychology, 106*(2), 419–434.

Berninger, V. W., Abbott, R. D., Abbott, S. P., Graham, S., & Richards, T. (2002). Writing and reading: Connections between language by hand and language by eye. *Journal of Learning Disabilities, 35*(1), 39–56.

Cunningham, J. W., & Fitzgerald, J. (1996). Epistemology and reading. *Reading Research Quarterly, 31*(1), 36–60.

Firth, J. R. (1957). A synopsis of linguistic theory 1930–1955. *Studies in Linguistic Analysis*, pp. 1–32.

Fitzgerald, J. (1984). The relationship between reading ability and expectations for story structures. *Discourse Processes, 7*(1), 21–41.

Fitzgerald, J. (1990). Reading and writing as mind meeting. In T. Shanahan (Ed.), *Reading and writing together* (pp. 81–97). Columbus, OH: Christopher-Gordon.

Fitzgerald, J. (2013). Constructing instruction for struggling writers: What and how. *Annals of Dyslexia, 63*(1), 80–95.

Fitzgerald, J., Elmore, J., & Relyea, J. E. (2021). Academic vocabulary networks matter for students' disciplinary learning. *The Reading Teacher, 74*(5), 569–579.

Fitzgerald, J., Elmore, J., Relyea, J. E., & Stenner, A. J. (2020). Domain-specific vocabulary network development in elementary years. *Journal of Educational Psychology, 112*(5), 855–879.

Fitzgerald, J., & Ramsbotham, A. (2004). First graders' cognitive and strategic development in Reading Recovery reading and writing. *Reading Research and Instruction, 44*(1), 1–31.

Fitzgerald, J., & Shanahan, T. (2000). Reading and writing relations and their development. *Educational Psychologist, 35*(1), 39–50.

Fitzgerald, J., & Teasley, A. B. (1986). Effects of instruction in narrative structure on children's writing. *Journal of Educational Psychology, 78*(6), 424–432.

Gravity. (n.d.). Merriam Webster. Retrieved from *www.merriam-webster.com/dictionary/gravity*.

Kim, Y.-S. G. (2020). Interactive dynamic literacy model: An integrative theoretical framework for reading-writing relations. In R. A. Alves, T. Limp, & R. M. Joschi (Eds.), *Reading–writing connections: Towards integrative literacy science* (pp. 11–34). Cham, Switzerland: Springer Nature.

Kim, Y.-S. G., Petscher, Y., Wanzek, J., & Al Otaiba, S. (2018). Relations between reading and writing: A longitudinal examination from grades 3 to 6. *Reading and Writing, 31*(7), 1591–1618.

Kintsch, W. (1988). The role of knowledge in discourse comprehension: A construction–integration model. *Psychological Review, 95*(2), 163–182.

Landauer, T. K., & Dumais, S. T. (1997). A solution to Plato's problem: The Latent Semantic Analysis theory of acquisition, induction, and representation of knowledge. *Psychological Review, 104*(2), 211–240.

Nystrand, M. (1989). A social-interactive model of writing. *Written Communication, 6*, 66–85.

Rosenblatt, L. M. (1978). *The reader the text the poem: The transactional theory of the literary work*. Carbondale and Edwardsville: Southern Illinois University Press.

Tierney, R. J., & Pearson, P. D. (1983). Toward a composing model of reading. *Language Arts, 60*(5), 568–580.

Whaley, J. F. (1981a). Readers' expectations for story structure. *Reading Research Quarterly, 17*(1), 90–114.

Whaley, J. F. (1981b). Story grammar and reading instruction. *The Reading Teacher, 34*(7), 762–771.

Preface

Writing and reading, reading and writing. Intuitively, the two activities are interconnected and interrelated. Readers write, and writers read their work. However, learning how to write does not necessarily mean one will be a frequent or enthusiastic reader, and learning to read can occur without learning to write. We can engage in writing without putting pen to paper, and we can write something without reading other material about the topic—or even what we wrote. Even so, when we use reading and writing in tandem to achieve our objectives, it can have a powerful effect (Tierney & Shanahan, 1991). This is evident when adults in their professional roles read information and take notes to understand or remember information they plan to use now or at a later time. It is also evident in school settings. From as early as kindergarten all the way through college, students use reading and writing together to learn content across different disciplines and contexts.

Because of the importance of writing and reading to academic progress and in our professional life, it seems logical that they both would receive equal attention in schools and be taught together. However, this is not the case in many classrooms; writing and reading often exist in silos. Indeed, for years reading and writing have been taught and treated as separate subject areas (Nelson & Calfee, 1998), as if they involved different skills and processes. Instructional schedules in many classrooms provided "boxed time" for the instruction of each without connections being made between writing and reading so that the teaching of each supported the learning of the other.

As a result of this disconnect between writing and reading instruction, many students learn to read, but little attention is placed on teaching them explicitly crucial aspects of literacy, such as the connections between decoding and encoding. This is essential as it helps young learners understand the alphabetic principle: knowledge of sounds (phonemes) and letters (graphemes) can be used to read and spell words, and taking advantage of the synchrony between them results in better readers and writers (Graham & Santangelo, 2014; Kim,

2020; Ouellette & Sénéchal, 2008). Similarly, students may learn how to read stories, but connections between the stories they read and the ones they and other authors compose are too often ignored. Making these connections allows students to better understand the interconnection between writing and reading and transfer knowledge and skills from one to the other (Klein, 1999). Even though writing and reading are not identical (Fitzgerald & Shanahan, 2000; Grabe & Zhang, 2016), students develop stronger reading and writing skills when they are taught together.

Unfortunately, an instructional divide that promotes the separate teaching of writing and reading persists. One reason this divide exists is because writing and reading are typically taught as different subjects and often at different times during the school day. It also may be the result of limited teacher professional development or teacher preparation by educational preparation providers (EPPs) on writing and reading integrations and on writing-to-learn tasks. A third possible explanation is that scholars studying writing and reading commonly focus on just one of these skills when developing and testing interventions and instructional procedures. Thus, many reading and writing teachers are not equipped with necessary knowledge and theoretical orientation for connecting these two essential skills, viewing themselves as teachers of writing or of reading, but not both.

The purpose of this book is indeed to provide a clear roadmap and the presentation of appropriate instructional activities that will lead teachers, researchers, and graduate learners, who are the future of academia, to better understand the relationships between writing and reading and offer guidelines for conducting instruction that connects both of these skills in classrooms of different grade levels and of different subject areas. It is our wish that this book will stimulate the development of additional research questions and generate studies to move forward the research in writing and reading.

As you read the book, you may wonder why we selected the term *writing and reading connections* instead of *reading and writing connections*, which is more often in use. This was not a typo, but rather a choice. That is, in our research we have seen firsthand the effects of systematic and evidence-based writing instruction on reading achievement (e.g., Graham & Hebert, 2011; Traga Philippakos, 2020a). We have also witnessed instruction that makes direct connections between writing and reading and how it strengthens students' understanding about how to compose and how to make meaning from text they read (Graham et al., 2018; Traga Philippakos & MacArthur, 2020). Finally, we have read research that explains the effects of writing instruction on reading achievement (Graham & Hebert, 2011) and the effects of writing on content learning and application (Graham, Kiuhara, & MacKay, 2020). We are not attempting to shift the attention from one to the other, but rather to point out that *writing matters* and that writing-to-reading connections can improve both (Philippakos, 2021).

We would like to close this section by arguing that the need for reading and writing to be integrated is without a doubt a prominent mandate (Shanahan, 2016), especially when the goal is for writing to be a vehicle for understanding and inquiry across the curriculum. However, for writing to function in this manner, teachers must be provided with time not only to deliver instruction on writing but also to support students' responses to reading (extended and short responses) and reflection for their own learning and goal setting (as readers and writers) (Traga Philippakos, 2020b). National surveys of teachers show that teachers do not spend a lot of time on writing, and when time is spent, it is more focused on instruction and less on student application (Cutler & Graham, 2008; Gilbert & Graham, 2010). Teachers need to have the time and flexibility to make connections between reading and writing (Philippakos & Graham, 2020)—writing and reading that go beyond only scripted programs and curricula. Finally, the research community should further conduct studies that integrate reading and writing and provide teachers with clear procedures and tasks that benefit the growth of both and support students' critical thinking.

Organization of the Book

The book is organized into four parts: Part I provides an introduction to the writing–reading connections, a historical overview of this relationship, and the research foundation for their relationship (Chapter 1). Part II includes specific applications of writing–reading connections in phonics and spelling (Chapter 2), vocabulary (Chapter 3), oral language (Chapter 4), comprehension (Chapter 5), genres and discourse (Chapter 6), assessment (Chapter 7), use of sources (Chapter 8), and digital contexts (Chapter 9). Part III focuses on specific ways that writing–reading connections can be applied in the content areas such as English language arts (Chapter 10), social studies (Chapter 11), science (Chapter 12), and mathematics (Chapter 13). Part IV, the final section of the book, addresses writing–reading connections with specific groups of learners such as second language learners (Chapter 14), struggling learners (Chapter 15), and underprepared college learners (Chapter 16).

ACKNOWLEDGMENTS

We would like to thank our colleagues who responded to our invitation and contributed to the 16 chapters in this book. We are aware that the timing of our request required them to manage the completion of this project in the midst of COVID-19 while they faced personal and professional challenges. We are grateful for their collaboration with us and excited about the wisdom, experience, and work they all brought to the task of developing bridges between writing and reading for the purpose of teaching these skills and using them to enhance students' learning. Their contributions will prepare students to be successful not only in school, but also in the broader context of their social connections and work.

Furthermore, we want to thank Jill Fitzgerald, who has been a consistent proponent of writing and reading connections, and has studied their relationships. Jill nicely threads together the content of all chapters in this book's Foreword, where she interweaves the meaningful relationships between writing, reading, speaking, and

listening. We would also like to thank our families who supported us during the pandemic while we worked and simultaneously faced the personal, health-related, and
professional challenges that the pandemic brought our way. In addition, we thank our
publisher, The Guilford Press, and Senior Editor Craig Thomas for being advocates
of writing and reading connections and for celebrating with us this book's entry into
schools, universities, and homes. In closing, as we do in all our books, we thank the
educators who work with us as they make a difference in developing learners, writers,
readers, and thinkers!

REFERENCES

Cutler, L., & Graham, S. (2008). Primary grade writing instruction: A national survey. *Journal of Educational Psychology, 100*(4), 907–919.

Fitzgerald, J., & Shanahan, T. (2000). Reading and writing relations and their development. *Educational Psychologist, 35*(1), 39–50.

Gilbert, J., & Graham, S. (2010). Teaching writing to elementary students in grades
4–6: A national survey. *The Elementary School Journal, 110*(1), 494–518.

Grabe, W., & Zhang, C. (2016). Reading–writing relationships in first and second
language academic literacy development. *Language Teaching, 49*(3), 339–355.

Graham, S., & Hebert, M. (2011). Writing to read: A meta-analysis of the impact
of writing and writing instruction on reading [Report]. *Harvard Educational
Review, 81*(4), 710–744.

Graham, S., Kiuhara, S., & MacKay, M. (2020). The effects of writing on learning in
science, social studies, and mathematics: A meta-analysis. *Review of Educational
Research, 90*(1), 179–226.

Graham, S., Liu, X., Bartlett, B., Ng, C., Harris, K., Aitken, A., . . . Talukdar, J.
(2018). Reading for writing: A meta-analysis of the impact of reading interventions on writing. *Review of Educational Research, 88*(2), 243–284.

Graham, S., & Santangelo, T. (2014). Does spelling instruction make students better
spellers, readers, and writers? A meta-analytic review. *Reading & Writing: An
Interdisciplinary Journal, 27*(1), 1703–1743.

Kim, Y.-S. G. (2020). Hierarchical and dynamic relations of language and cognitive
skills to reading comprehension: Testing the direct and indirect effects model of
reading (DIER). *Journal of Educational Psychology, 112*(4), 667–684.

Klein, P. (1999). Reopening inquiry into cognitive processes in writing-to-learn. *Educational Psychology Review, 11*(3), 203–270.

Nelson, N., & Calfee, R. C. (1998). *The reading–writing connection*. Chicago: The
University of Chicago Press.

Ouellette, G. P., & Sénéchal, M. (2008). A window into early literacy: Exploring the
cognitive and linguistic underpinnings of invented spelling. *Scientific Studies of
Reading, 12*(2), 195–219.

Philippakos, Z. A. (2021). Writing-reading integration. In S. Parsons & M. Vaughn
(Eds.), *Principles of effective literacy instruction* (pp. 163–180). New York: Guilford Press.

Philippakos, Z. A., & Graham, S. (2020). *Research Advisory: Teaching writing to
improve reading skills*. Newark, DE: International Literacy Association.

Shanahan, T. (2016). Relationships between reading and writing development. In C.
A. MacArthur, S. Graham, & J. Fitzgerald (Eds.), *Handbook of writing research*
(pp. 194–207). New York: Guilford Press.

Tierney, R., & Shanahan, T. (1991). Research on the reading–writing relationship: Interactions, transactions, and outcomes. In R. Barr, M. Kamil, P. Mosenthal, & D. Pearson (Eds.), *The handbook of reading research* (Vol. 2, pp. 246–280). New York: Longman.

Traga Philippakos, Z. A. (2020a). A yearlong, professional development model on genre-based strategy instruction on writing. *The Journal of Educational Research, 113*(3), 177–190.

Traga Philippakos, Z. A. (2020b). Developing strategic learners: Supporting self-efficacy through goal setting and reflection. *The Language and Literacy Spectrum, 30*(1), 1–24.

Traga Philippakos, Z. A., & MacArthur, C. A. (2020). Integrating collaborative reasoning and strategy instruction to improve second graders' opinion writing. *Reading & Writing Quarterly, 36*(4), 379–395.

Contents

Writing and Reading Connections

PART I

INTRODUCTION TO WRITING AND READING CONNECTIONS

CHAPTER 1

The History of Writing and Reading Connections

Timothy Shanahan

The way things are—our current instructional practices, for instance—is often presumed to be the result of long enduring arrangements. It is natural to think that the way we do things now must stretch far into the past, well beyond our own personal admissions to teaching. This makes history appear to be inevitable. But when it comes to how writing is dealt with in America's classrooms—particularly in elementary school, and the integration of writing and reading, such presumptions will be wide of the mark.

This chapter will explore that history. Its purpose is to help teachers contextualize this aspect of their practice. How has writing been dealt with over time? What attention has been paid to the writing–reading relationship and how has that changed? This kind of historical exploration can help us to construct our own professional identities within a changing field. Understanding how things have been, how they have changed in the past, and the reasons for this "progress" can prepare us for the future choices that are sure to come our way. The focus here will be mainly on the pedagogical aspects of the writing–reading connections during the American experience.

Some Preliminaries

Which came first, reading or writing? This is no chicken or egg proposition. It should be obvious that writing had to precede reading at the dawn of history. Writing refers to the use of written symbols to represent ideas and language (Ong, 1982); writing renders language into a form that allows it to be communicated over space or preserved through time (Schmandt-Besserat & Erard, 2008). Human attempts to record ideas were initially limited to cave paintings or the accounting symbols for representing items like sheep or sheaves of wheat. That changed about 5,000 years ago in Mesopotamia (what is now Iraq, Kuwait, Syria, and Turkey).

What changed was that written symbols began to be used to emulate oral language itself—embodying both the sounds of language (the phonemes) and the ways we organize our ideas into sentences (e.g., syntax). This made writing much more useful than its forerunners, but its utility depended on the availability of someone who could read it; an essential feature of any writing system because writing is basically a social agreement. Without this agreement, there can be no communication.

Given that, writing must have come first. Somebody—the unknown person who came up with it in the first place—was able to write. Then in order to make the system work, others had to be taught to read that writing, making it one of the few times in history that learning to write had to come first. Once there was a writing system, then things change. Reading (and readers) tend to take precedence over writing and writers. Fewer writers are needed to make the system work. The advantages of literacy can be enjoyed to a great extent by a society with few writers and many readers. That is almost as true now as it was in 3000 B.C.E., and it may be the major reason why schools continue to emphasize reading over writing, especially early on.

In ancient times, reading usually came before writing in curriculum (Muir, 1984). For example, Quintilian, in 68 C.E., encouraged the teaching of reading and writing, but the sequence introduced young readers to letters and sounds first so that they could make sense of text. Then later, students returned to those letters for tracing practice at the advent of writing. Students went from tracing to copying texts they could already read, and from there to producing their own compositions—transcribing their own thoughts rather than copying someone else's. Nevertheless, this sequence of instruction has been disrupted occasionally throughout history. During the French Revolution, for example, Condorcet proposed an elementary curriculum with equal emphasis on reading and writing and with a simultaneous introduction of these two skills (Duce, 1971). Such instances have been recognized as being sufficiently unusual to invite remark. In the United Kingdom at the dawn of the 18th century, a school organized around the idea of equal tutelage in reading and writing was lauded at the time as a "new principal of instruction" and an "extraordinary discovery" (Ensor, 1811, p. 226). Despite those occasional attempts to alter the sequence of reading and writing, writing tends to follow reading in today's curriculum.

Another fairly consistent historical concern has been the relative difficulty of reading and writing. In ancient times, scribes needed to know not only how to be adept with the agreed-upon written code, but also in how to prepare writing materials—trimming a reed stylus, molding a clay tablet, soaking papyrus, or scraping the entrails off of an animal skin. These technical demands alone made writing harder than reading (one could read without having to slaughter a lamb). Although the technical demands of writing have decreased greatly over the centuries, it continues to be more challenging than reading. According to psychological studies, writing tends to be a somewhat more challenging to develop skill than reading for most students. There are, for instance, fewer children who manage to learn to write well than there are children who learn to read well (Stotsky, 1983). The difficulty of certain cognitive processes, such as dealing with phonology, is greater in writing than reading (Del Campo, Buchanan, Abbott, & Berninger, 2015), and recognition tasks generally are learned more easily than production tasks (Putnam, Ozubko, MacLeod, & Roediger, 2014). Think of the different memory demands between answering multiple-choice questions (recognition) and having to generate answers for questions (production).

Some particular reading and writing tasks may appear to contradict this appraisal of relative difficulty. Reading places specific demands on a reader—the author has made all the choices of content, text structure, and so on. Writing, on the other hand, leaves the choices to the writer. Readers have to negotiate the author's vocabulary choices, no matter how unfamiliar those words may be, whereas writers can stick to word choices with which they feel comfortable. In this example, reading appears to be harder than writing. Despite that sense, the example is a bit misleading. Difficulty involves not just the issue of how one feels affectively about a task but also the criteria that are used to evaluate success. The only reason a reader would need to make sense of the author's vocabulary would be to comprehend the text. What are the criteria for evaluating writing? It is not clear in the example. One possibility might be that readers would evaluate the quality of the composition, considering the writer's diction or word choice. With comparable evaluation criteria, writing will again turn out to be the more demanding skill.

One final basic premise: Reading is a skill that writers must have, if only to monitor success, while readers can usually go about their business without becoming writers. Cognitive analyses of what writers do when composing disclose the importance of reading and rereading to writing (Rijlaarsdam et al., 2005). A writer who cannot reread a composition during and after production will not end up communicating well, while readers can often make sense of a text without resorting to writing.

These basic premises—the relative value of reading and writing, their historical placement within instruction, their comparative difficulty, their dependence on each other—have conspired to relegate writing to a lesser position than reading in the school curriculum. Because of them, reading has usually been introduced earlier and accorded greater attention in the school curriculum. This has tended to mean minimal attention is given to writing—and with little or no writing, there would be no interest in the connection of writing to reading. An examination of the historical record will reveal how and why some of these basic premises have been challenged or reinterpreted to bring writing and reading–writing connections into teaching.

Early American Education

It is often claimed that public education in the American experience began in 1642 with the introduction of compulsory education in Massachusetts

(Cremin, 1970). That pioneering law is widely noted as the original source of the American commitment to universal education in reading, writing, and arithmetic. However, a closer examination of the primary document reveals that this popular claim is not true. The original public education law of the Puritans and their descendants referred to neither writing nor math. The law required that children's education be addressed, "especiallity of their ability to read and understand the principles of religion and the capital lawes of the country" (Whitmore, 1887). Reading was viewed as a necessary support to both religious practice and the duties of citizenship. During that early period, only the New Haven Colony required instruction in both reading and writing, and that was only for boys. Girls were to be taught reading, but not writing. "The sonnes of all the inhabitants within this jurisdiction, shall (under the same penalty) be learned to write a ledgible hand, so soone as they are capable" (Jernegen, 1918, p. 747).

By the 1700s, this particular educational gender bias was still evident in the schools, though many girls may have gained some spelling and handwriting practice in the home. "In America the little girls of colonial times very often wrought out their own primers with needle and thread, in samplers containing the alphabet with vowels and consonants, Bible quotations, prayers, verses, and sometimes illustrations in the various designs and styles of type" (Huey, 1908/1968, p. 247).

At that time, the most widely used schoolbook in American education was the *New England Primer*. In fewer than 100 pages, it led students from alphabet to graduate-level texts on religious creed. This primer was the primary means for teaching reading and yet, it included no writing guidance, even in its most vestigial form (such as transcribing the alphabet or writing one's own name).

However, the *New England Primer* was not without competition in colonial America, and according to Nila Banton Smith (1965), the major alternatives were the spelling books of the time. For example, there was *Instructions for Right Spelling* by George Fox. The aims of this speller were stated forthrightly on the title page: "Instructions for right spelling and plain directions for reading and writing true English" (Smith, 1965, p. 26). Unfortunately, such books did not include much explicit pedagogical guidance. Mainly, according to Smith, the instruction focused on memorization. This speller included three pages of letters, three pages of syllables, several short religious sentences, and various passages taken from scripture, with the writing emphasizing copying in the main. Authors of those early spelling books may have had some notion that copying spellings would improve reading by boosting word memorization; if so, they left no written records of those ideas.

During that period, reading instruction almost always preceded writing, if writing were included at all. And, when penmanship and transcription were included, they were usually separated from reading. In some instances, reading and writing would be taught by different teachers, perhaps even at different places (Monaghan, 1987)! "Seventeenth-century New England sometimes offered separate schools for reading and writing, in accordance with European custom. The writing schools were considered more advanced, included some practice—but typically no instruction—in the rudiments of reading" (Nelson & Calfee, 1998b, p. 3).

At the beginning of the 19th century, a new generation of "spellers" became the predominant means of teaching beginning reading. These spelling books rarely include writing—beyond penmanship. Spelling practice tended to be oral in focus (think of the spelling bee), with an emphasis on articulation rather than writing. Reading, at that time, also had a heavy articulatory emphasis. It was taught first with a spelling book that emphasized letters and syllables and simple brief passages, and this was followed by one or two other books that encouraged the oral reading of more complex texts (Smith, 1965). At that time, writing was more likely to be combined with arithmetic than reading; penmanship exercises were sometimes included in the arithmetic books, but not in the readers. The idea of integrating school subjects was carried out in pursuit of fundamental social purposes rather than any purported psychological similarities (Clifford, 1989). Reading had been taught first for religious purposes and then for political ones (supporting the development of a new republic). Arithmetic and penmanship, on the other hand, were viewed as economic assets, so combining these pedagogically made sense to the textbook writers of that time.

By the mid-1800s, "reading wars" had emerged. Some programs continued to use spelling as the basis of reading instruction, as a precursor to what eventually would become explicit phonics instruction (the oral spelling replaced by letter sounding), and some of these spellers even recommended that students copy sentences from their primers and letters and syllables from the chalkboard (Tower, 1853). Alternative programs emphasized whole word learning, being careful never to ask a student to spell a word "before he has so far learned it to be able to read it" (Huey, 1908/1968, p. 259). In this approach, if there was a relationship between spelling and reading, it was thought to go in one direction only—from reading to writing; reading could benefit spelling but not the opposite. It was this approach that came to dominate American reading instruction during much of the 20th century (Huey, 1908/1968; Smith, 1965).

In the first 250 years of public education in the United States, writing was often excluded from the curriculum altogether, and when it was there, the emphasis was almost entirely on penmanship, copying, and spelling, with little formal attention to composition. If writing contributed to learning to read, it was solely at the initial levels and came mainly through the support it provided to the memorization of letters, syllables, and sentences. By the end of that period, even this very limited role for writing in early literacy development had lost favor in American pedagogy. Students learned to read, and they learned penmanship and spelling, but these realms of instruction were rarely linked explicitly—and composition played almost no role whatsoever.

A notable exception to this saga arose late in the 19th century with the "sentence method" of George L. Farnham (1870/2015). According to Edmund Burke Huey (1908), Farnham experimented with this method in Binghamton, New York schools during the 1870s and it achieved some popularity by 1890:

In using the sentence method, the teacher has come to make much use of the blackboard. A sketch of some object or scene interesting to the child suggests to the child a thought which he expresses in a sentence. The teacher writes this sentence and it is read, naturally with expression since the child's own thought here leads the expression. Other sentences are suggested, written, and read, until perhaps a little story of the picture is finished, all of which the child can soon "read" with natural expression. (Huey, 1908/1968, pp. 273–274)

But even in this instance, though oral composition is seen as the genesis of reading, its purpose is solely to support the initial reading of words—which is gained largely from the memorization that arises from working with the students' oral composition that the teacher has transcribed. The teacher's transcription gives birth to reading, but the students' own writing is not integral to the equation.

In their exceptionally cogent history of the connections between reading and writing, Nelson and Calfee (1998b) point out that the situation had been somewhat different at the college level throughout American history. Colonial colleges taught rhetoric, which focused on writing about literature and other canonical works. By 1890, English had become an established discipline within colleges and universities—with curriculum in language, literature, and composition (especially literature). In 1894, the Committee of Ten was established by the National Education Association to try to reshape the high school experience. It recommended that this college approach be adopted in the American high school, and vaguely encouraged the introduction of writing into the elementary curriculum (though not until third grade, by which time it was assumed the children would have safely learned to read).

The First Half of the 20th Century

The reading–writing relationship in America's schools during the first 60–70 years of the 20th century could be summed up in much the same way as the 19th—very limited attention to writing instruction, except penmanship and spelling; a predominance of reading in both the elementary and secondary (literature) curriculum; and little or no attention to integrating or combining writing and reading instruction.

That summary is not incorrect, but it may be misleading. The reason for this is because it neglects the tensions or dissatisfactions that lingered below the surface of these practices, which were brought about by the opposing forces of progressive education and the scientific measurement movement. Early in the 20th century, progressive educators like John Dewey championed the ideas of hands-on learning, experiential learning, thematic units, critical thinking, and so on. Simultaneously, the scientific measurement movement touted the creation of tests and the value of psychology-based research into learning. Nelson and Calfee (1998b) describe this period as being marked by competing "centripetal" and "centrifugal" forces—the former promoting a more integrated literacy curriculum and the latter bolstering their separation. Though these forces may have pulled in different directions initially, more recently they have come to be allied, which has allowed for clear progress in increasing elementary writing instruction and the integration of reading and writing.

It would be wrongheaded to conclude that there were widespread or extensive commitments to the teaching of writing in America's elementary schools for much of the 20th century, and yet, it would be disingenuous to ignore the ferment that existed. Various pro-writing, pro-integration forces were gathering throughout the 1900s. For instance, although the Committee of Ten had rather confusedly claimed the equal value of reading and writing while arguing for double the instructional time commitment to literature over composition, their pronouncements bore some fruit. High school English departments were reorganized, and their curriculum was built around a foundation of literature instruction. When writing was included at all, it typically came late to the table, and its role was decidedly secondary; writing tended to be an adjunct to the literature program, with students mainly writing about what they had read.

Clifford (1989) tells a complex tale of the decades-long disagreement between the progressives and the measurement experts over the place of writing in the elementary curriculum and whether writing and reading should be connected. She details the historical and economic factors that had long divided reading and writing, and that continued to keep them at arm's length for decades—including the nature of research publication, time demands of classroom instruction, textbook emphasis, assessment and testing resources, and professional organizations.

High school curriculum was influenced to such an extent that some secondary teachers pushed back, a conflict that led to the creation of the National Council of Teachers of English (NCTE), a professional group dedicated to the unification of the English language arts. Drawing heavily on the work of John Dewey and other progressive educators who endorsed child-centered approaches and the engagement of students in purposeful activities that would draw on a combination of school subjects, these teachers argued for a commitment to all of the language arts (including oral language) and for their integration.

But while the formation of the National Council of Teachers of English (NCTE)—and its later expansion to the elementary grades—guaranteed ongoing attention to these issues, it did not necessarily alter the direction of many schools. There were simply more reasons to focus on reading, and more powerful forces for its primary emphasis. The political, economic, and social need for reading in American society continued to grow, while the value of writing was more circumscribed and particular, with many needing reading, and fewer able to benefit directly from being able to write. Within the profession, textbook companies continued to find big markets for programs of reading instruction, and they advocated for a strong reading emphasis. To this day, writing is not a particularly textbook-oriented aspect of the curriculum, so it lacked for economic advocates. Likewise, the testing of reading got off to a much faster start than writing assessment, and the reading scores provided by such tests came to be valued by schools that never bothered to evaluate students' writing. Long before there were official testing mandates, teachers and parents often were informed of how well or poorly their students read without comparable feedback on writing performance. By midcentury, the efforts of the NCTE were matched by those of the International Reading Association (now International Literacy Association), which as its name implies, was focused not on all of the language arts, but on reading specifically.

What of those tensions below the surface? First, there were the efforts to develop reading and spelling tests, and researchers like Ernest Horn who explored the relationship between spelling and reading as early as the 1910s (e.g., Horn, 1926, 1929). These nascent psychological investigations suggested that the abilities to read and spell were intricately connected, a notion that later in the century would contribute to the eventual integration of reading and writing.

Even more exciting were the efforts of Alvina Treut Burrows and her teaching companions who pioneered the idea of teaching writing in the elementary grades (1939). Their book encouraging the instruction of writing went through three editions, an uncommon success at that time. This book claimed that all children wanted to write and that elementary school teachers could create classrooms that would fulfill these desires successfully. Some schools or districts may have taken on this challenge institutionally, but most often it was individual teachers who were enthralled with the idea of bringing writing into their classrooms and who on their own, here and there, took on this challenge.

Single discrete events may look to be significant turning points in history and particular persons may appear to drive those moments: *Pearl Harbor, 9/11, Abraham Lincoln,* and so on. In reality, history is rarely this simple or straightforward. Change most often comes about as a result of a confluence of conflicting incidents and efforts. That certainly has been the case with writing and reading–writing connections. The emergence and expansion of writing in the elementary curriculum and the increased attention to reading–writing connections have neither emerged due to a signal event, nor as the result of the efforts of one or two thought leaders. From 1960 through 2020, the pedagogical ferment of the first half of the century coalesced into the writing instruction that is now offered to millions of children. Figure 1.1 provides a rough timeline of some of the changes that got us here over these past 60 years, and the rest of this chapter provides a more detailed exploration of those more recent events. Despite the timeline—which should provide some sense of sequence—there were actually three lines of advancement: the publication of empirical research that has informed these efforts, the development and adoption of curriculum and testing policies by governments and educational institutions, and the expansion of relevant professional development and publications to encourage and support teachers' efforts. It would be easiest, of course, if research led to institutional change that necessitated professional development for teachers; the reality has been infinitely more complicated, with each new event building on the others and impelling what has followed—with practice leading research and policy as much as following from them.

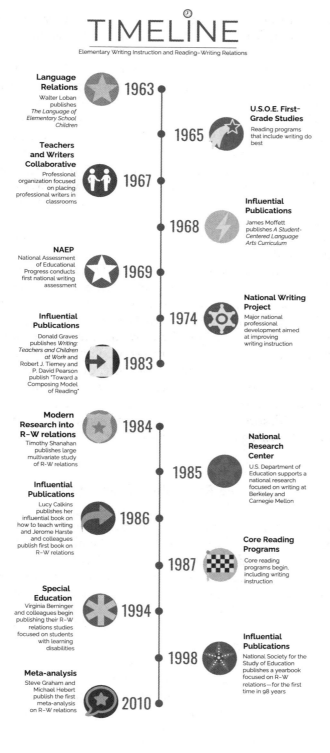

TIMELINE
Elementary Writing Instruction and Reading–Writing Relations

Language Relations
Walter Loban publishes *The Language of Elementary School Children*

1963

U.S.O.E. First-Grade Studies
Reading programs that include writing do best

1965

Teachers and Writers Collaborative
Professional organization focused on placing professional writers in classrooms

1967

Influential Publications
James Moffett publishes *A Student-Centered Language Arts Curriculum*

1968

NAEP
National Assessment of Educational Progress conducts first national writing assessment

1969

National Writing Project
Major national professional development aimed at improving writing instruction

1974

Influential Publications
Donald Graves publishes *Writing: Teachers and Children at Work* and Robert J. Tierney and P. David Pearson publish "Toward a Composing Model of Reading"

1983

Modern Research into R–W relations
Timothy Shanahan publishes large multivariate study of R–W relations

1984

National Research Center
U.S. Department of Education supports a national research focused on writing at Berkeley and Carnegie Mellon

1985

Influential Publications
Lucy Calkins publishes her influential book on how to teach writing and Jerome Harste and colleagues publish first book on R–W relations

1986

Core Reading Programs
Core reading programs begin, including writing instruction

1987

Special Education
Virginia Berninger and colleagues begin publishing their R–W relations studies focused on students with learning disabilities

1994

Influential Publications
National Society for the Study of Education publishes a yearbook focused on R–W relations—for the first time in 98 years

1998

Meta-analysis
Steve Graham and Michael Hebert publish the first meta-analysis on R–W relations

2010

FIGURE 1.1. Fifty-year timeline of elementary writing instruction and writing–reading relations.

As valuable as that early ferment was, by 1960 there was still no wide-spread or major emphasis on writing in American elementary schools and the notion of combining reading and writing was espoused by only a small handful of advocates whose influence was decidedly limited. That began to change in the 1960s and 1970s, both as a result of the instructional efforts of the time, but also due to the tremendous political and social changes wrought by the assassination of a president, far-ranging rulings of an activist Supreme Court, the civil rights movement, anti-Vietnam War protests, the emergence of modern feminism, and foundational economic dislocations, all of which combined to effect profound social changes in America. Such revolutionary transformation could not help but affect education, and one of the ways it did this was to encourage giving voice to children through their writing. Initially, progressive education influences began insinuating writing into the curriculum in a substantial if grassroots way, and later these efforts were reshaped and extended institutionally as well.

The previously mentioned book by Alvina Treut Burrows (*They All Want to Write*, 1939) was a landmark achievement that presaged the development of the "writing workshop" approach which has gained so much prominence in recent years. *They All Want to Write* has been reissued four times since then. It was the most prominent but not the only instance of teachers and scholars exploring how to teach elementary writing. A compendium of writing sources from the 1950s and 1960s provided annotations of more than 700 books and articles on the teaching of "creative writing" in the elementary and secondary school (Day & Weaver, 1978). Although such instruction may not have been either official or widespread, there clearly was a growing and vocal agitation for the teaching of writing at the grassroots level.

Writing Gains More Equal Status

During the 1960s, there were important advancements in research and professional development—though still no institutional embrace of such ideas. Walter Loban (1963) rediscovered the correlational studies that had taken place early in the century and began reporting a series of such contemporary studies (this work continued for more than a decade). These studies conducted in the 1960s and 1970s showed that various listening, speaking, reading, and writing skills were intercorrelated, suggesting the possibility that learning benefits could be derived from integrated instruction.

Earlier, the 19th-century contributions of George Farnam were noted. This approach that based reading instruction on oral composition had been lost to history. By the 1950s and 1960s, it was not as much rediscovered as born anew—this time with more substantial roots. Sylvia Ashton-Warner in New Zealand (Ashton-Warner, 1963), and Roach Van Allen (Van Allen, 1969) and Russell G. Stauffer (1970) in the United States apparently with no awareness of Farnham's earlier work, advocated what then was called the "language-experience approach" (LEA), which engaged students in the reading of oral compositions transcribed by teachers. Stauffer's role was particular notable, since he envisioned this as not just a method for introducing reading to young children, but as one that based writing on oral composition as well. Much like the scientific measurement advocates early in the 20th century and the yet-to-come scientific-based reading research advocates of the 21st century, Stauffer recognized the value of empirical data and showed the effectiveness of combining reading and writing in the primary grades (Stauffer, 1970).

Stauffer's studies of LEA were part of one of the most comprehensive research efforts in education. The U.S. Office of Education (prior to the establishment of the U.S. Department of Education) provided funding for 21 separate research studies, aimed at determining the superiority of one or another approach to beginning reading instruction. Each research team agreed to use the same research procedures and assessments and to share their data. This allowed comparisons of several approaches to beginning reading instruction: basal readers, phonics, LEA, linguistic readers, programmed instruction, technology, and so on. The U.S.O.E. Cooperative First Grade Studies (Bond & Dykstra, 1967) found that all of these approaches worked under some circumstances, but none were consistently more effective than the others. They also reported that LEA and any of the other approaches that included early writing tended to be particularly effective (the same was true for programs with explicit decoding instruction). A good deal of reading research during the 20th century had focused on trying to identify the best approach for beginning reading, and these findings essentially brought an end to that quest, redirecting those efforts to a focus on specific aspects of an instructional program, including reading–writing relations.

Another particularly influential research publication of that time was Jeanne S. Chall's *Learning to Read: The Great Debate* (1967). This popularly published book provided a qualitative review of the research on phonics instruction. Not only did she conclude that phonics gave beginning readers a decided advantage in learning to read, she also claimed that phonics instruction that emphasized early spelling or writing as part of the pedagogical regime conferred a learning advantage.

Such research reports may in the long run have contributed to the changes that were to come. Nevertheless, their influence was not immediate. Professional development efforts in the 1960s—both in terms of publications for teachers and institutionalized professional training—neither commonly referred to these sources nor were obviously based on them. For instance, James Moffett's innovative and influential *Teaching the Universe of Discourse* and *A Student-Centered Language Arts Curriculum, K–12* (both published in 1967) and a later commercial curricula that he based on these (*Interaction Active Voice*). In these books, Moffett argued persuasively for a progressive approach to English language arts, proposing a writing-based curriculum that connected reading and writing. These books were drawn more from Moffett's philosophy and personal teaching experiences than from the empirical research of the day. Moffett eschewed the traditional annual report writing that was evident in many schools in favor of a more ongoing and creative enterprise.

Separately and simultaneously, the Teachers and Writers Collaborative (TWC; *www.twc.org*) was founded by a group of writers and teachers in New York City. The idea was that professional writers by working in schools and providing writing workshops for teachers could help to vitalize writing and literature instruction in America's classrooms. Initially, this work was local in focus, but it quickly spread throughout the nation, both through in-person presentations and a widely distributed newsletter. Not surprisingly, given the poets, novelists, and short story writers who led (and lead) this effort, the focus of the work was mainly literary, personal, or creative in emphasis.

If the 1960s were pioneering and innovative with regard to writing instruction, the 1970s would by contrast appear to be a period of consolidation and extension. One important area of advancement was assessment. Through much of educational history, testing has been strictly a local affair. This began to change with the inception of the National Assessment of Educational Progress in 1969–1970 (NAEP; *www.nationsreportcard.gov*). In that first round of assessment, the writing abilities of 9-, 13-, and 17-year-olds were evaluated, and a year later, the first national reading assessment was reported. The initial results of those tests are not of importance here, but their existence is. Once the federal government began monitoring learning, several states began to get into the act, too. By 1980, about a dozen states were evaluating students' writing ability, and a common experience was that as the testing expanded, increased amounts of writing instruction followed in its wake (e.g., Schlawin, 1981). Teachers who previously had shown little interest in writing instruction were suddenly persuaded of its importance once their states began monitoring student progress. Early in the century, the development of reading assessment discouraged attention to writing—in spite of the progressives' desires. Now that writing became the focus of assessment, schools began teaching it, and this often meant turning to progressive instructional approaches. Despite the increases in writing, these early assessments did not consider reading–writing connections.

Professional development witnessed the creation of the National Writing Project (NWP; *www.nwp.org*)—what had begun as the Bay Area Writing project in San Francisco under the direction of James Gray. The program began in 1974 and in 2 years it had expanded to six states and continued to grow quickly. The basic idea was to support teachers' classroom efforts, less through professional development in specific curriculum and teaching approaches, and more by transforming teachers into writers. As teachers themselves became comfortable and proficient in the writing process and in employing writing as a tool for learning, they were more willing to include writing across the curriculum. Ultimately, tens of thousands of teachers participated in NWP programs providing a valuable resource for expanding writing instruction.

One other idea burst on the scene, which encouraged many primary grade teachers to include writing in their daily instructional routines. Although the pedagogical idea of "invented spelling" tracks back to the 1960s and the work on LEA, the intellectual undergirding of the idea was not much developed until the 1970s (Henderson & Beers, 1980; Read, 1975). The appearance of studies that revealed the logic behind those inventions went a long way toward encouraging teachers to allow young children to initially spell the words the way they thought they were spelled. If young children were left to their own devices during writing, then teachers would not have to spend inordinate amounts of time providing standard spellings. Many parents and educators were fearful that allowing such spelling would reinforce misunderstandings instead of rooting them out, in spite of research indicating that this would not be the case. Later, there would be angry pushbacks against these procedures, but initially the approach allowed the introduction of writing to many primary classrooms.

Thus, the 1980s began both with institutional imperatives for expanding writing (in pursuit of the new assessments) and with rich institutional resources for teacher education (WTC and NWP). This set the stage for substantial increases in the teaching of writing and more serious attention to the connections of reading and writing in the classroom. Accordingly, the 1980s witnessed important progress both on the research and instructional fronts, none more influential than Donald H. Graves's emergence as an influential educational leader. Graves had gained some notice during the previous decade, but his important role came to full flower after the publication of his first book, *Writing: Teachers and Children at Work* (Graves, 1983). Graves was a professor at the University of New Hampshire where he had worked with Donald Murray, a journalism professor and Pulitzer Prize-winning author. Murray was a pioneer in describing and promoting engagement in the processes of writing, and Graves translated this work into an approach viable for the elementary grades. He also mentored Lucy Calkins, who went on to articulate and make practical these ideas to an even greater extent, particularly in her widely used *The Art of Teaching Writing* (Calkins, 1986). As a result of these books and associated workshops—and the work of many other educators who followed in these footsteps—the idea of engaging students in the process of planning, drafting, revision, editing, and publishing became commonplaces in American classrooms, practices found in later research studies to be effective (Graham & Perrin, 2007); another example of how the scientific measurement and progressive approaches were beginning to support rather than undermine each other. Likewise, during this period, many colleges of education began offering preparation for elementary teachers to teach these aspects of writing.

But then, proponents of the progressive approaches went too far. In pursuit of the idea that children would best learn to read and write from reading and writing—and without explicit instructional support in skills like decoding or spelling—California adopted a so-called whole language English language arts framework. It required writing, but mainly of a personal nature rather than public writing (diaries over writing to learn, for instance); it emphasized the reading of high-quality literature (again without explicit teaching) and largely ignored informational text. This approach, when coupled with surprisingly low reading test scores, eventually led to a conservative backlash against the framework and the forms of teaching it had upheld. Before that happened, however, this progressive policy had managed to become very influential, because all textbooks had to adhere to the framework and California is one of the major purchasers of textbooks. At the time, this meant that if California wanted something in their textbooks, Nebraska (and everyone else) was going to get it, too. The benefit of all of that? Later, when California retreated from whole language, textbook publishers continued to include writing instruction in their reading textbooks.

While these events transpired, there were big increases in research support for writing instruction and reading–writing relations. Particularly important was a prominent article published by Robert J. Tierney and P. David Pearson in 1983, "Toward a Composing Model of Reading." This was a theoretical piece exploring how we might enhance reading comprehension that was published in *Language Arts*, NCTE's elementary teacher-oriented publication. This article argued for the idea that writers were particularly insightful readers, and that if children were taught to read like writers, it would lead to a stronger critical sense and richer comprehension development. This persuasive essay kicked off more than a few doctoral dissertations at the time and other research efforts as well and encouraged the idea of including writing lessons in reading programs. More immediately, it generated interest in any existing research on these topics, something from which I personally benefited. My doctoral dissertation had been the first large-scale multivariate investigation of reading–writing relations. In other words, I examined the correlations among several reading and writing variables including decoding, comprehension, vocabulary, spelling, syntax, and text organization simultaneously. Past studies had considered these one at a time—indicating that there were correlations—but not allowing importance or value to be sorted out. That work was ready to publish (Shanahan, 1984) just at the point that the Tierney and Pearson article had created such an extensive and receptive audience. That work gave some clues as to how reading and writing connections might be exploited instructionally and how those relations changed across grade levels (second and fifth graders). It was followed soon thereafter by another large investigation of reading–writing relations that examined processes that readers and writers engage in—such as the use of knowledge or prediction (Langer, 1986). Soon, there was enough such work that Jerome C. Harste and his colleagues were able to publish a professional development book on reading–writing relations (Harste, Short, & Burke, 1988)—and several more such books followed shortly afterward; making it possible to emphasize reading–writing relations in teacher education courses. In fact, research on this topic was burgeoning to such an extent at the time that the Educational Resources Information Center (ERIC) added "reading–writing relationships" to its thesaurus and began organizing studies using this indexing term.

With so much attention on writing, the U.S. Department of Education finally created a National Writing Center, at Berkeley and Carnegie Mellon University, and invested millions of dollars in examining ways to effectively teach writing at a variety of grade levels. This came more than 10 years after the creation of a similar center devoted to reading research. In any event, it presaged a continued commitment to increasing knowledge about writing—a commitment still honored today in the funding priorities of the Institute of

Education Science, the U.S. Department of Education's research arm (there are currently no federal research centers devoted to either reading or writing).

Given the continued growth of academic research on writing and reading–writing relations, the scholarly community began to produce a series of land-mark handbooks summarizing these bodies of knowledge (Bazerman, 2007; MacArthur, Graham, & Fitzgerald, 2005, 2016); long after such handbooks with regard to reading had begun to appear. Also, the National Society for the Study of Education (NSSE), for the only time in its century-long history, devoted its yearbook to reading–writing connections (Nelson & Calfee, 1998); over that history, there had been several NSSE yearbooks devoted to reading and none to writing. Such publications are unlikely to exert direct influences on classroom instruction. However, they serve to stabilize efforts aimed at increas-ing knowledge about writing instruction and interconnections—efforts that eventually do tend to influence teaching in the long run.

Most of the discussion up to this point has focused on general education. However, this lens was widened during the 1990s by Steve Graham, Virginia Berninger, and their colleagues. Graham did groundbreaking work on the writ-ing abilities of students with learning disabilities (e.g., Graham, 1990), and Berninger and her research team improved and extended my research line, looking for reading–writing connections for those with learning disabilities (e.g., Berninger, 2000). These studies were valuable. Not only did they reveal that reading and writing were even more closely related than had been previ-ously suspected—suggesting potentially greater benefits from closer instruc-tional alignments—but they also identified the value of explicit handwriting and spelling instruction to support beginning writers, something that had long been neglected.

The late 1990s and the first decade of the new century witnessed the adop-tion of educational standards in the English language arts by all 50 states (a government-led movement that had begun in the 1980s). This required that all states make a commitment to elementary writing instruction. Unfortunately, this bit of progress was unwittingly reversed by the passage of No Child Left Behind (2001). The heavy emphasis on standardized tests in reading and math-ematics, and the large amounts of money devoted to reading, led many teach-ers, schools, districts, and even states to lessen their emphasis on writing. Some states even stopped evaluating writing altogether. If schools were to be evalu-ated mainly or solely in terms of reading and math, then many educators would constrict their efforts to those outcomes alone.

This unfortunate and unintended retreat began to be arrested in 2010, with the adoption of the Common Core State Standards (CCSS) and an influ-ential meta-analysis of instruction that combined reading and writing in par-ticular ways. The CCSS represented the first attempt at states cooperating with each other to establish common educational goals and more than 40 states adopted those standards. The CCSS standards matter here because they refo-cused attention on writing instruction and encouraged explicit instructional attention on using reading and writing in combination (Shanahan, 2015). Some states stayed out of CCSS—and since then others have withdrawn—but the

CCSS emphasis on ambitious writing goals is now universal in American education.

On the research front, Steve Graham and Michael Hebert issued a meta-analysis of more than 100 research studies showing the power of having students writing about text—a particular approach to reading–writing connections, using writing to think about the ideas in a text (Graham & Hebert, 2011). When students wrote in response to text—summarizing the ideas, analyzing and critiquing them, and synthesizing the ideas across multiple texts—reading comprehension and learning from text were improved. This research was published right at the point that the CCSS standards were being adopted, and they emphasized this kind of integration of reading and writing. In the 1960s, Moffett had contended that traditional writing about text—such as report writing—was discouraging writing instruction. Now, a significant expansion of writing instruction is being instigated by evidence challenging those claims. Progressive educational efforts encouraged teachers to give children voice and to integrate curriculum. Now, testing, instructional standards, and quantitative research are promoting writing across the curriculum as well, rather than solely as an opportunity for personal or creative expression.

Where Does That Leave Us?

History is a river. It runs continuously and its appearance may be altered by a falling tree, a sudden snowfall, or a shift in vantage. Other observers may have chosen to highlight a different set of events, issues, or thought leaders. Nevertheless, there is enough here to suggest some important lessons for today.

1. **Reading *and* writing matter.** American society is complex—in terms of our economic, civic, and social lives. There have been times in history when a much greater need for readers than writers has existed; 21st-century America is not one of those times. Full participation in our society requires that all students gain both reading and writing during their schooling. In any event, there will be no reading–writing relations to exploit if both reading and writing are not part of the curriculum.

2. **Reading development precedes writing, but never by much.** Because literacy is a shared social system, reading necessarily precedes writing—an arrangement long honored in Western education. But it would be wrong to assume that writing instruction should tail far behind. History shows that children can begin to learn reading and writing in preschool, kindergarten, and grade 1—there is no reason to wait, once reading instruction begins.

3. **Reading and writing share essential skills.** A century ago, school subjects were grouped on the basis of their purpose or function (combining writing and math since their uses are economic). Over time, educators learned that it was more productive to combine subjects based on their psychological and

linguistic similarities and overlaps. Researchers started pursuing such issues in the 1910s, but it was not until the 1980s and 1990s that we gained a clear idea of the degree of overlaps between reading and writing, suggesting that exploiting these overlaps could allow for greater instructional efficiency and effectiveness. As we teach any aspect of reading—letter recognition, decoding, comprehension of simple messages—we should introduce their writing counterparts simultaneously, including, for instance, spelling or word writing in phonics lessons.

4. **Writing can play an important role across the curriculum.** During the past half century, there have been professional disagreements as to the kind of writing to emphasize. Those promoting writing from 1965 to 1985 mainly encouraged personal writing (diaries) or literary writing (stories, poetry); they saw writing's purpose as mainly expressive or therapeutic, and inveighed against the corruption of writing about the ideas from books. Recently, more public kinds of writing have been in vogue—with research, standards, and assessments all requiring greater attention to writing as a way to increase learning. This does not necessarily have to be an either–or proposition—opportunities for both public and personal writing can be made available. Nevertheless, learning to do the kinds of writing that can best provide academic and, perhaps, economic benefits fits the tenor of our times.

5. **Don't forget the fundamentals.** Research has found that explicitly teaching basic writing skills like handwriting (or manuscript hand) and spelling makes a difference in how much and how students will write. This appears to be particularly true with students with learning disabilities. Just as in reading when students struggle over the words, it can disrupt their comprehension, if students are distracted by spelling or handwriting demands, they won't provide quality writing. Again, an either–or approach may not be the best one; invented spelling or developmental writing provides valuable opportunities for children to explore the English writing system. Likewise, the information gained from explicit teaching becomes part of the store of knowledge that students use when they try to puzzle out a spelling.

6. **Teachers need support.** At various times in history, teachers have been successfully influenced by persuasive thought leaders (e.g., Farnham, Burrows, Moffett, Graves) to add writing to their classroom routines. Enticing encouragement can be valuable. However, if writing—and reading–writing connections—are to be universal in our classrooms, then teachers require more than great models and powerful rhetoric. Some of the most lasting gains in this regard have come from institutionalized professional development opportunities, explicit educational standards, and the use of more standardized curricula that promote more evidence-based approaches to writing instruction.

7. **Research must guide our actions.** Research did not become a major driver of educational practice until the last 50 years. As studies began to accumulate,

showing the benefits of teaching writing and of combining reading and writing in instruction and practice, it has become easier to convince school leaders to invest in writing. Research, however, can provide more than general guidance (e.g., we need to include writing in the curriculum and reading and writing can be combined). Research also can offer more specific directions in terms of what we teach and how we should teach those things. Over the past half century, research has revealed both how writing can be taught most effectively and how reading and writing can be combined in ways that help students. Developing pedagogy in close alignment with what has been learned from research is the surest way to advantage our students.

REFERENCES

Ashton-Warner, S. (1963). *Teacher.* New York: Simon & Schuster.

Bazerman, C. (2007). *Handbook of research on writing.* New York: Routledge.

Bond, G. L., & Dykstra, R. (1967). The cooperative research program in first-grade reading instruction. *Reading Research Quarterly, 2*(4), 5–142.

Berninger V. W. (2000). Development of language by hand and its connections with language by ear, mouth, and eye. *Topics in Language Disorders, 20*(4), 65–84.

Burrows, A. T., with Jackson, D. C., Saunders, D. O., & Ferebee, J. (1939). *They all want to write.* New York: Bobbs Merrill.

Calkins, L. M. (1986). *The art of teaching writing.* Portsmouth, NH: Heinemann.

Chall, J. S. (1967). *Learning to read: The great debate.* New York: Macmillan.

Clifford, G. J. (1989). A Sisyphean task: Historical perspectives. In A. H. Dyson (Ed.), *Collaboration through writing and reading* (pp. 25–84). Urbana, IL: National Council of Teachers of English.

Cremin, L. A. (1970). *American education: The colonial experience, 1607–1783.* New York: Harper & Row.

Day, R., & Weaver, G. C. (1978). *Creative writing in the classroom: An annotated bibliography of selected resources* (K–12). Urbana, IL: National Council of Teachers of English.

Del Campo, R., Buchanan, W. R., Abbott, R. D., & Berninger, V. W. (2015). Levels of phonology related to reading and writing in middle childhood. *Reading and Writing: An Interdisciplinary Journal, 28*(2), 183–198.

Duce, C. (1971). Condorcet on education. *British Journal of Educational Studies, 19*(3), 272–282.

Ensor, G. (1811). On national education. *Critical Review, 24*(3), 511–512.

Farnham, G. L. (1870/2015). *The sentence method of teaching reading writing, and spelling.* Charleston, SC: Bibliolife.

Graham, S. (1990). The role of production factors in learning disabled students' compositions. *Journal of Educational Psychology, 82*(4), 781–791.

Graham, S., & Hebert, M. (2011). Writing to read: A meta-analysis of writing and writing instruction on writing. *Harvard Educational Review, 81*(4), 710–744.

Graham, S., & Perrin, D. (2007). A meta-analysis of writing instruction for adolescent students. *Journal of Educational Psychology, 99*(3), 445–476.

Graves, D. H. (1983). *Writing: Teachers and children at work.* Exeter, NH: Heinemann.

Harste, J. C., Short, K. G., & Burke, C. (1988). *Creating classroom for authors: The reading–writing connection*. Portsmouth, NH: Heinemann.

Henderson, E., & Beers, J. (Eds.). (1980). *Developmental and cognitive aspects of learning to spell: A reflection of word knowledge*. Newark, DE: International Reading Association.

Horn, E. (1926). *A basic writing vocabulary*. University of Iowa Monographs in Education, 4. Iowa City: State University of Iowa.

Horn, E. (1929). The child's early experience with the letter A. *Journal of Educational Psychology, 20*(3), 161–168.

Huey, E. B. (1908/1968). *The psychology and pedagogy of reading*. Cambridge, MA: MIT Press.

Jernegen, M. W. (1918). Compulsory education in the American colonies: New England. *School Review, 26*(10), 731–749.

Langer, J. (1986). *Children reading and writing: Structures and strategies*. New York: Ablex.

Loban, W. (1963). *The language of elementary school children*. Urbana, IL: National Council of Teachers of English.

MacArthur, C. A., Graham, S., & Fitzgerald, J. (Eds.). (2005). *Handbook of writing research*. New York: Guilford Press.

MacArthur, C. A., Graham, S., & Fitzgerald, J. (Eds.). (2016). *Handbook of writing research* (2nd ed). New York: Guilford Press.

Moffett, J. (1967a). *Teaching the universe of discourse*. Boston: Houghton Mifflin.

Moffett, J. (1967b). *A student-centered language arts curriculum, K–12*. Boston: Houghton Mifflin.

Monaghan, J. (1987). Readers writing: The curriculum of the writing schools of eighteenth century Boston. *Visible Language, 21*, 167–213.

Muir, J. (1984). A note on ancient methods of learning to write. *Classical Quarterly, 34*(1), 236–237.

Nelson, N. N., & Calfee, R. C. (Eds.). (1998a). *The reading–writing connection. Yearbook of the Society for the Study of Education, 97* (Part II). Chicago: University of Chicago Press.

Nelson, N. N., & Calfee, R. C. (1998b). The reading–writing connection viewed historically. In N. Nelson & R. C. Calfee (Eds.), *The reading–writing connection. Yearbook of the National Society for the Study of Education, 97* (Part II, pp. 1–52). Chicago: University of Chicago Press.

Ong, W. J. (1982). *Orality and literacy: The technologizing of the world*. London: Methuen.

Putnam, A. L., Ozubko, J. D., MacLeod, C. M., & Roediger, H. L. (2014). The production effect in paired-associate learning: Benefits for item and associative information. *Memory & Cognition, 42*(3), 409–420.

Read, C. (1975). *Children's categorization of speech sounds in English*. Urbana, IL: National Council of Teachers of English.

Rijlaarsdam, G., Braaksma, M., Couzijn, M., Janssen, T., Kieft, M., Broekkamp, H., & Van Den Bergh, H. (2005). Psychology and the teaching of writing in 8000 and some words. *Pedagogy—Learning for Teaching, BJEP Monograph Series II*(3), 127–153.

Schlawin, S. A. (1981). *The New York State Testing Program in Writing: Its influence on instruction, 1–7*. Albany: State of New York.

Schmandt-Besserat, D., & Erard, M. (2008). Origins and forms of writing. In C.

Bazerman (Ed.), *Handbook of research on writing: History, society, school, individual, text* (pp. 7–22). Philadelphia: Routledge.

Shanahan, T. (1984). Nature of the reading–writing relation: An exploratory multivariate analysis. *Journal of Educational Psychology, 76*(3), 466–477.

Shanahan, T. (2015). Common Core Standards: A new role for writing. *Elementary School Journal, 115*(4), 464–479.

Smith, N. B. (1965). *American reading instruction.* Newark, DE: International Reading Association.

Stauffer, R. G. (1970). *The language-experience approach to the teaching of reading.* New York: Harper & Row.

Stotsky, S. (1983). Research on reading/writing relationships: A synthesis and suggested directions. *Language Arts, 60*(5), 627–642.

Tierney, R. J., & Pearson, P. D. (1983). Towards a composing model of reading. *Language Arts, 60*(5), 568–580.

Tower, D. B. (1853). *The gradual primer.* Boston: Sanborn, Carter, Bazin, & Co.

Van Allen, R. (1969). *Language experiences in early childhood.* Chicago: Encyclopedia Britannica.

Whitmore, W. H. (Ed.). (1887). *The general laws and liberties of the Massachusetts Colony.* Boston: State of Massachusetts.

PART II

SPECIFIC APPLICATIONS
OF WRITING AND
READING CONNECTIONS

CHAPTER 2

A Tale of Two Closely Related Skills
Word Reading and Spelling
Development and Instruction

Young-Suk Kim

Imagine reading the following text: 어느 마을에 한 소녀가 살았습니다. One will not be able to comprehend this sentence unless he or she can read Korean—is able to decode words in the Korean orthography and has an understanding of the Korean language. This example illustrates the absolutely necessary role of word reading in reading comprehension. Similar is the case of spelling for writing— that is, spelling is necessary for writing texts. Although the ultimate goals of reading and writing instruction are not word reading and spelling per se, there is no reading comprehension or written composition without word reading and spelling skills. In this chapter, we focus on word reading and spelling, with particular attention to their connections and instructional implications. To this end, we briefly review the roles of word reading and spelling in theoretical models of reading comprehension and written composition as well as the developmental progression of word reading and spelling skills. We then focus on building foundations of word reading and spelling—emergent literacy skills such as phonological, orthographic, and morphological awareness—and research-informed teaching practices of emergent literacy skills, word reading, and spelling. The following are guiding questions for this chapter.

GUIDING QUESTIONS

- What is the developmental progression of reading and spelling skills?
- What skills contribute to the development of word reading and spelling skills?
- What research-informed teaching practices support the synergistic development of word reading and spelling skills?

The Roles of Word Reading and Spelling
in Reading Comprehension and Written Composition

Reading comprehension and written composition are two of the most complex tasks in which individuals engage during schooling and in their adult lives. Multiple theoretical models have been proposed to explain reading and writing processes, and the skills that contribute to reading and writing development. Although the nature and focal aspects of these various theoretical models differ, all recognize the roles of the ability to read/decode words in reading comprehension, and the ability to spell/encode words in written composition. For example, according to the simple view of reading, word reading and listening comprehension are two global skills necessary for reading comprehension (Gough & Tunmer, 1986; Hoover & Gough, 1990). Other models such as the Reading Systems Framework (Perfetti & Stafura, 2014) and the direct and indirect effects model of reading (Kim, 2017, 2020a, 2020b) include greater details about processes and skills that are involved in word reading and listening comprehension.

The essential role of spelling in writing texts is also recognized in theoretical models such as the simple view of writing (Juel, Griffith, & Gough, 1986), not-so-simple view of writing (Berninger & Winn, 2006), and the direct and indirect effects model of writing (Kim, 2020c; Kim & Park, 2019; Kim & Schatschneider, 2017). Writing requires generation, translation, and transcription of ideas, and spelling is part of the transcription process. Simply put, writing by definition requires a written product, and therefore, writing requires spelling skills. In addition, dysfluency with spelling skill hinders the writing process by interfering with idea generation and the coherence-building process. An abundance of evidence indicates the necessary role of spelling in written composition (Abbott & Berninger, 1993; Graham, Berninger, Abbott, Abbott, & Whitaker, 1997; Graham, Harris, & Chorzempa, 2002; Kim et al., 2011; Kim, Al Otaiba, Wanzek, & Gatlin, 2015; Kim & Schatschneider, 2017).

Although the theoretical models above focus on either reading or writing, another line of work has recognized reading–writing connections (see Kim, 2020d, and Shanahan, 2016, for a review). According to this rich body of work, reading and writing are interdependent systems, drawing on highly similar skills (Fitzgerald & Shanahan, 2000; Kim, 2020d). This applies to lexical-level skills, word reading and spelling, such that word reading and spelling are founded on the same skills and knowledge, and they develop interactively, mutually supporting each other (see below for details).

Phases of Word Reading and Spelling Development

Word reading and spelling skills are not *either–or* phenomena. Instead, they develop on a continuum through phases with practice and exposure that is greatly facilitated by systematic instruction, and ultimately children need to develop automaticity whereby their word reading and spelling are automatic and do not require mental effort. According to Ehri (2005), the developmental progression of word reading is as follows: (1) pre-alphabetic phase, (2) partial alphabetic phase, (3) full alphabetic phase, (4) consolidated alphabetic phase, and (5) development of automaticity. The word *alphabetic* here refers to the alphabetic principle that graphemes—letters and groups of letters (e.g., *sh* in *ship*)—represent sounds or phonemes. In the *pre*-alphabetic phase, the child has not developed an understanding of the alphabetic principle and adopts a visual cue approach in reading. For example, the child would recognize a word, say, *McDonald's*, for its visual cue as a whole (e.g., an arch). In the *partial* alphabetic phase, the child uses partial phonological cues (including knowledge of letter names) for word reading. In the *full* alphabetic phase, the child is able to "form connections between all of the graphemes in spellings and the phonemes in the pronunciations to remember how to read words" (Ehri, 2005, p. 148) and has complete knowledge of grapheme–phoneme correspondences. In the *consolidated* phase, the child develops an understanding of a consolidated unit of letter sequences (e.g., <u>caught</u>, <u>taught</u>; <u>re</u>act, <u>re</u>do) and reads by these units rather than graphemes. In the *automaticity* phase, word reading is not only accurate but also fast because spellings of words are fully secured to their pronunciations in memory, and as such they are retrieved automatically and immediately without analytic retrieval (i.e., not using the process of retrieving and assembling phonemes associated with each grapheme). In this phase, whole words are recognized by sight without requiring attentional resources.

Spelling development has been described as having five stages: (1) emergent/ precommunicative, (2) letter name, (3) within word, (4) syllables and affixes, and (5) derivational relations (Bear, Invernisi, Templeton, & Johnston, 2016; Gentry, 1982). The emergent/precommunicative stage is similar to the pre-alphabetic stage in reading development in which children lack an understanding of the systematic relation between letters and sounds. In the letter name phase, children use their knowledge of letter–sound correspondences, but accuracy tends to be limited to consonants at the beginning and end of a word, and short vowels. In the within word phase, children can spell most single-syllable words with short vowels but have difficulties with silent long-vowel patterns. In the syllables and affixes phase, the errors tend to occur at syllable junctures and in unaccented syllables. In the derivational relations phase, errors are with low-frequency multisyllabic words involving derivational morphemes. These developmental phases are not lockstep, and children access and utilize knowledge of multiple sources (e.g., phonology, orthography, and morphology) across the phases, depending on the nature of the words and the availability of children's knowledge (see Apel & Masterson, 2001; Siegler, 1996; also see Pollo, Treiman, & Kessler, 2008; Treiman, 2017a, 2017b).

Emergent Literacy Skills and Word Reading and Spelling Skills

What skills contribute to the development of word reading and spelling skills? Here, we introduce the concept and term *emergent literacy skills*. The concept of "emergent" literacy skills is that literacy skills such as reading and writing develop or emerge from prereading or precursor skills that are foundational for reading and writing development. These include knowledge and awareness of phonology, orthography, and morphology, and oral language skills such as vocabulary and listening comprehension (Kim, 2020a). In this chapter, we focus on phonological awareness, orthographic awareness, and morphological awareness as they are critical for word reading and spelling.

Phonological awareness is one's knowledge and awareness of structure of speech sounds in a language (National Institute of Child Health and Human Development [NICHD], 2000). For example, in English, the word *cat* is a single-syllable word pronounced as /kæt/. The syllable can be broken into smaller units of sounds: onset /k/ and rime /æt/. Onset is the consonant(s) before the vowel within a syllable. Rime is the vowel and following consonant(s) within a syllable; although a vowel is necessary, consonants are not. The rime /æt/ can be segmented into phonemes /æ/ and /t/. Phonemes are the smallest unit in a speech sound. In the word *cat*, the onset /k/ is also a phoneme and therefore *cat* consists of three phonemes, /k/, /æ/, and /t/. Figure 2.1 shows the phonological structure of a syllable in English for the word *cat*. The same breakdown can be applied to the multisyllabic word *react*, which is composed of two syllables, /ri/ and /ækt/. In this case, the syllable /ri/ has an onset /r/ and rime /i/. The rime does not contain a consonant in this case. In the syllable /ækt/, there is no onset. The rime /ækt/ can be broken into three phonemes, /æ/, /k/, and /t/. Notice that there are two consonant phonemes /k/ and /t/ without a vowel in between, which is called a consonant cluster (see Moats, 2010). Phonological awareness develops from a larger unit (syllables) to a smaller unit (phonemes).

Orthographic awareness is the knowledge and awareness of print functions (print concepts), graphemes, and permissible patterns in an orthography (e.g., *tr*, but not *tl*, is allowed in the syllable initial position in English). Graphemes

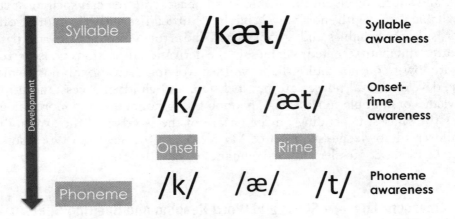

FIGURE 2.1. Phonological structure of a syllable in English, using the word *cat* as an example.

include individual letters (shapes, names, and sounds of alphabet letters) and groups of letters (e.g., the digraph *sh* in *ship*). Learning to read or spell in English is not as simple as mapping individual letters to individual sounds (e.g., letter *t* representing /t/). Groups of letters, called digraphs or trigraphs, and so on, also represent a phoneme. High-frequency consonant digraphs include *th* (*that, thin*); *sh* (*ship*); *ch* (*chip*); *wh* (*what*); and *ph* (*phone*). In some consonant digraphs, one of the consonant letters is silent (e.g., *wr-, kn-, ps-, -bt, -lm*). There are also vowel digraphs (e.g., *ea, ei, ee, ou, a_e, i_e, o_e*) as well as digraphs and trigraphs that include both consonants and vowel letters (e.g., *qu-, -dge*). Because phonemes map onto graphemes, not just individual letters, knowledge of grapheme–phoneme correspondences is the key to word reading and spelling (see Figure 2.2).

Morphological awareness refers to the knowledge and awareness of morphological structure of a word. Morphemes are the smallest unit of meaning. Intuitively, it might appear that individual vocabulary words are the smallest unit of meaning, but morphemes are. For example, the word *cats* has two morphemes, *cat* and *-s* for plural. The word *react* is composed of two morphemes, *re* and *act*. The word *incredible* has three morphemes (*in-cred-ible*). Morphemes are classified into categories such as base words, derivational prefixes, derivational suffixes, and inflectional suffixes (see Figure 2.3).

Why are phonological awareness, orthographic awareness, and morphological awareness important to word reading and spelling in English?

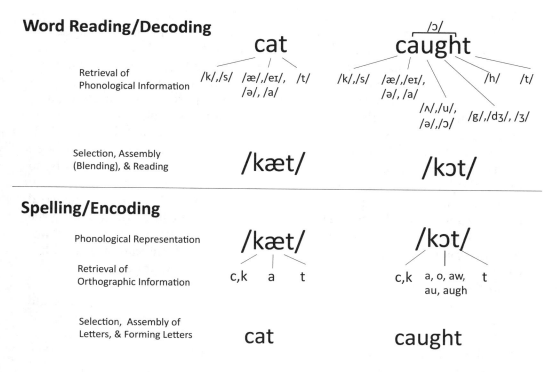

FIGURE 2.2. Word reading and spelling processes for the words *cat* and *caught*.

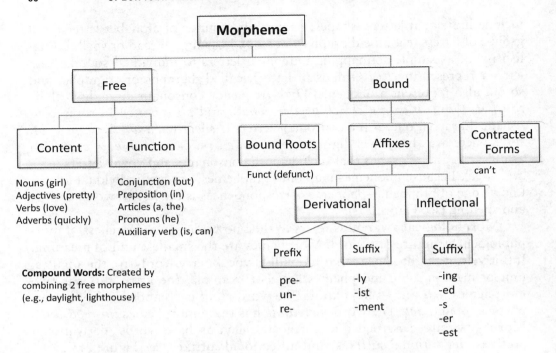

FIGURE 2.3. Categories of morphemes and examples.

Understanding the writing system of English—an alphabetic or a morphophonological writing system—gives a clue. In the alphabetic writing system, orthographic symbols like alphabet letters principally represent speech sounds, not meanings. Therefore, the key to decoding words in alphabetic writing systems is an understanding of the alphabetic principle and correspondences between letters and groups of letters to appropriate speech sounds. For instance, we read the word *cat* as /kæt/, not anything else, because the letters *c-a-t*, respectively, represent /k/, /æ/, and /t/. As shown in Figure 2.2, when the child sees the word *cat*, they have to retrieve sounds associated with each letter. Letters *c* and *a* are often associated with multiple sounds, so the reader has to select one sound over the other options. They then have to assemble and blend the sounds in correct order to pronounce /kæt/. The word *caught* is more complex because it involves a grapheme *augh* representing the phoneme /ɔ/. The child's attempt to use the letter-by-letter processing will not be a successful strategy for this word (see Figure 2.2). Instead, the child has to process, recognize, and use their knowledge of the grapheme *augh* for /ɔ/ or *aught* for /ɔt/ as a unit.

The process of spelling is the reverse of that for word reading. The child needs to have an accurate representation of the sounds in a target word, say, /kæt/, and therefore the child's lack of understanding of the sounds (i.e., phonological awareness) would lead to an incorrect spelling. The child then has to retrieve their knowledge of graphemes or larger units associated with each identified phoneme, followed by selecting correct graphemes, assembling them in correct order, and forming letters accurately (see the bottom panel of Figure 2.2).

Morphological awareness also plays an important role in word reading and spelling, particularly for multimorphemic words. Consider the example of *react*. If one applies the knowledge of vowel digraph *ea*, it is reasonable to read this word as /rikt/ (*reeked*) because *ea* frequently represents /i/ in English (e.g., *reap*, *cheap*). Of course, /rikt/ is not an accurate reading of *react*. Then what knowledge is needed to correctly read the word? English has a morphophonological writing system in which morphemic information, in addition to phonological information, is represented in the spelling of words. Therefore, morphological information overrides what appears to be vowel digraph *ea* so as to read *react* correctly as /riækt/. The same applies to spelling. If the child has an understanding of the morphemic structure of the word *react*, they are more likely to accurately spell the word. Morphology is particularly prominent for words in academic content areas such as social studies and science, where words are frequently composed of multiple morphemes (e.g., *photosynthesis*, *chronology*, *magnification*).

The roles of phonological, orthographic, and morphological awareness in word reading and spelling are well established in theoretical models of word reading (Adams, 1990; Seidenberg & McClelland, 1989) and spelling (Bahr et al., 2012; Treiman, 2017a). This is widely referred to as the triangle model of word reading (Adams, 1990) or triple word form theory (Bahr, Silliman, Berninger, & Dow, 2012). It is important to highlight that both word reading and spelling draw on essentially the *same* skills. This has three important implications. First and foremost, early literacy instruction should target these skills to promote development of word reading and spelling. Abundant research indicates that teaching these skills improves word reading and spelling, and no explicit and systematic teaching of these skills puts children at risk for reading and writing difficulties (National Early Literacy Panel, 2008; NICHD, 2000). Second, if word reading and spelling draw on the same skills, children's word reading and spelling skills should be strongly related and indeed they are (r = .82; Kim, Wolters, & Lee, 2022). It also entails that children who are strong in word reading will likely be strong in spelling and vice versa, and similarly those who are weak in word reading will likely be weak in spelling and vice versa. In fact, it is well documented that children with dyslexia also have persistent difficulties with spelling (e.g., Berninger, Neilsen, Abbott, Wijsman, & Raskind, 2008; Graham et al., 2021).

The third important implication is that integrated teaching of word reading and spelling has a synergistic effect and facilitates the acquisition of both word reading and spelling (Graham et al., 2017). Teaching of word reading promotes spelling, and teaching of spelling promotes word reading because quality teaching of word reading or spelling involves teaching emergent literacy skills, and word reading and spelling experiences support memory representations of words, enhancing lexical quality. Spelling practice, particularly during the early phase of spelling development, involves attention to sounds of words (phonemes) and representing them with letters, and this experience reinforces the mapping between phonological information and graphemes (Arra & Aaron, 2001; Ellis & Cataldo, 1990). Similarly, word reading involves converting graphemes to phonemes, which reinforces grapheme–phoneme correspondences. Therefore, an effective phonics instruction involves both ways of conversion—grapheme–phoneme conversion (word reading) and phoneme–grapheme conversion (spelling)—as these are two sides of the same coin (Ehri, 1997). Phonics is not just a reading instructional approach; it is also a spelling instructional approach. In fact, effective phonics instruction systematically integrates word reading and spelling instruction to reinforce and support coding into memory and analyzing phonological, orthographic, and morphological information.

Note that the strong relation between word reading and spelling does not entail that word reading and spelling are identical (Ehri, 1997; Shanahan, 2016). Word reading requires recognizing and identifying graphemes, retrieving associated phonemes, and assembling the phonemes in correct sequence. Spelling, on the other hand, requires identifying phonemes in the target words, retrieving associated graphemes, and assembling the graphemes in correct sequence, and forming the letters in correct shapes (see Figure 2.2). Word reading largely requires a *recognition* of patterns, whereas spelling requires a *production* of a series of letters in accurate sequence. In other words, spelling requires greater precision of mental representation of words and is typically more difficult than word reading. For instance, to read the word *caught* accurately, one needs to recognize the pattern *-aught* for /ɔt/, whereas in spelling, one needs to accurately sequence the five letters *a*, *u*, *g*, *h*, *t* in correct order.

How Can Teachers Support Development of Word Reading and Spelling Skills?: Foundations for Effective Teaching

Decades of research have revealed several general principles for effective instruction. The first principle is that children differ in the rate at which they acquire word reading and spelling skills; therefore, for maximally effective instruction, teachers need to identify their students' strengths and needs and provide instruction that is tailored to those needs—that is, differentiated or individualized instruction. This type of instruction involves assessments of students' word reading and spelling skills as well as phonological awareness, orthographic awareness, and morphological awareness, and using assessment data to make instructional decisions such as grouping students by their strengths and needs. This practice is called data-based instructional decision making (see McMaster et al., 2020). Children differ in their needs of target skills because some children are already proficient in target skills (e.g., phonological awareness), while others are not. Children also vary in their learning time for mastery. It is important to recognize that differentiated instruction is *not* tracking. In tracking, students are not allowed to flexibly move into and out of ability groups. In differentiated instruction, students are grouped and regrouped flexibly throughout the year depending on their progress in target skills. The goal of differentiated instruction is to best meet students' needs, and grouping would differ depending on individual student progress.

The second principle is consideration of students' language backgrounds in planning and delivery of instruction. Students in modern classrooms are from diverse linguistic backgrounds, including monolingual learners, multilingual learners, those who have limited proficiency in language of instruction, and those who speak nonmainstream American English (e.g., African American Vernacular English [AAVE]). This implies that teachers need to have knowledge about the language development and language experiences of children from diverse backgrounds (see Fillmore & Snow, 2000). For example, students with limited English proficiency by definition need instruction on English language in addition to literacy instruction. These children bring their first language (L1) language skills that can be transferred to support their learning of the English language and their word reading and spelling in English (Vaughn et al., 2006; Wawire & Kim, 2018). Multilingual learners (e.g., those who are proficient in more than one language, including the language of instruction, English) are different from English learners as they already have proficiency in English as well as other languages. Essentially, they are akin to monolingual learners of English but have proficiency in additional languages. Those who speak AAVE speak proficient English but not the "standard" or "general" English dialect. Phonological and morphological features of AAVE have important implications for word reading and spelling acquisition for AAVE speakers (see Craig, Thompson, Washington, & Potter, 2003, for details). The good news is that effective teaching of word reading and spelling (see below) works for all children regardless of children's linguistic or cultural backgrounds (August, Shanahan, & Escamilla, 2009) as long as teachers recognize, understand, and value children's linguistic backgrounds and make appropriate adaptions.

The third principle concerns instructional delivery—using evidence-based pedagogical approaches. This includes explicit and systematic teaching and establishing evidence-based instructional routines. Explicit instruction refers to "a structured, direct, clearly articulated methodology for teaching target skills" (Kim & Davidson, 2019, p. 2). Systematic instruction is step-by-step teaching in manageable steps and logical sequences (e.g., easy tasks to more challenging tasks). Explicit and systematic teaching deliberately includes opportunities for practice. Practice refers to carefully prepared opportunities "for rehearsing, reviewing, and retrieving newly learned material in order to support robust learning" (Kim & Davidson, 2019, p. 2) and should not be confused with a "drill." Another important aspect of instructional delivery is establishing instructional routines. Humans learn new material best when it is presented in the context of their existing knowledge network, and a brief review of previous learning before presenting new material facilitates learning (Rosenshine, 2012). This is followed by teacher modeling of target skills and opportunities for guided and independent practice along with teachers' corrective feedback. This is widely known as the I Do, We Do, You Do model. The key point of this pedagogical approach is the provision of instructional scaffolding, which is gradually reduced for eventual independent work by students (see Kim & Davidson, 2019, for details).

Research-Supported Recommendations for Teaching Word Reading and Spelling

For the majority of children, word reading and spelling skills do not develop "naturally" (Rayner, Foorman, Perfetti, Pesetsky, & Seidenberg, 2001), and development from the pre-alphabetic phase to the automaticity phase largely depends on devoted explicit and systematic teaching of emergent literacy skills, word reading, and spelling, not just an exposure to print. This is widely known as phonics, which is an instructional approach that explicitly teaches grapheme–phoneme correspondences. The following are four recommendations for effective teaching of word reading and spelling based on theory and empirical evidence.

Teach Phonological Awareness and Grapheme–Phoneme Correspondences

Although a starting place for phonological awareness instruction depends on assessment results, instruction should consider grain size (syllables, rimes, and phonemes) and task/activity demands. Recognition of sounds precedes manipulation of them, and tasks/activities increase in difficulty from matching to oddity, counting, blending, segmenting, deletion/elision, and substitution. Table 2.1 shows an example of these phonological awareness activities. For instance, for a syllable task, the student can be asked to identify the number of syllables in the words *homework* and *ballpark*. This can be followed by blending of these words, *home-work* to *homework*, and *ball-park* to *ballpark*. In phonemic awareness tasks, difficulty also depends on the position of the sound. Identifying phonemes in the initial position is easiest, followed by the final position and then the middle position. For instance, for the word *cat*, the easiest sound to identify is the first sound, /k/, followed by /t/ and then /æ/. Note that pronouncing consonants in isolation without a vowel is not natural for children, and therefore, drawing their attention to articulation of isolated consonants can be helpful (e.g., using pictures that show the mouth when articulating a sound or drawing attention to the teacher's mouth). Picture sorting is also another approach. In picture sorting, the child is shown pictures of familiar objects that contain target sounds (e.g., pictures of *sun, sock,* and *ball; fan, pants, five*) and is asked to sort them according to the shared sounds (a matching task) or different sounds (an oddity task). Elkonin boxes are also widely used, where a square box is mapped onto sounds (and graphemes) because boxes add concreteness to understanding sound manipulation.

Teaching letters and groups of letters (e.g., digraphs) is also a crucial part of word reading and spelling instruction. A few things to be mindful of when teaching letters are as follows.

• Provide opportunities for frequent exposure. The relation between letter shapes and letter names is artificial just like vocabulary words (there is no inherent relation between an object *desk* and why we call it *desk* in English).

TABLE 2.1. Phonological Awareness Tasks/Activities and Examples

Task/activity	Example for the onset–rime unit
Matching	Say the word: *sun, sock, ball.* Which two words begin with the same sound? (*sun* and *sock*)
Oddity	Say the word: *sun, sock, ball.* Which word begins with a different sound? (*ball*)
Counting	Say *s-un.* How many sounds are there? (two)
Blending	Say *s-un.* Put these sounds into a word. (*sun*)
Segmenting	Say *sun.* Break this word into two. (*s-un*)
Deletion/elision	Say *ball.* Say ball without /b/. (*all*)
Substitution	Say *ball.* Say the word replacing /b/ with /f/. (*fall*)

Therefore, learning letter shapes and names requires the same principle as learning vocabulary—children need to be exposed to letters and their names frequently (Kim, Petscher, Treiman, & Kelcey, 2021). One research-based approach to facilitate the connection between letters and their names is embedded/integrated picture mnemonics. In this approach, the shapes of letters are linked to familiar objects, for example, *B* resembling a bee, or *S* a snake (Ehri, Deffner, & Wilce, 1984; Shmidman & Ehri, 2010).

• Consider visual similarity. Many letters in English share visual similarity. For example, letters *b* and *d* are identical shapes when reversed. Many other letters also share similarity (e.g., *p-q, m-n, n-h, g-q, i-l, i-j, E-F, B-D, B-P, U-V*). Visual similarity creates confusion (Kim, Petscher, et al., 2021; Treiman & Kessler, 2003). Not surprisingly, some children show reversal in their letter writing, and persistent use of reversal is related to poorer spelling performance at a later time (Treiman, Kessler, & Caravolas, 2019). One strategy when teaching visually similar letters is not to introduce them in adjacent sequence. For instance, although *n* immediately follows *m* according to the alphabet sequence, they do not have to be taught back to back. In addition, drawing students' attention explicitly to distinguishing features between target letters can help mitigate confusion (e.g., *h* has a long stick compared to *n*). Another strategy is spending a different amount of time for teaching more difficult letters rather than the widely popular approach of a letter a week.

• Make the connection between letter names and letter sounds explicit. Some letter names provide concrete clues about their sounds. For example, the letter name for *b* contains the sound value /b/ in the beginning of the name /bi/. The letter name for *f* contains the sound value of /f/ at the end of the name /ɛf/. Explicitly identifying these clues aids students' letter sound learning. Note though that some consonant letters such as *h* and *w* do not provide a clue about letter sounds. Vowel letters in English represent many sounds in different contexts, and in fact, the phoneme–grapheme correspondences for vowels are a persistent challenge for children; thus, explicit and systematic instruction is critical.

• Teach for accuracy *and* speed. Like any learning, achieving automaticity for letter names and sounds is important. In other words, children should reach mastery so that their identification of letter names and sounds is automatic. This means fast retrieval of information, which facilitates children's application of letter knowledge during word reading and spelling processes.

• Teach letter writing. In addition to letter name and sound knowledge, students should be taught letter writing as well. This is important for two reasons. First, multimodal learning helps secure learning of letters in children's memory (see dual coding theory; Paivio, 1991), and thus, letter writing supports the learning of letter shapes. Second, letter writing automaticity helps the development of spelling and written composition (Kim & Park, 2019; Santangelo & Graham, 2016). Instruction of letter writing should include the order of the strokes and well-formedness. Beyond accuracy, sufficient practice opportunities should be provided for speed and automaticity of letter writing.

Teach Chunking

As noted above, in the beginning phase of word reading and spelling development, children learn the correspondences between individual graphemes and phonemes, the foundation for word reading and spelling. As children develop their word reading skill, however, this approach is inefficient and slow. Instead, they need to recognize chunks larger than individual graphemes, store them in memory, and use them in word reading and spelling. Ultimately, recognizing words as a whole by sight automatically is the goal (see the automaticity phase above). Figure 2.4 shows the mapping of speech sounds (phonology) and meaning (morphology) to a written representation (orthography) for various gain sizes such as phonemes and graphemes, rimes and phonograms, and syllables and syllable types as well as morphemes. Chunking can be done in phonograms, syllables, and morphemes.

Phonograms as a Unit for Chunking

Phonograms are technically a letter or groups of letters (i.e., graphemes). The term is also widely used to refer to spellings that correspond to the rime unit in phonology. For example, -*ock* in the following words is a phonogram: *sock*, *lock*, and *rock*. These words share the same rime and share the same spelling. Therefore, applying this knowledge facilitates word reading and spelling. For example, a child does not know how to spell the word *dock*, but if they know how to read and spell the word *sock*, they can use this knowledge to spell *dock* (this is called analogy; Goswami, 1994). Word building and word sort are effective activities for phonics in general and can be applied to teaching phonogram as a unit. Examples can be found below.

WORD BUILDING

The word *sock* is written on the board. The teacher models reading the word according to the onset–rime units, *s-ock*. Then the teacher brings attention to the spelling of *ock* for the /ak/ sound; replaces the letter *s* in *sock* with the letter *l* (lock) and points out the spelling of *ock* for the sound; and repeats with other words (e.g., *rock, dock, shock*).

WORD SORT

Word cards are prepared for the words *sock, lock, rock,* and *dock* and for the words *bag, tag,* and *rag*. The teacher does a model think-aloud, explicitly articulating the target patterns: *-ock* and *-ag* (I Do). Next, with the help of children, the teacher moves a word under one of the patterns (We Do). Then children are asked to sort the words according to shared sounds and spelling patterns (You Do). Throughout the week, students work with these patterns engaging in varied versions of word sort. See Bear et al. (2016) for excellent details and resources for word study for word reading and spelling instruction.

Syllables as a Unit for Chunking

The transition to reading and spelling multisyllabic words is formidable for many children. Therefore, recognizing syllables as a chunk is part and parcel of effective phonics instruction. For example, unaccented vowel schwa (e.g., /ə/ as in *about*) is a challenge in reading and spelling because children have difficulty identifying the sound as it is unstressed vowel, and it is spelled with all the five vowel letters in English (*a, e, i, o, u*). Also challenging are unaccented final syllables such as *-al* (e.g., *trial, annual, causal, mammal, signal*); *-il* (e.g., *tonsil, pupil, fossil*); *-el* (e.g., *fuel, tunnel, pretzel, cruel*); or *-le* (e.g., *fiddle, beetle, circle, cradle*). R-controlled vowels /ɪ/ or /ɚ/ also present challenges because they are spelled in different ways: *-ar* (e.g., *dollar, solar, lunar*); *-er* (e.g., *toaster, trouser, pitcher*); *-or* (e.g., *rumor, motor, razor*); and *-ure* (e.g., *culture, feature, lecture, pressure, leisure, conjure*). Because there are no strong rules for these patterns and there are always exceptions, word study or word sort is a great way to teach these patterns (see Bear et al., 2016).

Other patterns that children confuse particularly in spelling are doubling of consonant letters and dropping the letter *e* (e.g., *shopping, jogging, skipping; reading, chewing, looking; writing, changing, shining*). Doubling of consonant letters is used as a means to indicate that preceding vowels are a short vowel (e.g., *hop → hopping* compared with *hope → hoping*). The letter *e* is dropped when it is at the end of the word and suffixes (e.g., *-ing, -ed*) are added. Although there are exceptions (e.g., *taxing* for the doubling consonant; *being* for dropping *e*), these general observations about these patterns are useful and thus should be taught. Again, word sort can be a great approach to teaching these patterns.

Morphemes as a Unit for Chunking

Recognizing morphemes and associated spellings, storing them in memory, and then using this knowledge help support development of word reading and spelling. As shown in Figure 2.3, morphemes can be classified into several categories. Students need to be taught that words are composed of meaningful units, and these units map onto spelling. For example, the past tense morphological marker is -ed (e.g., want*ed*, paint*ed*, play*ed*, learn*ed*, walk*ed*, jump*ed*). In spelling, students need to learn that the sounds of the -ed differ depending on the nature of words, but they are all spelled with -ed. In word reading, it should be explicitly pointed out that although these words end with the same spelling pattern (-ed), their sounds differ because of the last sound in the preceding part (e.g., when -ed is preceded by /t/, it is pronounced as as /ɪd/).

An instructional approach incorporating morphological awareness is widely known as morphemic analysis or structural analysis, and typically involves recognizing morphemes and associated spellings. This is important for beginning readers. However, morphological awareness instruction should not wait until children develop initial word reading and spelling skills. Instead, morphological awareness should be taught to prereaders just like phonological awareness. For example, counting and substitution can be used to teach prereaders that words are composed of multiple morphemes (e.g., *jumped* has two meaningful units, *jump-ed*; *redo* and *active* have two meaningful units, *re-do* and *act-ive*).

Teach Decoding and Encoding

The aforementioned instructional approaches—teaching phonological awareness and grapheme–phoneme correspondences, and chunking—are not end goals by themselves, but instead they are in service of word reading and spelling. This implies that instruction of phonological awareness and letters should explicitly address blending the decoded sounds into a word for word reading, and encoding sounds into a series of graphemes and assembling them for spelling. Studies have shown that combining instruction on phonological awareness and letter–sound correspondences with word reading and spelling better develops students' word reading and spelling skills (e.g., Ehri, Satlow, & Gaskins, 2009). Powerful tools for decoding and encoding are word building and word study/sort (see above). Word dictation is another powerful tool. Although dictation is typically used as an assessment tool for spelling, it can be a useful instructional tool as well. For example, the teacher can model dictating a target word as follows:

> "My word is *cat*. /kkæætt/. I hear three sounds /k-æ-t/. The word /kæt/ begins with a /k/ sound and has /æ/ and /t/ sounds. What letters make a /k/ sound? I know letters *c* and *k* do. For this word, I am going to write down the letter *k*. Which letter makes an /æ/ sound? I know that the letter *a* does so I am going to write down the letter *a* right after the letter *k*. Now

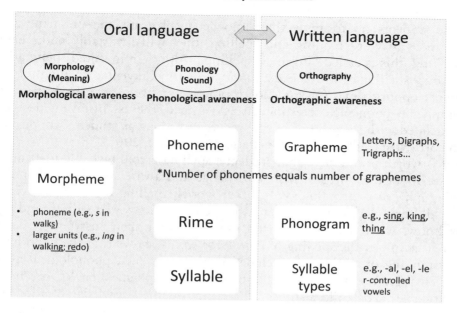

FIGURE 2.4. Mapping between oral language and written language for word reading and spelling.

I need a letter for the /t/ sound so I am going to write down the letter *t* right after the letter *a*. Now I have *k-a-t* for the word /kæt/. Hmm, this does not look quite right. The letter *k* in the beginning seems odd. I am going to try replacing it with a *c*, so now I have *c-a-t* for the word /kæt/. Does this look right to you all? That's right. Let's read this word together /kkæætt/ (moving your finger under each letter as it is read). How do you spell the word /kæt/? *c-a-t*."

This can be followed by a We Do practice with another word, for example, *bat*. Then, students can try on their own with other words such as *pat* and *rat*.

Another important aspect of word reading and spelling instruction is the teaching of irregular words, words that do not follow common grapheme–phoneme correspondences, such as *was*, *you*, *to*, *should*, *of*, *have*, *give*, *listen*, *answer*, and *come*. These are typically taught as sight words, using a whole word approach, where students are asked to memorize the word as a whole without analyzing it using their knowledge of grapheme–phoneme correspondences. However, this approach does not capitalize on the letter–sound relations that exist in these words. For example, the word *should* /ʃʊd/ follows the common letter–sound correspondences for the letters *sh* and *d*, but the silent letters *oul* are an exception. Therefore, an analytic approach for *sh* and *d* is applicable for *should* and other irregular words as well, and this approach to word reading and spelling instruction improves students' learning (Miles, Rubin, & Gonzalez-Frey, 2017).

As students try to apply their knowledge of grapheme–phoneme correspondences in word reading and spelling, they will invariably make errors. In spelling, this is called "invented spelling." Although invented spelling is an inaccurate spelling of words (e.g., *kande* for *candy*), invented spelling provides excellent opportunities for students to practice and reinforce their knowledge of grapheme–phoneme correspondences. As such, the use of invented spelling is associated with the growth of spelling skills as long as students are provided with corrective feedback (e.g., Ouellette & Sénéchal, 2008).

It is worth noting here that students' spelling errors reveal a great deal of insights about the status of their knowledge and awareness about phonology, orthography, and morphology. In other words, spelling errors are a window into children's developmental stage of spelling *and* word reading, and what they know, what they use but confuse, and what their instructional needs are. For example, the spelling of *kande* for *candy* shows that the child has an understanding of the sounds included in the word (i.e., phonological awareness). Furthermore, the child has knowledge of graphemes for /k/, /æ/, /n/, and /d/ phonemes. The child also used their letter–name knowledge of *e* for an /ɪ/ sound. In terms of immediate instructional planning for this child, the teacher may teach the child that letter *c* is used before the vowel letters *a*, *o*, and *u*. By analyzing patterns of errors in the child's spelling, the teacher can identify their knowledge and needs, and plan word reading and spelling instruction accordingly (see Bear et al., 2016, for a spelling inventory associated with developmental phases).

Incorporate Connected Texts

The end goal of word reading and spelling instruction is for students to use these skills in reading connected texts and producing connected texts. Therefore, it is important to provide opportunities to practice reading and spelling words in isolation *and* in connected texts. In terms of reading, connected texts include decodable texts and authentic texts. Decodable texts are texts in which the decodability of words is controlled such that the majority of words in the text are phonetically regular words and taught spelling patterns. Decodable texts, of course, should not be driven solely by decodability; they should have a coherent storyline. Decodable texts are typically used as a *transitional* text for beginning readers before students move to authentic connected texts because authentic texts typically include many words that are too challenging and overwhelming for beginning readers. Decodable texts afford opportunities to read and practice taught words in context for accuracy and automaticity, as well as comprehension. Studies have shown that the use of decodable texts as part of beginning literacy instruction is beneficial for students' reading development (Cheatham & Allor, 2012; Juel & Roper-Schneider, 1985).

Likewise, opportunities to practice spelling in writing connected texts should be systematically incorporated as part of reading and writing instruction. As students engage in daily writing activities, they should be encouraged to use their learned patterns, try their best spelling (which may be invented spelling), and read their own writing. This provides an opportunity to practice orthographic patterns, spelling, and word reading, and also to engage in meaning-making processes (e.g., comprehension and composition).

Conclusion

There is no doubt that word reading and spelling are the foundational skills for reading and writing development. Word reading and spelling are strongly related and draw on essentially the same skills, namely phonological awareness, orthographic awareness, and morphological awareness. Therefore, these skills should be taught explicitly and systematically. In particular, phonics that includes explicit and systematic teaching of all these aspects should be part and parcel of early literacy instruction. Word reading and spelling are also mutually supportive, and thus, instruction should also capitalize on the synergy between word reading and spelling. Word reading and spelling instruction, like the teaching of any skill, should be built on research-informed pedagogical practices. Last but certainly not least, teaching of word reading and spelling is only *part* of a larger effective early literacy instruction, which also should include explicit and systematic teaching of other skills that are important for reading comprehension and written composition (e.g., vocabulary, listening comprehension, higher-order thinking skills).

ACKNOWLEDGMENTS

This work was supported by a grant from the Institute of Education Sciences, U.S. Department of Education (R305A180055, R305A170113, and R305C190007) and the National Institute of Child Health and Human Development (P50HD052120). The content is solely the responsibility of the authors and does not necessarily represent the official views of the funding agencies.

REFERENCES

Abbott, R. D., & Berninger, V. W. (1993). Structural equation modeling of relationships among developmental skills and writing skills in primary- and intermediate-grade writers. *Journal of Educational Psychology, 85*(3), 478–508.

Adams, M. A. (1990). *Beginning to read: Thinking and learning about print*. Cambridge, MA: MIT Press.

Apel, K., & Masterson, J. J. (2001). Theory-guided spelling assessment and intervention: A case study. *Language, Speech, and Hearing Services in the Schools, 32*(3), 182–195.

Arra, C. T., & Aaron, P. G. (2001). Effects of psycholinguistic instruction on spelling performance. *Psychology in the Schools, 38*(4), 357–363.

August, D., Shanahan, T., & Escamilla, K. (2009). English language learners:

Developing literacy in second-language learners—Report of the National Literacy Panel on Language-Minority Children and Youth. *Journal of Literacy Research, 41,* 432–452.

Bahr, R. H., Silliman, E. R., Berninger, V. W., & Dow, M. (2012). Linguistic pattern analysis of misspellings of typically developing writers in grades 1–9. *Journal of Speech, Language, and Hearing Research, 55*(6), 1587–1599.

Bear, D. R., Invernizzi, M., Templeton, S., & Johnston, F. (2016). *Words their way: Word study for phonics, vocabulary, and spelling instruction* (6th ed.). Boston: Pearson.

Berninger, V. W., Nielson, K. H., Abbott, R. D., Wijsman, E., & Raskind, W. (2008). Writing problems in developmental dyslexia: Under-recognized and under-treated. *Journal of School Psychology, 46,* 1–21.

Berninger, V. W., & Winn, W. D. (2006). Implications of advancements in brain research and technology for writing development, writing instruction, and educational evolution. In C. MacArthur, S. Graham, & J. Fitzgerald (Eds.), *Handbook of writing research* (pp. 96–114). New York: Guilford Press.

Cheatham, J. P., & Allor, J. H. (2012). The influence of decodability in early reading text on reading achievement: A review of the evidence. *Reading and Writing, 25,* 2223–2246.

Craig, H. K., Thompson, C. A., Washington, J. A., & Potter, S. L. (2003). Phonological features of child African American English. *Journal of Speech, Language, and Hearing Research, 46,* 623–635.

Ehri, L. C. (1997). Learning to read and learning to spell are one and the same, almost. In C. A. Perfetti, L. Rieben, & M. Fayol (Eds.), *Learning to spell: Research, theory, and practice across languages* (pp. 237–269). Mahwah, NJ: Erlbaum.

Ehri, L. C. (2005). Development of sight word reading: Phases and findings. In M. J. Snowling & C. Hulme (Eds.), *Blackwell handbooks of developmental psychology. The science of reading: A handbook* (pp. 135–154). Malden, MA: Blackwell.

Ehri, L., Deffner, N., & Wilce, L. (1984). Pictorial mnemonics for phonics. *Journal of Educational Psychology, 76,* 880–893.

Ehri, L. C., Satlow, E., & Gaskins, I. (2009). Grapho-phonemic enrichment strengthens keyword analogy instruction for struggling young readers. *Reading & Writing Quarterly, 25*(2/3), 162–191.

Ellis, N., & Cataldo, S. (1990). The role of spelling in learning to read. *Language and Education, 4*(1), 1–28.

Fillmore, L. W., & Snow, C. E. (2000). *What teachers need to know about language.* Retrieved from *https://eric.ed.gov/?id=ED444379.*

Fitzgerald, J., & Shanahan, T. (2000). Reading and writing relations and their development. *Educational Psychologist, 35,* 39–50.

Gentry, J. R. (1982). An analysis of developmental spelling in GNYS AT WRK. *The Reading Teacher, 36,* 192–200.

Goswami, U. (1994). The role of analogies in reading development. *Support for Learning, 9*(1), 22–26.

Gough, P. B., & Tunmer, W. E. (1986). Decoding, reading, and reading disability. *RASE: Remedial & Special Education, 7*(1), 6–10.

Graham, S., Aiken, A. A., Hebert, A., Camping, A., Santagelo, T., Harris, K. R., . . . Ng, C. (2021). Do children with reading difficulties experience writing difficulties? A meta-analysis. *Journal of Educational Psychology, 113*(8), 1481–1506.

Graham, S., Berninger, V. W., Abbott, R. D., Abbott, S. P., & Whitaker, D. (1997). Role of mechanics in composing of elementary school students: A new methodological approach. *Journal of Educational Psychology, 89,* 170–182.

Graham, S., Harris, K. R., & Chorzempa, B. F. (2002). Contribution of spelling instruction to the spelling, writing, and reading of poor spellers. *Journal of Educational Psychology, 94,* 669–686.

Graham, S., Liu, X., Aitken, A., Ng, C., Bartlett, B., Harris, K. R., & Holzapfel, J. (2017). Effectiveness of literacy programs balancing reading and writing instruction: A meta-analysis. *Reading Research Quarterly, 53*(3), 279–304.

Hoover, W. A., & Gough, P. B. (1990). The simple view of reading. *Reading and Writing: An Interdisciplinary Journal, 2,* 127–160.

Juel, C., Griffith, P. L., & Gough, P. B. (1986). Acquisition of literacy: A longitudinal study of children in first and second grade. *Journal of Educational Psychology, 78,* 243–255.

Juel, C., & Roper-Schneider, D. (1985). The influence of basal readers on first grade reading. *Reading Research Quarterly, 20,* 134–152.

Kim, Y.-S. G. (2017). Why the simple view of reading is not simplistic: Unpacking component skills of reading using a direct and indirect effect model of reading (DIER). *Scientific Studies of Reading, 21*(4), 310–333.

Kim, Y.-S. G. (2020a). Hierarchical and dynamic relations of language and cognitive skills to reading comprehension: Testing the direct and indirect effects model of reading (DIER). *Journal of Educational Psychology, 112*(4), 667–684.

Kim, Y.-S. G. (2020b). The simple view of reading unpacked and expanded: The direct and indirect effects model of reading. *The Reading League, 1*(2), 15–22.

Kim, Y.-S. G. (2020c). Structural relations of language and cognitive skills, and topic knowledge to written composition: A test of the direct and indirect effects model of writing (DIEW). *British Journal of Educational Psychology, 90*(4), 910–932.

Kim, Y.-S. G. (2020d). Interactive dynamic literacy model: An integrative theoretical framework for reading and writing relations. In R. Alves, T. Limpo, & M. Joshi (Eds.), *Reading–writing connections: Towards integrative literacy science* (pp. 11–34). New York: Springer.

Kim, Y.-S., Al Otaiba, S., Puranik, C., Folsom, J. S., Greulich, L., & Wagner, R. K. (2011). Componential skills of beginning writing: An exploratory study. *Learning and Individual Differences, 21*(5), 517–525.

Kim, Y.-S., Al Otaiba, S., Wanzek, J., & Gatlin, B. (2015). Toward an understanding of dimensions, predictors, and the gender gap in written composition. *Journal of Educational Psychology, 107*(1), 79–95.

Kim, Y.-S. G., & Davidson, M. (2019). *Promoting successful literacy acquisition through structured pedagogy.* Global Reading Network Critical Topics Series. Washington, DC: U.S. Agency for International Development. Retrieved from *www.globalreadingnetwork.net/resources/promoting-successful-literacy-acquisition-through-structured-pedagogy.*

Kim, Y.-S. G., & Park, S. (2019). Unpacking pathways using the direct and indirect effects model of writing (DIEW) and the contributions of higher order cognitive skills to writing. *Reading and Writing: An Interdisciplinary Journal, 32*(5), 1319–1343.

Kim, Y.-S. G., Petscher, Y., Treiman, R., & Kelcey, B. (2021). Letter features as predictors of letter-name acquisition in four languages with three scripts. *Scientific Studies of Reading, 25*(6), 453–469.

Kim, Y.-S. G., & Schatschneider, C. (2017). Expanding the developmental models of writing: A direct and indirect effects model of developmental writing (DIEW). *Journal of Educational Psychology, 109*(1), 35–50.

Kim, Y.-S. G., Wolters, A., & Lee, W. J. (2022). *Reading and writing relations are not uniform. They differ by the linguistic grain size, developmental phase, and measurement.* Manuscript submitted for publication.

McMaster, K. L., Lembke, E. S., Shin, J., Poch, A., Smith, R. A., Jung, P., . . . Wagner, K. (2020). Supporting teachers' use of data-based instruction to improve students' early writing skills. *Journal of Educational Psychology, 112*(1), 1–21.

Miles, K. P., Rubin, G. B., & Gonzalez-Frey, S. (2017). Rethinking sight words. *The Reading Teacher, 71*(6), 715–726.

Moats, L. (2010). *Speech to print: Language essentials for teachers.* Paul H. Baltimore, MD: Brookes.

National Early Literacy Panel. (2008). *Developing early literacy: Report of the National Early Literacy Panel.* Washington, DC: National Institute for Literacy. Retrieved from *www.nifl.gov/earlychildhood/NELP/ NELPreport.html.*

National Institute of Child Health and Human Development. (2000). *Report of the National Reading Panel. Teaching children to read: An evidence-based assessment of the scientific research literature on reading and its implications for reading instruction* (NIH Publication No. 00–4769). Washington, DC: U.S. Government Printing Office.

Ouellette, G. P., & Sénéchal, M. (2008). A window into early literacy: Exploring the cognitive and linguistic underpinnings of invented spelling. *Scientific Studies of Reading, 12*(2), 195–219.

Paivio, A. (1991). Dual coding theory: Retrospect and current status. *Canadian Journal of Psychology/Revue canadienne de psychologie, 45*(3), 255–287.

Perfetti, C., & Stafura, J. (2014). Word knowledge in a theory of reading comprehension. *Scientific Studies of Reading, 18*(1), 22–37.

Pollo, T. C., Treiman, R., & Kessler, B. (2008). Three perspectives on spelling development. In E. L. Grigorenko & A. J. Naples (Eds.), *Single-word reading: Behavioral and biological perspectives* (pp. 175–189). Mahwah, NJ: Erlbaum.

Rayner, K., Foorman, B., Perfetti, C. A., Pesetsky, D., & Seidenberg, M. S. (2001). How psychological science informs the teaching of reading. *Psychological Science in the Public Interest, 2*(2), 31–74.

Rosenshine, B. (2012). Principles of instruction: Research-based strategies that all teachers should know. *American Educator, 36*(1), 12–19.

Santangelo, T., & Graham, S. (2016). A comprehensive meta-analysis of handwriting instruction. *Educational Psychology Review, 28*(2), 225–265.

Seidenberg, M. S., & McClelland, J. L. (1989). A distributed, developmental model of word recognition and naming. *Psychological Review, 96*(4), 523–568.

Shanahan, T. (2016). Relationships between reading and writing development. In C. A. MacArthur, S. Graham, & J. Fitzgerald (Eds.), *Handbook of writing research* (pp. 194–207). New York: Guilford Press.

Shmidman, A., & Ehri, L. (2010). Embedded picture mnemonics to learn letters. *Scientific Studies of Reading, 14*(2), 159–182.

Siegler, R. S. (1996). A grand theory of development. *Monographs of the Society of Research in Child Development, 61,* 266–275.

Treiman, R. (2017a). Learning to spell: Phonology and beyond. *Cognitive Neuropsychology, 34*(3–4), 83–93.

Treiman, R. (2017b). Learning to spell words: Findings, theories, and issues. *Scientific Studies of Reading, 21*(4), 265–276.

Treiman, R., & Kessler, B. (2003). The role of letter names in the acquisition of literacy. In R. V. Kail (Ed.), *Advances in child development and behavior* (Vol. 31, pp. 105–135). Cambridge, MA: Academic Press.

Treiman, R., Kessler, B., & Caravolas, M. (2019). What methods of scoring young children's spelling best predict later spelling performance? *Journal of Research in Reading, 42*(1), 80–96.

Vaughn, S., Cirino, P. T., Linan-Thompson, S., Mathes, P. G., Carlson, C. D., Hagan, E. C., . . . Francis, D. J. (2006). Effectiveness of a Spanish intervention and an English intervention for English-language learners at risk for reading problems. *American Educational Research Journal, 43*(3), 449–487.

Wawire, B. A., & Kim, Y.-S. G. (2018). Cross-language transfer of phonological awareness and letter knowledge: Causal evidence and nature of transfer. *Scientific Studies of Reading, 22*(6), 443–461.

CHAPTER 3

The Role of Vocabulary in and for Writing

Margaret G. McKeown

What is the relationship between vocabulary and writing, beyond the very obvious one—words? That relationship might be interpreted in two ways: one is the role of vocabulary knowledge in a writer's ability to write; the other is the role of vocabulary used within a piece of writing in determining the quality of that writing.

Consideration of those two aspects of this relationship initiates this chapter. The rest of the chapter focuses on the kind of vocabulary knowledge a writer needs to produce good writing, whether vocabulary instruction influences students' writing, and finally, samples of instructional activities that promote vocabulary in and for writing. Thus, the following questions become the blueprint for this chapter.

GUIDING QUESTIONS

- What is the role of vocabulary knowledge in the writing process?
- What aspects of vocabulary characterize good writing?
- What kind of vocabulary knowledge do writers need?
- Does vocabulary instruction enhance writing?
- What kinds of instructional activities support both vocabulary and writing?

What Is the Role of Vocabulary Knowledge in the Writing Process?

Theories and models of writing generally consider the processes that a writer engages to produce written text and the knowledge and resources that a writer brings to bear to engage those processes. Cognitive theories of writing, dominant since the 1980s, attend to the mental processes that take a writer from ideation to a written product. Sociocultural theories focus more on the influences of a writer's resources, experiences, and context for writing. The role of vocabulary is not well specified in either type of model, and as Olinghouse and Wilson (2013) note, there has been scant attention to the relationship between vocabulary and writing. In particular, they point out that the Flower and Hayes (1981; Hayes, 1996) and Bereiter and Scardamalia (1987) models do not include an explicit role for vocabulary. However, Olinghouse and Wilson infer a link from components within those models, hypothesizing that vocabulary may connect knowledge stored in long-term memory with a writer's ability to express that knowledge through the use of the most appropriate word.

Linguistic processes are frequently included as a component of the writing process, and one might expect vocabulary to be included there, too. However, the focus is generally on lower-level processes involved in actually getting words on paper—transcription and handwriting skills. For example, MacArthur and Graham (2016) review five models of the writing process, but none include vocabulary or language skills beyond transcription. Linguistic skills have a somewhat higher profile in McCutchen's cognitive capacity model (1996, 2011), which views fluency of linguistic processes as underlying writing ability. However, specification of those processes is limited to phonological and orthographic knowledge.

Vocabulary receives direct attention in recent work by Kim and colleagues (2015, 2016; Kim & Schatschneider, 2017). A motivation for this work was that some critical aspects of prior models are underspecified, particularly in the realm of text generation relative to the transcription aspect of writing. The work investigates discourse-level oral language, which refers to comprehension and production of multiple extended oral text such as conversations or stories. The skill is assessed with a narrative retelling task. In the authors' view, discourse-level oral language draws on a range of skills, including vocabulary and grammatical knowledge. Kim and Schatschneider (2017) constructed models based on foundational language and cognitive skills (vocabulary, grammatical skills, working memory) and higher-order cognitive skills (inference, perspective taking) related to discourse-level oral language and tested the models using first-graders' writing samples. They found that vocabulary predicted discourse-level language skills, which in turn predicted writing ability. Thus, Kim and Schatschneider's data suggest that the ability to use words helps a writer create a high-quality text, but that knowledge of those words alone does not directly predict good writing.

Another finding from their work that may bear on the relationship of vocabulary knowledge to writing is the role of working memory. Kim and Schatschneider found that working memory was not directly related to writing once all the language and cognitive skills were accounted for. However, the total effect of working memory on writing was substantial, and pointed to working memory as an important cognitive underpinning of writing skill.

The relationship of working memory to vocabulary comes into focus if we consider McCutchen's (1996, 2011) model of writing, which highlights cognitive capacity. According to McCutchen (2011), two key components in writing expertise are development of fluent language generation processes and extensive knowledge relevant to writing. Although not specified in McCutchen's model, there is reason to believe that fluency of vocabulary knowledge may play a role as well. According to the lexical quality hypothesis (Perfetti, 2007), high-quality lexical representations of orthographic and phonological form and of meaning underlie successful reading comprehension. High-quality representations allow for rapid and reliable retrieval of word identities, which frees up cognitive resources for comprehension processing. If the fluent processing needed for reading requires both form and meaning knowledge, it makes sense that fluent vocabulary knowledge, as well as fluency of linguistic forms, would support writing. Fluent access to a greater number and variety of words and their relationships might free up resources for idea development, monitoring coherence, and so on.

What Aspects of Vocabulary Characterize Good Writing?

The specific words an author chooses to get their point across are critical to good writing. What characterizes good word choices in writing? Often cited aspects include diversity of vocabulary within a text; use of lower-frequency versus common high-frequency words, often labeled maturity of vocabulary; precision of vocabulary to the concept or situation; and appropriateness to the tone, mood, or purpose of a text. Of those traits, diversity and maturity of vocabulary are the easiest to communicate and measure, but less likely to guarantee writing quality. Regarding diversity, any of us who have taught language arts recognize the naive writing move of opening the thesaurus and haphazardly selecting a bunch of synonyms for a target word in an essay. The outcome is rarely a higher-quality text.

Indeed, Durrant and Benchley's (2019) study of young writers demonstrated that measuring frequency of words does not tell the whole story of the quality of vocabulary in a piece of writing. The authors used a corpus of school-based writing from students 6 to 16 years old. They found that the writing of students in primary grades was distinct from that of older students in its greater repetition of low-frequency nouns and high-frequency adjectives, adverbs, and verbs. The nouns that young students used, although low frequency, tended to be concrete and narrow in utility, such as *fairy* and *turtle*. Thus, as Durrant and Benchley conclude, "the relationship between vocabulary frequency and development in children's writing is far more complex than simply equating low-frequency with sophistication" (p. 1951).

Olinghouse and Wilson (2013) examined the role of vocabulary in writing by studying characteristics of vocabulary use across three genres: story, persuasive, and informative text. Fifth-grade students were asked to write in each genre on the topic of outer space. The vocabulary constructs measured included diversity, maturity (frequency), content vocabulary, academic vocabulary, and register (words of Latinate origin).

They found that vocabulary played a different role in the different genres. Narrative text had greater vocabulary diversity than informative text and higher maturity than persuasive text. Persuasive text had higher diversity than informative text, and higher register than both of the other genres. Informative text included more content words than narrative or persuasive text and higher maturity than persuasive text. Their work suggests that writing in different genres calls for different aspects of vocabulary. Similarly, Olinghouse and Wilson (2013) report that different vocabulary measures predicted writing quality in each genre. For narrative text, vocabulary diversity was a unique predictor; for persuasive text, content words and register were unique predictors; and for informative text, use of content words was the strongest unique predictor.

More broadly, one might conclude that it is likely easier to recognize the contribution of word choice to writing—for example, as a reader delights in an author's apt description of a character—than it is to measure or describe in general terms. Effective word choice in writing is rooted in an author's facility to mentally sort through words and select ones that best represent what the author is trying to communicate. Viewing effective word choice from the author side brings us to the question of what kind of knowledge a writer needs to produce effective text.

What Kind of Vocabulary Knowledge Do Writers Need?

First and most obvious, as the sections on the role of vocabulary knowledge and characteristics of word choice make clear, writers benefit from a large and diverse vocabulary. Yet as the work cited suggests, especially that of Kim and Schatschneider, knowledge of those words on its own does not lead to good writing. Coxhead and Byrd (2007) assert that knowing a word in order to use it in writing involves at least understanding and expressing meaning in a range of contexts, regular grammatical patterns of occurrence, words that commonly occur with the word (collocations), word families, formality, word parts, and synonyms and antonyms.

Coxhead and Byrd put particular emphasis on extended sets of words that occur in "relatively fixed sequences and that are likely to be stored in memory as sets" (p. 134), which they point to as characteristic of academic English. This includes phrases such as *the extent to which*, *as a result of*, phrasal verbs and prepositional verbs *look up*, *agree to*, and what they term lexical bundles such as *in order to* and *there is no*. Coxhead and Byrd also highlight collocational patterns, such as the word *widespread* being most often followed by *adoption*, *acceptance*, or *agreement*.

Coxhead and Byrd's (2007) depiction of vocabulary knowledge for writing aligns well with descriptions of effective vocabulary knowledge developed in work on reading comprehension. The high-quality lexical representations that are the centerpiece of the lexical quality hypothesis (Perfetti, 2007) constitute richly connected networks of word meaning, linking words that are similar or opposite in meaning and words that occur together.

The broad, multifaceted depiction of vocabulary knowledge by Coxhead and Byrd can also be likened to the consensus in the reading comprehension field that effective knowledge supporting comprehension is complex, flexible, and nuanced (Beck, McKeown, & Kucan, 2013). Rich flexible knowledge allows a reader to adjust features of word meaning to make sense of particular contexts encountered in texts.

McKeown, Deane, Scott, Krovetz, and Lawless (2017) provide a perspective on the components of vocabulary knowledge that underlie effective reading, writing, and critical thinking, which parallels Coxhead and Byrd's (2007) description. McKeown et al. view vocabulary knowledge as consisting of specific knowledge of words and multiword expressions, which includes various senses of a word's meaning, its connotations, its relationship to similar or associated words, and generative patterns of morphology, syntax, and semantics within and across words.

McKeown et al. highlight another aspect of language knowledge, which is also the heart of work by Nagy and Scott (2000; Scott & Nagy, 2004). That is metalinguistic knowledge, a language user's awareness that patterns apply across words, thus making new examples of them familiar and predictable. For example, recognizing that words are made up of morphological constituents, or that the same words can have both physical and metaphorical meanings, boosts the learning of unfamiliar words. Metalinguistic knowledge includes understandings about language such as the awareness of how words work, and the ability to reflect on and manipulate units of language (McKeown, Deane, et al., 2017; Scott & Nagy, 2004).

Understanding underlying patterns of word meaning, syntax, and morphology supports students in making sense of newly encountered words and their contexts. That same repertoire of generative knowledge supports students in making appropriate and precise word choices when they write. Knowing not only specific words, but also how language operates—the ways that words can be put together to express meaning—helps a writer reach for and select among apt words to evoke a feeling, portray an idea with clarity, or subtly shade how information is interpreted.

Metalinguistic skill also likely contributes to audience awareness and a related construct, theory of mind—the ability to understand other's thoughts and take perspectives. Kim's work (2015, 2016; Kim & Schatschneider, 2017) found that perspective taking was predictive of discourse-level language skills. This suggests that good writing takes account of the audience and considers how the message will be received, or tailors the message to a desired audience. Will it be comprehensible, persuasive, engaging? Choosing words carefully and precisely both reflects audience awareness and partly determines a text's success in prompting the targeted audience reaction.

To summarize, the knowledge a writer needs for effective writing is grounded first in a deep knowledge about individual words and multiword expressions. But an effective writing process also calls for knowledge of generative patterns that apply to individual words and across words. Finally, the metalinguistic awareness of how words work is key to supporting a writer's felicitous choice of words.

Does Vocabulary Instruction Enhance Writing?

It seems reasonable to hypothesize that vocabulary instruction that effectively enhances knowledge of words, especially depth of word knowledge, would impact writing. The characteristics of vocabulary knowledge that underlie successful comprehension are those that promote writing quality as well. That is, knowledge of word use beyond merely definitional meaning, application of words in different contexts, relationships to associated words, morphological structure of words. But what do we know about whether that impact actually exists? Precious little research has explored that relationship.

Improvement in writing is generally not a stated goal of vocabulary intervention studies, and thus studies of vocabulary instruction do not include measures of writing ability as a matter of course. There are, however, a few studies that have explicitly examined the impact of teaching vocabulary on writing. These are mostly represented in the second language literature, with the most prominent being work by Webb (2009) and Lee (2003). Both of these studies were rather narrow, but led to potentially informative results.

Webb's study asked Japanese students learning English to study word translations in either a receptive or productive mode. Students either looked at target words and tried to recall their translations (receptive) or looked at translations and tried to recall the target word (productive). Students were then asked to write sentences with each word to describe a picture. Target words were generally concrete and of limited utility, such as *dagger, doze, boulder,* and *sprint*. The result was that the productive learners scored significantly better in terms of sentences that accurately used the word. Thus, even in this narrow study, the result suggested that knowledge needed to support writing ability needs to be greater than recalling a definition.

Lee's (2003) study was richer, but still rather limited; for example, all the instruction took place in one day. Participants were secondary multi-L1 English learners. This study involved (1) a vocabulary pretest, (2) reading a text that contained the target words, (3) a writing task, (4) vocabulary instruction, and (5) a postwriting task. The target words were academically relevant, such as *serious, defeat, effects,* and *prohibit*. The instruction, though brief, was multifaceted—including discussion of definitions and uses of words, relationships to other words, and using the word in writing. This resulted in a significant increase in use of target words in the post-instruction writing. But perhaps more interesting was the result about recognition versus productive knowledge. The study found that words whose meanings students recognized on the pretest were rarely used in their writing (about 13% of the words were used productively). But after instruction, about two-thirds of the words were used in the writing task. Thus, the study suggests that learners do not automatically put their recognition vocabulary to productive use, but are able to expand that use after explicit vocabulary instruction.

Ecologically richer studies are even rarer than the kind of studies Webb and Lee conducted. There are several dissertations cited in the literature, but beyond that, the only study seems to be Duin and Graves, and that was published in 1987! In 2000, Johnson examined the literature for studies of vocabulary instruction and writing and found only Duin and Graves and two studies "too flawed to be included."

Fortunately, Duin and Graves's (1987) study is intriguing and informative. The authors investigated the effect of vocabulary instruction on writing an essay. There were three instructional conditions, each provided over 6 days. One was traditional instruction, which involved practicing dictionary definitions and completing worksheets. The other two conditions featured rich instruction involving a variety of contexts and uses for words, and active processing. One of the rich vocabulary conditions also involved a daily writing activity with the target words. Students were then asked to write an essay about space. The words were selected for their utility in writing on the topic, and each group also discussed what they knew about space prior to vocabulary instruction. Essays were scored for overall impression and on scales for composition quality by independent raters. Also, a vocabulary multiple-choice assessment was given as a pretest and a posttest.

The results were that on the vocabulary test, all groups exhibited significant gains, with the two rich vocabulary groups' gains significantly higher than the traditional group's. For the writing task, the rich vocabulary and writing, and rich vocabulary alone groups made significant gains on composition quality scales, and the traditional vocabulary group showed a significant loss. Thus, it seems that rich vocabulary instruction did lead to improved writing while traditional instruction did not; but incorporating writing activities into the rich vocabulary instruction led to even greater improvement.

Also of interest to this discussion is a relatively recent dissertation completed at the University of Pittsburgh (Yonek, 2009). Yonek also investigated the effect of different types of vocabulary instruction on a writing task. One group of students received traditional, definition-based instruction and the other received rich instruction. The number of encounters with each target word was the same for both conditions. Students were then asked to write a persuasive essay in the form of a newspaper editorial about the importance of keeping parks clean. The fourth-grade participants had received instruction in writing in different genres, including persuasion, in the fall of the year, and the parks editorial had been a district assessment. Yonek used the assessment as a pretest and gave the same assignment as a posttest, about 7 months later.

The study assessed both vocabulary and writing. Vocabulary was assessed with both a multiple-choice test of definitions and a depth of knowledge test. Writing was assessed by counting the number of target words used and by the same qualitative writing scale used by the district. Yonek found no differences on the multiple-choice vocabulary test between groups, but significant advantage for the rich vocabulary group on the depth of knowledge test and on both writing measures. However, the traditional instruction group did improve their writing scores and included some target words in their essays. Of course, this happened 7 months later, and the same assignment as students had completed previously, which may have supported writing improvement.

Both the Duin and Graves (1987) and Yonek (2009) studies confirm the emerging pattern that vocabulary instruction that includes rich word information and active processing supports writing development compared to narrow, definition-focused instruction. Duin and Graves's study further indicates that if such vocabulary instruction includes writing using the target words, it provides an even greater boost for writing ability.

The question of a vocabulary instruction and writing relationship can also be asked in the other direction; does a writing component in vocabulary instruction enhance knowledge of the words? Writing activities are included in several vocabulary intervention studies (e.g., WordGen: Jones et al., 2019; ALIAS: Lesaux, Kieffer, Faller, & Kelley, 2010; RAVE: McKeown, Crosson, Moore, & Beck, 2018), but not in a way that can be readily measured. It seems that vocabulary researchers often surmise that students' use of target words in writing will enhance their knowledge of the words, as productive use likely instigates active processing.

One vocabulary intervention project that more explicitly emphasized writing to influence word knowledge was conducted by Judith Scott and colleagues (Henry et al., 1999; Scott, Miller, & Flinspach, 2012). The project began as A Gift of Words, a small researcher–teacher collaborative aimed to develop word-rich reading and writing strategies for enhancing vocabulary. Built around the concept of word consciousness, the project's goal was to enhance students' awareness of words that would transfer to their ability to notice and learn other words—producing generative word knowledge. Fundamental to the researchers' concept of word consciousness, which is a type of metalinguistic awareness, was helping students understand differences between spoken and written English, and particularly the role of precise word choice in effective writing (Scott & Nagy, 2004). Well-written novels and poems were the foundation for the project.

Attention to high-quality texts provided models of language use that students could analyze and critique toward developing a sense of how authors use words. Teachers read books aloud to prompt class discussions of word use, and students were encouraged to borrow words from the readings and explore them in their own writing. Students were also encouraged to analyze patterns of word use and use them as models to build their own phrasing. Classrooms kept a Gift of Words collection, words and phrases gathered from the texts they read, and students were encouraged to consult the collection when they wrote.

Teachers and researchers both observed marked changes in students' awareness and use of words. Gift of Words led to a larger project, Vocabulary Innovations in Education (VINE) (Scott et al., 2012). VINE was also a researcher–teacher collaborative, which aimed to both enhance teachers' own word consciousness and offer instructional ideas for teachers to use in their classrooms to enhance the word consciousness of their students. Word-conscious instruction was not prescribed in VINE; each teacher adapted and invented strategies. Thus, the range of strategies was much broader than in Gift of Words and beyond prioritizing writing. However, core components remained, including awareness of the difference between spoken and written language and the role of word choice in effective communication.

Of particular interest is that the VINE project was able to assess the effects of word consciousness on students' vocabulary growth (Scott, Flinspach, Miller, Gage-Serio, & Vevea, 2009). The project-developed assessment was based on words drawn from grade-level texts used in the school district. These words had not been directly taught, and in fact teachers in the project remained unaware of which words were tested. Students in the project significantly outperformed control students on the assessment. These results suggest that vocabulary interventions based on boosting students' awareness of word meaning and word use, with strong grounding in the use of texts and connected to student writing, can enhance students' general vocabulary learning.

Summing up the relationship of vocabulary instruction to writing, evidence is scanty that vocabulary instruction affects writing, chiefly because that question is rarely asked in vocabulary intervention studies. When the question has been explicitly posed, the answer seems to be "yes." And even more strongly "yes" when the vocabulary instruction includes the use of target words in writing. The caveat is that the knowledge built needs to be multifaceted and flexible, the kind of knowledge developed from instruction that offers active processing of words and their uses and presents information about word relationships and the fit of words to language contexts. Even though the lack of broad evidence is frustrating, the strength of the theoretical connection between flexible multifaceted language and the abilities it fosters is strong enough to build confidence in the evidence that is available.

What Kinds of Instructional Activities Support Both Vocabulary and Writing?

The issue of what kinds of instructional activities to recommend can be focused in a number of ways. Are we talking about vocabulary activities that involve writing? Or writing activities designed to boost vocabulary? And where does reading fit in? The good news is that vocabulary, reading, and writing are so tightly interconnected that activities that help one help all. But there are characteristics that make activities more effective in general, and more likely to promote the range of literacy knowledge and abilities. In other words, just a tad of thoughtful planning can buy you a three-fer! However, not every activity will be, or needs to be, equally balanced among vocabulary, reading, and writing. What unites the effectiveness of the enterprise in each domain is, again, active processing. Let's start with activities that have vocabulary learning as the main goal.

Vocabulary Focus

Vocabulary focus means activities designed for students to practice word use in writing, usually a particular word or words that are the current target of instruction. Here, the written product is fairly brief, because effort is targeted on deepening understanding of the word through creating a context for it.

First, mention should be made of a classic practice to be discouraged—asking students to write a sentence using their vocabulary words. This one is especially problematic if used early in learning, when students have just been introduced to a word's meaning. For example, they learn that *cozy* means "something that gives a feeling of comfort," and then are asked to write a sentence with the word. Often that comes out as "I feel cozy." Such sentences provide no practice in exploring what the word's meaning can bring to a context. So it does little to advance vocabulary learning, nothing to support writing, and likely nothing to increase students' interest in either.

The sentence creation activity can be recreated to support vocabulary, and likely writing, in a variety of ways. One that my colleagues and I used often in our vocabulary intervention studies was offering sentence stems, such as "My cat looks cozy when _____." Here, students need to create and explain a situation of coziness that involves a cat. Even though the stem provides half of the sentence for the students, it requires much more thinking than developing empty sentences. Students can write "I feel cozy" sentences all day and hardly fire a brain cell! Here are a few other examples, drawn from the Robust Academic Vocabulary Encounters (RAVE) intervention that my colleagues and I developed (McKeown et al., 2018; for more examples, see Beck et al., 2013, p. 91):

- "We decided to *confine* our pet rabbit by _____."
- "The new kid and I are *compatible* because _____."

The following are a couple of other variations on sentence-creating activities:

- Present stems that prescribe a target word to be used in the sentence, such as:
  - (*abandon*) "After the tornado, we had to _____."
  - (*isolate*) "You'd better _____."
  - (*eliminate*) "I never thought I'd have to _____."

An advantage of this latter format is that students have to write the target word, and as we know from the lexical quality hypothesis (Perfetti, 2007), building an orthographic representation of a word contributes to high-quality word knowledge.

- Provide students with pairs of their vocabulary words that need to be used within one sentence or in a brief paragraph, such as *abandon* and *adjacent*; *interact* and *isolate*; *compatible* and *unify*.

- An activity that combines the stem activity and the two-words activity involves analogy stems, such as "An *isolated* person spends all his time alone, while a person who *interacts* with others _____."

This activity promotes students considering how a pair of words contrasts or has similarities. *Isolate* and *interact* are not opposites, but have features in opposite directions. Considering such properties of words strengthens a word's mental representation as well as the more general understanding of the range and nuances of meanings of words. Below are a few more examples of analogy stems that ask student to reflect on words that have both overlapping and distinctive features:

- "If Joe was *eliminated* from the basketball team, he was cut and is not going to be part of the team. If Joe was *abandoned* by the basketball team, _____."
- "An *isolated* village is one that is all alone and where the residents never see people from other villages. An *abandoned* village _____."
- "If orangutans were *eliminated* from the national zoo, they would be removed from all exhibits. If orangutans were *isolated* at the national zoo, _____."

The key here is to make use of the words meaningful, requiring students to reflect on their meanings and how to use them.

Formats and Upping the Ante

For the activities presented above, as with nearly all that will be offered here, formats can vary that extend the learning benefits as well as spur motivation. An activity can be assigned for students to complete individually, of course, or can be assigned to pairs or groups to complete together. Another take on pairs or groups is to divide the word list and have half the class work on creating stems for half the list and then switch, so students complete the stems created by their peers.

A further step in this sequence would be to have students read some of their favorite sentences aloud, or even vote on class favorites. Up the ante a bit further by asking students to explain why a specific sentence is good. Interactions such as these deepen learning by prompting students to reflect on word uses and the types of contexts in which words appear. More connections are built to the words in students' mental representations. In addition—they're fun!

Writing Focus

The activities in this section are more likely to accompany writing assignments than vocabulary work, but they easily benefit vocabulary knowledge. Probably the most ubiquitous activity that combines vocabulary and writing is a class prewriting activity to brainstorm words that might be used in the assignment.

This activity is not usually aimed at boosting vocabulary, but at stoking students' thinking, or prompting them to use a wider range of words in their writing.

A caveat for brainstorming activities is that free-range thesaurus hunting is not recommended! This can lead to inaccurate choices and give students the mistaken idea that many words mean exactly the same thing and can be substituted for each other in any context. For example, students are writing about living on a desert island, and brainstorming begins with *lonely*. A Google search finds *solitary* and *despondent* both listed with *lonely*. Thesaurus.com includes *destitute* and *homeless*. The thesaurus activity can be transformed into a useful one, if students are given nuanced support, such as choosing one or two of the words and exploring the kind of loneliness it characterizes, or when it might or might not overlap with their concept of loneliness. This kind of exploration enriches planning for writing as it prompts students to reflect on the different qualities of loneliness or aloneness and which of those might be present on a desert island.

Another activity directed at writing with a focus on vocabulary is the creation of classroom word collections, which was a centerpiece of Scott and colleagues' Gift of Words program (Henry et al., 1999). Students were asked to be on the lookout for interesting words in their reading and add those to a public collection. The word collections were then an inherent part of prewriting activities, as students were reminded to consult the collection for words that might serve the topic they were writing about. The idea of word collections serves as a bridge to connecting reading to activities aimed at writing and vocabulary development.

Integrating Reading, Writing, and Vocabulary

Let's explore the ways in which reading, writing, and vocabulary interact in instruction. Word collections involve gathering words from texts to be used in writing. But it also involves noticing the role of those words in the text and what they bring to the message that an author is trying to create. Noticing word use helps students develop the kind of analytic eye toward text that underlies successful comprehension. This can be thought of as mining text for word choice—reading with a deliberate goal of noticing how an author uses words to portray ideas or produce a response in readers. Of course, just assigning students to notice words may not be an effective technique on its own. For best effects, this text work would be part of an interaction, discussing and exploring an author's words choices, considering alternatives or why a particular choice is effective. We see descriptions of such interactions in Scott's work (McKeown, Deane, et al., 2017, pp. 115–116; Scott et al., 2012). Another natural component of this sequence is explicitly considering how a noticed word or language pattern might be used in one's own writing. This is what Scott saw happening in classrooms, for example, when students read an author's description of "a potato of a woman" and then described a character in their own writing as a "string bean of a man" (Scott & Nagy, 2004).

Reading, writing, and vocabulary can also be integrated by embedding vocabulary moments into text interactions, directed at specific words. These moments can bolster both students' vocabulary knowledge and their analysis of author word choice. For example, Beck, McKeown, and Sandora (2021) include a story about a bridge that is in such disrepair that it is about to fall down, threatening a town's livelihood. The author describes that bridge, saying "it's a disgrace" and could "cave in at any moment" (p. 37). Later the author refers to the bridge as *dilapidated*. The teacher pauses and asks, "Given what the author has told us about the bridge, what do you think *dilapidated* means?"

A vocabulary moment can also provide the meaning of an unfamiliar word and then explore its fit for the context. For example, a story character is described as carrying out an action "with malicious swiftness." The teacher can stop, describe *malicious* as "wanting to cause harm," and then direct students to consider a character's nature by asking, "If he is acting with malicious swiftness, what does that tell us about this character?" or "How does this fit in with what we already know about this character?" These points of departure, especially against the backdrop of interactive discussion, provide acutely effective prompts for subsequent writing.

Interactive discussion of text is at the heart of supporting writing in response to text. Graham (2018) describes writing as a social activity that involves a dialogue between writers and readers. Effective reading is the flip side of that dialogue. Both writing and reading are processes of sense-making using language. Both comprise gathering information, identifying what's most important, and establishing connections among ideas in order to create a coherent whole. An approach to reading instruction that makes those processes visible supports comprehension and also writing.

This kind of approach to reading proceeds by having students identify important information and connect ideas through discussion that is interspersed with reading segments of text. My colleagues and I developed one such approach, Questioning the Author (Beck, McKeown, Sandora, Kucan, & Worthy, 1996; Beck et al., 2021), in which a teacher and students move through text with the teacher prompting discussion with open questions such as "What is the author trying to say?" and "How does that connect to what the author told us before?" Because such an approach prompts students to explicitly consider and think through text ideas, one result is that text ideas are "laid open," making them available for students to access later on when writing.

Examples of Reading–Vocabulary–Writing Sequences

In this section, several sample sequences are provided for interactive reading of a text with attention to vocabulary of the text, leading to writing activities. An example is presented for two narratives, one for primary grades using a read-aloud and one that suits upper elementary through middle school, followed by an example using expository text with a genre focus. The general pattern for the narrative text sequences is as follows:

- Before reading: Identify vocabulary to introduce during reading and identify points in the text at which to stop and initiate a brief discussion to promote comprehension of major ideas, themes, and events.
- Plan one or more writing assignments. Consider a series of assignments, such as
  - a wrap-up of a story theme, event, or character
  - a series of separate sentences about a theme, event, or character that require using a target word
  - a prompt for a fuller piece of writing
- Read the text together, as a class or group, stopping at pre-identified discussion points and to explain and contextualize target words.
- After reading: Introduce any opportunity words—words that were not used in the text but that fit ideas, themes, characters, events. Select these with an eye toward words judged to be useful in writing.
- Engage in prewriting brainstorming and later postwriting sharing, underscoring word choice. Provide and encourage commentary on interesting words or how words were used in interesting or apt ways.

STORY READ-ALOUD: *WOLF*

Wolf, by Becky Bloom (1999), is a hilarious tale of animals who read, sprinkled with lots of sophisticated vocabulary. The story opens with a hungry wolf sneaking up on some farm animals with plans to devour them. Turns out they are engaged in reading and pay little attention to the wolf, despite how "big and dangerous" he tries to be. This motivates the wolf to learn to read, so he attends a local school. As he learns to read, he returns to visit the animals several times before finally mastering reading, and becoming an accepted part of their group of educated animals. Table 3.1 illustrates some key points in the text and how discussion of them might be prompted.

The extent to which the following writing activities would be done as a class or assigned for students to do individually will vary among grade levels and the writing ability of such young writers. To kick off writing in response to this text, a wrap-up activity might be to write about three ways in which the wolf changed from the beginning to the end of the story. Discussion of the assignment could be primed by introducing and discussing words from the text, such as *admire, impressed, confident, improved,* along with words that are likely familiar (*dangerous, educated*).

A subsequent writing activity might ask students to imagine an animal joining their classroom. What kind of animal might it be, and what do they want to learn? What would you do? Using specific words could be optional for this activity, but this is a good one to share afterward, because there may be an interesting variety of responses from students. Discussion could then also turn to word choices.

A vocabulary-centered writing activity might involve the wolf's learning to read "with confidence and passion." Students could be asked to consider

TABLE 3.1. Story Segments and Discussion Prompts for _Wolf_

Story segment content	Discussion/vocabulary prompts
The wolf is introduced as very hungry and approaches the farm.	What do we know about the wolf so far?
The wolf notices the animals reading, but approaches trying to scare them. They brush him off, telling him the farm is for educated animals.	The wolf told the animals he was dangerous. How did that turn out?
. . . After the wolf attends school and begins to learn to read, he decides to return to the farm, saying, "They'll be impressed with my reading now."	The wolf thinks that the animals will be _impressed_. This means he believes they will think his reading is very good and that he is pretty special. But what happened?
After yet more practice, the wolf returns, to read with "confidence and passion." The animals listen as he reads story after story.	The wolf read with _confidence_ and _passion_. Confidence means he knew that he was doing it well, and passion means that he was loving being able to read.
	How is this different from the last time the wolf read to the animals?

in their essay how he came to be such a good reader, and then to write about something they do with confidence, or would like to do with confidence.

UPPER ELEMENTARY THROUGH HIGH SCHOOL: _RAVEN AND THE WHALE_

This is an indigenous tale, one of many featuring the Raven. The reading level is appropriate for upper elementary levels, but the content allows it to stretch well beyond that. The story begins as the raven flies into the mouth of a whale and finds inside a small home with a lamp tended by a young woman. He is told never to touch the lamp, which is the whale's heart. Of course, he touches the lamp, and the whale and the woman die. The raven flies out of the whale, sees a ship approaching, and tells the crew he is a great hunter who just slayed the whale. The sailors do not believe him, challenge him to a hunt, and the raven dies.

The goal for reading the text is to build an understanding of the raven, including the tricky nature of his character and his dastardly deeds. Table 3.2 offers key points in the text and discussion prompts.

For a story wrap-up assignment, any of the questions suggested for the final segment would serve well. The text is rich with possibilities—including words that were not used in the story, but that apply conceptually to the story's ideas. From the vocabulary perspective, it is possible to identify four areas that speak to the raven's character, and then several words to choose from within each:

TABLE 3.2. Story Segments and Discussion Prompts for *Raven and the Whale*

Story segment	Discussion prompts
There was once a raven who flew into the mouth of a bowheaded whale. . . . Inside this house was a young woman minding a blubber lamp. "You may stay here as long as you like," she told him, "but you must never touch this lamp." For the lamp was the whale's heart.	How has the author started things off for us?
"Is there anything you would like?" the woman would ask him. "Yes," said the raven. "I would like to touch the lamp." "You must never, never touch the lamp," she told him. But this made the raven all the more curious. More than anything else, he wanted to touch that lamp. . . .	What do you see going on here?
He saw a ship floating toward a human village, so he turned himself into a man. "Behold!" he exclaimed, "I've just killed this enormous whale without even using a harpoon. . . . "	What's this raven up to now? How does this fit in with what we already know about the raven character?
One day a herd of narwhals was sighted in the harbour. "Leave this to me," he said. The kayak was knocked over and he was pierced by a narwhal's horn. Thus did the mighty hunter die. But as he died, he turned back into a raven, and was eaten by one of the narwhals.	What do you think about the way the author has finished up this story? How do you think this ending fits in with the events within the story? Why do you suppose the author chose to kill him twice?

- His curiosity, which leads to the death of the whale and the woman—*inquisitive, impertinent, meddling*
- The consequences he brings on himself—*deserve, merit, warrant, justify, apt, fitting, appropriate, his just deserts*
- The deception at the heart of his nature—*duplicity, devious, cunning, betray*
- His pride—*self-confidence, arrogance, disdain, insolence, hubris*

An initial activity could involve introducing a couple of words in each domain and talking about whether they apply to the raven and how they differ in meaning. Students could then be assigned to write a sentence using each word to describe the raven, how they feel about the raven, or whether the raven got what he deserved, for example. A later assignment could ask students to expand on those responses, for example, to create one connected essay about their view of the raven. Or they might be asked to imagine they were an eyewitness to the events in the story and to describe what occurred.

A particularly intriguing activity, especially if working with older students, might be to write an obituary for the raven. This would mean familiarizing students with obituaries, for example, reading together several literary ones, and talking about their form and the kind of information included. But it could be worth the time investment, as the form could be used with any character-rich text and might prove motivating. The assignment could require some number of target words to be included.

Integrating Reading, Writing, and Vocabulary for Teaching Argument Skills

Beyond its utility for general writing and reading ability, writing in response to text is a necessary component for building academic skill (Coxhead & Byrd, 2007). One important example of integrating reading, writing, and vocabulary for academic success is in a domain such as argumentation. Providing students with the vocabulary of claim, reasons, evidence, and explanation equips them with a means to analyze and explore text, both for comprehension and for understanding the features of argument. Such vocabulary-led analysis activities, in turn, furnish a structure for constructing an argument.

My colleagues and I developed an instructional intervention to teach argument writing to middle school students designed around integrating reading, writing, and vocabulary, (McKeown, Crosson, et al., 2017). The program, called Triple Q, was centered on three types of questions to guide students' reading and writing of arguments: gist, argument, and language choice. Gist questions such as "What is the author saying here?" were interspersed during initial reading to help students develop deep-level comprehension. Argument questions such as "What is the author claiming? What reasons does the author give?" were used in revisiting a text to help students identify and examine argument elements. As students developed their own argument essays, language choice questions helped students examine how authors use specific words to communicate their argument. This included recognizing words that signal relationships and words used to explain things, and how to paraphrase text to report information accurately, without copying it word for word.

Our project implemented three 15-lesson units that guided students from reading and analyzing argument texts to developing, writing, and revising their own arguments. (These materials may be downloaded for free at *www.serpinstitute.org/educator-resources*.) Results showed that students in the Triple Q intervention made greater improvement in their argument writing over a 9-week period compared to students in a control condition (Crosson, Correnti, Matsumura, & McKeown, 2020).

Final Thoughts

Thoughtful activities that ask students to write about what they read can and should also deepen comprehension and, if designed to do so, enhance vocabulary. Likewise, effective comprehension instruction also builds capabilities that underlie writing. Consider the following action questions as you plan your instruction:

- How can I organize writing activities to take advantage of words that students are learning?
- How can I integrate responding to language into text reading and into writing?
- How can I prompt students to explore words they've met in reading in their own writing?

REFERENCES

Beck, I. L., McKeown, M. G., & Kucan, L. (2013). *Bringing words to life: Robust vocabulary instruction* (2nd ed.). New York: Guilford Press.

Beck, I. L., McKeown, M. G., & Sandora, C. A. (2021). *Robust comprehension instruction with questioning the author: 15 years smarter.* New York: Guilford Press.

Beck, I. L., McKeown, M. G., Sandora, C., Kucan, L., & Worthy, J. (1996). Questioning the Author: A yearlong classroom implementation to engage students with text. *Elementary School Journal, 96*(4), 385–414.

Bereiter, C., &. Scardamalia, M. (Eds.). (1987). *The psychology of written composition.* New York: Routledge.

Bloom, B. (1999). *Wolf.* New York: Orchard Books.

Coxhead, A., & Byrd, P. (2007). Preparing writing teachers to teach the vocabulary and grammar of academic prose. *Journal of Second Language Writing, 16*(3), 129–147.

Crosson, A. C., Correnti, R., Matsumura, L. C., & McKeown, M. G. (2020). *Effects of the Triple Q intervention on argument writing quality in the middle school grades.* Manuscript submitted for publication.

Duin, A. H., & Graves, M. F. (1987). Intensive vocabulary instruction as a prewriting technique. *Reading Research Quarterly, 22*(3), 311–330

Durrant, P., & Benchley, M. (2019). Development of vocabulary sophistication across genres in English children's writing. *Reading and Writing, 32,* 1927–1953.

Flower, L., & Hayes, J. (1981). A cognitive process theory of writing. *College Composition and Communication, 32*(4), 365–387.

Graham, S. (2018). A revised writer(s)-within-community model of writing. *Educational Psychologist, 53,* 258–279.

Hayes, J. (1996). A new framework for understanding cognition and affect in writing. In M. Levy & S. Ransdell (Eds.), *The science of writing: Theories, methods, individual differences, and applications* (pp. 1–27). Mahwah, NJ: Erlbaum.

Henry, S., Scott, J., Wells, J., Skobel, B., Jones, A., Cross, S., . . . Blackstone, T. (1999).

Linking university and teacher communities: A "think tank" model of professional development. *Teacher Education and Special Education, 22*(4), 251–267.

Johnson, D. D. (2000). Just the right word: Vocabulary and writing. In R. Indrisano & J. R. Squire (Eds.), *Perspectives on writing: Research, theory, and practice* (pp. 162–186). Newark, DE: International Reading Association.

Jones, S. M., LaRusso, M., Kim, J., Yeon Kim, H., Selman, R., Uccelli, P., . . . Snow, C. (2019). Experimental effects of Word Generation on vocabulary, academic language, perspective taking, and reading comprehension in high-poverty schools. *Journal of Research on Educational Effectiveness, 12*(3), 448–483.

Kim, Y.-S. (2015). Language and cognitive predictors of text comprehension: Evidence from multivariate analysis. *Child Development, 86,* 128–144.

Kim, Y.-S. G. (2016). Direct and mediated effects of language and cognitive skills on comprehension or oral narrative texts (listening comprehension) for children. *Journal of Experimental Child Psychology, 141,* 101–120.

Kim, Y.-S. G., & Schatschneider, C. (2017). Expanding the developmental models of writing: A direct and indirect effects model of developmental writing (DIEW). *Journal of Educational Psychology, 109*(1), 35–50.

Lee, S. H. (2003). ESL learners' vocabulary use in writing and the effects of explicit vocabulary instruction. *System, 31*(4), 537–561.

Lesaux, N. K., Kieffer, M. J., Faller, S. E., & Kelley, J. G. (2010). The effectiveness and ease of implementation of an academic vocabulary intervention for linguistically diverse students in urban middle schools. *Reading Research Quarterly, 45*(2), 196–228.

MacArthur, C. A., & Graham, S. (2016). Writing research from a cognitive perspective. In C. A. MacArthur, S. Graham, & J. Fitzgerald (Eds.), *Handbook of writing research* (2nd ed., pp. 24–40). New York: Guilford Press.

McCutchen, D. (1996). A capacity theory of writing: Working memory in composition. *Educational Psychology Review, 8,* 299–325.

McCutchen, D. (2011). From novice to expert: Implications of language skills and writing—relevant knowledge for memory during the development of writing skill. *Journal of Writing Research, 3*(1), 51–68.

McKeown, M. G., Crosson, A. C., Correnti, R., Matsumura, L. C., Quintana, R., & Sartoris, M. (2017, July). *Enhancing students' argument writing: Effects of an instructional intervention.* Paper presented at Exploring Intervention Effects on Students' Argument Writing, at Scientific Studies of Reading Conference, Halifax, Nova Scotia.

McKeown, M., Crosson, A. C., Moore, D., & Beck, I. (2018). Word knowledge and comprehension effects of an academic vocabulary intervention for middle school students. *American Educational Research Journal, 55*(3), 572–616.

McKeown, M. G., Deane, P. D., Scott, J. A., Krovetz, R., & Lawless, R. R. (2017). *Vocabulary assessment to support instruction: Building rich word-learning experiences.* New York: Guilford Press.

Nagy, W. E., & Scott, J. A. (2000). Vocabulary processes. In M. L. Kamil, P. B. Mosenthal, P. David Pearson, & R. Barr (Eds.), *Handbook of reading research,* Vol. III (pp. 69–284). Mahwah, NJ: Erlbaum.

Olinghouse, N. G., & Wilson, J. (2013) *Reading and Writing, 26,* 45–65.

Perfetti, C. (2007). Reading ability: Lexical quality to comprehension. *Scientific Studies of Reading, 11*(4), 357–383.

Scardamalia, M., & Bereiter, C. (1986) Written composition. In M. Witttrock (Ed.), *Handbook of research on teaching* (3rd ed., pp. 778–803). New York: Macmillan.

Scott, J. A., Flinspach, S. L., Miller, T. F., Gage-Serio, O., & Vevea, J. L. (2009). An analysis of reclassified English learners, English learners, and native English fourth graders on assessments of receptive and productive vocabulary. In *58th Yearbook of the National Reading Conference* (pp. 312–329). Oak Cree, WI: National Reading Conference.

Scott, J. A., Miller, T. F., & Flinspach, S. L. (2012). Developing word consciousness: Lessons from highly diverse fourth-grade classrooms. In J. F. Baumann & E. J. Kame'euni (Eds.), *Vocabulary instruction: Research to practice* (pp. 169–188). New York: Guilford Press.

Scott, J., & Nagy, W. E. (2004). Developing word consciousness. In J. F. Baumann & E. J. Kame'euni (Eds.), *Vocabulary instruction: Research to practice* (pp. 201–217). New York: Guilford Press.

Webb, S. A. (2009). The effects of pre-learning vocabulary on reading comprehension and writing. *The Canadian Modern Language Review/La Revue Canadienne des Langues Vivantes, 65*(3), 441–470.

Yonek, L. M. (2009). *The effects of rich vocabulary instruction on students' expository writing*. PhD dissertation, University of Pittsburgh.

CHAPTER 4

From Talk to Text
Implementing Student Discussions That Matter

Deanna Kuhn
Mariel Halpern
Sybille Bruun

Never has it seemed more critical to prepare young people for their roles as citizens of a democracy. Societies that don't prepare their next generation risk not surviving. Education has long seemed the answer, with reading and writing as the foundational skills that open the door to deep thinking about critical, typically complex issues. Here, we highlight discourse as a third foundational skill, essential in its own right but also as a powerful bridge to individual thinking and writing (Clarke, Resnick, & Rose, 2015; Kuhn, 2019; Mehan & Cazden, 2015). Such a bridge may be crucial for students who struggle to master traditional literacy skills, especially writing, or fail to recognize their value in accomplishing one's goals.

Serious discussion is intellectually demanding, requiring the envisioning and weighing of possibilities as well as bringing evidence to bear on claims. Leading such discussions is similarly challenging, requiring skill and experience. Teachers have been inclined to see them as optional "enrichment," once curriculum content coverage has been achieved. Here, we take the contrasting position that discourse with peers about significant, challenging real-world issues is an educational core and necessity, preparing students for futures that will depend on it. Even more, we see discourse as a bridge to developing what have long been termed critical thinking and critical writing. Everyone is in favor of students becoming critical thinkers, but less is known about how to get them there (Kuhn, 2019). We propose good talk as a path to good thinking and, in turn, effective written communication.

In authentic peer-to-peer discourse, the teacher relinquishes a role of authority as mediator of all discourse or sole source of knowledge and replaces it with shared construction of meaning and another basis for authority—that of evidence and argument. This evolution comes only with consistent practice, and both teacher and students must develop the confidence and commitment it requires. While whole-class discussion remains the most common format for classroom discourse, the approach we describe here transfers a greater share of management of the discourse from the teacher to students themselves. It has dual advantages, one for students and one for teachers. It provides students the opportunity for dense engagement in peer-to-peer discourse—much greater than they experience when all dialogue is mediated by the teacher and hesitant students risk becoming only passive listeners—while making more manageable (yet not eliminating) the guiding role of a more practiced adult. Readers can contemplate in advance the following questions.

GUIDING QUESTIONS

- What does *talk* consist of in student-to-student interactions? What forms might we encourage such talk to take?
- What practices can support students, especially bilinguals or other language-challenged students, and in what ways?
- How can students' discourse lead to and support individual writing activity?
- Since talk is collaborative, might writing be profitably so as well?

Students Talking to Students

An initial issue vital to the success of student-to-student discussions is topic selection. A critical question to ask is: *Does addressing this topic have an evident purpose, one that students, as well as teachers, can buy into and see value in?* Contemporary issues of concern that students hear their elders talking about outside the classroom meet this criterion, but it's also good to start with issues close to home before moving further afield. One we illustrate later, appropriate for middle and high school students, is how best to treat delinquent behavior by teens. Another is working first before attending college.

Students soon come to see themselves as worthy and capable of expressing their own ideas on such topics and being listened to by others, while in turn hearing their peers' ideas. With practice, we have found, they become able to recognize opposing positions as having arguments and evidence to support them, making these positions worthy of consideration. In short, they feel the empowerment of entering into and being accepted as members of a community of discourse.

To achieve these outcomes, of foremost importance is that students talk directly to one another, rather than primarily to or through a teacher. This means responding directly and thoughtfully to what a peer says. The consequence is a heightened density of talk, reducing time students spend as passive listeners—the role students spend most time occupying in most class discussions. Instead, all students are engaged, all or most of the time. Rather than a traditional teacher role, teachers play more the role of coach, providing "on the spot" guidance as needed, to clarify and answer questions, but also to pose to students occasional questions of their own, asking a student to elaborate or clarify for their teammates what they were saying or recording in writing.

Unique to the approach we describe here, students engage deeply with a topic, over multiple class sessions and across a range of formats. By the end, they've learned a good deal about it and brought much of what they've learned to bear on their own and others' positions. Critically, students choose the side to take on the issue (although they may later change their position) and begin with each team of same-side peers working in small groups to construct their position and bring evidence to bear on it, and to prepare for what is the core of the experience—a series of dialogues with rotating opposing-side peers. These dialogues are conducted as written exchanges, typically (but not necessarily) electronic, between a same-side pair and successive pairs of opposing-side peers. (See also Chapter 9, this volume, on writing–reading connections in the digital world.) The written format provides a record that externalizes thought into tangible, retrievable form (in contrast to verbal discourse, which disappears as soon as it is uttered) and supports reflection on what has been said. The written record of the dialogue thus becomes the object of various reflective activities students engage in (see Figures 4.1 and 4.2).

A small dose of initial reading can be productive to arouse interest in the topic, but in our projects and work we see advantage in employing it sparingly out of concern that a deluge of information up front may not only be met with disinterest but also shut down students' own thinking and inquisitiveness about a topic. We let students' own ideas dominate at first and offer information related to the topic only gradually, in individual short questions and answers one or two at a time, suggesting to students that this information might be helpful to them in making their arguments. Soon they begin generating their own questions and are assisted in obtaining answers.

Stimulating interest, however, is only the first function of reading matter that is intended to support student discourse on a challenging topic. It is essential that students gain relevant information to draw on if their discourse is to be rich and informed, and reading research has established that comprehension is superior when students identify a purpose to their reading, this purpose in the present case being engaging in argumentation. But purpose in the service of comprehension, while essential, is not enough. In the context of argumentation, students confront the challenge of making use of new information by transforming it from information to evidence. Information becomes evidence when it is invoked in the service of a claim, either to support or weaken the claim. Claim–evidence coordination lies at the heart of argumentation and is a skill that is developed only gradually with extended practice. We note later research evidence that the employment of newly gained information as evidence is enhanced when it has a purpose for being comprehended, when it is easily digestible (as in the small bits we employ), and when

Team members _____
Date _____

Let's think...Starting with the other side's argument

One of the other side's MAIN ARGUMENTS was:

_____

_____

_____

Our COUNTERARGUMENT against their argument was:

_____

_____

_____

Give a specific example of an improved, more effective COUNTERARGUMENT.

_____

_____

_____

_____

FIGURE 4.1. Other and own reflection sheets—Example 1. Photograph by Steve Carmichael. Photograph was isolated from the original license available at *https://creative commons.org/licenses/by/2.0/deed.en*

it is framed dialogically (Iordanou, Kuhn, Matos, Shi, & Hemberger, 2019; Kuhn & Modrek, 2021).

Reading (or listening) is, of course, closely linked to writing (or speaking), as the entire present volume attests. And in this chapter, we highlight discourse (inter- or intrapersonal) as a powerful link between reading and writing. In our program (for more detailed descriptions, see Kuhn, 2018; Kuhn, Hemberger, & Khait, 2016; Rapanta, 2021; Iordanou & Rapanta, 2021), a same-side pair must verbally agree on what to communicate in writing to an opposing pair, essentially doubling the amount of discourse (verbal or written) that occurs.

FIGURE 4.2. Other and own reflection sheets—Example 2. Photograph by Steve Carmichael. Photograph was isolated from the original license available at *https://creative commons.org/licenses/by/2.0/deed.en*

Both forms provide an opportunity for metacognitive planning and reflection, since the pair must reflect on the opponents' statements and decide what to reply ("What can we say back to this?"). Rather than a traditional teacher role, they play the role of coach, providing "on the spot" guidance as needed, to clarify and answer questions, but also to pose to students occasional questions of their own, asking a student to elaborate or clarify for their teammates what they were saying or recording in writing.

Following these dialogues with a number of different opposing pairs, students reassemble in same-side teams to prepare for a whole-class "showdown" debate in which members of each team take turns verbally debating a member of the opposing team. While engaged in this exchange, either speaker may request a "huddle" to consult with their team (who has available all material that team members prepared in the previous phase). Team members may also call a huddle if they view their teammate in the speaker's position to need assistance.

The showdown is followed by a full-group debrief and reflection, and lastly individual final essays written as a newspaper "op-ed." During this writing, the preceding purposeful discourse hopefully remains alive, although confined now to students' own thought (Vygotsky, 1937/1987), as they envision what the now only imagined opponent might say and how they can address it. The discourse serves to make the opposing position and its accompanying arguments clear and vivid enough so that the writer can represent and address them, and, moreover, sees the relevance of doing so. These are typically written individually, although recently we have found it productive when final essays are written collaboratively by a student pair (Matos, 2021; Shi, 2019).

Teachers will want to choose their own topics to fit particular curriculum content and students' interests, but we suggest that topics begin close to home. An early topic that has worked well for us, for example, is "Should misbehaving students be expelled or given another chance?" Topics can then extend gradually to ones of wider scope—community, nation, and world. The most important criteria for a good topic are that it invokes a rich set of reasons on either side of the issue and that a straw poll indicates students have diverging positions. Teachers may find useful as a reference *Building Our Best Future* (Kuhn, 2018), a book written directly for middle and high school students, as a source of topic ideas. Suggested topics, 47 in all, are accompanied by informational Q&As and further reading sources. An accompanying teacher edition contains supplementary materials for reflective activities, and a separate edition of the book (Kuhn, 2022) is available tailored for English language learners, where the activities provide this population with rich practice in all four language skills (listening, talking, reading, writing). Suggested topics fall into the categories of "A personal future" (e.g., *When you finish high school, you have the choice of going right to college or of working for a few years first*), then proceed to "A community future" (e.g., *Should town taxes help to pay the cost of buses and trains, or should the cost be covered entirely by the people who use them?*), "A national future" (e.g., *Should people be required to pay a Social Security tax from each paycheck that will provide money when they retire, or should people save on their own for their retirement?*), and "A world future" (e.g., *Should a nation allow people from other countries to come live in their country based on what they can contribute or how bad life is where they come from?*). The teacher's edition of *Building Our Best Future* contains a detailed guide to the sequence of activities for the topic cycle, along with accompanying materials and suggestions for implementation, albeit one with considerable flexibility to accommodate student needs and classroom circumstances. Also downloadable at low cost from the book's publisher is a set of videos that portray a middle school group in action as they participate in the program (Kuhn, 2020).

Moving Operations Online

The discourse-based approach to developing argumentation skills that we have described in overview here allows considerable flexibility as to its implementation, which can vary considerably as a function of students' ability and experience and how a teacher chooses to fit it into the curriculum and class schedule. These circumstances will influence the number of sessions devoted to the topic cycle and the number of topics students engage. The amount of teacher guidance students need will also vary accordingly, but our experience indicates that the amount invariably decreases over time, regardless of initial level.

Other particulars are fully adjustable to fit best with student and classroom characteristics. The nature of the post-showdown debrief, for example, will vary with the extent of students' experience within the program and more generally. One end of a continuum is illustrated in a 30-minute video (available as an embedded video in our earlier book; Kuhn et al., 2016) that illustrates a teacher taking students through their showdown, applying a pluses-and-minuses scoring system. At the other end, beginning groups receive elementary, broad feedback, encouraging them, for example, to simply listen to their opponent and respond to what they say. The bar gradually rises, however, to successively higher standards of counterargument and evidence use, as it similarly does in the nature of feedback that students receive on the post-showdown final essays they write.

We have implemented the approach in various forms, either as a freestanding class in argumentation or situated within the English language arts (ELA) or social studies curriculum. Most often, we have implemented it with middle school students, but it also has been used productively with high school students. The most common schedule has been a twice-weekly class session, with 8–12 class sessions devoted to the activity cycle for a given topic, after which a new topic is introduced and the cycle repeated. The most effective, we have found, and for students most enjoyable, schedule is an intensive workshop format over 4 full days during a school vacation, allowing students to become deeply immersed in the topics and the activity (Iordanou et al., 2019).

All of this changed abruptly, however, in March 2020, just after we had completed and filmed one such workshop. Schools closed widely and indefinitely, and face-to-face contact between students was prohibited. These circumstances have led to our developing an entirely online version of the curriculum, consisting largely of just the electronic dialogue and essay components. When we began the online program, public middle school students were largely attending school from home, listening to a teacher appearing on a screen, so they welcomed the opportunity to engage in discourse with peers. These were not their friends from school, however, but agemates unknown to them, as students came from different schools and all participants assumed animal code names, while their real names remained undisclosed. They interacted only by electronic text, in a chat software program we chose that was well suited for the purpose. Only introductory and concluding video presented by the program coordinator, not the students, appeared at each session.

The anonymity that this format provides to students turned out to be an unanticipated benefit of the online program. It accords students a freedom that their social media exchanges outside of school don't provide. Several have given us feedback suggesting that it has made them feel freer to express ideas that they might otherwise not have shared. At the same time, they are reminded to criticize only ideas, not persons.

During each session of the online program, students engaged in two 25-minute dialogues with two different peers on a single topic. This continued for 5 consecutive days, each day with different partners. Q&As, each with a website address provided for further information, were made available, a few per session. On the final day for the topic, students were asked to prepare a final "position piece" written as a newspaper op-ed intended for someone new to the topic. In the several such programs we have carried out in 2020–2021, students engaged with four topics over a 4-week period, but this program length can, of course, be adjusted to any desired length.

Despite its positive features, the online version of the program does lose much with respect to the range of human interaction it supports. As it is now configured, students lack the experience of collaborative interaction with same-side peers in constructing their arguments and coordinating them with evidence and in anticipating counterarguments. Just as important, they miss the experience of individualized interaction with an adult coach or teacher. We have now configured the program to provide this in next-best fashion through "Friday Feedbacks"—which the coordinators provide at the final session for a topic, just before students begin their essay assignment. (See *https://youtu.be/hy1t-pHqN36I* for an example.) In these brief Friday online presentations, the coach focuses on discourse skills, drawing on examples from students' exchanges on the topic from that week's work. See Table 4.1 for illustrations.

The fact that these illustrations are tied to the topic and to work students have been engaged with during the week is a very positive feature. Students show great interest at this point. Still, this feedback is of a broad scope in scaffolding students' discourse skill development well beyond the week's topic.

Outcomes

We have now conducted around the globe formal studies of students' skill gains in both discourse and writing for programs using our model, most often in a twice-weekly format across the school year, over periods from one semester to 3 academic years (see Kuhn, 2018, for a brief summary). We are in the process of analyzing data on the most recent online version of the program. Formal reports of these studies document quantitatively measured gains in both discourse and argumentative writing following participation in our dialogic curriculum. Here, we highlight qualitative evidence, in particular in the form most familiar to teachers, written essays. These essays were written near the end of the school year by a middle school social studies class at a low-performing Title 1 urban school whose teacher implemented our curriculum that year. Three

TABLE 4.1. Illustrations from Friday Afternoon Feedback Sessions

Coach shares excerpts from student dialogues enclosed in quotation marks, and the coach's feedback appears in bold. *Topics:* Should animals be used to test new medical procedures, drugs, or other products? Should teens who commit serious crimes be tried in regular adult court or a special court for juveniles? Should all schools have the same school curriculum, or should this decision be left up to local communities? When you finish high school, is it better to go right to college or work for a few years first? Should high school graduates be required to do community service? Should everyone be allowed to vote, or should voters be required to show they have studied the candidates and issues?

1. **Be sure to explain your thinking, so your partner has something to react to. One person, for example, when a partner asked them for their reasons, just said, "Same as yours." Neither person gains much from such a response. Explaining your thinking includes defining your terms carefully.**

   a. One student said, "I agree with your statement," and the other student replied, "Well, I have nothing more to say." **This doesn't move the dialogue forward for either participant.**

   b. [*animal topic*] "What do you mean by an animal being tortured?" The partner responds, "Being put in insanely small cages, fattened up extremely quickly. . . . "

   c. [*juvenile justice topic*] One student asked, "Shouldn't the person who robs the bank be given a longer sentence than the guy in the getaway vehicle?," and their partner responded, "No, I think they should get the same sentence because they each had a hand in the crime. While the driver did a less serious thing, they essentially let the robber get away with it." **The response is specific and explains the opposing view clearly.**

   d. [*juvenile justice topic*] A student asked, "How do we know harsh punishment is better?," and their partner replied, "It's not a punishment, it's an experience. Harsh experiences are better because if it is not harsh, then the kid would be like 'oh it's not so bad, I can do it again' but a harsh punishment would really stick in the kid's memory."

2. **React to what the other person has said. The worst option is to ignore, by saying, for example, "Well that's your opinion. Here's my opinion." What your partner has put out there deserves a response. You might say, "I totally agree" or "I agree" or "I partially agree BUT" or "I disagree and here's why." You could even say what one debater said, "I didn't think about that. That's a good reason" (they could have added WHY they think it's a good reason).**

   a. [*juvenile justice topic*] One student said, "I think because of what they did, they should be tried in a serious manner," and their partner asked for specifics: "Can you explain what you mean by serious manner?"

   b. [*national curriculum*] One student asked their partner: "What about having local curriculums is making you unsure?," and the partner responded, "I don't know." **What one partner has put out there deserves a response.**

   c. [*animal topic*] One person said, "One reason is that it's better to test on animals before people [in order] to know they are safe." The other responded, "But testing is cruel to the animals." **This could be true and is an important issue. But where does this response leave the first person's reason? Safety to humans is an important issue, and the second person needs to respond to it and not simply introduce their own reason.**

TABLE 4.1. (continued)

3. Compliment your partner on a good idea, but also tell them why you think it's good.	a. "I liked your reasoning because you came up with a strong reason that was very convincing." **This is a good start but would benefit from an example of the "strong reason" mentioned.**
	b. [*juvenile justice topic*] One student said, "Juvenile court is more expensive for the government," and their partner kindly responded by saying, "That is interesting about how juvenile court is more expensive, I had no idea. That's a good point as well."
4. Get your partner to explain their thinking if they haven't said enough for you to understand it.	a. [*juvenile justice topic*] One partner said, "I think it depends on the age of the teen and the crime." **The strongest response would be "Can you explain why those factors are important?" Instead, their partner responds by introducing their own ideas: "Well, one of my reasons is . . . " and ignoring what their partner has said.**
	b. [*college vs. work topic*] "Are you saying they're wasting money because they haven't explored their interests?
	c. [*national/community service*] One partner said, "I think that once people realize the many benefits coming from community/international service, they will not refuse," and their partner asked them to clarify: "What *are* some of the benefits?" **This allowed their partner to explain their thinking and share evidence by responding:** "college credits, learning self-confidence and responsibility, and feeling satisfied and happier when giving to poor communities."
	d. [*juvenile justice topic*] One student said, "[Adult courts] are better because they get more punishments," and their partner responded, "Why is it good to get a harsher punishment? What good does punishment do for them?"
5. Be careful not to drift away from the topic entirely, even if your point is a good one.	a. [*juvenile justice topic*] One person said, "I also think they should have some sort of help when they come out of jail." **This is a good point, but it does not address the question of whether the teen vs. adult system is better.**
	b. [*animal topic*] One person said, "I actually have a friend who works with mice." **An interesting anecdote, but it does not address the question of whether animals should be used as test subjects.**
	c. [*voting topic*] For example, one partner said, "I think that they should pass a competency test. What do you think?," and the other partner responded, "I agree." **Neither partner offers or asks for reasons why, and that makes it tough to continue the debate and move into increasingly meaningful dialogue. Still, the first partner asking, "What do you think?" is a good start to probe their partner's thinking. They could follow up with "Why do you think that?"** *(continued)*

TABLE 4.1. (*continued*)

6. Make sure what you or your partner say really addresses the question. If your partner's point doesn't answer the question, tell them and bring them back to the main question.	a. [*national curriculum*] One student stated, "Lots of things you learn in school are boring, but if they are talking about something that you are interested in, you pay attention." **Their partner attempts to address the disconnect between the statement and the topic by responding, "Yes, but not liking the topic and having the same curriculum are unrelated."**
	b. [*juvenile justice topic*] For example, one debater said, "I think that teens can change and it's harder for adults to change." And the partner responded, "So why does that mean teen court is better?" **The partner likely has a reason for introducing this opinion but should make them explain the reason. It's okay to say, "What point are you trying to make?" It's better to ask them to repeat if you're not sure, so then the discussion can go forward.**
	c. [*voting topic*] One debater said, "Here's a better solution—just fund schools better so everyone has a good education and understands how the government works. Then we can make an informed decision without having to deny people the right to vote." **We do not know that better school funding would produce informed voters. While it is an interesting statement, the question being debated is not school funding.**
	d. [*college vs. work topic*] One debater said, "My main reason is that a college degree is a required step in many job opportunities." **The question being debated is not whether to go to college, but WHEN to go to college.**
7. Consider why your partner is telling you this. Why do they think it's important? What are they trying to show? If you're not sure, ask.	a. [*juvenile justice topic*] One debater said, "In teen court they get special treatment but in adult court they don't." **Their partner could have just asked, "Why is that important?," but they do something even better by responding, "We should find out if this special treatment really does them any good." That will get to the point of whether special treatment is an important factor.**
	b. [*voting topic*] One debater said, "The president can get us into wars." **The debater may have a reason to present that piece of information, and their partner can respond with "Why is that important?" in order to get to the heart of whether or not that piece of information is relevant.**
	c. [*juvenile justice topic*] A student said, "Teens can commit the same crimes as an adult could," and their partner replied, "Yeah, that's a good point. But why does it matter?"

TABLE 4.1. (continued)

8. Always consider whether it's certain the other's claim is correct. What's the evidence to support this claim?	a. [*juvenile justice topic*] For example, one person said, "Usually, people that commit crimes are poor, so even if you help them, they will go back out and do it again because they need to." **You need to question their starting assumption—"people who commit crimes are poor." If the starting assumption isn't necessarily true, nothing can follow from it.**
	b. [*national curriculum*] A student said, "Most of the adults right now have jobs that don't interest them at all. If they were given the chance to study different things . . . they would be happy with their jobs." **The partner can add to their understanding by asking in response: "What evidence do you have that most adults have jobs that don't make them happy?"**
	c. [*voting topic*] One person said, "Voting is a human right, and taking that away from someone who is eligible is technically illegal." **You need to question their starting assumption—"voting is a human right." If the starting assumption isn't necessarily true, nothing can follow from it.**
	d. [*national/community service*] One student mentioned that kids might "risk their lives" if they engaged in mandatory service after high school, and their partner responded, "Do you have evidence that they risk their lives for community service?"
9. If you have doubts, ask your partner, "How do WE KNOW that's true?" Don't say, "How do YOU know that's true?," making it sound like a challenge. We KNOW together. If one of us can show for sure it's false (or true), then we both know. So, together, find the facts you need.	a. [*college vs. work topic*] One debater said, "After high school most people have a plan; if they don't go to college, it might make it harder to achieve." **You need to question their starting assumption—"most people have a plan." Is that accurate?**
	b. [*juvenile justice topic*] A student said, "Just because teens get harsher punishments, doesn't mean they'll behave better." Their partner responded, "Can you provide evidence?"
	c. [*juvenile justice topic*] A student said, "If they go to prison with the adults, they are more likely to be attacked," and their partner asked, "Do you have any proof of this?"
10. Know and point it out if you don't have the evidence you need. Figure out where to get it.	a. [*animal topic*] "I think we'd need some additional info to show that the testing does benefit humans."
	b. [*animal topic*] "I thought they were careful to avoid or minimize an animal's suffering, so we should find that out."

(continued)

TABLE 4.1. (continued)

11. **Question the assumptions underlying the issue.**	a. [*juvenile justice topic*] One debater asked, "Why do teens need different treatment than adults?" Their partner was able to respond with a reason: "Their minds are quite underdeveloped."
	b. [*juvenile justice topic*] One person said, "It sounds like you are suggesting it's better to give teens a smaller punishment. Why?" Their partner disagreed and redefined what they are debating: "It should not be a question of punishment; rather, their future threat to society." **So, is the goal to punish the wrongdoer or keep others safe? Debaters need to get these silent assumptions out in the open and settled if they're going to make progress in deciding the best course of action— which will depend on the purpose.**
	c. [*voting topic*] One debater said, "What if they [the voters] are mentally ill and doing bad stuff for our country on purpose?" Their partner responded, "Something that might be bad to you might not be bad to them."
12. **Explore your partner's reasoning, especially when you think you don't agree with it.**	a. [*college vs. work topic*] Your partner says, "Going to college directly can put a load of stress on a young person." **You disagree and want to counter this argument, but if you just say, "that's not true," you haven't weakened their reason by saying what's wrong with it and you haven't moved the discussion forward. You need to do that, but first try to better understand your partner's thinking, by asking, for example, "Why do you think it will put a load of stress on them?"**
	b. [*juvenile justice topic*] A student let her partner know that she had changed her mind at the end of a debate, and the partner responded: "And what is your main reason [for changing your mind]? It's okay to change your mind as long as you have good reasons."
	c. [*juvenile justice topic*] One student said: "[Teens] get special help and they get to finish work in teen court," and their partner responded by asking for clarification: "And why do you think the special help is good?"

modules of ten consecutive class sessions each across the year had been devoted to one of three topics. Each topic was set in a concrete scenario, for example, "Which applicant should be given priority—Al, who sought to escape the life-threatening violence in his own war-torn country, or Ben, a highly educated computer specialist who wished to fill a U.S. job vacancy in this field?" As their final essay on the topic, students wrote an argument to the immigration judge on behalf of Al or Ben, and in a final whole-class reflection, it was emphasized that Al and Ben represent large classes of individuals and hence the arguments being offered were, in fact, made on behalf of more than a single individual.

Did discourse or writing gains reflect more than knowledge gains with respect to the specific topic? To address this question, we asked students to write an additional year-end essay on a topic they had not debated: whether teen offenders should be tried in an adult or a juvenile court. They were given access to 10 short Q&A items providing information on the topic but told they were not required to include it in their essays.

A comparison class not participating in the program received the same writing assignment. This class's essays extended little beyond stating their position with minimal to no justification. Less than a third cited any evidence. In the participant class, in contrast, all but one essay referred to evidence, citing an average of nearly three pieces. The following are two representative essays:

(*Anna*) Teens who commit serious crimes should go to juvenile prison because they don't have a fully developed brain. [*Cites evidence.*] This is important to me cause as a teen they don't think as carefully as adults. Meaning a teen might of just made a mistake and doesn't deserve adult prison. Also a teen is most likely to be more of a target in adult prison. [*Cites evidence.*] Also, teens have not gotten their high-school diploma and may succeed in life if the court lets them get their education. I think its not fair that a teen's future could be on the line because of a mistake. Evidence shows that "teens in juvenile prisons attend school regularly." This shows that a teen has a better chance at getting their education in juvenile prison. Evidence also shows that juvenile prisons do not keep records. This also give a teen a better chance at life.

(*Carmen*) Teens who commit serious crimes should be charged/judged in a adult court. Maybe if they make decisions as a adult (like to kill somebody), they should be charged as a adult. And maybe going to a real jail can put them in check! if they go to a juvenile prison they may take that punishment lightly because it doesn't go on their record. [*Cites evidence.*] The real jail may scare them to stop killing or doing bad things because in real jail you can get assaulted by other inmates. [*Cites evidence.*] And if they don't like being assaulted and not go back to jail they'll stop doing what they did to be in jail. Also, teens were involved in one quarter of violent crimes. [*Cites evidence.*] And that's a lot for teens to be involved with killings. Also adult courts cost less to operate. [*Cites evidence.*] This shows it'll cost more for juvenile court. But they can still get educated in regular jail.

The writers of these essays were able to coordinate evidence and claims to build an argument. They also made two-sided arguments, weighing the merits and drawbacks of both conditions. Furthermore, the dialogic structure of the program frequently makes its way into the essays (Kuhn, 2019; Shi, Matos, & Kuhn, 2019), for example, "The opposition's side might say that they might repeat their crime if not taken to a higher level like adult court. But our comeback could be . . . "

We were pleased to find that the essays of students who participated for 4 weeks (20 sessions) in the virtual version of the program showed equally promising performance. Below is one such essay, a postprogram essay on a new topic that had not been one of the program's topics. Notable are its coordination of claims with supporting evidence and address of an opposing position in an argument/counterargument structure, as well as use of available evidence.

> (*Nico*) Dreamers, aka undocumented kids that grew up in America, economically benefit America. Since 2012, the deferred action for childhood arrivals program has guaranteed access for hundreds of thousands of dreamers to attend public schools for occupations later on. According to *Science Daily* and researchers, disadvantaged students or dreamers from poor areas prove similar learning rates as most other pupils from wealthy backgrounds; in addition, most of those undocumented students have hardworking parents that influence them to work in school for a better life. Consequently, years later, the 400,000 now employed dreamers contributed 48 billion dollars to the American economy, with a four billion dollar tax rate towards hospitals, schools, federal funds, Medicare, etc. Further, an estimated 15 billion dollars more could've been attained if the problems for getting jobs or going to college were expunged for the illegal youngsters. The economics in America can be improved with dreamers.
>
> Dreamers are a vital part of America's workforce and society. Twenty percent of DACA members work jobs which directly assist others, amounting to approximately 50,000 as healthcare workers, schoolteachers, and soldiers. According to "America's voice," they are more prone to work in high-need areas where communities face challenges in recruiting other physicians, be bilingual, come from diverse cultural backgrounds, and understand challenges in certain ethnic communities. These aspects help their understanding, communications, and aid with the people in need. In addition, the current pandemic has sparked the need for 1.25 million healthcare professions by 2024. The 30,000 healthcare dreamers, which is expected to increase, can really help fill that number. Kids, the disabled, and adults are assisted by DACA members.
>
> Although dreamers aid American economics, **some may say** they're affiliated with the job loss of many natives. **Opposers believe** citizens should always come first, and the thousands of dreamers in America are stealing their jobs. **However, new studies show** we have a relatively low level of unemployment, and among college educated, a really low level. Nevertheless, according to NPR, most dreamers are still in school with 17% earning a college degree, possibly filling in for our large unemployment gap in the future. In addition, statistics prove the now employed dreamers contribute with their jobs more in taxes than the top 1% of American taxpayers, proving more worthy for America than the average citizen. [*Boldface is ours for emphasis.*]

As noteworthy as their writing are students' own reports of their experience in the program. It was "serious but fun" as one student put it. Their responses regarding the benefits of their experience ranged from self-expression ("It helped me come out more as a person and speak out more") to the even greater challenges of embracing norms of discourse ("In order for you to come back at them with your evidence and your reasons, you have to be able to understand what they are saying and understand their point of view before you form your own reasons.") Several students made explicit that they had acquired the standards of what Resnick and colleagues call "accountable talk." One student, for example, evaluated successive partners differently: "My first partner used good evidence, and they had good points too. My second partner, however, stated their four reasons, in one line, with zero evidence" and "They used opinionated facts, but treated them as statistical facts."

Well-controlled experimental studies have documented student gains in individual argumentative essay writing following participation in the kind of student-centered, discourse-based activity described here among middle school (Hemberger, Kuhn, Matos, & Shi, 2017) and high school student populations (Rapanta, 2021). We've also conducted studies designed to identify the effectiveness of individual program components. For example, students did not advance as much in the use of evidence in their arguments when instead of our Q&A method, we compiled the same information in a text provided at the outset that then remained available (Iordanou et al., 2019). It lost its immediate purpose and usefulness. This finding we believe has potentially broad implications with respect to reading instruction and reading comprehension. Too commonly in classrooms, students are told to "read first" and "then we'll talk about and make some sense of what you've read and then we can explore how it might be put to use." Why is this the optimal order rather than the reverse?

In another recent study (Kuhn & Modrek, 2021), we found that students gained more from their reading about opposing views on a controversial social issue when these were framed as a dialogue between two individuals, than they did when the same material was presented as separate position statements by the two individuals. Presented with the dialogic framing, students made more reference to these individuals' ideas in their own discussions of the issue. In current work, we are investigating whether this effect may be observed when students listen to the dialogue or individual statements, rather than read them.

In another study (Iordanou & Kuhn, 2020), we followed J. S. Mill (1859/1996) in exploring his claim that it is necessary that opposing views be embodied in another person to be engaged most effectively. Our results supported Mill's claim. Students' argumentation skill did not advance to the same extent when they examined the same arguments and evidence but discussed it only with peers who shared their own position. Thus, both purpose and personification are implicated in bringing new knowledge or perspectives to bear on contrasting claims.

Conclusions and Suggestions

Young people's civic engagement has lately become a topic of considerable interest—not only how to encourage it but also devising appropriate assessment tools to measure it. Before worrying overly about how to assess or promote civic engagement, perhaps a first step is to engage students in deep thinking and talking about the issues they might take action with regard to. A similar point can be made regarding the transition from discourse to writing. There are many old and new approaches to supporting students in their writing, as the present volume reflects, but in the end the success of these efforts requires that students have something to say, have ideas they believe in enough to regard them as worth sharing. Exploring such ideas in discourse with peers may in the end prove the best path for the individual student in developing those ideas and refining and even reformulating them.

The approach we have described here emphasizes getting both young and older learners involved, early on and deeply, in reading, thinking, talking, and writing about both local and global issues of the day. How else can they envision future selves as informed, thoughtful contributors to improving life in a democratic society, especially in today's world with as many poor public role models as good ones? And how else can they get the needed practice in thinking, talking, reading, and writing about such issues?

Our experience with students of diverse backgrounds and abilities confirms they are able to debate even the most difficult contemporary topics—immigration, abortion, and many others—and do so productively in multiple respects. At least as important, they come to appreciate the value of doing so. As educators, we engage them deeply in the practice, so they can discover its value for themselves.

- What can you make use of in your classroom from the ideas presented in this chapter? What oral language discourse practices take place most often in your classroom?
- How can you encourage students not only to listen carefully but also to respond to their peers' ideas?
- How can you nurture students' appreciation of argument, counterargument, and evidence as norms a community of discourse must abide by?

REFERENCES

Clarke, S., Resnick, L., & Rose, C. (2015). Dialogic instruction: A new frontier. In L. Corno & E. Anderman (Eds.), *Handbook of Educational Psychology* (pp. 378–389). New York: Routledge.

Hemberger, L., Kuhn, D., Matos, F., & Shi, Y. (2017). A dialogic path to evidence-based argumentive writing. *Journal of the Learning Sciences, 26,* 575–607.

Iordanou, K., & Kuhn, D. (2020). Contemplating the opposition: Does a personal touch matter? *Discourse Processes, 57,* 343–359.

Iordanou, K., Kuhn, D., Matos, F., Shi, Y., & Hemberger, L. (2019). Learning by arguing. *Learning and Instruction, 63.*

Iordanou, K., & Rapanta, C. (2021). "Argue with me": A method for developing argument skills. *Frontiers in Psychology, 12,* 631203.

Kuhn, D. (2018). *Building our best future: Thinking critically about ourselves and our world.* New York: Wessex Learning. Retrieved from *https://wessexlearning.com/collections/k-12-education.*

Kuhn, D. (2019). Critical thinking as discourse. *Human Development, 62,* 146–164.

Kuhn, D. (2020). *Argue with me* [video]. New York: Wessex Learning. Retrieved from *https://wessexlearning.com/collections/k-12-education.*

Kuhn, D. (2022). *Let's discuss: Second-language learners share ideas.* New York: Wessex Learning. Retrieved from *https://wessexlearning.com/collections/k-12-education.*

Kuhn, D., Hemberger, L., & Khait, V. (2016). *Argue with me: Argument as a path to developing students' thinking and writing* (2nd ed.). New York: Routledge.

Kuhn, D., & Modrek, A. (2021). Mere exposure to dialogic framing enriches argumentive thinking. *Applied Cognitive Psychology, 35,* 1349–1355.

Matos, F. (2021). Collaborative writing as a bridge from peer discourse to individual argumentative writing. *Reading and Writing, 34*(3), 1–22.

Mehan, H., & Cazden, C. (2015). The study of classroom discourse: Early history and current developments. In L. Resnick, C. Asterhan, & S. Clarke (Eds.), *Socializing intelligence through academic talk and dialogue* (pp. 13–34). Washington, DC: AERA.

Mill, J. S. (1859/1996). On liberty. In D. Wooton (Ed.), *Modern political thought: Readings from Machiavelli to Nietzsche* (pp. 592–651). Indianapolis: Hackett.

Rapanta, C. (2021). Can teachers implement a student-centered dialogical argumentation method across the curriculum? *Teaching and Teacher Education, 105.*

Shi, Y. (2019). Enhancing evidence-based argumentation in a Mainland China middle school. *Contemporary Educational Psychology, 59.*

Shi, Y., Matos, F., & Kuhn, D. (2019). Dialog as a bridge to argumentative writing. *Journal of Writing Research, 11,* 107–129.

Vygotsky, L. (1937/1987). *The collected works of L. S. Vygotsky: Problems of general psychology* (R. Rieber & A. Carlton, Eds.). New York: Plenum.

CHAPTER 5

Writing to Promote Better Reading Comprehension

Steve Graham
Adiba Nusrat

Writing provides a powerful and flexible tool for promoting learners' comprehension of the text they read as well as the development of stronger reading comprehension skills (Graham et al., 2020; Shanahan, 2016). Unfortunately, elementary and secondary students and teachers do not always take full advantage of the benefits of writing as a tool to facilitate comprehension and learning. This chapter presents evidence-based writing practices that enhance younger as well as older students' reading. For these evidence-based practices (EBP), we also suggest additional procedures that should enhance their effectiveness. We offer the following three questions to guide your reading of this chapter.

GUIDING QUESTIONS

- How can writing enhance reading comprehension?
- What instructional writing practices make students better readers?
- How can these practices be improved?

Have Students Write More

How Does Extra Writing Improve Reading Comprehension?

One way to help students learn to better comprehend text is to increase how much they write (Graham & Hebert, 2011). This EBP is a win-win situation for elementary and middle school students because it improves not only their skills in comprehending text, but also the overall quality of their writing (Graham,

Harris, & Santangelo, 2015). The impact of increased writing for high school students, however, is uncertain. Even so, it is important to ensure that these older students write frequently, as they need to use and practice applying this versatile tool in multiple situations if it is to become a common and useful part of their literacy toolkit.

Readers of this chapter may ask, "Why does increasing how much students write help them become better at comprehending the text they read?" Simply put, writing and reading are both communication activities (Tierney & Shanahan, 1991), and engaging in either of these processes should allow students to gain insight into the operation of the other process. Accordingly, as writers create text for others to read, even when the author is the intended audience, they gain insight about the process of reading. For example, writing requires that students make their assumptions and premises explicit and observe the rules of logic as they write. This can make them more aware of the same issues when reading text produced by others. Similarly, students have to think about the needs of their audience as they write, so increasingly the likelihood they will consider how authors of the material they read attend to this same issue. In essence, writing can make students more reflective about the material they read.

Examples of EBP for Extra Writing

For students who are just learning to write, relatively small increases in time spent writing can produce positive gains in their reading comprehension. This was illustrated in a study by Sussman (1998) with first-grade students. Students in this study spent between 75 to 100 minutes each week writing. Over the course of 23 weeks, they were asked to write for an additional 20 minutes 1 day a week. Students were encouraged to use invented spellings for all of their writing. For the extra writing they did each week, they were provided with a picture and asked to write something about it. At the end of the 23 weeks, their reading comprehension scores on a norm-referenced reading test were 9 percentile points higher than the scores of their peers who were not assigned extra picture writing.

It is also important that the extra writing students produce has a purpose and a real audience (Graham, Harris, & Santangelo, 2015). This was illustrated in a study by Dana and her colleagues (1991). They asked sixth-grade students to exchange a total of five letters with local college students, providing the sixth graders with an audience that would respond to their writing. This extra writing resulted in a 10-point percentile jump in their reading comprehension scores when compared to students who did not write to a pen pal.

There are many different writing activities that can enhance students' comprehension of content material (Graham, Kiuhara, & MacKay, 2020), including journal, narrative, informational, and persuasive writing. Extra writing instruction can involve these different types of writing, but it can also involve extra writing to create possible semantic representations of material that is to be read. This was demonstrated in a study by Reutzel (1985) with fifth-grade students. Before reading a story, but after a brief introduction to it, students created a written map in response to questions such as: "What do you think this story is about? Who do you think the first character is in the story? Do we know anything about this character? Do you think a story like this could be true?" Using these questions as a guide, students created a semantic map showing the relationships between their ideas about the story (e.g., main idea map, a compare and contrast map). They then read the story to see if their guesses were accurate. When compared to students who were not engaged in this extra writing, students who created these story maps evidenced a 31-point percentile jump in the comprehension of the stories they subsequently read.

Extensions

With the exception of the example involving extra writing through creating story maps above, reading comprehension gains occurred without explicit guidance, hints, or help from the teacher. We believe that the positive benefits of extra writing might be enhanced by explicitly directing students' attention to how their writing can inform their reading. One possible way of accomplishing this is to have students set a goal to address the needs of their audience. First, students can identify the specific audience need(s) they will address. This can be facilitated by providing students with a list of possible audience needs (e.g., make sure each point makes sense, provide adequate detail for each idea, make sure each idea logically leads to the next idea, define unusual words, write neatly), and asking them to choose one or more of these goals to address. Once goals are established, students should develop a plan for how they will accomplish their goal (e.g., check each sentence to be sure it connects to the next idea). After they have written their paper, they should be asked to reread it to determine if they met their desired goals. If not, they should be encouraged to revise their paper.

Another possible avenue for making the link between writing and reading more concrete is to have students write something and then view how their audience reacts (Couzijn & Rijlaarsdam, 2005). For instance, they can write directions for carrying out a specific activity, and then watch what happens as another student applies these directions. If the directions are not adequate, they can be encouraged to revise them. Likewise, they can be asked to write a paper on a controversial topic and to participate in a discussion where their ideas are examined and debated. These types of activities should make the connections between writing and reading as communication activities even clearer to students.

As students are encouraged to write more, teachers can also conference with them, asking them questions about their composition in progress. Some questions can focus specifically on the needs of the writer's audience. This includes questions such as: "Will your reader understand what you mean here? Does your reader need additional information to understand what you are saying here? What does this word mean? Will your reader think you are providing too much detail here?"

Have Students Write about What They Read

How Does Writing about Material Read Improve Reading Comprehension?

When students write about material they read, it helps them understand it better (Fitzgerald & Shanahan, 2000). It can facilitate comprehension of text in one or more of the following ways:

1. It fosters explicitness, as students must decide which information in text is most important.
2. It supports integration, as it encourages students to organize ideas in text into a coherent whole, creating explicit relationships between ideas.
3. It promotes reflection, as students can easily review, reexamine, connect, critique, and construct new understandings of reading material they commit to paper.
4. It generates a personal connection with text, as students must make active decisions about what is to be written and how it is to be treated.
5. It involves students putting ideas from text into their own words, making them think about what these ideas mean.

More specifically, writing about text facilitates comprehension because it provides students with a tool for visibly and permanently recording, connecting, analyzing, personalizing, and manipulating key ideas in material read (Graham & Hebert, 2011).

Writing about material read can also facilitate learning and comprehension as it provides students with a tool that helps them integrate information from text with their current knowledge held in long-term memory (Silva & Limongi, 2019). As students write about text, they rehearse information read, modifying and elaborating on it as they integrate these ideas with what they already know. For example, recording in a journal information taken from text acts as a rehearsal strategy, increasing students' exposure to the material read and extending time on task. Similarly, writing a response to a particular passage can evoke the use of organization and elaboration learning strategies, as students build a structure for presenting text ideas in writing, including linking new ideas in the text with their current understandings. Specific writing activities may further encourage comprehension monitoring. This can happen when a writing activity prompts students to reconsider old ideas in light of new information presented in a passage.

Writing can further facilitate comprehension when students transform material read into an argument, informational text, creative stories, or personal narratives (Klein, 1999). Genres are particular kinds of text, with specific purposes and text structures (Langer & Applebee, 1987). When students use a specific genre structure to organize relationships among ideas in the material they are reading, it helps them better understand how these ideas are related (see also Chapter 6, this volume). As students bring together ideas from text using the organizing structure of a specific genre (e.g., evidence, claims, and warrants when writing an argument), they acquire new understanding as they construct corresponding relations among the knowledge in the text and their own knowledge.

Writing is clearly a powerful tool for helping students better understand the material they read. In the next section, we present EBP examples of different types of writing that can enhance students' comprehension of text.

Examples of EBP for Writing about Material Read

Table 5.1 presents seven writing activities that are effective at improving students' comprehension of text. Drawing on research with younger and older students, as well as students who find literacy challenging, we provide examples of each of these writing activities.

Answering Questions in Writing

Perhaps one of the easiest ways of using writing to enhance comprehension is to have students answer in writing questions about the material they are reading. While this can be done verbally, writing the answers to such questions makes them more memorable because it provides a second form of rehearsal and the answers are available for review, reevaluation, and reconstruction (Graham & Hebert, 2011).

An example of this approach involves a study by Berkowitz (1986) with sixth-grade students. After being introduced to new vocabulary and needed background knowledge, students read a social studies text and answered in writing 10 main idea and 10 detail questions about it. They then discussed their answers with the teacher, with the goal of identifying the correct answer for each question. Students studied their answers and shared with a peer all they could remember from the social studies material read. Students applied these procedures to six social studies texts over a 6-week period, resulting in a 14-point percentile jump in students' comprehension of social studies materials.

An even more active approach to using writing to answer questions about material read is to have students generate their own written questions about

TABLE 5.1. Seven EBP Writing Activities for Promoting Text Comprehension

Use writing to . . .

- Answer questions about text
- Create written questions about text and answer them
- Take written notes about text
- Produce a summary of material read
- Generate a story about material read
- Describe how to apply information taken from text
- Develop an argument to support or reject a position presented in text

the material they read. Andre and Anderson (1979) applied this approach as a way to improve high school students' comprehension of expository text. Students were taught how to generate their own questions about the material they were reading. This involved the following three steps: (1) directing students to identify the main idea for each paragraph in a three-paragraph composition, (2) generating a question for each idea that focused on generating new instances or ideas that would logically flow from the main idea, and (3) generating a written question about a concept in text if the second step proved too difficult. The teacher modeled how to carry out these procedures, provided students with examples of self-generated written questions, and had them practice generating their own written questions for the main ideas presented in several practice paragraphs. The use of this question generation process resulted in a 20-point percentile increase in students' reading comprehension.

As these two examples illustrate, responding to questions about text in writing or students creating their own questions about the text they are reading enhances understanding of this material. The examples above do not exhaust the types of questions that students can answer or generate. Questions can range from those that ask students to make inference, focus on text organization, or evaluate an idea in text. They can involve answers that are directly presented in text, only exist in the reader's head, or both. They can focus attention on clarifying new meanings, making predictions, or considering an author's intent. These various purposes provide teachers with multiple avenues for using questions and writing as a means for helping students understand what they read.

Note Taking

Taking notes about material read requires students to shift through text to determine what is most relevant and transform these ideas into written words, phrases, and even sentences (Graham & Hebert, 2011). It can also involve connecting one text idea to another and blending this information from text with what a student already knows, resulting in new understandings.

Two basic approaches to note taking for reading have been studied scientifically. With one approach, students are directed to take notes but provided with little guidance on how to do so. For example, fifth- and sixth-grade students in a study by Leshin (1989) were simply told to take notes about passages they were reading, whereas Ryan (1981) directed middle school students to take written notes after each paragraph read and Kulhavey and colleagues (1975) directed students to take up to three lines of notes after reading each page. Despite the relative simplicity of these approaches, they resulted in gains ranging from 14 to 20 percentile points in reading comprehension.

With the other approach to taking notes from reading materials, students apply a much more structured strategy. This approach was illustrated in a study by Berkowitz (1986) with sixth-grade students who were good and poor readers. These students were taught how to construct a semantic map of the social studies material they were reading. For instance, when reading a passage entitled "What Makes a Nation?," they would construct a map with this question in the center and main ideas in this text connected to this hub with arrows or straight lines. Each main idea was represented by a labeled box (e.g., national unity, territory, government) with relevant notes included within the box.

To teach this note-taking procedure, the teacher introduced students to the reading topic prior to reading about it. This included introducing the topic, defining unfamiliar vocabulary words in the social studies text, and presenting background information needed to understand the passage. Students then read the text and constructed a map on a blank sheet of paper. Students wrote the title of the passage in the center of the page. Next, they skimmed the article to find four to six main ideas. They rewrote these ideas in their own words in a clockwise direction around the title. They again skimmed the article to find two to four important details to mention under each main idea. Finally, they connected the main idea and supporting details to the title of the passage. They then studied their map, reciting main ideas as well as the details until they could do this without looking back at the map. They further told a partner all they could remember from their reading. Students practiced applying these procedures under teacher direction, and they received feedback on the maps they produced. This approach to note taking was effective, as students made a 31-point percentile jump in reading comprehension.

A variety of structured note-taking procedures have positively enhanced students' reading comprehension. This includes outlining reading material, using a two-column note-taking method, and taking notes on a structural/graphic organizer that provides already designated categories (Graham & Hebert, 2011).

Summarizing Text in Writing

When students summarize text read into writing, they must decide what is and is not most important and transform this into a written statement that captures the essence of the material (Graham & Hebert, 2011). Written summaries present a synopsis of what was read, and they can readily be critiqued and reworked. This makes summary writing a powerful tool for understanding text.

Summarization is a complex skill, and we recommend teaching students how to apply this skill when writing a summary. A study by Hare and Borchardt (1984) provides one example of how students can be taught to summarize material read. They taught eleventh-grade students rules for writing a summary. This involved the following four steps: (1) Read the text and ask questions to be sure you understand it ("What is the text about? What did the writer say? Try to state the general theme to yourself"); (2) reread the text to be sure you got the theme right, be sure you understand important parts, and star these parts; (3) apply four summarization rules to create a summary of the passage read (i.e., collapse lists of ideas to a single word or phrase, use topic sentences as they often summarize a paragraph, get rid of unnecessary details, collapse paragraphs by deleting unimportant ones or combining those talking about the same topic); and (4) write and double-check your summary to polish it and make sure you didn't repeat yourself, leave in lists of items, or omit important information.

Hare and Borchardt (1984) taught these summarization rules in three 2-hour sessions. On the first day, the teacher and students defined a summary, and the teacher introduced the rules for writing a summary presented above. The teacher modeled how to use these rules on a selected passage, receiving help from the students. After they completed this summary, students compared what they had produced to a polished summary of the passage read, and they reviewed the rules for writing a summary. As a group and individually, students practiced writing summaries of materials read, receiving feedback form the teacher. On Day 2 of instruction, the teacher again modeled all the summarization rules for students, and students practiced writing summaries on materials more similar to what they would use in class. On the final and third day of instruction, students again practiced using the summarization rules, but now applied them to longer passages. This approach to teaching summarization was successful, as the students in this study experienced a 17-point percentile jump in reading comprehension.

Another approach to teaching summarization is illustrated in a study by Chang et al. (2002) with fifth-grade students. Students were first introduced to an expert summary of material read, and they examined and discussed it with their teacher. They then completed an expert summary that was missing a piece of key information from the material read. Missing information from the expert summary was signaled with a blank line. As students practiced completing expert summaries of material read, more and more information was deleted until students were writing the full summary by themselves. As they completed the incomplete expert summaries, they were provided feedback on the number of blank lines completed successfully. Students who learned to create summaries through this fading method evidenced a 20-point percentile jump in reading comprehension.

We share one additional approach to teaching summarization of material read that was applied with grade 3 to 6 students with learning disabilities (Jenkins et al., 1987). This involved three phases of instruction whereby students were taught to write brief restatements of the main ideas as they read each paragraph. In Phase 1, students were provided with retyped narrative stories with lined space between each paragraph. Using modeling, practice, and corrective feedback, students were taught to name the most important character/person and the main event in each paragraph. This was guided through the use of two supportive questions for formulating restatements: who and what is happening. If students were unable to generate a restatement, they were asked to read the paragraph a second time, and if they were still unable to identify an important event from the paragraph, the teacher provided corrective feedback. During Phase 2, students worked individually writing their restatements on the lined spaces given after each paragraph, receiving feedback as needed. When students finished writing restatements, the reading material was removed, and students were asked to elaborate on material read in each paragraph. In the third phase of instruction, students read regular narrative passages with no spaces for writing notes and practiced recording their restatements on a separate piece of paper. Students taught these procedures evidenced a 10-point percentile jump in reading comprehension.

Extended Writing

Writing a more extended response to reading material provides students with the opportunity to express a personal reaction to it, analyze and interpret it, or both (Graham & Hebert, 2011). Newer and better understanding of text are likely to occur when students write about reading material in such ways.

To date, scientifically tested extended writing activities involve a variety of narrative, information, or persuasive writing tasks. This includes writing a personal response to material read, writing about a personal experience evoked by reading text, writing an analysis of a character in a story, showing or explaining in writing how to apply knowledge presented in text, and analyzing a particular point of view presented in text.

To illustrate the use of extended writing, we share procedures applied in two different studies. Wong and her colleagues (2002) used journal writing as a way of helping grade 12 students better understand themes and main characters in F. Scott Fitzgerald's novel *The Great Gatsby*. For selected chapters in the novel, students responded to specific questions about the chapter by writing their responses in a journal they completed in class. For example, for Chapter 7, where Gatsby forces Daisy to choose between himself and her husband Tom, students responded to a series of questions about what they noticed (e.g., "Do you notice anything ironic?"), questioned (e.g., "Do you question Gatsby's soundness in forcing Daisy to choose?"), and felt (e.g., "Does the story leave you feeling sad, angry, scared?"). For the final chapter in the book, students responded to questions about what they had learned (e.g., Nick's view of Gatsby's vigil) and felt (e.g., "How do you feel about Gatsby?"). Once they completed their journal entries, they discussed as a group their reactions to the guiding questions. Once students began talking, the teacher maintained the flow of class discussion by using open-ended questions, incorporating students' comments in her follow-up comments or questions, and validating student's responses. This use of extended writing through journal entries increased students' comprehension of the novel by 33 percentile points.

In a study with much younger second-grade students, Denner et al. (1989) applied an interesting writing activity where students constructed a story before reading it (see also Reutzel, 1985, presented earlier where an outline of a story was created). This was done by giving students clues and hints concerning how the events and characters interacted in the story to be read. After writing their story impression, students shared their stories in class. Students then read the actual story that inspired the narrative they wrote. Creating such impressions of the story to be read led to a 30-point percentile increase in comprehension of it.

Extensions

While research has demonstrated that writing about text can enhance a student's comprehension of it, studies of writing as a tool to promote comprehension have only tested a relatively small number of writing activities. It is likely that other writing activities can also increase students' comprehension of text. Table 5.2 presents a variety of writing activities that can potentially enhance students' text comprehension. These eight writing activities were drawn from a meta-analysis demonstrating that writing about material presented in class can improve students' learning of such content (Graham et al., 2020). As a result, we believe these writing activities are also viable candidates for improving the comprehension of text read.

Because the writing activities in Table 5.2 have not been scientifically tested with reading material specifically, we make three important recommendations. First, it is important to identify what you want students to understand or learn as a result of reading a particular text. Such learning can take many forms, including determining the central ideas in a reading selection, comparing different ideas in a text, connecting text information to current knowledge, extending thinking about a topic, generating solutions and outcomes, or better understanding specific ideas presented in a text. Once you identify what students are to learn or better understand as they read a particular passage, you can identify one or more activities that will help them meet these goals. For example, if you want students to extend their thinking about the basic ideas in a text, you could ask them to write a poem or story using these ideas.

Second, it is important that students possess the prerequisite writing skills needed to use the selected writing activity effectively. The best way to ensure this is to teach students how to apply the writing activity when reading. This includes describing the writing activity, why it is useful, when and when not to use it, as well as modeling how it is used and providing students with guided practice doing so until they can apply it correctly and effectively. We find that it is advisable to use the writing activity yourself before teaching your students

TABLE 5.2. Eight Additional Writing Activities for Promoting Text Comprehension

Use writing to . . .

- Compare and contrast ideas in text
- Connect new information in text with information already known
- Describe the possible effects of an idea presented in text
- Present one or more solutions for a problem presented in text
- Create a written image of information, ideas, or processes presented in text
- Explain in your own words ideas presented in text
- Create a poem to illustrate or extend text ideas
- Construct analogies to describe information, ideas, or processes presented in text

to use it. This will help you think more clearly about how to teach it and how it is applied.

Finally, please do not assume that any writing activity, an EBP or not, will automatically be effective with your students. The best advice we can give is to carefully monitor if the selected writing activity achieves the desired goals you have set for it. If it does not enhance your students' comprehension of text, investigate why this is the case and make needed adjustments in its use as needed.

Teach Students to Write to Improve Their Reading

How Does Teaching Writing Improve Students' Reading?

While writing and reading are not identical skills, they both draw on common sources of knowledge (Fitzgerald & Shanahan, 2000). Students draw on knowledge stored in long-term memory to help them understand what they read and to obtain ideas to write about. Students also apply what they know about the functions and purposes of written language to help them create text for others to read and interpret text written by others. Students further use their knowledge of words, syntax, usage, and the features of text to decode and write words as well as comprehend and produce larger units of text. Moreover, students use their knowledge of cognitive activities such as goal setting, accessing information, questioning, predicting, summarizing, visualizing, and analyzing to understand text read and write what they intend. As a result, instruction that enhances writing knowledge, skills, and processes should improve students' reading, too.

Examples of EBP for Teaching Writing to Improve Reading

Spelling

Teaching students how words are spelled provides them with schemata about specific connections between letters and sounds. This should make it easier for them to identify and remember words in text containing these connections (Ehri, 2000; see also Chapter 2, this volume). There are multiple examples of studies where teaching spelling to young students improved their word reading, reading fluency, and reading comprehension (see Graham & Santangelo, 2014). We share one example here from a study by Graham and colleagues (2002) conducted with second-grade students experiencing difficulty with reading, spelling, and writing.

Each 2-week unit (six 20-minute sessions) in the spelling program devised by Graham and his colleagues (2002) began with a word-sorting activity where students determined the underlying rules of the two or three spelling patterns presented in that unit (e.g., consonant–vowel–consonant and consonant–vowel–consonant and letter *e* patterns for short and long /a/). The instructor placed two or more word cards next to each: one for each spelling patterns. The word was pronounced twice, with the instructor emphasizing the target sound the second time. New words were then introduced that included the target spelling patterns, and the teacher solicited students' help in placing each new word under the word that illustrated the same spelling pattern. To help students do this, the instructor provided hints, pointing out similarities and differences in sounds and letters. The instructor encouraged students to identify a rule for each of the target spelling pattern, and to test these rules as they carried out the word-sorting activity. Once the instructor believed students were ready, they generated a rule for each spelling pattern.

After the word study activity and throughout the unit, students were encouraged to "hunt" for words in their reading and writing that fit the spelling pattern they were working on in that unit. These were shared and discussed with the instructor and other classmates to ensure that they, in fact, fit the specified spelling pattern.

On the second day of each unit, students were provided with a list of spelling words to study that fit the spelling rules targeted. They had misspelled these words on an earlier assessment administered before the start of the study. They were taught a specific strategy for studying the words. They were taught to: (1) say the word and study the letters, (2) close their eyes and say the letters, (3) write a word three times without looking at it, and (4) check to see if their spelling were correct (correcting any misspellings). They graphed how many words were spelled correctly and set a goal for how many words they would spell correctly during the next session.

Students not only set goals for how many practice words would be spelled correctly, but also created a plan for studying these words. This could involve the strategy described above as well as the use of a variety of games, such as tic-tac-toe or hangman, which were played with a peer. Moves in these games depended on how many letters in a word were spelled correctly.

For four of the six sessions in each spelling unit, students began the lesson with a spelling warm-up activity. This involved identifying the letter that represented onset, medial, or final sounds in simple words. This warm-up activity was done in pairs, with one student holding up a card with a picture on one side and a corresponding letter on another side. The child said the word depicted by the picture and made the sound and identified the location of the sound in the word (beginning, middle, or end). The student's partner then identified the letter(s) that correspond to that sound. If an incorrect letter was identified, the student holding the card said the correct response. Students spent several minutes as the tutor and the tutee in each session.

Students also built words from the spelling patterns they were studying. For long and short /a/, they were provided with rimes such *ad* and *ade*, and directed to work with a partner to build as many real words as possible by adding consonants, blends, and diagraphs.

Throughout the spelling program, review of spelling patterns provided in previous units occurred. For example, in each unit, students built words from rimes introduced in the previous unit. This program enhanced not only students' spelling, but also resulted in an 18-point percentile increase in students' word-reading skills.

Sentence Construction

Teaching students how to construct more complex sentences by combining smaller, less complex ones should result in greater skill in recognizing and understanding such sentences when reading (Neville & Searls, 1991). This was illustrated by Neville and Searls (1985) in a study with sixth-grade students who were taught how to construct more complex sentences over a period of 10 weeks as well as identify kernel sentences (i.e., short simple sentences used to make longer more complex ones). First, students were given an assigned text to read. They then practiced combining kernel sentences from this text into more complex sentences. In the first three exercises, they combined 2 to 7 kernel sentences into a single sentence. In the next two exercises, they combined 7 to 19 kernel sentences into as few sentences as possible. Students shared the sentences they produced with the class, defending the choices they made. Students also completed kernel-recognition exercises by identifying kernel sentences taken from more complex sentences in the assigned text they were reading. Each recognition activity included kernel sentences that were and were not included in the more complex sentence. Again, students shared and defended their answers with their peers. This sentence construction program resulted in a 12-point percentile jump in reading comprehension.

Extensions

The EBPs presented here involved teaching spelling and sentence construction skills. It is also likely that instructional practices designed to increase students' knowledge of text structure as well as cognitive process used when writing, such as goal setting, self-monitoring, planning, evaluating, visualizing, questioning, creating analogies, and accessing information, provide students with strategies that can also be used when reading. For example, when students are taught to produce content for a narrative they are writing by generating possible writing ideas around the basic building block of a story ("Who is the story about? Where does it take place? When does it occur? What are the main characters' goals? What do they do to achieve them? What emotions do characters display? How does the story end?"), this provides them with schema for interpreting stories read. Likewise, teaching students how to visualize a scene so that they can make it more vivid when writing about it provides students with a tool they can use to better imagine a described setting in a story, characters' actions, or even their own feelings and emotions.

Instead of assuming such transfer occurs, however, we encourage teachers to make sure students see and understand how such knowledge and processes can be applied across both reading and writing. This includes not only teaching students how to use these processes when writing, but also making explicit connections on how to profitably use them when reading. This can be illustrated with the visualization example above. Students can be taught how to form images of scenes, characters, or actions they want to include in their story, while at the same time using the process of imagery to form mental pictures of the same aspects of stories they are reading. Such integration makes the connections between reading and writing even more concrete and visible to students.

Concluding Comments

The effectiveness of using writing or writing instruction as a tool to support students' understanding of text and growth as a reader depends on how writing is valued in the classrooms where it is applied (Smagorinsky, 1995). It is more likely to be a successful tool in classrooms where it is sanctioned and valued, and less likely to be useful in classrooms where this is not the case and writing occurs infrequently (Graham, 2018). The best way to ensure that the effects of writing on reading comprehension are maximized is to make writing a common and typified action in your class. Have students write frequently, ask them to use writing to think about what they read, teach students how to write, and make connections between writing and reading visible and as concrete as possible.

In closing, we ask you to consider the following questions as you apply procedures and information presented in this chapter in your own classroom:

- What writing activities presented here can you successfully apply with your students?
- How will you need to use these writing activities to maximize their success with your students?
- How will you evaluate if the writing activities applied were successful?

REFERENCES

Andre, M., & Anderson, T. H. (1979). The development and evaluation of a self-questioning study technique. *Reading Research Quarterly, 14*(4), 605–623.

Berkowitz, S. J. (1986). Effects of instruction in text organization on sixth-grade students' memory for expository reading. *Reading Research Quarterly, 21*(2), 161–178.

Chang, K., Sung, Y., & Chen, I. (2002). The effect of concept mapping to enhance text comprehension and summarization. *Journal of Experimental Education, 71*(1), 5–23.

Couzijn, M., & Rijlaarsdam, G. (2005). Learning to read and write argumentative text by observation of peer learners. In G. Rijlaarsdam (Series Ed.) & G. Rijlaarsdam, H. Van den Bergh, & M. Couzijn (Vol. Eds.), *Studies in writing: Vol. 14. Effective learning and teaching of writing, Part 1, Studies in learning to write* (2nd ed., pp. 241–258). Dordrecht, Netherlands: Kluwer Academic.

Dana, M. E., Scheffler, A. J., Richmond, M. G., Smith, S., & Draper, H. S. (1991).

Writing to read: Pen palling for a purpose. *Reading Improvement, 28*(2), 113–118.

Denner, P. R., McGinley, W. J., & Brown, E. (1989). Effects of story impressions as a prereading/writing activity on story comprehension. *Journal of Educational Research, 82*(6), 320–326.

Ehri, L. (2000). Learning to read and learning to spell: Two sides of a coin. *Topics in Language Disorders, 20*(3), 19–49.

Fitzgerald, J., & Shanahan, T. (2000). Reading and writing relations and their development. *Educational Psychologist, 35,* 39–50.

Graham, S. (2018). The writer(s)-within-community model of writing. *Educational Psychologist, 53,* 258–279.

Graham, S., Harris, K. R., & Fink-Chorzempa, B. (2002). Contributions of spelling instruction to the spelling, writing, and reading of poor spellers. *Journal of Educational Psychology, 94*(4), 669–686.

Graham, S., Harris, K. R., & Santangelo, T. (2015). Research-based writing practices and the Common Core: Meta-analysis and meta-synthesis. *Elementary School Journal, 115,* 498–522.

Graham, S., & Hebert, M. (2011). Writing to read: A meta-analysis of the impact of writing and writing instruction on reading. *Harvard Educational Review, 81,* 710–744.

Graham, S., Kiuhara, S., & MacKay, M. (2020). The effects of writing on learning in science, social studies, and mathematics: A meta-analysis. *Review of Educational Research, 90,* 179–226.

Graham, S., & Santangelo, T. (2014). Does spelling instruction make students better spellers, readers, and writers? A meta-analytic review. *Reading & Writing: An Interdisciplinary Journal, 27,* 1703–1743.

Hare, V. C., & Borchardt, J. (1984). Direct instruction of summarization skills. *Reading Research Quarterly, 20*(1), 62–78.

Jenkins, J. R., Heliotis, J. D., & Stein, M. L. (1987). Improving reading comprehension by using paragraph restatements. *Exceptional Children, 54*(1), 54–63.

Klein, P. (1999). Reopening inquiry into cognitive processes in writing-to-learn. *Educational Psychology Review, 11*(3), 203–270.

Langer, J., & Applebee, A. (1987). *How writing shapes thinking: A study of teaching and learning.* Champaign, IL: National Council of Teachers of English.

Kulhavey, R., Dyer, J., & Silver, L. (1975). The effects of notetaking and test expectancy on the learning of text material. *Journal of Educational Research, 68*(10), 363–365.

Leshin, C. (1989). *Spatial representation and reading comprehension in 5th and 6th grade students.* Unpublished PhD dissertation, Arizona State University.

Neville, D. D., & Searls, E. F. (1985). The effect of sentence-combining and kernel-identification training on the syntactic component of reading comprehension. *Research in the Teaching of English, 19*(1), 37–61.

Neville, D., & Searls, E. (1991). A meta-analytic review of the effect of sentence-combining on reading comprehension. *Reading Research and Instruction, 31*(1), 63–76.

Reutzel, D. R. (1985). Story maps improve comprehension. *The Reading Teacher, 38*(4), 400–404.

Ryan, M. T. (1981). *Effects of paraphrase note taking on prose learning.* Unpublished PhD dissertation, University of Connecticut.

Shanahan, T. (2016). Relationships between reading and writing development. In C.

MacArthur, S. Graham, & J. Fitzgerald (Eds.), *Handbook of writing research* (2nd ed., pp. 194–207). New York: Guilford Press.

Silva, A., & Limongi, R. (2019). Writing to learn increases long-term memory consolidation: A mental-chronometry and computational-modeling study of "epistemic writing." *Journal of Writing Research, 11*(1), 211–243.

Smagorinsky, P. (1995). Constructing meaning in the disciplines: Reconceptualizing writing across the curriculum as composing across the curriculum. *American Journal of Education, 103*(2), 160–184.

Sussman, G. L. (1998). *The effects of phonologically constructed spelling on first graders' literacy development.* Unpublished PhD dissertation, Fordham University.

Tierney, R., & Shanahan, T. (1991). Research on the reading-writing relationship: Interactions, transactions, and outcomes. In R. Barr, M. Kamil, P. Mosenthal, & D. Pearson (Eds.), *The handbook of reading research* (Vol. 2, pp. 246–280). New York: Longman.

Wong, B. Y. L., Kuperis, S., Jamieson, D., Keller, L., & Cull-Hewitt, R. (2002). Effects of guided journal writing on students' story understanding. *Journal of Educational Research, 95*(3), 179–193.

CHAPTER 6

Genre and Text Structure in Writing and Reading Instruction

Zoi A. Philippakos

Writing and reading performance can influence learners' professional and academic career, their motivation, and confidence. Writing can support reading performance (Graham & Hebert, 2011) and reading interventions can lead to improvements in writing (Graham et al., 2018a), while approaches that integrate reading and writing further advance academic performance (Graham et al., 2018b; see also Chapter 12, this volume). Jouhar and Rupley (2021), in a systematic review of studies on independent reading and writing, found that independent reading led to improvements on narrative and descriptive writing, resulting also in improvements on mechanics, spelling, and text organization, a finding that is in line with another meta-analysis on the effects of reading on writing (Graham et al., 2018a). Reading can also support learners' understanding about how text is structured and what elements of a specific genre are commonly used (MacArthur, 2016).

Chapter 1 of this book explains in detail the historical relationship between the two as they connect at a rhetorical, cognitive, and pragmatic level (also see Philippakos, 2021). The International Literacy Association in its research advisory on reading and writing connections (Philippakos & Graham, 2020) made a strong claim that writing and reading need to be integrated. Indeed, this integration is imperative, as writing and reading both draw from common cognitive, linguistic, and pragmatic resources. Readers should keep in mind that someone may be a reader, but not a writer, and will not become a writer without systematic instruction and opportunities to write for different genres and audiences. The purpose of this chapter is to explain how genre and text structure instruction can support writing and reading performance. The next section presents practices that refer to text structure as well as evidence-based methodologies for learners' transfer of knowledge and skills across writing and reading genres. But first, a brief definition of terms will be provided in order to better navigate through these ideas. The guiding questions that follow can be used to support readers' navigation across meanings.

GUIDING QUESTIONS

- What is the function of genre and text structure in reading comprehension?
- What is the function of genre in writing?
- What is the role of explicit instruction of genre?
- What instructional practices support students' understanding about and use of genres?
- How can writing and reading be authentically integrated across the curriculum?

Genre and Text Structures

Genre refers to the function and features of a written form. Based on the social semiotic theory (Halliday & Hasan, 1985), genres reflect specific sociocultural contexts and are shaped by the specific expectations of those developing linguistic forms (Martin, Christie, & Rothery, 1987). Text structure refers to the organization of written text that addresses the expectations of the discourse and of the community that will read it or, in simple terms, to the ways ideas are organized to communicate a message to a reader. In an argumentative text, for example, the structure will include:

- a statement of position,
- reasons with supporting evidence,
- opposing position with reasons and a rebuttal, and
- ending with a restatement of position.

In the case of a story, there will be a story grammar (Stein & Glenn, 1979), and inclusion of elements such as:

- character/s,
- time, place (together called setting),
- problem,
- actions and complications,
- solution, and
- emotions.

Some text structures have common organizations, as is found in narrative and story writing. Informative writing can pose more challenges because there are different types of text structure depending on the goals of the writer (Meyer, 1975). Challenges can also arise due to lack of familiarity with concepts and vocabulary that appear in expository text and make the processing of content and reading for understanding more demanding compared to narratives (Hiebert & Mesmer, 2013). Informative texts can be compare–contrast, cause–effect, sequence, descriptions, and problem–solution. In general, authors' purposes lead to specific genres and text structures. Cues and signaling words are associated with specific structures (Meyer, 1975). For example, when writing to inform and examine similarities and differences between different topics, the genre of compare–contrast will be used, with the elements of:

- issue,
- purpose,
- similarities with explanations,
- differences with explanations, and
- restatement of purpose.

While reading, learners will notice signal words such as *similar, both, on the one hand*, and *on the other hand* that authors used to present information. Table 6.1 presents purposes and genres with common text structures and signal words (based on Meyer & Ray, 2011; Philippakos, 2021).

Understanding of text structure can support learners' reading comprehension (e.g., Pyle et al., 2017), organization of their writing and quality of recorded meanings (e.g., Harris et al., 2012; Traga Philippakos, 2019), and also note taking for reading (Hebert, Bohaty, Nelson, & Roehling, 2018; Reynolds & Perin, 2009; MacArthur, Traga Philippakos, May, & Compello, 2022). Students may be able to write on the genres they are exposed to and are familiar with but systematic instruction is required for less familiar ones (Duke, 2000). Systematic instruction of such structures can support students' academic paths, reading comprehension, and writing as this relates to given discourses (Gersten, Fuchs, Williams, & Baker, 2001), yet lack of this knowledge restricts students' ability to communicate effectively through such forms (Kress, 1989; Martin, 2009).

It is important to be clear what is meant by *systematic instruction*. This involves no guessing of the processes and tasks learners are expected to complete, but rather instruction that includes direct explanations and gradual release of responsibility (Pearson & Gallagher, 1983) with clear transition of locus of control from the teacher to the student. Strategy instruction is such an approach that addresses systematic and methodical instruction of tasks and processes building on the premise that strategies are conscious processes that learners use to achieve goals. They are plans that are thoughtfully considered and followed but are also flexible, and readers can apply and adapt them in texts they read (Pressley, Borkowski, & Schneider, 1987) and in texts they write (MacArthur, 2011). *Strategies*, contrary to *skills*, are conscious plans that readers use to think what to do, when, and why. Strategies require and are based on critical thinking and problem solving as well as active cognitive

TABLE 6.1. Genre, Purposes, Elements, and Signal Words

Genre	Purpose	Elements	Sample signal words
Opinion/ argument	Persuade	*Beginning:* Topic and opinion/ position/thesis *Middle:* Reasons, evidence/ explanations opposing position, reasons, rebuttal *End:* Restatement and message to reader	*opinion, perspective on issue, view, reason, claim, evidence, opposing view, should, should not, support the claim, controversy, argument, argue, others say/believe/ claim, even though, despite, although*
Report	Inform	*Beginning:* Topic and purpose *Middle:* Categories (main ideas) and evidence/ explanations *End:* Restatement of purpose and message to reader	*characteristics, categories, classify, classification, also, in addition*
Procedural	Inform	*Beginning:* Topic, purpose, materials–skills *Middle:* Steps and explanations *End:* Evaluation, restatement of purpose, message to reader	*materials, steps, how to, first, second, third, steps, if you do not _____, then _____*
Compare– contrast	Inform	*Beginning:* Topic, purpose (to make a decision, to learn) *Middle:* Similarities with examples and evidence/ explanations Differences with examples and evidence *End:* Restate purpose, message for reader to think/take action	*differ, similar, differences, both, on the one hand, on the other hand, contrary to, common, despite, although, more, less than, alternatively*
Cause–effect	Inform	*Beginning:* Topic, purpose *Middle:* Causes or effects with evidence and examples. *End:* Restate purpose, message for reader to think/take action	Causes: *reasons for, causes, because, due to, bring about, leads to* Effects: *consequences, effect, affects, outcomes, thus, therefore, as a result*

engagement with a text. Strategies must be adaptable and flexible so readers can apply them in different situations. Strategies also include metacognitive thinking and reflection on their use. Effective readers and writers use strategies to navigate a text and construct meaning, and to develop a text and convey meaning to outside readers.

Effects of Genre and Text Structure
Instruction on Reading Comprehension

Readers and their processes of meaning-making are affected by text characteristics (Dole, Duffy, Roehler, & Pearson, 1991). Good readers and comprehenders have specific schemata (Meyer, 1985) about rhetorical purpose and organization they employ while reading (Englert & Hiebert, 1984). When good readers process text, they identify those structures and look for specific elements or genre characteristics to develop memory representations of the information they read, and recall it later or summarize it (Kintsch & Van Dijk, 1978; Meyer, Brandt, & Bluth, 1980). While reading, cues or signal words can lead readers to appropriately identify text structure (see Table 6.1). For instance, while reading a text, the signaling words *controversy, position, reason*, and *argue* will lead a reader to conclude that the author's purpose is to argue for a specific position. This, in turn, signals that they need to identify, comprehend, and recall the elements of an argument (position, reasons, evidence, opposition, conclusion) as they read.

Knowledge of top-level structures of text allows learners to recall more information from text they have read compared to readers who are not able to identify such structures (Meyer & Rice, 1984). Furthermore, such knowledge allows learners to better anticipate and predict content and organize the presented information (Zwaan, 1994). For example, while reading a story, once readers are introduced to the characters and the setting, they anticipate that a problem will exist. Similarly, when reading a mystery text, they anticipate that there is a false clue that misleads the character. Also, they ask questions about the specific information and genre elements they have encountered to better monitor meaning-making and recall essential information (Wolman, 1991). Overall, understanding how a text is organized and how an author has structured a text can support reading comprehension across grades and ability levels.

A meta-analysis by Hebert et al. (2016) reviewed 44 studies and found that when students with and without reading difficulties are taught expository text structure, their reading comprehension improves. Furthermore, when instruction includes more than one text structure, and when it is followed by writing text structure instruction, the effects on reading comprehension are greater.

Instructional Approaches to Text Structure for Reading Comprehension

Several approaches are effective for teaching text structure when reading. Students can be taught the elements of a genre and use this knowledge to identify and recognize that structure while reading. Meyer and Ray (2011) shared a comprehensive review of studies that address text structure recognition and are based on the Meyer (e.g., 1975) text structure characteristics. For example, students can be taught the elements of story writing or story grammar and then use this knowledge to determine who a character is and what the problem is throughout their reading. However, instruction to identify those elements while reading may not always be sufficient. Considering that some students may not be able to activate knowledge on text structure as they process a text, systematic instruction on questioning and question generation can better support their reading and comprehension monitoring. To illustrate, Singer and Donlan (1982) investigated whether teaching students story elements and showing them genre-based questions would evoke answers from the text about those elements and would support students' own abilities to develop such questions and use them when reading. The 11th-grade students in this investigation daily learned about specific elements of a story (character, goal, obstacles, outcome, theme) and content-based questions specific to these elements (e.g., "Who is the leading character?" "What is the character trying to accomplish?"). As they listened to a story and read it, students were asked to consider questions they wanted to answer. When compared to students who answered questions about specific content in a story (e.g., "What do you think will happen to X?") (Singer & Donlan, 1982, p. 174), students who received the story genre questions evidenced improved comprehension and were better able to ask genre-related questions about the material they were reading. In effect, the story-genre instruction helped readers identify specific information from a story as well as classify it under specific structures instead of just memorizing words from the story.

An additional approach to supporting text structure comprehension instruction involves the use of maps or graphic organizers (see also Chapter 5, this volume). Reutzel (1985) conducted a study with fifth graders using visual maps (called *story maps*) for story structure and expository texts. Students who were provided with and were instructed to ask questions with visual maps for reading were able to recall more information across the narrative and descriptive text structures.

McLaughlin (1990) investigated the effects of teaching text structures to fifth-grade students experiencing reading difficulties. Students were taught the compare–contrast text structure and how to identify similarities and differences during a 60-minute session. Teachers introduced and explained how to use a Venn diagram, highlighting similarities and differences. Then, students predicted the topics that were compared and contrasted by reading a Venn diagram that had information about those two things. Next, students practiced completing a Venn diagram using a different passage that included information about two things that were compared and contrasted. Finally, students completed a recall task after reading passages that were at different grade levels. When compared to students who did not receive such instruction, teaching students to use these procedures led to better recall of information presented in text.

Bartlett (1978) in his seminal work taught ninth-grade learners to identify the structures of compare–contrast, cause–effect, description, and problem–solution (Meyer, 1975). Instruction involved five 1-hour sessions. The control group had access to the same texts as the treatment group and read the same information; however, instead of learning about the text structures, students in the control group engaged in grammar-based instruction (punctuation work). Students in both groups responded to questions about texts before instruction, immediately after training, and at 3-week maintenance. Students who received text structure instruction remembered far more content (twice as much) compared to control students both at posttest and at the 3-week maintenance task.

Cue words and signal words (e.g., *both*, *differ*, and *on the other hand* in compare–contrast texts) can be used to support students' ability to recognize text structures, and students may often highlight text or record the genre-signal words they encounter in texts. Chambliss (1995) conducted a study with 12th graders who engaged in reading arguments of different levels of familiarity, a variety of signal words, and different argument structures. The use of signaling words and the understanding of text structure at the introduction and conclusion of the texts affected students' ability to recognize the argumentative structure, the presence of a claim, the evidence that supported it, and increased their ability to provide a gist.

Williams and colleagues (2004) developed and refined a strategy for teaching reading comprehension that addressed text structure and combines the use of reading, rereading, analysis, graphic representation, use of signal words, and summarization (i.e., see Williams, Hall, & Lauer, 2004). The Close Analysis of Texts with Structure (CATS) involves the analysis of short paragraphs on targeted structures utilizing three specific strategies: the use of cue words, graphic organizers, and targeted questions. Teachers provided direct instruction that includes the reading of texts and vocabulary conversations while students read trade books. In a study where lessons were provided in a social studies curriculum for second graders, students in the CATS intervention had higher comprehension scores compared to the content and the business-as-usual group as measured by the summaries students wrote on paragraphs that addressed the taught text structures (sequence, comparison, causation, description, and problem–solution).

Points to Remember

- Teaching students the elements of text structure can support their ability to recognize content related to those structures when they read texts.
- Teaching students the elements of genre can support them in monitoring the text they read.
- Teaching students text structure and schema-generated questions that refer to genre elements can support their recall, meaning-making, and ability to monitor comprehension.
- Teaching students to ask questions about the elements in relation to the content as they progress through a text can support active engagement with meaning-making and strategy use.

Instructional Approaches to Text Structure and Genre for Writing Instruction

Systematic instruction of text structure and genre elements is common in writing strategy instruction. Strategy instruction refers to the systematic instruction of processes and tasks and includes the following components (MacArthur, 2011, 2016):

- Instruction of the cognitive processes that students find challenging
- Instruction using evidence-based methodologies
- Instruction that supports students' independence and increases self-regulation

Cognitive Strategy Instruction in Writing

A model of strategy instruction developed by Englert and colleagues (1991) called Cognitive Strategy Instruction in Writing (CSIW) demonstrates instruction of organizational structures for planning and revising. Englert et al. conducted a study with fourth- and fifth-grade students to examine the effects of CSIW on students' composition of expository texts. Instruction included teacher modeling of self-talk, explanation of steps to use and information about the organization of the text, collaboration with students, use of think-sheets to facilitate students' application of the strategy, peer discussions and collaboration during conferencing. Students were taught a strategy that was captured by the acronym POWER, which referred to Plan, Organize, Write, Edit, and Revise. Each step of POWER was supported with a think-sheet, which guided students' work. For example, when reading the work of a peer, students were instructed to identify areas of confusion. The results demonstrated that students who participated in the CSIW group improved significantly in audience awareness, in the composition of the taught expository text, and in the quality of their texts. Furthermore, students' writing improved on a transfer task in which they were asked to compose an unknown text structure.

Self-Regulated Strategy Development

One of the most effective approaches of teaching text structure and elements of genre to students is the Self-Regulated Strategy Development (SRSD) approach (Harris, Graham, & Mason, 2006; Harris & Graham, 2009). SRSD has positive effects on the writing quality of elementary (e.g., Harris, Graham, & Mason, 2006; Graham, 2006), secondary (e.g., Graham & Perin, 2007; see also Chapter 8, this volume), postsecondary and adult learners (MacArthur, Philippakos, & Ianetta, 2015; Traga Philippakos & MacArthur, 2019; see also Chapter 16, this volume). Such effects are evident for students with and without learning disabilities and struggling writers, and is effective when instruction is provided by classroom teachers, undergraduate students, or paraprofessionals (see Graham, 2006; Graham & Perin, 2007). SRSD instruction is based on six steps or stages of instruction that are meant to be used flexibly:

1. Develop and activate background knowledge on the type of writing that will be taught,
2. discuss it,
3. model it,
4. memorize it,
5. support it, and
6. practice it.

SRSD involves a gradual release of responsibility where learners engage in understanding the genre, its purposes, vocabulary and terms related to it, modeling, and scaffolded application until they have mastered the strategy. One of the major contributions of SRSD is the development of students' self-regulation through goal setting and monitoring of their performance across writing tasks.

At the *develop background knowledge* stage, the teacher explains the elements of the genre and the specifics of the text structure. Students' prior knowledge about this genre is activated and discussed. A model paper may be also provided for the students to make the connection between the elements and their function. A mnemonic that is used to support the specific structure is then explained. For instance, when working on opinion writing, the POW+TREE mnemonic can be introduced (Harris, Graham, Mason, & Friedlander, 2008):

Pick my idea and pay attention to the prompt.

Organize.

Write and say more.

+

Topic sentence: Tell what you believe.

Reasons three or more: Why do I believe that? Will my readers believe this?

Explain reasons: Say more about each reason.

Ending: Wrap it up right.

Baseline data are collected.

At the *discuss it* stage, texts that represent the genre are provided to students and the instructors explain how each letter of the mnemonic is present in those texts. The instructor models the identification of the elements, and then as a group they identify those elements in additional texts. Students discuss goal setting. Students analyze their own paper and develop goals. Their performance may be also graphed.

At the *model it* stage, teachers review the mnemonic and model how to use it to complete the writing task. In the case of TREE, they will use each letter to organize their ideas while they also use self-statements that address the process and their progress (e.g., "What shall I do next?"). The instructor completes the writing, examines the presence of elements, and graphs the progress that is made on the chart.

The *memorize it* stage consists of the students learning the mnemonic and of the teachers examining whether students know and can recall it. This stage is important, as lack of automaticity on recall of elements can affect students' production and motivation.

The *support it* stage includes collaborative writing tasks and scaffolding for students to gradually apply the taught strategy without support of the use of visual aids. For example, an organizer will be faded and students organize their ideas without the use of such a facilitator.

At the final stage, students apply the mnemonic to complete their writing without support, as this independent, self-regulated performance is the goal of the SRSD model.

SRSD has a wealth of research support, both with regular-education learners and students with learning disabilities. Graham et al. (2005) conducted a research study with third graders who were randomly assigned to three groups: SRSD instruction only, SRSD with peer support, and practice–control. Students wrote essays on four different genres: story, persuasion, personal narrative, and informative essay before and after instruction. The results showed that students in the SRSD with peer support condition showed transfer to informative writing that was not part of the instructed genres. Furthermore, the students in both SRSD conditions included more story elements in their stories and their persuasive essays compared to the students without SRSD instruction, and this pattern was also shown at maintenance. Overall, SRSD includes several text structures that can be taught using those six steps and stages (Harris et al., 2008).

Genre-Based Strategy Instruction

The genre-based strategy instruction approach draws from the works of Englert et al. (1991), SRSD (Harris & Graham, 2009), and genre focus (Rose, 2016) and provides systematic instruction of genre as this relates to text structure, syntax, and vocabulary or linguistic forms. Experimental studies with primary (e.g., Traga Philippakos, 2019; Traga Philippakos & MacArthur, 2020) and intermediate learners (Traga Philippakos, 2020a), and design-based research with secondary learners (Traga Philippakos & MacArthur, 2021) show improvements on students' writing quality across genres and reading performance. The approach addresses purposes, elements of genre, cues, and signals, while it also includes a strong emphasis on genre-based evaluation and utilizes read-alouds for the identification of elements as well as readings for note taking and retelling. Instruction is provided using an approach called Strategy for Teaching Strategies (STS) (see Philippakos & MacArthur, 2020; Philippakos et al., 2015):

Introduction to the Writing Purposes

Teachers explain writing purposes (Persuade, Inform, Entertain, or Convey Experience) (see Philippakos, 2018), discuss the purpose for the specific genre (e.g., persuade), and introduce the genre (opinion) and its organizational elements as well as additional linguistic and syntactic characteristics. Teachers record the elements of the genre while they explain that reading and writing tasks include a Beginning, a Middle, and an End (BME), and the content of each section is determined by the writing purpose and genre. (See Table 6.2 for the elements of genres and BME structure.) Teachers share that prior to writing learners consider the Form, Topic, Audience, Author, and Purpose to analyze the assignment and better understand the task, determine the writing purpose and genre, and select the strategies used for planning, drafting, and evaluation to revise.

1. **Introduction of genre via read-alouds.** Teachers conduct a read-aloud and use the information from it to take notes using the genre's organizational elements and summarize/retell. The task is completed with the purpose of showing students how knowledge of the elements and of the text structure characteristics can support students' note taking and retelling.

2. **Evaluation of good and weak examples.** Teachers display an evaluation rubric that includes the same genre elements (BME) and explain its scoring system and the process of evaluating by critically reading. Teachers model the process using a well-written and poorly written samples discussing the writer's goals. Students reread their own papers, evaluate them, and set genre-specific and other goals (e.g., use of specific vocabulary and sentence frames).

3. **Think-aloud modeling.** Teachers explain the writing process and model how to plan, draft, evaluate to revise, and edit a paper. For this purpose, they use charts and graphic organizers (GO) that are based on text structure. For the generation of ideas in opinion writing, they brainstorm in favor and against the given topic, develop ideas for both sides, and select the side that is more persuasive (e.g., see Philippakos & MacArthur, 2020). Then they use an outline with the genre elements to transfer and expand on ideas from the brainstorming stage. Teachers use the information from the organizer/outline to draft using the aid of sentence frames. At this point, they may say the intended sentence out loud to first hear it and auditorily examine the clarity of the intended meaning before writing it or typing it (say it, hear it, write it, reread it, fix it if you need to fix it; Traga Philippakos, 2019). Once the paper is completed, they use the same genre elements and a scoring system of 0 (element is absent), 1 (element is present but either insufficient or unclear to reader), and 2 (element is well developed and clear to reader) to evaluate the clarity of the content. In addition,

teachers examine the use of sentence frames and qualitative aspects of the genre (e.g., tone, the use of convincing reasons).

4. **A focus on self-regulation.** Students and teachers comment on the strategies, the language used to support their motivation and progress monitoring, behavior, and attitude (e.g., it is okay to get stuck, it is not okay to quit; use the strategy to find the way) (Traga Philippakos & MacArthur, 2020). Together or individually, they develop language they can use to remember to apply the strategies when they work, to monitor their use, and to manage their behavior and affect.

5. **Collaborative practice.** Teachers work with students to complete the planning, drafting, evaluation to revise, and editing of a paper in which the teacher scaffolds students' application of the writing process, and together they write a paper on a new topic using the same strategies.

6. **Guided practice.** Students begin their work while teachers support the application of strategies and, when needed, differentiate by working in small groups or with individuals.

7. **Preparation for self-evaluation and peer review.** Teachers model giving feedback and goal setting (Traga Philippakos, 2020b). They explain the difference between editing and revising, model how to evaluate a paper, and set revision goals for immediate correction as well as goals for their next assignment. Students collaboratively practice evaluating papers, self-evaluate their work, and reexamine the goals they had set and their progress toward them. Then they meet for peer review and determine their revision goals.

8. **Editing.** Teachers explain the role and importance of editing and model it using a mnemonic that refers to Spelling, Capitalization, Indentation, Punctuation, and Sentences (SCIPS). Students reread and edit their work focusing on a specific skill teachers have modeled that is part of their grade-level standards or addresses the needs of the students.

9. **Continuous practice to mastery and independence.** Students identify the goals for their next paper and continue applying the strategies to other topics and/or contexts.

This instructional process underwent cycles of design-based research (see Reinking & Bradley, 2008; Philippakos, 2021) and experimental studies in traditional and virtual settings (e.g., Traga Philippakos & Voggt, 2021). In a study with second graders (Traga Philippakos & MacArthur, 2020) that investigated the effects of genre-based strategy instruction on the quality of second graders' persuasive papers, 4 classroom teachers and their 80 students were randomly assigned to two conditions: the genre-based strategy instruction

TABLE 6.2. Genres across a BME Structure

	Genre	Opinion	Argument	Procedural	Report	Effects
	Genre	Persuade	Persuade	Inform	Inform	Inform
Beginning		Topic	Topic	Topic	Topic	Topic
		Opinion/position/thesis	Opinion/position/thesis	Purpose Materials/skills	Purpose	Purpose
Middle		Reasons	ME: Reasons	Steps	Categories (main ideas)	Effects
		Evidence/explanations	Evidence/explanations	Explanations	Evidence/explanations Explanations	Explanations
			OTHERS: Opposing position			
			Reasons Rebuttal			
End		Restate position	Restate position	Evaluation	Restate position	Restate position
		Message to reader for the reader to take action	Message to reader for the reader to think more/take action	Restatement of purpose Message to reader	Message to reader	Message to reader

plus collaborative reasoning condition, and the units of study approach that was already in place at the site. Instruction was provided by the teachers who were virtually coached. The results showed that students in the genre-based strategy instruction plus collaborative reasoning group wrote papers of better quality compared to students in the control condition. Furthermore, even though elements of persuasion increased for both groups, the treatment group included more elements for the *beginning* and *end* of their paper that referred to the statement of purpose and explanation of the issue/problem statement and restatement of the position with a message to the reader, respectively.

This instruction, when integrated in the curriculum and applied to teach more than one genre across time, can potentially support students' reading and writing performance as well as transfer across genres. Traga Philippakos (2020a) examined a yearlong professional development model on genre-based strategy instruction with students learning and applying the genres of opinion, story, and compare–contrast writing. Instruction was provided to 273 students by their teachers, and students' written responses across all genres were collected at the beginning of this work and after each genre's instruction. The results showed that the quality of students' written responses improved after instruction of each genre, writing quality was retained for each taught genre across time, and students transferred knowledge from the genre of opinion to compare–contrast prior to that instruction. An important finding is that no gender differences were found, a result that shows systematic genre instruction can potentially increase students' writing performance independently of gender and socioeconomic status. Furthermore, students' performance on reading comprehension increased across time.

Points to Remember

- Teaching students the elements of text structure supports their ability to develop ideas, plan their papers, and outline or organize their thoughts.
- Teaching students the elements of genre supports their ability to draft without omitting information that can affect the quality of their response (e.g., excluding evidence for reasons in persuasion or explanations to steps in procedural writing).
- Teaching students the elements of a genre allows them to critically reread and evaluate their work examining whether their paper includes those elements and whether they are clearly communicated to readers.
- Teaching students the elements of a genre helps them better monitor their progress and set specific goals for improvement (e.g., include a statement of purpose in an effect paper).
- Teaching students the elements of the genre, signal words, and sentence frames helps them address the communicative needs of the discourse.
- Teaching students the elements of genre can support them in monitoring the text they write and read.

Text Structure and Genre-Based Instruction in Combined Approaches of Reading and Writing

The meta-analysis by Hebert et al. (2016), among its other findings, shared that instruction on text structure that addressed both reading comprehension and writing was more effective. Studies of SRSD have combined instruction on reading and writing strategies addressing text structure (e.g., Mason, Davison, Hammer, Miller, & Glutting, 2013; see also Chapter 8, this volume). Similarly, genre-based strategy instruction has incorporated the use of genre across reading and writing tasks, and other promising approaches examine the ways in which writing and the inclusion of readings that address cognitive overload can support writing (Hebert et al., 2021).

The genre-based writing instruction approach engages students in a reading–writing integration through the use of read-alouds that learners process to identify genre elements, take notes on a graph, and summarize information (orally or in writing). Furthermore, students are taught how to evaluate written text by carefully rereading and identifying the elements, underlining them, and circling signaling words and phrases (Philippakos & MacArthur, 2016; Philippakos, 2017). In a study that examined the effects of giving feedback using genre-evaluation criteria, fourth and fifth graders were able to make revisions that affected the quality of their papers compared to readers who had access to the same training resources but did not practice evaluation using genre-specific criteria (Philippakos & MacArthur, 2016).

In order to better support students' writing-to-reading and reading-to-writing pathways, a rhetorical analysis was designed to support students' analysis of reading tasks, note taking, and summary writing (Philippakos, 2018; Traga Philippakos & MacArthur, 2020, 2021). Instruction always follows a gradual release of responsibility, can occur across content areas and not only in English language arts (ELA) (Traga Philippakos & MacArthur, 2021).

- **Application of FTAAP (rhetorical task analysis process) to determine the purpose and genre.** Prior to reading a text or book or any reading resource, teachers identify the Form (e.g., article), Title (e.g., vocabulary), Audience, Author (e.g., possible biases, other works), and Purpose (e.g., inform, persuade, entertain, convey experience).

- **Identification of the genre.** Based on the information provided in the title, readers may be able to identify the genre. Furthermore, they may identify text features that guide them. Otherwise, they read at least the first paragraphs, examine cue words and what the authors attempt to communicate with the reader to identify the genre, and record its elements.

- **Note taking.** Teachers then read each paragraph while asking, "What did I learn? What is this paragraph about? Is this information a reason? Is it general about the topic? What did I learn about the topic?" Using this information, they paraphrase and take notes. The process for this is a commonly used one:

- Read the information.
- Look away from the text, and say it in your own words.
- Write the note without writing complete sentences.

- **Oral summary using the notes.** Teachers review their notes and provide a summary of the gist of the reading using them.

- **Use of notes to compose.** Teachers provide a written summary by using sentence frames (e.g., According to _____, _____) and the notes. A sample summary structure for story writing follows:

> The _____ (*author*) of _____ presented a story that addressed the theme of _____. In this story, the characters are _____, and the story develops in _____. The problem _____. In order to resolve this, the following events take place: _____. Eventually, _____. The characters were _____.

- In the case of opinion writing, the guide for a summary may also include a few sentences for students to share their own reflection on the argument and their comments on the quality of the information the author shared:

> Author _____ of _____ in this _____ addresses the controversy _____. The author claims _____ and provides several reasons to support this view. _____. Overall, the argument that is presented accurately addresses _____. Even though as a reader I _____, _____.

Bridging Writing and Reading Using Genre Instruction, or Breaking the Silos of Curricula

Thus far the information presented shows common patterns across writing and reading using genre instruction. First, systematic instruction of text structures with clarity in the presentation and identification of genre elements is applicable in both reading and writing. In the case of reading, this information can be used to identify main ideas, take notes, and summarize, while in writing, it can be used to evaluate the quality of written work and set goals. Second, the inclusion of signal words supports students' ability to determine a genre and monitor understanding. This knowledge is also essential in writing for students to include words that allow readers to navigate through information and make meaning. Finally, in all approaches, systematic instruction was present. There was a gradual release of responsibility with teacher modeling, collaboration, guided practice with teacher support, and students' independent practice. This is an important component to remember when working on any instructional task, as simple presentation of information and exposure do not benefit learners; neither addresses their needs.

Caveats for Prudent Pedagogical Choices

A concern sometimes shared among teachers is that a focus on text structure makes writing formulaic and removes learners' creativity. Text structure and genre instruction for note taking, summarizing, and writing can be applied in social studies, science, and mathematics. It is widely acceptable that authentic reading and writing tasks are essential in genre learning (Reid, 1987), and learning in the content areas allows for such creativity. However, the learning benefits are larger when instruction addresses text structure and content (see Williams, 2018) and is systematic. Regarding the presence of a formula, once students are aware of the traditional organization of a genre (e.g., opinion), teachers can expand students' repertoire of organizational schemes (e.g., begin with opposing position) and sentence-frame choices or linguistic choices in representing those elements in their writing. However, students should be instructed in a systematic manner so that all have an equal opportunity to learn those genres.

Students should be able to learn and actively apply genre elements and text structure across the curriculum and across their academic practices. Realistically speaking, teachers are not able to teach in one academic year all types of story writing (e.g., fable, tall tale, fairy tale, historical fiction, science fiction, mystery) or all types of expository writing (sequence, description, compare–contrast, cause–effect, problem–solution). However, students will read such texts across the ELA, science, and social studies' curricula. Consequently, if students are taught the main genre elements for stories, they can discuss the specific variations in a genre they read and apply their knowledge of text structure to determine characters, the plot, and theme. In other words, by increasing the understanding of text structure awareness through systematic, strategic instruction, students' reading and writing performance are supported and they are empowered to confidently approach such tasks.

A possible challenge involves teachers' knowledge about text structures and genres. Teacher education programs and graduate schools have a responsibility to teach their graduates the applications of text structure in reading and writing. Furthermore, districts and departments of education have a responsibility to support the implementation of evidence-based approaches in reading and writing and to implement a model of professional development that connects with those approaches. Challenges may also arise because the texts and resources used in the classroom may not align with text structures targeted for instruction. These contextual challenges can also affect students' learning. Consequently, text structure instruction in writing and reading may require systemic changes that are beyond a teacher's control (Williams et al., 2018), but cannot be ignored.

In conclusion, readers can use the following action questions to reflect on and inform their instruction:

- What genres do you currently address in your reading and writing instruction?

- How can ELA, science, and social studies colleagues address genre and text structure in reading and writing instruction?
- What tasks can you incorporate in your instruction to support students' genre-based reading and writing?

REFERENCES

Bartlett, B. J. (1978). *Top-level structure as an organizational strategy recall of classroom text.* Unpublished PhD dissertation, Arizona State University.

Chambliss, M. J. (1995). Text cues and strategies successful readers use to construct the gist of lengthy written arguments. *Reading Research Quarterly, 30*(4), 778–807.

Dole, J. A., Duffy, G. G., Roehler, L. R., & Pearson, P. D. (1991). Moving from the old to the new: Research on reading comprehension instruction. *Review of Educational Research, 61*(1), 239–264.

Duke, N. K. (2000). 3.6 minutes per day: The scarcity of informational texts in first grade. *Reading Research Quarterly, 35*(1), 202–224.

Englert, C. S., & Hiebert, E. H. (1984). Children's developing awareness of text structures in expository materials. *Journal of Educational Psychology, 76*(1), 65–74.

Englert, C. S., Raphael, T. E., Anderson, L. M., Anthony, H. M., & Stevens, D. D. (1991). Making strategies and self-talk visible: Writing instruction in regular and special education classrooms. *American Educational Research Journal, 28*(1), 337–372.

Gersten, R., Fuchs, L. S., Williams, J. P., & Baker, S. (2001). Teaching reading comprehension strategies to students with learning disabilities: A review of research. *Review of Educational Research, 71*, 279–320.

Graham, S. (2006). Strategy instruction and the teaching of writing: A meta-analysis. In C. A. MacArthur, S. Graham, & J. Fitzgerald (Eds.), *Handbook of writing research* (pp. 187–207). New York: Guilford Press.

Graham, S., Harris, K., & Mason, L. (2005). Improving the writing performance, knowledge and self-efficacy of struggling young writers: The effects of self-regulated strategy development. *Contemporary Educational Psychology, 30*(1), 207–224.

Graham, S., & Hebert, M. (2011). Writing to read: A meta-analysis of the impact of writing and writing instruction on reading. *Harvard Educational Review, 81*(4), 710–744.

Graham, S., Liu, X., Aitken, A., Ng, C., Bartlett, B., Harris, K., & Holzapfel, J. (2018b). Effectiveness of literacy programs balancing reading and writing instruction: A meta-analysis. *Reading Research Quarterly, 53*(3), 279–304.

Graham, S., Liu, X., Bartlett, B., Ng, C., Harris, K., Aitken, A., . . . Talukdar, J. (2018a). Reading for writing: A meta-analysis of the impact of reading interventions on writing. *Review of Educational Research, 88*(2), 243–284.

Graham, S., & Perin, D. (2007). *Writing next: Effective strategies to improve writing of adolescents in middle and high school: A report to Carnegie Corporation of New York.* Washington, DC: Alliance for Excellent Education.

Halliday, M. A. K., & Hasan, R. (1985). *Language, context and text: Aspects of language in social-semiotic perspective.* Geelong, VIC, Australia: Deakin University Press.

Harris, K. R., & Graham, S. (2009). Self-regulated strategy development in writing: Premises, evolution, and the future. *British Journal of Educational Psychology, 2*(6), 113–135.

Harris, K. R., Graham, S., & Mason, L. H. (2006). Improving the writing, knowledge, and motivation of struggling young writers: Effects of self-regulated strategy development with and without peer support. *American Educational Research Journal, 43*, 295–340.

Harris, K. R., Graham, S., Mason, L., & Friedlander, B. (2008). *Powerful writing strategies for all students*. Baltimore: Brookes.

Harris, K. R., Lane, K. L., Graham, S., Driscoll, S. A., Sandmel, K., Brindle, M., & Schatschneider, C. (2012). Practice-based professional development for self-regulated strategies development in writing: A randomized controlled study. *Journal of Teacher Education, 63*(2), 103–119.

Hebert, M., Bazis, P., Bohaty, J., Roehling, J., & Nelson, J. R. (2021). Examining the impacts of the structures writing intervention for teaching fourth-grade students to write informational text. *Reading and Writing: An Interdisciplinary Journal, 34*, 1711–1740.

Hebert, M., Bohaty, J. J., Nelson, J. R., & Brown, J. A. (2016). The effects of text structure instruction on expository reading comprehension: A meta-analysis. *Journal of Educational Psychology, 108*, 609–629.

Hebert, M., Bohaty, J., Nelson, J., & Roehling, J. (2018). Writing informational text using provided information and text structures: An intervention for upper elementary struggling writers. *Reading & Writing, 31*(9), 2165–2190.

Hiebert, E. H., & Mesmer, H. A. E. (2013). Upping the ante of text complexity in the Common Core State Standards: Examining its potential impact on young readers. *Educational Researcher, 42*(1), 44–51.

Jouhar, M., & Rupley, W. (2021). The reading–writing connection based on independent reading and writing: A systematic review. *Reading & Writing Quarterly, 37*(2), 136–156.

Kintsch, W., & van Dijk, T. A. (1978). Toward a model of text comprehension and production. *Psychological Review, 85*(5), 363–394.

Kress, G. (1989). *Linguistic processes in sociocultural practice*. Oxford: Oxford University.

MacArthur, C. A. (2011). Strategies instruction. In K. R. Harris, S. Graham, & T. Urdan (Eds.), *Educational psychology handbook*. Vol. 3, *Applications of educational psychology to learning and teaching* (pp. 379–401). Washington, DC: American Psychological Association.

MacArthur, C. A. (2016). Instruction in evaluation and revision. In C. A. MacArthur, S. Graham, & J. Fitzgerald (Eds.), *Handbook of writing research* (pp. 272–287). New York: Guilford Press.

MacArthur, C. A., Philippakos, Z. A., & Ianetta, M. (2015). Self-regulated strategy instruction in college developmental writing. *Journal of Educational Psychology, 107*(3), 855–867.

MacArthur, C. A., Traga Philippakos, Z. A., May, H., & Compello, J. (2022). Strategy instruction with self-regulation in college developmental writing courses: Results from a randomized experiment. *Journal of Educational Psychology, 114*(4), 815–832.

Martin, J. R. (2009). Genre and language learning: A social semiotic perspective. *Linguistics and Education, 20*(1), 10–21.

Martin, J. R., Christie, F., & Rothery. J. (1987). Social processes in education. In I.

Reid (Ed.), *The place of genre in learning* (pp. 58–82). Melbourne, Australia: Centre for Studies in Literary Education, Deakin University Press.

Mason, L., Davison, M., Hammer, C., Miller, C., & Glutting, J. (2013). Knowledge, writing, and language outcomes for a reading comprehension and writing intervention. *Reading & Writing, 26*(7), 1133–1158.

McLaughlin, E. M. (1990). *Effects of graphic organizers and levels of text difficulty on less-proficient fifth-grade readers' comprehension of expository text* (Doctoral dissertation). Retrieved from *https://about.proquest.com/en/products-services/pqdtglobal* (UMI No. 9030955).

Meyer, B. J. F. (1975). *The organization of prose and its effects on memory.* Amsterdam: North-Holland.

Meyer, B. J. F. (1984). Text dimensions and cognitive processing. In H. Mandl, N. Stein, & T. Trabasso (Eds.), *Learning and comprehension of texts* (pp. 3–52). Hillsdale, NJ: Erlbaum.

Meyer, B. J. F. (1985). Prose analysis: Purposes, procedures, and problems. In B. K. Britton & J. Black (Eds.), *Analyzing and understanding expository text* (pp. 11–64). Hillsdale, NJ: Erlbaum.

Meyer, B. J. F., Brandt, D. M., & Bluth, G. J. (1980). Use of the top-level structure in text: Key for reading comprehension of ninth-grade students. *Reading Research Quarterly, 16*(1), 72–103.

Meyer, B. J., & Ray, M. N. (2011). Structure strategy interventions: Increasing reading comprehension of expository text. *International Electronic Journal of Elementary Education, 4*(1), 127–152.

Meyer, B. J., & Rice, G. E. (1984). The structure of text. In P. D. Pearson (Ed.), *Handbook of reading research* (pp. 319–351). New York: Longman.

Pearson, P. D., & Gallagher, M. C. (1983). The instruction of reading comprehension. *Contemporary Educational Psychology, 8*(3), 317–344.

Philippakos, Z. A. (2017). Giving feedback: Preparing students for peer review and self-evaluation. *The Reading Teacher, 71*(1), 13–22.

Philippakos, Z. (2018). Using a task analysis process for reading and writing assignments. *Reading Teacher, 72*(1), 107–114.

Philippakos, Z. A. (2021). Writing-reading integration. In S. Parsons & M. Vaughn (Eds.), *Principles of effective literacy instruction* (pp. 163–180). New York: Guilford Press.

Philippakos, Z. A., & Graham, S. (2020). *Research Advisory: Teaching writing to improve reading skills.* Available at *www.literacyworldwide.org/docs/default-source/where-we-stand/ila-teaching-writing-to-improve-reading-skills.pdf.*

Philippakos, Z. A., & MacArthur, C. A. (2016). The effects of giving feedback on the persuasive writing of fourth- and fifth-grade students. *Reading Research Quarterly, 51*(4), 419–433.

Philippakos. Z. A., & MacArthur, C. A. (2020). *Developing strategic, young writers through genre instruction: Resources for grades K–2.* New York: Guilford Press.

Pressley, M., Borkowski, J. G., & Schneider, W. (1987). Cognitive strategies: Good strategy users coordinate metacognition and knowledge. *Annals of Child Development, 4*(1), 89–129.

Pyle, N., Vasquez, A. C., Lignugaris Kraft, B., Gillam, S. L., Reutzel, D. R., Olszewski, A., . . . Pyle, D. (2017). Effects of expository text structure interventions on comprehension: A meta-analysis. *Reading Research Quarterly, 52*(4), 469–501.

Reid, I. (Ed.). (1987). *The place of genre in learning: Current debates.* Geelong, VIC, Australia: Deakin University, Centre for Studies in Literary Education.

Reinking, D., & Bradley, B. (2008). *On formative and design experiments: Approaches to language and literacy research.* New York: Teachers College Press.

Reutzel, D. R. (1985). Story maps improve comprehension. *Reading Teacher, 38*(4), 400–404.

Reynolds, G., & Perin, D. (2009). A comparison of text structure and self-regulated writing strategies for composing from sources by middle school students. *Reading Psychology, 30*(3), 265–300.

Rose, D. (2016). New developments in genre-based literacy pedagogy. In C. A. MacArthur, S. Graham, & J. Fitzgerald (Eds.), *Handbook of writing research* (pp. 227–242). New York: Guilford Press.

Singer, H., & Donlan, D. (1982). Active comprehension: Problem-solving schema with question generation for comprehension of complex short stories. *Reading Research Quarterly, 17*(2), 166–186.

Stein, N., & Glenn, C. (1979). An analysis of story comprehension in elementary school children. In R. O. Freedle (Ed.), *New directions in discourse processing* (pp. 53–120). New York: Ablex Publishing.

Traga Philippakos, Z. (2019). Effects of strategy instruction with an emphasis on oral language and dramatization on the quality of first graders' procedural writing. *Reading & Writing Quarterly, 35*(5), 409–426.

Traga Philippakos, Z. A. (2020a). A yearlong, professional development model on genre-based strategy instruction on writing. *The Journal of Educational Research, 113*(3), 177–190.

Traga Philippakos, Z. A. (2020b). Developing strategic learners: Supporting self-efficacy through goal setting and reflection. *The Language and Literacy Spectrum, 30*(1), 1–24.

Traga Philippakos, Z. A., & MacArthur, C. A. (2019). Writing strategy instruction for low-skilled postsecondary students. In D. Perin (Ed.), *Wiley handbook of adult literacy* (pp. 495–516). New York: Wiley.

Traga Philippakos, Z. A., & MacArthur, C. A. (2020). Integrating collaborative reasoning and strategy instruction to improve second graders' opinion writing. *Reading & Writing Quarterly, 36*(4), 379–395.

Traga Philippakos, Z. A., & MacArthur, C. A. S. (2021). Examination of genre-based strategy instruction in middle school English language arts and science. *The Clearing House: A Journal of Educational Strategies, Issues and Ideas, 94*(4), 151–158.

Traga Philippakos, Z. A., & Voggt, A. (2021). The effects of a virtual professional development model on teachers' instruction and the quality of second graders' procedural writing. *Reading & Writing, 34,* 1791–1822.

Williams, J. (2018). Text structure instruction: The research is moving forward. *Reading & Writing, 31*(9), 1923–1935.

Williams, J. P., Hall, K. M., & Lauer, K. D. (2004). Teaching expository text structure to young at-risk learners: Building the basics of comprehension instruction. *Exceptionality, 12,* 129–144.

Wolman, C. (1991). Sensitivity to causal cohesion in stories by children with mild mental retardation, children with learning disabilities, and children without disabilities. *The Journal of Special Education, 25*(2), 135–154.

Zwaan, R. A. (1994). Effect of genre expectations on text comprehension. *Journal of Experimental Psychology: Learning, Memory, and Cognition, 20*(4), 920–933.

CHAPTER 7

Assessment in Writing and Reading

Paul D. Deane

It is easy to conceive of assessment as externally imposed. That is how standardized tests are often experienced (Hillocks, 2002; Smagorinsky, 2009). But assessment is evaluation against standards, which makes it integral to both writing and reading. For example, a basic writing process—monitoring—happens when writers reread to evaluate what they have written and determine their next steps (Rijlaarsdam & Van den Bergh, 2006). People become better writers when they self-reflect (or obtain feedback). Assessment plays an equally important role in reading development. Students are more likely to learn when reading teachers use formative assessment methods, provide strategy instruction, and build up student awareness of language and text structure (McLaughlin & DeVoogd, 2018). The purpose of this chapter is to address the role of assessment in writing and reading and explain practices teachers can use to inform their instruction and to support students' literacy growth. The following guiding questions can support readers as they process the next sections:

GUIDING QUESTIONS

- What are the major purposes for reading and writing assessment?
- What assessment practices directly support learning?
- What are the advantages and limitations of specific types of assessment?

Purposes for Assessment

Assessment enters the classroom in multiple forms. It includes *formative assessment*, which happens when teachers assess student learning informally during instruction; *diagnostic assessment*, used to identify which students may benefit from targeted interventions; and *summative and interim summative assessment*, used to track student progress within the academic year and between successive school years. Assessment can also take the form of self-assessment and self-evaluation for students' goal setting (e.g., Philippakos, 2017).

Formative Assessment

Black and Wiliam (2009) define formative assessment as the situation that arises when

> evidence about student achievement is elicited, interpreted, and used by teachers, learners, or their peers, to make decisions about the next steps in instruction that are likely to be better, or better founded, than the decisions they would have taken in the absence of the evidence that was elicited. (p. 7)

Formative assessment therefore covers several different learning mechanisms, including self-assessment, teacher and peer feedback, and peer tutoring, that work together to produce more effective learning in the classroom.

Self-Assessment

Self-assessment plays a critical role in both writing and reading. Skilled writers analyze the writing task, evaluate what strategies will be most successful, and develop a writing plan. They monitor progress during writing and evaluate the final written product. In complex writing tasks, there may be multiple self- and peer-evaluations leading to successive drafts and revisions, reflecting metacognitive planning, monitoring, and evaluation processes (Hacker, 2018). Skilled readers evaluate a text during prereading to determine genre and select reading strategies (see Chapter 6, this volume). They monitor themselves during reading and select strategies to repair comprehension failures and deepen understanding. Afterward, they critically review what they have learned, and if necessary, reread and analyze the text to achieve an appropriate standard of coherence (O'Brien & Cook, 2016).

Writers and readers attend to and evaluate texts at multiple levels (Deane, 2011, Fig. 1, p. 8). Texts are orthographic objects in which sequences of characters correspond to linguistic elements, such as words, phrases, and sentences. Texts are also linguistic objects, sequences of words, phrases, and sentences whose grammatical arrangement conveys specific propositions. Texts also instantiate specific organizational structures. Their content may be accurate or inaccurate, valid or invalid, straightforward or misleading. They are designed to achieve specific rhetorical purposes in specific social contexts. Thus, depending on task and purpose, writers (and readers) may evaluate texts against orthographic, grammatical, textual, factual, logical, and/or social/rhetorical standards. Thus, self-assessment, as a form of self-regulated learning, depends on metalinguistic and metacognitive awareness (Schunk & Zimmerman, 1998).

However, metalinguistic and metacognitive awareness must be cultivated. Naïve readers may misunderstand texts like *A Modest Proposal* by Jonathan Swift (1729) because they miss the distinctive cues that indicate satire. Similarly, naive writers may choose inappropriate organizational patterns, styles, or content due to ignorance of the constraints that govern specific genres or registers.

Thus, self-assessment is one of the central drivers of reading and writing development. Effective literacy programs teach students to self-assess using explicit evaluation criteria (Andrade & Valtcheva, 2009).

Rubrics, Checklists, and Exemplars

Formative assessment only works when the teacher and the students develop common standards of evaluation (Black & Wiliam, 2009). This support often takes the form of checklists, rating scales, or rubrics. When the same standards are used for self-assessment, peer review, and teacher review, students are more likely to internalize standards for evaluation (Brookhart, 2018). Students also benefit when they collaborate to generate their own rubrics (Fraile, Panadero, & Pardo, 2017).

However, it would be a mistake to assume that students already know how to use rubrics and checklists. Rubrics and checklists tend to be short and use general, abstract language, which makes them open to interpretation, yet they reference multiple standards of evaluation, which requires students to make multiple abstract judgments (Li & Lindsey, 2015). It is therefore important that rubrics used for instructional purposes should be easy to understand and clearly define high-quality responses and potential weaknesses (Andrade, 2001). In practice, people learn to use rubrics by applying them to exemplars (sometimes called benchmarks) (de Leeuw, 2016). Analyzing exemplars or "mentor texts" can facilitate learning even before students have mastered a rubric (Culham, 2016). In genre-based strategy instruction (Philippakos, MacArthur, & Coker, 2015), teachers model the application of genre-specific rubrics on well-written and poorly written writing samples and practice with students how to identify genre elements, score their quality and clarity, and set goals. For instance, in compare–contrast, such elements will be:

Beginning
   Topic
   Purpose

Middle
   Similarities and differences with evidence

End
   Restatement of purpose
   Message to reader

Ultimately, students need both models and rubrics. Reading comprehension strategies can be modeled by teacher think-alouds that demonstrate how to apply them to a specific text (Schunk & Zimmerman, 2007). Oral reading fluency can be modeled by teacher readings designed to prepare students to do interpretive readings of their own (Mraz et al., 2013). Similarly, teachers can use mentor texts to illustrate specific writing techniques (Gallagher, 2011).

Teacher Questioning

A key contributor to the effectiveness of classroom discussion is the nature of the questions that teachers ask (Black & Wiliam, 2009). Effective class discussion depends on teachers developing questions that ask students to apply, analyze, synthesize, evaluate, and generate ideas (Bloom, 1956). Following Slack (1998), Afflerbach (2017) argues that well-designed questions:

- Gather evidence of student understanding, while enabling students to demonstrate what they have learned. For example, if the teacher assigns a mentor text (cf. Marchetti & O'Dell, 2021), they could ask students to highlight passages from the text that illustrate particular techniques (such as providing worked out illustrations or considering and responding to opposing points of view). Alternatively, teachers might provide students with already highlighted passages and ask them to discuss why the author chose to use the highlighted language and what effect that choice has on the reader.

- Are well aligned with lesson learning objectives and the materials being covered. For example, if the teacher assigns a mentor text as part of a unit on how to structure an argument, guiding questions might focus on getting students to notice and analyze specific structural choices that the author has made in the course of building an argument.

- Are clearly worded so that students understand exactly what is being asked. For instance, guided questions about mentor texts must strike a balance between using plain language that students already know and introducing specific metalanguage (such as names for "craft moves") that make it easier for students to participate in future conversations about writing.

- Are logically ordered and allow for modifications and follow-up questions that depend on how students respond. For example, initial questions about a mentor text might focus on getting students to notice and, later, to imitate specific craft moves. Later questions might get students to examine the benefits and costs of using specific craft moves and to consider other choices the writer might have made.

- Represent the complexity (Paul & Dylan, 1998) of the content and of skills students are expected to acquire. For instance, when introducing a mentor text, teachers might want to ask some questions that help students see how the author has used moves they already know, and others designed to help them expand their personal repertoire of writing strategies.

• Provide evidence of the thinking process for students who are not able to answer in full. For example, it might be better to walk students through a scaffolded series of questions, graduated in difficulty, rather than asking open-ended questions that only the strongest students will be comfortable answering at length. For example, questions that ask students to highlight text that uses a specific craft move, or which ask them to explain why they highlighted the text they did, may provide more useful information than broad, open-ended questions that struggling students may be unprepared or unwilling to answer.

Effective formative questions are also designed to get responses from the whole class, not just a few selected students.

Teacher Feedback

Teacher feedback plays an important role in learning (Black & Wiliam, 2009). However, feedback can be a two-edged sword. It can reduce rather than improve learning, so it is important to provide the *right* kind of feedback. Shute (2008) indicates that effective feedback has the following properties:

• **Effective feedback comes after students try to solve a problem on their own.** For instance, feedback about using an outline is more likely to be adopted if students see that it will solve a problem they have already experienced (such as hitting a dead end or a mental block halfway through writing an essay).

• **Effective feedback tells students objectively where they stand.** Such feedback on students' writing might be, "Your introduction clearly stated your position."

• **Effective feedback focuses on the task, not the learner.** For example, if an essay had a weak introduction, effective feedback might be, "Your introduction would be stronger if it started with an engaging hook to capture the readers' attention."

• **Effective feedback is concrete and specific.** Feedback on the body of an argumentative essay might state, "The second reason is not well supported. Review the reading to include evidence from the text. Make sure you cite the information."

• **Effective feedback provides no more information than necessary and offers it in a form that is easy to process.** A common formative assessment technique, "two stars and a wish," illustrates this strategy (Lee & Wiliam, 2005), because it forces reviewers to identify two strengths of the text they are reviewing, and limits them to identifying a single (highest-priority) weakness.

- **Effective feedback is calibrated to meet students where they are.** For instance, if students need additional support in order to produce a fully developed, coherent text, an effective teacher may prioritize that goal over other goals, such as teaching them how to correctly format citations.

Comprehension is improved when feedback is provided after students finish reading (Swart, Nielen, & Sikkema-de Jong, 2019). Writers benefit more from content feedback than feedback on form (Biber, Nekrasova, & Horn, 2011).

Peer Review; Peer Tutoring

Peer review is central to writing instruction (Beach & Friedrich, 2006). In reading instruction, peer-to-peer interaction usually includes more explicitly instructional activities, such as peer tutoring (Annis, 1983). Peer instructional activities are most effective under the following conditions (e.g., Cho & Cho, 2011; Cho & MacArthur, 2010; Flores & Duran, 2013; Patchan, Schunn, & Clark, 2017; Patchan & Schunn, 2016; Philippakos & MacArthur, 2016; Topping, Dehkinet, Blanch, & Corcelles, 2013; Topping, Duran, & Van Keer, 2015):

- **Students are expected to generate evaluations that will be used by their peers.** Nothing will kill student uptake of peer feedback faster than the sense that they are doing it only to check off a box in a protocol that they do not perceive as providing any practical benefit.

- **Students receive enough feedback to show them what they should address, but not so much that it overwhelms them.** There is a balance between getting limited feedback from only one reviewer (which may fail to address the student's needs), and getting so much detailed feedback that the student loses track of what is important and what is not.

- **Peer interactions are structured to motivate and encourage students.** Peer review can go off the rails if students approach it with a competitive attitude, or with a focus on identifying weaknesses without providing actionable advice. Anonymous peer reviews can help to minimize these risks.

- **Students are held accountable for the quality and usefulness of their work.** It can be useful, for instance, if students are graded for the quality of their contributions to peer activities, especially if these evaluations reflect the judgment of the students who worked with them.

- **Teachers model the skills students are expected to use with their peers and train them in their use.** Untrained students conducting peer reviews often prioritize form over content and focus on identifying weaknesses, rather than providing actionable advice.

- **The training that students receive shows them how to give feedback that students are likely to use.** When conducting peer review activities, it is never safe to assume that students know how to provide actionable feedback. It is often much easier to see what is wrong with a text than it is to identify concrete ways to improve it.

- **Students are grouped to maximize the benefit for all students.** It is often useful to pair stronger with weaker students, or students with specific strengths with students who have corresponding weaknesses. Such pairings often provide unexpected benefits, since participants make their implicit knowledge explicit during the peer feedback and tutoring.

Diagnostic Assessment

Diagnostic assessment enables teachers and schools to target students for intervention and help them personalize learning. In the United States, following approaches mandated by federal laws and regulations, most schools use a response-to-intervention (RTI) framework (Mesmer & Mesmer, 2008). Several forms of diagnostic assessment are coordinated to identify student needs (Wixson & Valencia, 2011):

- *Screeners*, to identify students at risk
- *Diagnostics*, to plan instruction and determine appropriate interventions
- *Progress monitors*, to track student progress and make decisions about how to revise and adjust instruction

Most schools focus on RTI for reading rather than writing, though there have been several proposals for how to extend RTI to writing (cf. Saddler & Asaro-Sadler, 2013; Philippakos & FitzPatrick, 2018).

Many different factors influence student performance, which means that it can be difficult to identify which students need intervention, much less determine which interventions will be most appropriate for specific students. It is therefore important to get a clear sense of the supporting skills for which diagnostic assessment may be needed.

Diagnostic Assessment of Working Memory and Motivation

Writing and reading are fundamentally strategic, purposeful activities (Flower & Hayes, 1977; Paris, Lipson, & Wixson, 1983). Effective instruction teaches students appropriate strategies that reduce the load on working memory and motivate students to write and read efficiently (Graham, Harris, & Mason, 2005; McNamara, 2007). However, issues of cognitive load and motivation become critical when students do not respond to intervention.

Working memory, time management, and aspects of executive function, including cognitive flexibility and inhibition, combine to enable students to handle complex tasks effectively (Carlson, Zelazo, & Faja, 2013). These include such critical writing tasks as planning and revision (Follmer, 2018; Graham, Harris, & Olinghouse, 2007). Disruption of executive function is characteristic of several learning disorders, including attention-deficit/hyperactivity disorder (ADD/ADHD), autism spectrum disorders, and dyslexia (Demetriou, DeMayo, & Guastella, 2019). Like other struggling students, students with learning disabilities may be overwhelmed, distracted, or inflexible in their approach to reading and writing tasks (Jenkins et al., 2014).

Of course, similar symptoms can be induced by low levels of motivation. There is a characteristic school dynamic by which stronger-performing students develop higher levels of intrinsic motivation, positive self-concepts, a greater sense of self-efficacy, and epistemic beliefs that value effort and persistence (Hidi & Boscolo, 2006; Schiefele, Schaffner, Moller, & Wigfield, 2012). However, lower-performing students may become demotivated, showing negative affect, low self-efficacy, and the belief that inherent ability, not skill, determines success.

Diagnostic Assessment of Vocabulary and Content Knowledge

The purpose of reading is to access meaning, and at a minimum, students need to understand the words they read (Perfetti, 2007). It can therefore be useful to assess vocabulary knowledge in the written mode (McKeown, Deane, & Lawless, 2017) (see also Chapter 3, this volume). This is particularly important for academic vocabulary, which mostly consists of Latinate vocabulary students are less likely to encounter outside of school (Nagy & Townsend, 2012).

Writing and reading are fundamentally concerned with content—and it is much easier to deal with new content if people can connect it with what they already know (McCutchen, 1986; Cervetti & Wright, 2020). But students enter school with vastly different stores of knowledge (Neuman & Celano, 2006), and if there are enough gaps in their knowledge, they will have difficulty learning anything from a text (O'Reilly, Wang, & Sabatini, 2019). Thus, it is important to screen students for low levels of background knowledge (Davis, Lindo, & Compton, 2007). Comprehension of domain-specific vocabulary can be used as a rough proxy for background content knowledge, by checking whether students recognize words relevant to the content they are going to read (O'Reilly et al., 2019).

Diagnostic Assessment of Foundational Reading Skills

Students who show apparent reading comprehension difficulties may actually be experiencing difficulty with low-level reading processes, such as decoding, word recognition, morphological analysis of unfamiliar words, reading vocabulary size and depth, or sentence processing. Weaknesses in these skills, even if not severe, increase the cognitive load and reduce the fluency of reading, even among adults (Tighe & Schatschneider, 2016).

PHONOLOGICAL AWARENESS

English is written in an alphabetic script, which means that it presupposes that the reader can break down a word into its component sounds (Nithart et al., 2011). While the relation between phonological awareness and reading development is complex (Thompson et al., 2015), there is clear evidence that instruction designed to develop phonological awareness can have a positive impact on student reading outcomes (Mahfoudhi & Haynes, 2009).

DECODING

In English, it is critical that readers learn how to sound out words. This skill is often assessed by asking students to pronounce nonsense words, since unfamiliar letter sequences must be sounded out (Cummings, Dewey, Latimer, & Good, 2011). Without effective decoding instruction, a large minority of students are at risk to become struggling readers (Wang, Sabatini, O'Reilly, & Weeks, 2019).

WORD RECOGNITION

While English uses an alphabetic script, it is not purely alphabetic (Venezky, 1999). Therefore, it is critical for readers to learn how to spell and pronounce words with unpredictable spellings (Ehri, 2014). When word recognition is not automatic, it increases the cognitive load on the reader, resulting in hesitations and dysfluencies in reading (Torgesen & Hudson, 2006). It is generally assessed by measuring the fluency and accuracy of word reading—the rate at which the reader produces correct word pronunciations during oral reading (Al Otaiba, Kosanovich, Torgesen, Kamhi, & Catts, 2012).

MORPHOLOGICAL AWARENESS

Many apparent irregularities in English spelling serve to clarify relationships between words. For instance, in the words *orthographic* and *orthography*, the second vowel is pronounced differently, but both sounds are spelled with an *o*. This helps the reader see that both words contain a common root (*ortho*, meaning "correct"). Since most words acquired between 4th and 12th grades are morphologically complex (Sullivan, 2007), morphological awareness plays a critical role in reading development (Tong, Deacon, Kirby, Cain, & Parrila, 2011). Morphological awareness can be assessed by asking students to identify common roots, prefixes, or suffixes (Berninger, 2007) or by asking them to choose which of two related words best fits in a specific sentence content (Sabatini et al., 2019).

SENTENCE COMPREHENSION AND READING EFFICIENCY

Word reading is not enough. Readers must be able to integrate words into sentences. For this purpose, structure matters. It is thus important to assess sentence-level comprehension skills (Scott, 2009). One assessment method is the Cloze technique, whereby information is blanked from a text at regular intervals, and the student is asked to fill each blank (Shanahan, Kamil, & Tobin, 1982). For instance, the student might be given a passage containing the sentence "I went to the _____ and bought a loaf of _____." If they have stronger reading comprehension skills, they should be able to fill in the blanks and provide the missing words (*store* and *bread*). Another method is the MAZE technique, whereby students are given a Cloze context and a multiple-choice item that asks them to select the word that best fills the blank (Fuchs & Fuchs, 1992; Sabatini et al., 2019). Unlike the Maze technique, they do not have to generate the missing words, only recognize them in a list of options. Yet another method is to ask students to judge whether two sentences express similar meanings (Ecalle, Bouchafa, Potocki, & Magnan, 2013). This may range from relatively simple judgments (such as recognizing that sentences like "The kangaroo bounds" and "The kangaroo leaps" are equivalent), to more complex judgments (such as recognizing the difference between sentences like "The square which is in the circle is brown" and "The brown circle is in the square").

Diagnostic Assessment of Foundational Writing Skills

Assessments of foundational writing skills focus primarily on transcription skills: handwriting, keyboarding, and spelling.

HANDWRITING

Teaching handwriting builds orthographic knowledge (Santangelo & Graham, 2016). The legibility and fluency of handwriting can have a strong impact on the fluency and quality of student writing (Graham, Berninger, Abbott, Abbott, & Whitaker, 1997). Conversely, slow, effortful handwriting increases cognitive load and reduces writing performance (Medwell & Wray, 2014).

KEYBOARDING

Keyboarding is typically assessed by examining typing speed—the rate at which characters are typed and then corrected for errors (Horne, Ferrier, Singleton, & Read, 2011). There is considerable variation in typing rates between expert and novice typists (Gentner, 1988). Keyboarding and handwriting fluency appear to have similar relations to writing quality, but students write faster and tend to write longer on a keyboard than when they are writing by hand (Feng, Lindner, Xi, & Malatesha, 2019). These facts are consistent with the larger finding that widespread use of word-processing tools tends to improve student writing (Morphy & Graham, 2012). However, when students have stronger handwriting than keyboarding ability (or have little experience with writing on a computer), their handwritten compositions tend to be of higher quality (Connelly, Dockrell, Walter, & Critten, 2012).

SPELLING

Students' orthographic knowledge about words can be assessed by measuring their spelling accuracy, which has a moderate relation to writing quality (Kent & Wanzek, 2016). In fact, handwriting and spelling skills may jointly account for nearly three-fourths of the total variance in writing quality in younger children (Harrison et al., 2016).

Together, handwriting, keyboarding, and spelling constitute *transcription* skills. Automatization of transcription skills enables the writer to devote more attention and effort to higher-order writing skills, such as planning, revision, and editing. Conversely, students for whom transcription is slow and effortful are less likely to apply effective writing strategies (Feng et al., 2019). Such students are therefore likely to benefit from interventions that combine transcription instruction with self-regulated strategy development (Limpo & Alves, 2018).

Diagnostic Assessment of Oral Language Skills

Assessments of oral language may address multiple skills, including oral vocabulary, oral sentence production and comprehension, and oral discourse production and comprehension. In the following section, assessments relevant to reading and writing are shared:

ORAL VOCABULARY

Vocabulary size and depth of vocabulary knowledge are relatively strong predictors of academic performance in general and of reading comprehension in particular (Perfetti, 2007). Preschool oral vocabulary size is a significant predictor of school performance even after accounting for demographic variables, such as ethnicity, gender, and socioeconomic status (Lee, 2011). However, these effects are moderated by literacy instruction. In schools with effective literacy programs, the effects of preschool oral vocabulary differences can be significantly reduced (Mancilla-Martinez & McClain, 2020).

ORAL SENTENCE PRODUCTION AND COMPREHENSION

The ability of students to understand spoken sentences (e.g., by following directions) is predictive of reading comprehension above and beyond other factors, such as vocabulary size and decoding (Muter, Hulme, Snowling, & Stevenson, 2004). In fact, the ability of students to understand simple sentences—sentences that follow patterns likely to appear in oral conversation—appears to be predictive of fifth-grade students' reading comprehension, whereas the ability to understand complex spoken sentences is not (Sorenson Duncan, Mimeau, Crowell, & Duncan, 2020). There is some evidence that oral sentence comprehension can be improved by exposing students to more complex syntactic structures and providing structured interventions (Vasilyeva, Huttenlocher,

& Waterfall, 2006). In this study, when young students listened to a story that contained a large number of passive sentences, their ability to produce and understand passive sentences increased. Similarly, students who demonstrate strong oral sentence generation skills are likely to show greater fluency and accuracy on writing tasks, and practice in oral text generation also appears to improve student writing (Arfé, Festa, Ronconi, & Spicciarella, 2020). In a study by Philippakos and MacArthur (2020), second graders engaged in collaborative argumentation and dialogic reasoning as teachers facilitated a dialogue with the text and supported the application of sentence frames for students to state their position, reasons, and evidence in response to questions about the characters and their actions. This task was combined with instruction on the writing process. Students' writing significantly improved compared to that of their peers.

ORAL DISCOURSE COMPREHENSION AND PRODUCTION

Ultimately, oral language includes higher-order comprehension and production skills. These are often assessed by testing students' memory for and ability to recall and retell stories or other orally presented performances. Such discourse-level measurements of listening and speaking skills make unique contributions to the prediction of reading comprehension (Kim, 2020) and writing development (Kim & Schatschneider, 2017).

Literacy instruction builds on oral language. Some students are developmentally delayed in their oral language development, and these students typically encounter writing and reading difficulties. But it is relatively rare for U.S. schools to screen for oral language difficulties as part of their RTI programs, which means that students with developmental language delays may be misidentified as having issues with reading comprehension or academic writing (Adlof & Hogan, 2019).

On the other hand, some students may have strong oral language skills—but in a different language or dialect. While such students may quickly acquire the oral language skills they need to use standard English in school settings, their learner status may depress their performance and cause them to be inappropriately routed into special education programs (Sullivan, 2011). Similar issues may arise for speakers of nonstandard dialects of English, such as African American Vernacular English (AAVE), if dialect features are misidentified as evidence of language disorder (Stockman, 2010).

Summative and Interim Assessment

Formative and diagnostic assessments are primarily intended for students and teachers. Summative and interim assessments have additional audiences—parents, educational administrators, and policymakers. Depending on state educational policies, schools may be shut down or reorganized and teachers may be rewarded or reassigned, depending on the outcome of state-mandated tests. These stakes guarantee a strong impact on school practice.

Summative assessments tend to be held to high (and potentially conflicting) standards. They are expected to be valid, reliable, and fair (American Educational Research Association, 2014), but also inexpensive to administer and easy to score. They are designed to measure specific, state-mandated educational standards (Lee & Wu, 2017) but intrinsically impose trade-offs: too much time devoted to high-stakes tests can reduce instructional time and stress both students and teachers (Popham, 2001), but a short assessment is less likely to be valid and reliable. Thus, different types of summative assessment reflect different decisions about which trade-offs to make.

Standardized Assessment

When the assessment goal is to compare students across contexts, testing constraints drive designers toward standardized formats that favor multiple-choice questions, broadly accessible reading passages, and stand-alone questions. They include *indirect* assessments of writing skill (Stiggins, 1982) and multiple-choice reading comprehension assessments (Afflerbach, 2017). Standardized assessments are usually optimized to give reliable scores. They are not usually optimized to provide diagnostic information. For example, the Test of Written Language (Hammill & Larsen, 2009) measures writing using a combination of indirect and direct measures. It includes items that measure such foundational writing skills as vocabulary, spelling, punctuation, sentence logic, and sentence-combining skills, and items that measure students' ability to produce interesting and well-structured stories. It is well designed to identify students who are struggling with foundational skills or who have difficulty producing simple stories, which is one of its intended applications. But that means it has limited usefulness in assessing students' ability to write flexibly across a variety of genres. This kind of standardized writing assessment necessarily prioritizes straightforward tasks anyone could do over more challenging tasks that might require higher levels of creativity or critical thinking.

Performance Assessment

When the assessment goal is to determine how well people can perform complex tasks, performance assessments are the natural choice. In a performance assessment, students may get a choice of topic, format, or even the modality of their response, though the higher the stakes, the more these variables may be standardized to ensure comparability of response. However, all performance assessments require learners to generate a performance—whether that performance is a research paper, an oral presentation, a song, a poem, or a multimedia slideshow (Madaus & O'Dwyer, 1999; Darling-Hammond, 2017).

Extended writing tasks can be considered performance assessments. However, the on-demand writing tasks typically used in standardized tests abstract away from the complexities of multiple-draft writing (Behizadeh & Pang, 2016). When performance assessments are used to assess reading, they usually assess *applied* reading comprehension, in which students are expected to use their reading ability to accomplish some larger goal (Chall, 1983).

Portfolio Assessment

When the assessment goal is to measure what students can do independently, portfolio assessments are the natural choice (Tierney, 1991). In this approach, students build annotated collections of their work that showcase what they can do. Since portfolios are not standardized, they may be best suited for use as local assessments, where the goal is to document student accomplishments within a specific setting (Lam, 2018). For instance, students may be collecting their writing across the year and across genres demonstrating their growth across an academic year.

Scenario-Based Assessment

Standardized assessments ask students to read and write without establishing a meaningful context or purpose for reading. On the other hand, performance tasks provide very little information about students who fail to put together a successful performance. Scenario-based assessments (SBAs) combine some of the best features of standardized assessments and performance tasks. SBAs consist of a sequence of standardized tasks, but each task is presented within a shared context and contributes meaningfully to the accomplishment of some overarching goal. As a result, they tend to emulate naturally occurring literacy activities and measure targeted prerequisite skills that indicate whether students are ready to perform the culminating performance task on their own (Deane et al., 2019; Sabatini, O'Reilly, Halderman, & Bruce, 2014).

An SBA for argument writing, such as that documented in Deane et al. (2019), might begin by having students read and summarize argument texts about a specific issue. It might then scaffold students through argument analysis tasks, such as filling in a T-chart containing arguments pro and con, or determining whether specific pieces of evidence strengthen or weaken an argument. After a sequence of additional argument reading and writing tasks designed both to measure and build student understanding, the culminating task might require them to build an argument of their own and express it in a well-structured essay.

SBAs are only just beginning to be available for use in the classroom (see, for instance, *https://edulastic.com/ets-testlets* and *https://gca.coe.uga.edu/assesslets*), but one of their potential strengths as an assessment tool is that they narrow the gap between summative and formative or diagnostic assessments. SBAs function well as summative instruments, but because their component tasks assess critical prerequisite skills, they may also be useful for formative or diagnostic purposes (Deane et al., 2019).

Conclusion

Assessment is about learning. It should support teaching, and to the extent that it is used to identify student needs, plan more effective instruction, and provide feedback that students can use, it will. It is important, however, for teachers to understand the kinds of assessments they use and the purposes for which they are suited. Formative assessment techniques provide a way for teachers to identify student needs in the moment, and to adjust their instruction dynamically from hour to hour, day to day, and week to week. Screeners can be very useful for the purpose of identifying critical student needs, but they are less closely linked to instruction, and care needs to be taken to choose appropriate interventions based on screener results. Standardized assessments provide useful information about student progress, but they tend to provide broader, less targeted information than formative assessments and screeners. Ultimately, the goal of literacy instruction is to train students to function as independent readers and writers, and for that purpose, performance tasks provide good information about which students are capable of independent performance. On the other hand, SBAs are designed to identify student progression along a sequence of skills necessary to achieving independent performance.

As we conclude this chapter, it might be useful to consider the following questions about the assessments used to evaluate writing and reading in your classrooms:

- What screening assessments do I currently use to assess students' reading and writing achievement? What foundational skills do they cover? Are there any gaps that need to be addressed?
- How do I and my grade-level colleagues monitor students' reading and writing performance? Are there any additional formative assessment techniques that I should consider incorporating into my teaching practice?
- How do I currently use data from standardized assessments, performance assessments, or SBAs? What adjustments should I make to my existing practice in order to improve instructional planning and provide better support for student learning?

REFERENCES

Adlof, S. M., & Hogan, T. P. (2019). If we don't look, we won't see: Measuring language development to inform literacy instruction. *Policy Insights from the Behavioral and Brain Sciences, 6*(2), 210–217.

Afflerbach, P. (2017). *Understanding and using reading assessment, K–12.* Alexandria, VA: Association of Supervision and Curriculum Development.

Al Otaiba, S., Kosanovich, M. L., Torgesen, J. K., Kamhi, A., & Catts, H. (2012). Assessment and instruction for phonemic awareness and word recognition skills. *Language and Reading Disabilities, 3,* 112–140.

American Educational Research Association. (2014). *Standards for educational and psychological testing.* Washington, DC: American Educational Research Association and American Psychological Association.

Andrade, H. G. (2001). *The effects of instructional rubrics on learning to write.* Albany: State University of New York.

Andrade, H. G., & Brookhart, S. M. (2016). The role of classroom assessment in supporting self-regulated learning. In D. Levault & L. Allal (Eds.), *Assessment for learning: Meeting the challenge of implementation* (pp. 293–309). New York: Springer.

Andrade, H. G., & Valtcheva, A. (2009). Promoting learning and achievement through self-assessment. *Theory into Practice, 48*(1), 12–19.

Annis, L. F. (1983). The processes and effects of peer tutoring. *Human Learning: Journal of Practical Research & Applications, 2*(1), 39–47.

Arfé, B., Festa, F., Ronconi, L., & Spicciarelli, G. (2020). Oral sentence generation training to improve fifth and 10th graders' writing. *Reading and Writing, 34,* 1851–1883.

Beach, R., & Friedrich, T. (2006). Response to writing. In C. A. MacArthur, S. Graham, & J. Fitzgerald (Eds.), *Handbook of writing research* (pp. 222–234). New York: Guilford Press.

Behizadeh, N., & Pang, M. E. (2016). Awaiting a new wave: The status of state writing assessment in the United States. *Assessing Writing, 29,* 25–41.

Berninger, V. W. (2007). *Process Assessment of the Learner (PAL-II): Diagnostic assessment for reading and writing.* Bloomington, MN: NCS Pearson.

Biber, D., Nekrasova, T., & Horn, B. (2011). *The effectiveness of feedback for L1-English and L2-writing development: A meta-analysis.* ETS Research Report Series. Princeton, NJ: Educational Testing Service.

Black, P., & Wiliam, D. (2009). Developing the theory of formative assessment. *Educational Assessment, Evaluation and Accountability (formerly Journal of Personnel Evaluation in Education), 21*(1), 5–31.

Bloom, B. S. (1956). *Taxonomy of educational objectives.* Vol. 1: *Cognitive domain.* New York: McKay.

Carlson, S. M., Zelazo, P. D., & Faja, S. (2013). Executive function. In P. D. Zelazo (Ed.), *Handbook of developmental psychology: Body and mind* (Vol. 1, pp. 706–743). New York: Oxford University Press.

Cervetti, G. N., & Wright, T. S. (2020). The role of knowledge in understanding and learning from text. In E. B. Moje, P. P. Afflerbach, P. Enciso, & N. K. Lesaux (Eds.), *Handbook of reading research* (Vol. 5, pp. 237–260). New York: Routledge.

Chall, J. S. (1983). *Stages of reading development.* New York: McGraw-Hill.

Cho, K., & MacArthur, C. (2010). Student revision with peer and expert reviewing. *Learning and instruction, 20*(4), 328–338.

Cho, Y. H., & Cho, K. (2011). Peer reviewers learn from giving comments. *Instructional Science, 39*(5), 629–643.

Connelly, V., Dockrell, J. E., Walter, K., & Critten, S. (2012). Predicting the quality of composition and written language bursts from oral language, spelling, and handwriting skills in children with and without specific language impairment. *Written Communication, 29*(3), 278–302.

Culham, R. (2016). *The writing thief: Using mentor texts to teach the craft of writing.* Portsmouth, NH: Stenhouse.

Cummings, K. D., Dewey, E. N., Latimer, R. J., & Good III, R. H. (2011). Pathways to word reading and decoding: The roles of automaticity and accuracy. *School Psychology Review, 40*(2), 284–295.

Darling-Hammond, L. (2017). *Developing and measuring higher order skills: Models for state performance assessment systems.* Palo Alto, CA: Learning Policy Institute and Council of Chief State School Officers.

Davis, G. N., Lindo, E. J., & Compton, D. L. (2007). Children at risk for reading failure: Constructing an early screening measure. *Teaching Exceptional Children, 39*(5), 32–37.

de Leeuw, J. (2016). Rubrics and exemplars in writing assessment. In S. Scott, D. E. Scott, & C. F. Webber (Eds.), *Leadership of assessment, inclusion, and learning* (pp. 89–110). New York: Springer.

Deane, P. (2011). *Writing assessment and cognition ETS Research Report Series.* Princeton, NJ: Educational Testing Service.

Deane, P., Song, Y., van Rijn, P., O'Reilly, T., Fowles, M., Bennett, R., . . . Zhang, M. (2019). The case for scenario-based assessment of written argumentation. *Reading and Writing, 32*(6), 1575–1606.

Demetriou, E. A., DeMayo, M. M., & Guastella, A. J. (2019). Executive function in autism spectrum disorder: History, theoretical models, empirical findings, and potential as an endophenotype. *Frontiers in Psychiatry, 10, 753.*

Ecalle, J., Bouchafa, H., Potocki, A., & Magnan, A. (2013). Comprehension of written sentences as a core component of children's reading comprehension. *Journal of Research in Reading, 36*(2), 117–131.

Ehri, L. C. (2014). Orthographic mapping in the acquisition of sight word reading, spelling memory, and vocabulary learning. *Scientific Studies of Reading, 18*(1), 5–21.

Feng, L., Lindner, A., Ji, X. R., & Malatesha Joshi, R. (2019). The roles of handwriting and keyboarding in writing: A meta-analytic review. *Reading and Writing, 32*(1), 33–63.

Flores, M., & Duran, D. (2013). Effects of peer tutoring on reading self-concept. *International Journal of Educational Psychology, 2*(3), 297–324.

Flower, L. S., & Hayes, J. R. (1977). Problem-solving strategies and the writing process. *College English, 39*(4), 449–461.

Follmer, D. J. (2018). Executive function and reading comprehension: A meta-analytic review. *Educational Psychologist, 53*(1), 42–60.

Fraile, J., Panadero, E., & Pardo, R. (2017). Co-creating rubrics: The effects on self-regulated learning, self-efficacy and performance of establishing assessment criteria with students. *Studies in Educational Evaluation, 53,* 69–76.

Fuchs, L. S., & Fuchs, D. (1992). Identifying a measure for monitoring student reading progress. *School Psychology Review, 21*(1), 45–58.

Gallagher, K. (2011). *Write like this: Teaching real-world writing through modeling & mentor texts.* Portsmouth, NH: Stenhouse.

Gentner, D. R. (1988). Expertise in typewriting. In M. T. H. Chi, R. Glaser, & M. J. Farr (Eds.), *The nature of expertise* (pp. 1–21). Mahwah, NJ: Erlbaum.

Graham, S., Berninger, V. W., Abbott, R. D., Abbott, S. P., & Whitaker, D. (1997). Role of mechanics in composing of elementary school students: A new methodological approach. *Journal of Educational Psychology, 89*(1), 170.

Graham, S., Harris, K. R., & Mason, L. (2005). Improving the writing performance, knowledge, and self-efficacy of struggling young writers: The effects of self-regulated strategy development. *Contemporary Educational Psychology, 30*(2), 207–241.

Graham, S., Harris, K. R., & Olinghouse, N. (2007). Addressing executive function problems in writing. In L. Meltzer (Ed.), *Executive function in education: From theory to practice* (pp. 216–236). New York: Guilford Press.

Hacker, D. J. (2018). A metacognitive model of writing: An update from a developmental perspective. *Educational Psychologist, 53*(4), 220–237.

Hammill, D. D., & Larsen, S. C. (2009). *Test of written language: TOWL 4* (4th ed.). New York: Pearson Education.

Harrison, G. L., Goegan, L. D., Jalbert, R., McManus, K., Sinclair, K., & Spurling, J. (2016). Predictors of spelling and writing skills in first-and second-language learners. *Reading and Writing, 29*(1), 69–89.

Hidi, S., & Boscolo, P. (2006). Motivation and writing. In C. A. MacArthur, S. Graham, & J. Fitzgerald (Eds.), *Handbook of writing research* (pp. 144–157). New York: Guilford Press.

Hillocks, G. (2002). *The testing trap: How state writing assessments control learning.* New York: Teachers College Press.

Horne, J., Ferrier, J., Singleton, C., & Read, C. (2011). Computerised assessment of handwriting and typing speed. *Educational and Child Psychology, 28*(2), 52.

Jenkins, L. N., Demaray, M. K., Wren, N. S., Secord, S. M., Lyell, K. M., Magers, A. M., . . . Tennant, J. (2014). A critical review of five commonly used social–emotional and behavioral screeners for elementary or secondary schools. *Contemporary School Psychology, 18*(4), 241–254.

Kent, S. C., & Wanzek, J. (2016). The relationship between component skills and writing quality and production across developmental levels: A meta-analysis of the last 25 years. *Review of Educational Research, 86*(2), 570–601.

Kim, Y.-S. G. (2020). Interactive dynamic literacy model: An integrative theoretical framework for reading-writing relations. In R. A. Alves, T. Limpo, & R. Malatesha Joshi (Eds.), *Reading–writing connections* (pp. 11–34). New York: Springer.

Kim, Y.-S. G., & Schatschneider, C. (2017). Expanding the developmental models of writing: A direct and indirect effects model of developmental writing (DIEW). *Journal of Educational Psychology, 109*(1), 35.

Lam, R. (2018). *Portfolio assessment for the teaching and learning of writing.* New York: Springer.

Lee, C., & Wiliam, D. (2005). Studying changes in the practice of two teachers developing assessment for learning. *Teacher Development, 2,* 265–283.

Lee, J. (2011). Size matters: Early vocabulary as a predictor of language and literacy competence. *Applied Psycholinguistics, 32*(1), 69.

Lee, J., & Wu, Y. (2017). Is the Common Core racing America to the top? Tracking changes in state standards, school practices, and student achievement. *Education Policy Analysis Archives, 25,* 35.

Li, J., & Lindsey, P. (2015). Understanding variations between student and teacher application of rubrics. *Assessing Writing, 26,* 67–79.

Limpo, T., & Alves, R. A. (2018). Tailoring multicomponent writing interventions: Effects of coupling self-regulation and transcription training. *Journal of Learning Disabilities, 51*(4), 381–398.

Madaus, G. F., & O'Dwyer, L. M. (1999). A short history of performance assessment: Lessons learned. *Phi Delta Kappan, 80*(9), 688.

Mahfoudhi, A., & Haynes, C. W. (2009). Phonological awareness in reading disabilities remediation. In G. Reid (Ed.), *The Routledge companion to dyslexia* (pp. 139–146). New York: Routledge.

Mancilla-Martinez, J., & McClain, J. B. (2020). What do we know today about the complexity of vocabulary gaps and what do we not know? In E. B. Moje, P. P. Afflerbach, P. Enciso, & N. K. Lesaux (Eds.), *Handbook of reading research* (Vol. 5, pp. 216–236). New York: Routledge.

Marchetti, A., & O'Dell, R. (2021). *A teacher's guide to mentor texts, grades 6–12.* Portsmouth, NH: Heineman.

McCutchen, D. (1986). Domain knowledge and linguistic knowledge in the development of writing ability. *Journal of Memory and Language, 24*(4), 431–444.

McKeown, M. G., Deane, P. D., & Lawless, R. R. (2017). *Vocabulary assessment to support instruction: Building rich word-learning experiences.* New York: Guilford Press.

McLaughlin, M., & DeVoogd, G. (2018). Reading comprehension, critical understanding: Research-based practice. In D. Lapp & D. Fisher (Eds.), *Handbook of research on teaching the English language arts* (pp. 85–110). New York: Routledge.

McNamara, D. S. (2007). *Reading comprehension strategies: Theories, interventions, and technologies.* London: Psychology Press.

Medwell, J., & Wray, D. (2014). Handwriting automaticity: The search for performance thresholds. *Language and Education, 28*(1), 34–51.

Mesmer, E. M., & Mesmer, H. A. E. (2008). Response to intervention (RTI): What teachers of reading need to know. *The Reading Teacher, 62*(4), 280–290.

Morphy, P., & Graham, S. (2012). Word processing programs and weaker writers/readers: A meta-analysis of research findings. *Reading and Writing, 25*(3), 641–678.

Mraz, M., Nichols, W., Caldwell, S., Beisley, R., Sargent, S., & Rupley, W. (2013). Improving oral reading fluency through readers theatre. *Reading Horizons: A Journal of Literacy and Language Arts, 52*(2), 5.

Muter, V., Hulme, C., Snowling, M. J., & Stevenson, J. (2004). Phonemes, rimes, vocabulary, and grammatical skills as foundations of early reading development: Evidence from a longitudinal study. *Developmental Psychology, 40*(5), 665.

Nagy, W., & Townsend, D. (2012). Words as tools: Learning academic vocabulary as language acquisition. *Reading Research Quarterly, 47*(1), 91–108.

Neuman, S. B., & Celano, D. (2006). The knowledge gap: Implications of leveling the playing field for low-income and middle-income children. *Reading Research Quarterly, 41*(2), 176–201.

Nithart, C., Demont, E., Metz-Lutz, M. N., Majerus, S., Poncelet, M., & Leybaert, J. (2011). Early contribution of phonological awareness and later influence of phonological memory throughout reading acquisition. *Journal of Research in Reading, 34*(3), 346–363.

O'Brien, E. J., & Cook, A. E. (2016). Coherence threshold and the continuity of processing: The RI-Val model of comprehension. *Discourse Processes, 53*(5–6), 326–338.

O'Reilly, T., Wang, Z., & Sabatini, J. (2019). How much knowledge is too little? When a lack of knowledge becomes a barrier to comprehension. *Psychological Science, 30*(9), 1344–1351.

Paris, S. G., Lipson, M. Y., & Wixson, K. K. (1983). Becoming a strategic reader. *Contemporary Educational Psychology, 8*(3), 293–316.

Patchan, M. M., & Schunn, C. D. (2016). Understanding the effects of receiving peer feedback for text revision: Relations between author and reviewer ability. *Journal of Writing Research, 8*(2), 227–265.

Patchan, M. M., Schunn, C. D., & Clark, R. J. (2017). Accountability in peer assessment: Examining the effects of reviewing grades on peer ratings and peer feedback. *Studies in Higher Education, 43*(1), 1–16.

Paul, B., & Dylan, W. (1998). Inside the black box: Raising standards through classroom assessment. *Phi Delta Kappan, 80*(2), 139–148.

Perfetti, C. A. (2007). Reading ability: Lexical quality to comprehension. *Scientific Studies of Reading, 11*(4), 357–383.

Philippakos, Z. A. (2017). Giving feedback: Preparing students for peer review and self-evaluation. *The Reading Teacher, 71*(1), 13–22.

Philippakos, Z. A., & FitzPatrick, E. (2018). A proposed tiered model of assessment in writing instruction: Supporting all student-writers. *Insights into Learning Disabilities, 15*(2), 149–173.

Philippakos, Z. A., & MacArthur, C. A. (2016). The effects of giving feedback on the persuasive writing of fourth- and fifth-grade students. *Reading Research Quarterly, 51*(4), 419–433.

Philippakos, Z. A., & MacArthur, C. A. (2020). Integrating collaborative reasoning and strategy instruction to improve second graders' opinion writing. *Reading and Writing Quarterly, 36*(4), 379–395.

Philippakos, Z. A., MacArthur, C. A., & Coker, D. L. (2015). *Developing strategic writers through genre instruction: Resources for grades 3–5.* New York: Guilford Press.

Popham, W. J. (2001). *The truth about testing: An educator's call to action.* Alexandria, VA: Association for Supervision and Curriculum Development.

Rijlaarsdam, G., & Van den Bergh, H. (2006). Writing process theory. In C. A. MacArthur, S. Graham, & J. Fitzgerald (Eds.), *Handbook of writing research* (pp. 41–53). New York: Guilford Press.

Sabatini, J. P., O'Reilly, T., Halderman, L., & Bruce, K. (2014). Broadening the scope of reading comprehension using scenario-based assessments: Preliminary findings and challenges. *LAnnee psychologique, 114*(4), 693–723.

Sabatini, J., Weeks, J., O'Reilly, T., Bruce, K., Steinberg, J., & Chao, S. F. (2019). *SARA Reading Components Tests, RISE forms: Technical adequacy and test design.* ETS *Research Report Series.* Princeton, NJ: Educational Testing Service.

Saddler, B., & Asaro-Saddler, K. (2013). Response to intervention in writing: A suggested framework for screening, intervention, and progress monitoring. *Reading & Writing Quarterly, 29*(1), 20–43.

Santangelo, T., & Graham, S. (2016). A comprehensive meta-analysis of handwriting instruction. *Educational Psychology Review, 28*(2), 225–265.

Schiefele, U., Schaffner, E., Möller, J., & Wigfield, A. (2012). Dimensions of reading motivation and their relation to reading behavior and competence. *Reading Research Quarterly, 47*(4), 427–463.

Schunk, D. H., & Zimmerman, B. J. (Eds.). (1998). *Self-regulated learning: From teaching to self-reflective practice.* New York: Guilford Press.

Schunk, D. H., & Zimmerman, B. J. (2007). Influencing children's self-efficacy and self-regulation of reading and writing through modeling. *Reading & Writing Quarterly, 23*(1), 7–25.

Scott, C. M. (2009). A case for the sentence in reading comprehension. *Language, Speech, and Hearing Services in Schools, 40*(2), 184–191.

Shanahan, T., Kamil, M. L., & Tobin, A. W. (1982). Cloze as a measure of intersentential comprehension. *Reading Research Quarterly, 17*(2), 229–255.

Shute, V. J. (2008). Focus on formative feedback. *Review of Educational Research, 78*(1), 153–189.

Slack, J. B. (1998). *Questioning strategies to improve student thinking and comprehension.* Austin, TX: Southwest Educational Development Laboratory.

Smagorinsky, P. (2009). The cultural practice of reading and the standardized assessment of reading instruction: When incommensurate worlds collide. *Educational Researcher, 38*(7), 522–527.

Sorenson Duncan, T., Mimeau, C., Crowell, N., & Deacon, S. H. (2020). Not all sentences are created equal: Evaluating the relation between children's understanding of basic and difficult sentences and their reading comprehension. *Journal of Educational Psychology, 113*(2), 268–278.

Stiggins, R. J. (1982). A comparison of direct and indirect writing assessment methods. *Research in the Teaching of English, 16*(2), 101–114.

Stockman, I. J. (2010). A review of developmental and applied language research on African American children: From a deficit to difference perspective on dialect differences. *Language, Speech, and Hearing Services in School, 41*(1), 23–38.

Sullivan, A. L. (2011). Disproportionality in special education identification and placement of English language learners. *Exceptional Children, 77*(3), 317–334.

Sullivan, J. (2007). *Developing knowledge of polysemous vocabulary.* PhD dissertation, Waterloo University, Ontario, Canada.

Swart, E. K., Nielen, T. M., & Sikkema-de Jong, M. T. (2019). Supporting learning from text: A meta-analysis on the timing and content of effective feedback. *Educational Research Review, 28,* 100296.

Swift, J. (1729). *A modest proposal.* Telltale Weekly.

Thompson, P. A., Hulme, C., Nash, H. M., Gooch, D., Hayiou-Thomas, E., & Snowling, M. J. (2015). Developmental dyslexia: Predicting individual risk. *Journal of Child Psychology and Psychiatry, 56*(9), 976–987.

Tierney, R. J. (1991). *Portfolio assessment in the reading–writing classroom.* Washington, DC: Education Resources Information Center.

Tighe, E. L., & Schatschneider, C. (2016). Examining the relationships of component reading skills to reading comprehension in struggling adult readers: A meta-analysis. *Journal of Learning Disabilities, 49*(4), 395–409.

Tong, X., Deacon, S. H., Kirby, J. R., Cain, K., & Parrila, R. (2011). Morphological awareness: A key to understanding poor reading comprehension in English. *Journal of Educational Psychology, 103*(3), 523.

Topping, K. J., Dehkinet, R., Blanch, S., Corcelles, M., & Duran, D. (2013). Paradoxical effects of feedback in international online reciprocal peer tutoring. *Computers & Education, 61,* 225–231.

Topping, K. J., Duran, D., & Van Keer, H. (2015). *Using peer tutoring to improve reading skills: A practical guide for teachers.* New York: Routledge.

Torgesen, J. K., & Hudson, R. F. (2006). Reading fluency: Critical issues for struggling readers. In S. J. Samuels & A. E. Farstrup (Eds.), *What research has to say about fluency instruction* (pp. 130–158). Newark, DE: International Reading Association.

Vasilyeva, M., Huttenlocher, J., & Waterfall, H. (2006). Effects of language intervention on syntactic skill levels in preschoolers. *Developmental Psychology, 42*(1), 164.

Venezky, R. L. (1999). *The American way of spelling: The structure and origins of American English orthography.* New York: Guilford Press.

Wang, Z., Sabatini, J., O'Reilly, T., & Weeks, J. (2019). Decoding and reading comprehension: A test of the decoding threshold hypothesis. *Journal of Educational Psychology, 111*(3), 387.

Wixson, K. K., & Valencia, S. W. (2011). Assessment in RTI: What teachers and specialists need to know. *The Reading Teacher, 64*(6), 466–469.

CHAPTER 8

Self-Regulated Strategy Development
Reading Source Materials to Learn and Write

Karen R. Harris
Linda H. Mason

Concerns regarding inadequate abilities to integrate reading and writing to learn among many K–12 students have become a worldwide issue (Harris, Kim, Yim, Camping, & Graham, 2021). Reading and writing are essential tools for functioning in today's world and critical tools for learning and work. Writing, in addition, is also vital for self-expression, communicating, self-advocacy, identity development, and social and political engagement. The majority of teachers, however, feel poorly prepared to teach writing and report that writing is a low priority in the school day and/or at the grade levels they teach (Brindle, Graham, Harris, & Hebert, 2016; Harris & Graham, 2016). Alarmingly, the latest data from the National Assessment of Educational Progress indicates that only 27% of eighth- and twelfth-grade students scored at or above proficient for writing (Aud et al., 2012). Underserved students living in high poverty areas and students with disabilities face even greater challenges (Harris, 2018, 2021).

Reading to learn across the curriculum, followed by writing to summarize, inform, persuade, respond to text read, and more, have become key goals in state and national standards for literacy. The majority of U.S. states have adopted or adapted the Common Core State Standards (CCSS), with the remaining developing their own college- and career-ready standards, often similar to the CCSS (Achieve, 2013). The CCSS language arts standards focus on students becoming proficient and skilled readers and writers, but that alone is not adequate. The language arts CCSS strongly stress emphasizing the use of reading and writing to support each other and highlight the role of both in supporting learning (Harris, Ray, Graham, & Houston, 2019; Harris et al., 2021). This has created new challenges for both students and teachers (Jones, Chang, Heritage, Tobiasman, & Herman, 2015). Students must learn to closely read and attend to text; gather, organize, and synthesize evidence from their reading; apply what they have learned by integrating it with what they know about effective writing for various purposes and readers; and more. Teachers must learn how to support this process and develop these abilities across grades and areas. Evidence-based instructional practices for reading texts to learn, integrated with evidence-based writing instruction, are critical for our students.

In this chapter, we share two examples of evidence-based instruction that teachers can use to help students integrate what they read and learn with their goals for writing and the writing process. The first set of strategies has been proven to empower students from grade 3 and above to read informative text and write powerful persuasive essays. The second set of strategies is proven to substantially improve adolescent students' comprehension of content-area informative text and written responses to the text. These responses can be either "quick writes" or more extended assignments, such as essays. Both sets of strategies for elementary and secondary learners are based on the Self-Regulated Strategy Development (SRSD) instructional model, for both reading and writing, that is explained in the next section.

GUIDING QUESTIONS

■ What is the SRSD model of instruction based on? What are critical components and aspects of SRSD instruction?

■ What is the evidence base for SRSD instruction in both writing and reading?

■ What strategies can teachers apply to help students in the third grade or higher learn close reading of text to learn and to then write to persuade?

■ What outcomes can teachers expect for their students?

■ What strategies can teachers select for adolescents to learn to read and write from text across disciplines?

■ What outcomes can their teachers expect?

What Is Special about SRSD Instruction, and How Does It Work?

SRSD instruction is based on what research has proven about both teaching and learning across multiple theories, rather than any single theory. For example, SRSD instruction is situated within a large body of research on the sociocognitive model of learning (e.g., Vygotsky, 1986); what we know about metacognition, self-regulated learning, and executive functioning (Harris, Graham, Brindle, & Sandmel, 2009; Harris, Graham, MacArthur, Reid, & Mason, 2011; Harris, Graham, Mason, McKeown, & Olinghouse, 2018; Schunk & Zimmerman, 2003); research and theories on memory, social emotional learning, and more (Harris, 1982; Harris & Graham, 2009, 2018; Harris, Graham, Mason, & Friedlander, 2008). This is one reason SRSD instruction has proven to be so powerful.

To illustrate, SRSD instruction for writing reflects strong respect for and reliance on teacher judgment, and situates writing development, and reading to learn before writing, within the writing process (Harris et al., 2008; Mason, Reid, & Hagaman, 2012). SRSD instruction begins with reading, analyzing, and discussing model texts that represent what students are learning to achieve. Weak texts are also read and evaluated, and then revised. This discussion aids in learning to read with a "writer's eye" and to think like a writer. Aspects of topic, audience, and purpose are investigated and discussed throughout six instructional stages in SRSD:

1. Develop background knowledge
2. Discuss it
3. Model it
4. Memorize it
5. Support it
6. Independent practice.

These stages are flexible and recursive; teachers differentiate across students' strengths and needs and allow students the time needed in each stage.

SRSD instruction involves rich discussion to develop academic vocabulary, concepts, and knowledge; active learning; and peer, group, and teacher collaborations. Students learn powerful reading and/or writing strategies and are given the level of support and scaffolding needed until they can use these strategies independently and effectively. Mnemonics are used to support long-term memory of these strategies. Students also learn that we all need to learn to write—no one is born a good or bad writer! Writing ability is something they can develop with effort on their part to both learn and use these strategies. Furthermore, they learn powerful strategies to self-regulate both reading to learn and the writing process (including goal setting, self-instructions, self-monitoring, and self-reinforcement) and the emotional (e.g., frustration) and behavioral (e.g., persistence) demands faced by writers. Multiple elements of SRSD instruction, therefore, help teachers support social emotional strengths such as development of motivation, positive attitudes toward writing, and students' belief in themselves as capable writers (i.e., self-efficacy). SRSD instruction takes place in a supportive community of learners and writers, is based in reading and writing processes, and must be individualized to teachers' context and students' development. According to our students, it is also often fun (see later student comments)! Table 8.1 provides a thorough summary of the six stages and characteristics of SRSD instruction.

SRSD for Close Reading of Source Text to Learn and to Write

Both learning to read and learning to write are complex areas of learning, as is learning to read to learn, and then writing for differing audiences and

TABLE 8.1. SRSD Instruction for Writing, or Reading and Writing[a]

1. Develop and Activate Knowledge	• Read and discuss works in the reading–writing genre being addressed to develop academic language and knowledge (e.g., "What does it mean to persuade?"), appreciation of characteristics of effective writing (e.g., "How did the writer grab your interest?"), and other knowledge and understandings targeted for instruction. Continue through the Model It stage as needed until all key knowledge and understandings are clear.
	• Introduce reading–writing strategies to be learned, the importance of each part, and how they can help us as readers and writers. Continue reading models of writing in the target genre (such as opinion essays) that exemplify what the students will learn to do, identifying each element of the genre being learned and the appropriate characteristics of effective writing.
	• Introduce goal setting and overview the goals you will be working on to read, learn, and write.
2. Discuss It— Discourse Is Critical!	• Discuss students' attitudes and beliefs about reading and writing, and what they say to themselves as they read and write ("What helps you?," "What gets in your way?," etc.).
	• Discuss reading, writing, and self-regulation strategies to be learned: purpose, benefits, how and when they can be used. Practice; support memorization in fun ways.
	• Establish each student's commitment to put in the effort needed to learn the strategies, and to participate as a collaborative partner with the teacher and other students. Establish the teacher's commitment to teach strategies that work as long as students put forth the effort to learn and use them.
	• Introduce a mnemonic and/or graphic organizer (GO) to be used, give a copy to each student, emphasize the purpose of each part.
	• Continue analyzing grade-level-appropriate model papers for genre elements, characteristics; take notes from these papers on a GO to assist students in learning to make notes.
	• With the teacher or peers, analyze poor essay(s), make notes for a better essay on a GO, and write this essay collaboratively.
	• Graph the number of genre-specific essay elements and other targeted goals included in a pretest[b] or prior essays to support goal setting and self-monitoring; this can be done later or left out if needed.
3. Model It	• Interactive, collaborative modeling of writing and self-regulation strategies (goal setting, self-instructions, self-monitoring, and self-reinforcement); teacher uses these strategies, referring to the mnemonic chart and GO during the writing process. Teacher maintains control of the writing process; students assist.
	• Peers act as models as appropriate; videotape, if allowed, for future use.
	• Students record personal self-statements to assist them in reading and writing.
	• Model self-monitoring and self-reinforcement through graphing of collaborative compositions; each student does this on their own graph.

(continued)

TABLE 8.1. *(continued)*

4. Memorize It	• Although begun earlier, confirm memorization of meaning and importance of each step for strategies. • Support memorization in the following stage; make sure students have memorized all before *Independent Performance*.
5. Support It	• Challenging initial goals for genre elements and characteristics of writing established with students and individualized as needed; goals increased gradually as appropriate. • GO handout replaced with student creating GO on scratch paper. • Teachers and/or peers work together using strategies collaboratively as needed to meet goals. • Prompts, guidance, and collaboration faded individually until a student can compose on their own. • Discuss plans for maintenance and generalization.
6. Independent Performance	• Students use writing and self-regulation strategies independently; teacher monitors and supports/enhances as needed. • Student graphing is continued; all other supports removed. • Continue to discuss plans for maintenance and generalization.

[a] A "stage" of instruction is not equivalent to a single lesson. Stages 1 and 2 are often combined in instruction; instruction is recursive across stages; students should progress across stages as they meet criteria for doing so. Students learning to read to learn, and then to write, should follow all SRSD stages for reading first; then writing based on close reading should follow using all stages (differentiate as appropriate).

[b] Have students do the best they can on a pretest before instruction begins, both to support differentiation and allow graphing of the pretest.

purposes (Flower & Hayes, 1980; Harris & Graham, 2018). The SRSD model of instruction, initially developed and refined over time by the first author of this chapter, is appropriate and powerful in these areas. SRSD for teaching writing was the first area to be researched, with over 100 studies conducted by 2013 from grades 1 to 12 (Graham, Harris, & McKeown, 2013) and more since (Harris & Graham, 2018). SRSD for writing has been deemed an evidence-based practice at elementary grades in inclusive classrooms by the IES What Works Clearinghouse (Graham et al., 2018) and has been shown to work across grades 2 through 12 in multiple meta-analyses (Graham & Harris, 2018). Researchers have found SRSD instruction effective among students in ethnically and racially diverse classrooms and across socioeconomic levels (Graham & Harris, 2018; Salas, Birello, & Ribas, 2020). SRSD for writing is effective at the whole-class, small-group, and individual levels across narrative, informative, and persuasive/argumentative writing (Harris & Graham, 2018), as well as with students with learning disabilities, emotional-behavioral disorders, and other special needs in special education or inclusive classrooms. Furthermore, a large body of research shows that classroom teachers can use SRSD instruction effectively in their classrooms with outcomes equal to those of researchers (Graham et al., 2013; Harris, 2021; Harris et al., 2012a, 2012b; Harris, Graham, & Adkins, 2015).

Researchers have studied SRSD for reading as well as writing. SRSD instruction for reading comprehension followed by writing for specific purposes enhances content knowledge as well as writing ability across grades 1 to 12 (Harris et al., 2021; Foxworth & Mason, 2017). The evidence base is growing for the integration of reading and writing using the SRSD model of instruction. Thus, SRSD instruction in reading and writing is well aligned with expectations for K–12 writing instruction and the CCSS for literacy (Harris et al., 2019; National Governors Association & Council of Chief School Officers, 2010).

Reading to Learn and Writing to Persuade: Grades 3 and Up

A powerful set of strategies has been successful in helping students from grade 3 and up learn to write to persuade the reader to agree with their view or stand on a topic (Harris et al., 2019; Harris & Graham, 2018). We often refer to these strategies by their mnemonics (see Figure 8.1). Instruction, however, goes far beyond simply learning what the mnemonic stands for. Next, we provide an overview of the specific strategies taught and a summary of SRSD instruction across the six stages described in Table 8.1. We also address what students learn about writing to persuade that goes beyond, and is as important as, the two strategies they learn to use.

POW + TREE: POWerful Strategies for Writing to Persuade

POW (Pick my idea, Organize my notes, Write and say more) is a general writing process strategy useful for most writing tasks. In *picking their idea*, students learn to think about the writing task, or "pull apart the prompt." Students learn to identify the task (e.g., write to persuade, inform, or narrate), determine who their reader is (students might write to persuade their classmates, principal, or parents, for instance), and their goals (e.g., to do your best to get the reader to agree with you, use all that you know, etc.). For writing to persuade, students may also need to decide what they believe or determine if the prompt asks them to write on a particular viewpoint.

Organize my notes begins with learning what it means to make notes for writing and why they are important. Writing short phrases takes less time than writing out sentences for our notes, and making notes helps us remember our ideas. Making effective notes is often new to most students and requires practice and guidance across the stages of instruction.

Write and say more reminds the student to continue thinking while writing, making changes or adding to their graphic organizers (GOs) and/or text as they work. Students know that POW will help guide them through the writing task and makes them a POWerful writer (some elementary teachers have expanded on this theme, creating Power Ranger Writers, dressing as a superhero POWer writer, etc.).

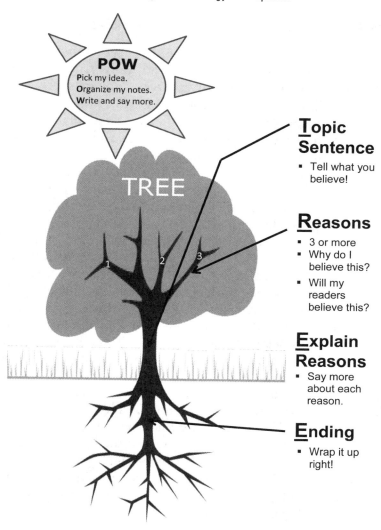

FIGURE 8.1. POW + TREE strategies.

TREE stands for the major elements of writing to persuade: Topic sentence, Reasons, Explain (or elaborate on) each reason further, and Ending. Students learn to make notes for each of these parts of persuasive writing using their own ideas and opinions. Students first learn to organize notes using a structured GO, and then learn to make their own GO on scratch paper. They learn that the topic sentence(s) needs to clearly tell what you believe and should hook the reader; you should have three or more strong reasons for why you believe something (these reasons should matter to your intended reader); each reason needs to be explained further to help persuade the reader, and your ending needs to wrap it up effectively for the reader.

SRSD Instruction for POW + TREE and Writing to Persuade

To prepare for instruction, teachers have students write an opinion essay on a topic relevant to them. Teachers then read and study their students' work to see what individual students are already capable of doing as well as what they need to learn. This informal assessment aids greatly in lesson planning and differentiating instruction (Harris et al., 2008). Teachers we have worked with have made learning to write opinion essays through SRSD instruction fun and engaging for their students. For example, teachers have developed raps, chants, songs, and/or hand and body movements to help students remember and internalize the strategy mnemonics, fun bulletin boards, games, and peer activities throughout instruction (including peer planning and composing, as well as peer feedback for revising; see Harris et al., 2008).

Teachers complete the six stages of SRSD instruction as outlined in Table 8.1. Across the first two stages of SRSD instruction, students learn the strategies POW + TREE, described previously, and how they are used to write to persuade. SRSD instruction always begins with reading model writing, written at a level these students are striving to attain. As seen in Table 8.1, these model pieces are discussed, allowing careful development of discourse knowledge about the writing process and this genre. Teachers take the time needed in these two stages, which are often combined flexibly in instruction, to address all of the topics noted in Table 8.1.

Teachers, in addition, develop goals for their students beyond learning and using POW + TREE. For example, important goals teachers set align with the CCSS and local standards and what we know about good writing. During these first two stages and continuing as needed in the following stages, young students learn that good opinion essays (i.e., have all the parts, are well written, and have a chance of convincing your reader to agree with you) should be fun for you to write and fun for your target audience to read, hook the reader, use strong sentences and effective vocabulary, make sense, use linking words, and make a strong attempt to convince your reader to agree with you.

Teachers model the use of these strategies in writing to persuade in stage 3 of SRSD instruction. Students do not, however, simply sit and listen. Rather, SRSD emphasizes interactive modeling, where students can assist the teacher in pulling apart the prompt and identifying their audience, making notes on a GO created on scratch paper (or the board, etc.), and so on until the essay is complete. The teacher stays in control, making sure all aspects of writing to persuade are used. In addition, the teacher models helpful self-instructions while writing. Students later create their own personal self-talk to use before, while, and after they write. Stage 4 is a check to see that students have memorized the key elements of POW and TREE, as well as key aspects of good writing to persuade. Stages 5 and 6 are the gradual release of control until each student is writing independently.

When POW and TREE are taught for writing to persuade using the six stages of SRSD instruction, a strong body of research shows significant and large effects on the holistic quality of students' essays, the use of critical genre elements, and length of essays (Graham et al., 2013). Studies have also shown that students find SRSD instruction enjoyable and successful; their attitudes about writing, engagement in writing, and self-efficacy for writing have also improved in multiple studies (cf. Graham et al., 2013; Harris et al., 2012a, 2012b, 2019; Harris, Graham, Chambers, & Houston, 2014; Mason, Kubina, Kostewicz, Mong Cramer, & Datchuk, 2013b). As one student said to us, "These strategies should be taught to all the students in the world." Another student noted, "Of course, I can write now, someone taught me how." Furthermore, these strategies have been taught successfully in inclusive classrooms, and in small groups that included special education students with learning disabilities, autism, or emotional-behavioral disorders. This instruction has been effective with students of differing races, ethnicities, and SES levels, and with boys and girls (Graham et al., 2013; Harris & Graham, 2018). POW has also been successfully combined with strategies for writing stories and writing to inform at the elementary grades (Harris et al., 2008, 2021). All student and teacher materials for teaching POW + TREE (which can be copied without asking permission from the publisher), as well as more detailed descriptions of each stage of instruction, can be found in Harris et al. (2008).

Adding Reading to Learn and to Support Persuasion: POW + TREE + TWA

Previously, students in the elementary grades typically learned to write to persuade based on their own opinions and ideas; use of source text began in later grades. Currently, however, the focus on reading to learn and writing to inform, persuade, or narrate is beginning to move into earlier grades. Research indicates that students in third grade and above who have learned to use POW + TREE, self-regulate their writing performance, and write good opinion essays can also learn to use source texts to strengthen their ability to write persuasive texts (FitzPatrick & McKeown, 2021; Harris & Graham, 2014; Harris et al., 2019).

Students can then learn to use a strategy for close reading, using the six stages of SRSD instruction seen in Table 8.1, such as TWA (Think before reading, While reading, and After reading; Mason, Dunn Davison, Hammer, Miller, & Glutting, 2013a). TWA focuses on reading, rereading, and marking up parts of text that can support your goals as a writer, emphasizing the use of facts as well as your own ideas. In the next section, readers will learn more about TWA and how it has been used with older students. TWA can be combined with POW + TREE using all of the parts of TWA seen in Figure 8.2. TWA may, however, be slightly modified for elementary grade students to stand for: Think *before* reading, think about the author's purpose, think about your own ideas for reasons and explanations; *While* reading, think about your reading speed (why not to read too slowly or too quickly), think about rereading and marking up the text for information or ideas you might use for reasons, explanations, or other aspects of your goals; *After* reading, think about: what will persuade your reader, think about and make notes for reasons and explanations to persuade your reader. This version of TWA has been taught successfully with

POW and TREE using the SRSD stages of instruction (Harris et al., 2019). A complete set of detailed professional learning lesson plans for POW + TREE + TWA and all teacher and student materials are provided for free at *https://brill.com.view/book/edcoll/9789004270480/B9789004270480_007.xml?rskey-7veuCS&result-1&body-figshare-43182.*

SRSD for Reading Comprehension and Writing with Adolescents

During middle and high school years, students are expected to read and write from text across disciplines such as English language arts, social studies/history, and science (Mason & Graham, 2008). Furthermore, students are expected to learn from both narrative and informational text and to demonstrate learning by writing in a variety of genres (i.e., narrative, informative, persuasive/argumentative) and for different writing tasks and assignments (e.g., essays, quick writes). We next describe how SRSD for two reading and writing strategy approaches, TWA + PLANS (Pick goals, List ways to meet goals, And make Notes, Sequence notes) and POW + TIDE (Topic Sentence, at least three Important Details, and an Ending), can address expectations for reading and writing successfully in upper grades. Strategies steps and tasks are highlighted in Figure 8.2.

Writing from Content Text

Mason and colleagues examined the effectiveness of SRSD instruction to teach adolescents the TWA strategy (Mason, 2004) for improving informative text reading comprehension with planning strategies for an extended constructed response, as in informational text essay writing (e.g., Mason et al., 2013a; Mason & Zheng, 2018), and for a short constructed response such as a quick write (e.g., Benedek-Wood, Mason, Wood, Hoffman, & McGuire, 2014; Ciullo, Mason, & Judd, 2021). In this integrated model of instruction (using the six stages of SRSD instruction described in the section above and in Table 8.1) developed for improving adolescent reading comprehension of, and writing about, content text, TWA for reading comprehension is taught first, followed by instruction in note taking from the text(s) read and instruction in planning an essay or a quick writing (i.e., a timed short constructed response).

    The nine strategy steps taught in TWA facilitate and support students' active engagement with text: (1) Think before reading—think about the author's purpose and why the topic is important, think about what you want to know about the topic, and think about what you want to learn about the topic; (2) think While reading—think about your reading speed—slow down if you are reading too fast!, think about linking new knowledge to what you already know about the topic, and think about rereading parts when you do not understand them; and (3) think After reading—think about the main ideas presented throughout the text, think about summarizing information by identifying important

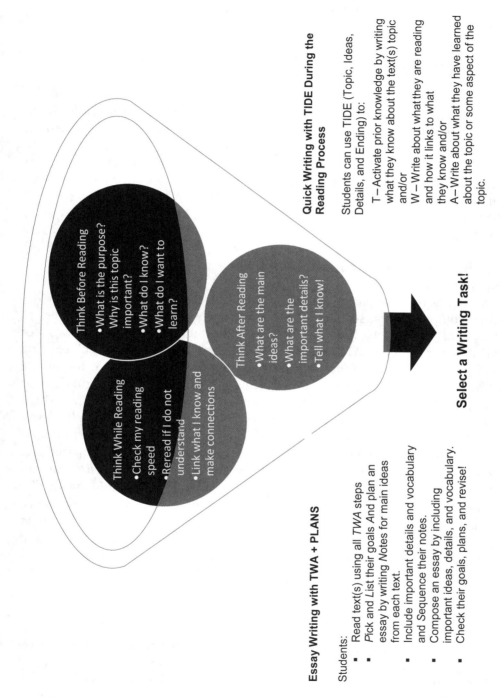

Essay Writing with TWA + PLANS

Students:

- Read text(s) using all *TWA* steps
- *Pick* and *List* their goals *And* plan an essay by writing *Notes* for main ideas from each text.
- Include important details and vocabulary and *Sequence* their notes.
- Compose an essay by including important ideas, details, and vocabulary.
- Check their goals, plans, and revise!

Think Before Reading
- What is the purpose? Why is this topic important?
- What do I know?
- What do I want to learn?

Think While Reading
- Check my reading speed
- Reread if I do not understand
- Link what I know and make connections

Think After Reading
- What are the main ideas?
- What are the important details?
- Tell what I know!

Select a Writing Task!

Quick Writing with TIDE During the Reading Process

Students can use TIDE (Topic, Ideas, Details, and Ending) to:

T – Activate prior knowledge by writing what they know about the text(s) topic and/or
W – Write about what they are reading and how it links to what they know and/or
A – Write about what they have learned about the topic or some aspect of the topic.

FIGURE 8.2. Writing from content text.

details for each main idea, and think about what you learned from reading the text. Many students have difficulty knowing what to write; therefore, it is critical that teachers are explicit about the task (e.g., writing an essay or writing a quick write) when teaching reading and writing strategies.

TWA + PLANS for Writing Informative Essays

The reading comprehension and essay planning strategies, TWA + PLANS, support students' personal writing goals as well as providing additional support for self-monitoring writing performance (Graham, MacArthur, Schwartz, & Page-Voth, 1992). Using the notes written before, during, and after reading with TWA, students completed PLANS by selecting goals for writing an informative essay. SRSD for TWA + PLANS instruction in two group experimental studies (Mason et al., 2013a; Mason & Zheng, 2018) indicated significant and large effects in improving students' oral and written retelling of main ideas.

Researchers and teachers, however, caution that instruction for writing about the complex text used in content classrooms must be carefully sequenced (e.g., Mason et al., 2013a). When introducing the reading and essay writing strategies to adolescents using SRSD instruction, for example, the TWA reading comprehension strategies should be taught first using all six stages of instruction, followed by note taking, and ending with using the six stages of SRSD instruction for PLANS (see Mason et al., 2012, for professional learning lesson plans and instructional materials). SRSD instruction should follow the six SRSD stages and all procedures for teaching students to self-regulate their learning in Table 8.1. Teachers should prepare for lessons by (1) establishing the students' current performance levels so that appropriate goals can be developed, (2) selecting the texts to be used throughout instruction—starting with simple text structures when introducing each new strategy, and (3) practicing effective modeling techniques with self-instructions appropriate for the students (e.g., "I need to reread my goals before writing about what I have read"). In addition, teachers should consider focused mini-lessons for specific skills, such as developing vocabulary and sentence construction. Instruction should be recursive and mastery-based—designed to be taught until the teacher- and student-determined objectives for students' reading comprehension and writing have been achieved.

TWA

Many adolescents have difficulty understanding the purpose for reading, linking what they know to what is read in text, monitoring comprehension during reading, and attending to and identifying important ideas and details in text. Reading with TWA should be explicitly modeled by the teacher, or by a peer who has been taught the strategy. When first learning TWA, students use highlighters or underline main ideas and details in the text. Later, students can mark text with a pencil, or can use a sticky note for locating important information. During the TWA lessons, students discuss the "think about" steps before, during, and after reading in small groups or with a peer.

TWA Note Taking

After students have orally demonstrated application of TWA for reading a text passage, instruction in writing notes for an essay is provided. To support informative writing, students are taught how to write notes for each main idea and all supporting details that were identified during reading with TWA. Students are encouraged to use academic vocabulary by writing key words from the text in their outline. A teacher-created GO is used initially; later, students are taught to create their own note-taking outline:

1. Topic
   a. Main idea (repeated for each main idea)
      i. Detail
      ii. Detail
      iii. Detail (minimum of three details for each idea)
2. Conclusion

The teacher discusses the purpose of writing notes, models how to write notes efficiently by encouraging students to write in phrases and not in complete sentences, provides examples of good note-taking, and provides ample guided practice. During note-taking lessons, students continue to orally practice with a peer, and/or to silently practice, summarizing and reviewing what was learned from the text.

PLANS Instruction

The PLANS strategy provides students with a framework for developing goals and methods for evaluating their writing performance (Graham et al., 1992). Three writing steps are included: (1) complete PLANS, (2) write and say more, and (3) test goals (Pick goals, List goals). Students complete PLANS by selecting planning, composing, revising, and editing goals to support writing from the notes that they create when reading text with TWA (And make Notes, Sequence notes). Goals are listed on a planning sheet that includes a goal section for "Starting My Essay," for "Writing My Essay," and for "Revising My Essay." PLANS goals include elements that are characteristic of good informative essays, good written expression, and good writing mechanics.

Goals should be specific, meet the writing needs of each student, and support curriculum objectives in developing content and vocabulary. For example, if the curriculum objective is for students to classify the types of rocks, "Starting My Essay" goals could include:

- *I will write an interesting first paragraph;*
- *I will write a paragraph for each main idea and include supporting details and examples for each classification (igneous, metamorphic, and sedimentary);* and/or
- *I will use at least two scientific vocabulary words from the text for each classification.*

"Writing My Essay" goals could include:

- *I will write transition words and sentences;*
- *I will write at least two complex sentences in each paragraph;* and/or
- *I will pay attention to my organization.*

"Revising My Essay" goals could include:

- *I will check for use of spelling, punctuation, and capitalization,* and/or
- *I will check and revise word choice.*

Students also need to identify ways to meet and evaluate goals. If the goal is to write a main idea statement and supporting details for each rock classification, the student may list on their goal planning sheet, "I will read my notes and check the text for types of rocks and vocabulary to describe them," as the method for monitoring and achieving the goal. Goals should be developed to ensure students' success in meeting their objectives and the teacher's expectations for writing (Graham et al., 1992). Providing goal choice is important in PLANS instruction; therefore, collaboratively establishing goals as a class, in a group of students, or for students individually is critical. Goals are not stagnant; a goal should be revised when a student has demonstrated success across multiple writing opportunities.

Informative Quick Writing

Quick writes are brief, 10- to 15-minute, informal writing activities that require students to produce a written response before, during, or after reading, and are most often used in science and social studies instruction (Frey & Fisher, 2012; Mason, Benedek-Wood, & Valasa, 2009). Quick writing prior to reading or before content learning is often used to activate prior knowledge or express an opinion about a specific topic. In this case, quick writes are used prior to reading and/or content instruction. Quick writing during reading or after reading, for students having difficulty reading informative text, should follow reading comprehension instruction as described for SRSD for TWA instruction. Once students have demonstrated success in identifying key information read in text(s), the three-step planning POW strategy is introduced (Graham, Harris, & Mason, 2005; Harris, Graham, & Mason, 2006). For informative quick writing, TIDE is embedded in the POW, "Organize my notes," strategy step. SRSD for quick writing has been validated as effective for improving students' writing quality in inclusive classrooms, learning support classrooms, in-school tutoring (see Mason & Basile, 2021, for a review of SRSD for quick writing research).

POW + TIDE

In the first strategy step, "Pick my idea," students' attention is drawn to the task and text. Students are taught, for example, that the task may require writing about all the main ideas in the text (e.g., "Write about what you have read and learned about the three branches of the U.S. government") or require elaboration about one main idea (e.g., "Select one branch of the U.S. government. Write about what you have read and learned about this branch of government"). After understanding the task, students look back at the main ideas and details they identified when reading with TWA, and note important key vocabulary words to begin brainstorming ideas for the quick write.

In the second writing step, "Organize my notes," students are taught to write brief notes (i.e., two- or three-word phrases to prompt memory and organization) for their topic and ending sentences, and for the ideas and details in the text read. Initially, students are provided with teacher-created GOs for organizing notes. These GOs are faded over time as the students learn to write their organized notes on a blank piece of paper. Notes for the branches of government, for example, could include:

- **T:** *Write about three branches.*
- **I and D:** *Legislative (makes laws; Congress: the House of Representatives and Senate), Executive (carries out laws, president, vice president, cabinet), Judicial (evaluates laws, Supreme Court, other courts).*
- **E:** *Sometimes they work together, sometimes not.*

During note-taking time, key vocabulary should be listed and included in the notes. As with note taking in TWA + PLANS, many students have difficulty writing notes; therefore, the teacher may need to model how to correctly write notes and to provide the students with additional practice in this skill. Writing notes quickly is especially important, given the time needed for planning and writing a quick write.

After organizing notes, students are taught to "Write and say more." This strategy step includes checking and revising word choice and enriching writing by extending the quick write beyond what is written for notes. Mini-lessons to support topic and concluding sentence development (e.g., sentence combining) can be included during instruction for developing the "Write and say more" strategy step.

Timeline for Instructional Planning

In content classes, many students who struggle with writing do not use the allotted time for writing productively (Mason, Kubina, & Taft, 2011). Hence, once students demonstrate quick writing with the POW + TIDE strategy elements, a fluency-building component can be added to support writing within an allotted time frame (see Mason et al., 2012, for lesson plans and instructional materials). After TIDE instruction, SRSD instruction for fluency building includes the same six stages of instruction as noted in Table 8.1.

Fluency building is supported by revisiting the "Discuss it" and "Model it" stages and by providing additional guided practice. The teacher discusses the need to use writing time wisely for many class activities. The teacher and students provide examples of times when writing quickly is needed. The teacher then cognitively models a second time to show students how to use POW + TIDE within a specified time limit, generally 10 to 15 minutes. Guided practice in writing a timed quick write is scaffolded over multiple lessons until students demonstrate mastery in writing a timed response. As with all SRSD instruction, fluency-building instruction is recursive; any stage may be revisited to support students' learning.

Extending POW + TIDE: Add TWA

POW + TIDE can also be extended to writing essays after reading content area or other source text, combining TWA with these two strategies as above, but extending TIDE to stand for: Topic Sentence, at least three important main/big Ideas, Details for each main idea, and an Ending. Instruction then proceeds as above and in Table 8.1. Recently, young students in the first and second grades have been successful in reading science text and writing to inform using TWA + POW + TIDE (Harris et al., 2022)!

Your Classroom

We began this chapter with a discussion of the many challenges teachers and students face in reading for writing. This chapter will help you address and overcome many of these challenges. We hope that you will use SRSD instruction for reading to learn and then writing for differing audiences and purposes in your classroom. Where will you start, what content areas, and what audiences can you address? What critical challenges in reading to learn and then writing face your students? Which of the strategies covered here, POW + TREE + TWA, TWA + PLANS, POW + TIDE, and POW + TIDE + TWA, are a good match to your students and their developing abilities in reading and writing?

Students from grades K to 12 indicate that they enjoy the SRSD instruction, like writing after this instruction, and show impressive growth in reading and writing. Learning more about SRSD is low cost or free. In Table 8.2, we share a set of resources for SRSD instruction in writing and/or reading so that

TABLE 8.2. Resources for SRSD

Publications for teachers

- Harris, K. R., Graham, S., Mason, L. H., & Friedlander, B. (2008). *Powerful writing strategies for all students*. Baltimore: Brookes.
- Mason, L., Reid, R., & Hagaman, J. (2012). *Building comprehension in adolescents: Powerful strategies for improving reading and writing in content areas*. Baltimore: Brookes.
- Graham, S., & Harris, K. R. (2005). *Writing better: Teaching writing processes and self-regulation to students with learning problems*. Baltimore: Brookes.
- Harris, K., & Graham, S. (1996). *Making the writing process work: Strategies for composition and self-regulation* (2nd ed.). Cambridge, MA: Brookline Books.

Web-based and other resources

- IRIS Center modules on SRSD and writing: *http://iris.peabody.vanderbilt.edu*.
- Two organizations that support PD for SRSD provide numerous free online videos and materials: *www.thinkSRSD.com* and *https://srsdonline.org*.
- Robert Mitchel, Superintendent: What Is Self-Regulated Strategy Development? SRSD Makes Students "love to write"! (2019). thinkSRSD: *www.youtube.com/watch?v=nSgx0T2DEqs*.
- SRSD: Changing Students Lives Forever with Writing to Learn. (undated). Teachers, students, and researchers talk about SRSD for writing. SRSD online: *https://honceoui.wistia.com/medias/n0dlewrxva*.
- SRSD: A Deep Dive. (undated). Eighteen short videos on key aspects of SRSD. LD online: *https://srsdonline.org/srsd-deep-dive*.
- Why writing matters, what does it take to write well. and why can it be so challenging? This is a short, fun video: *www.youtube.com/watch?v=gZJcW2niRDc*.
- See YouTube, Pinterest, and Teachers Pay Teachers for many more videos, instructional support, and materials for SRSD instruction.

readers can go beyond this chapter in learning about SRSD instruction. There are many more proven reading and writing strategies at elementary, middle and high school grades, as well as strategies for revising, editing, and collaborating with peers. Strategies exist across multiple genres, including informational, persuasive/argumentative, and narrative writing (Harris et al., 2008; Mason et al., 2012). This chapter and these resources will help you work effectively with your students as they learn to read to learn, and write for multiple purposes using what they have learned. Because SRSD instruction works with diverse students, this instruction not only supports learning in many ways, but also fosters equity and addresses inequality in learning to write.

REFERENCES

Achieve. (2013). Closing the expectations gap: 2013 Annual Report on the Alignment of State K–12 Policies and Practice with the Demands of College and Careers.

Washington, DC: Author. Retrieved from *www.achieve.org/files/2013Closingthe ExpectationsGapReport.pdf.*

Aud, S., Hussar, W., Johnson, F., Kena, G., Roth, E., Manning, E., . . . Zhang, J. (2012). *The Condition of Education 2012* (NCES 2012–045). Washington, DC: U.S. Department of Education, National Center for Education Statistics. Retrieved from *http://nces.ed.gov/pubsearch.*

Benedek-Wood, E., Mason, L. H., Wood, P. H., Hoffman, K. E., & McGuire, A. (2014). An experimental examination of quick writing in the middle school science classroom. *Learning Disabilities: A Contemporary Journal, 12*(1), 69–92.

Brindle, M., Graham, S., Harris, K. R., & Hebert, M. (2016). Third and fourth grade teachers' classroom practices in writing: A national survey. *Reading and Writing: An Interdisciplinary Journal, 9,* 929–954.

Ciullo, S., Mason, L. H., & Judd, L. (2021). Persuasive quick writing about text: Intervention for students with learning disabilities. *Behavior Modification, 45*(1), 122–146.

FitzPatrick, E. R., & McKeown, D. (2021). Writing from multiple source texts: SRSD for fifth grade learners in inclusive settings. *Learning Disabilities Research and Practice.* Advance online publication.

Flower, L., & Hayes, J. (1980). The dynamics of composing: Making plans and juggling constraints. In L. Gregg & E. Steinberg (Eds.), *Cognitive processes in writing* (pp. 31–50). Mahwah, NJ: Erlbaum.

Foxworth, L., & Mason, L. H. (2017). Writing to learn instruction that works. In R. Fidalgo, K. R. Harris, & M. Braaksma (Eds.), *Design principles for teaching effective writing* (pp. 66–86). Amsterdam: Brill Editions.

Frey, N., & Fisher, D. (2012). *Improving adolescent literacy: Content area strategies at work.* Upper Saddle River, NJ: Pearson Prentice Hall.

Graham, S., Bollinger, A., Booth Olson, C., D'Aoust, C., MacArthur, C., McCutchen, D., & Olinghouse, N. (2018). *Teaching elementary school students to be effective writers: A practice guide* (NCEE 2012- 4058, rev. ed.). Washington, DC: National Center for Education Evaluation and Regional Assistance, Institute of Education Sciences, U.S. Department of Education. Retrieved from *https://ies.ed.gov/ncee/wwc/Docs/PracticeGuide/WWC_Elem_Writing_PG_Dec182018.pdf.*

Graham, S., & Harris, K. R. (2018). Evidence-based writing practices: A meta-analysis of existing meta-analyses. In R. Fidalgo, K. R. Harris, & M. Braaksma (Eds.), *Design principles for teaching effective writing: Theoretical and empirical grounded principles* (pp. 13–37). Leiden, the Netherlands: Brill.

Graham, S., Harris, K. R., & Mason, L. H. (2005). Improving the writing performance, knowledge, and self-efficacy of struggling young writers: The effects of self-regulated strategy development. *Contemporary Educational Psychology, 30*(2), 207–241.

Graham, S., Harris, K. R., & McKeown, D. (2013). The writing of students with LD and a meta-analysis of SRSD writing intervention studies: Redux. In L. Swanson, K. R. Harris, & S. Graham (Eds.), *Handbook of learning disabilities* (2nd ed., pp. 405–438). New York: Guilford Press.

Graham, S., MacArthur, C., Schwartz, S., & Page-Voth, V. (1992). Improving the compositions of students with learning disabilities using a strategy involving product and process goal setting. *Exceptional Children, 58*(4), 322–334.

Harris, K. R. (1982). Cognitive-behavior modification: Application with exceptional students. *Focus on Exceptional Children, 15*(2), 1–16.

Harris, K. R. (2018). Educational psychology: A future retrospective. *Journal of Educational Psychology, 110*(2), 163–173.

Harris, K. R. (2021). SRSD instructional research for students with or at-risk for LD across the content areas: History and reflections. Using Self-Regulated Strategy Development to support students with and at-risk for learning disabilities across the content areas [Special issue]. *Learning Disabilities Research and Practice, 36*(3), 235–241.

Harris, K. R., & Graham, S. (2009). Self-regulated strategy development in writing: Premises, evolution, and the future. *British Journal of Educational Psychology, 6,* 113–135.

Harris, K. R., & Graham, S. (2014). Integrating reading and writing instruction. In B. Miller, P. McCardle, & R. Long (Eds.), *Teaching reading and writing: Improving instruction and student achievement* (pp. 35–44). Baltimore: Brookes.

Harris, K. R., & Graham, S. (2016). Self-regulated strategy development in writing: Policy implications of an evidence-based practice. *Policy Insights from Behavioral and Brain Sciences, 3,* 77–84.

Harris, K. R., & Graham, S. (2018). Self-regulated strategy development: Theoretical bases, critical instructional elements, and future research. In R. Fidalgo, K. R. Harris, & Braaksma, M. (Eds.), *Design principles for teaching effective writing: Theoretical and empirical grounded principles* (pp. 119–151). Leiden, the Netherlands: Brill.

Harris, K. R., Graham, S., & Adkins, M. (2015). Practice-based professional development and self-regulated strategy development for Tier 2, at-risk writers in second grade. *Contemporary Educational Psychology, 40,* 5–16.

Harris, K. R., Graham, S., Brindle, M., & Sandmel, K. (2009). Metacognition and children's writing. In D. Hacker, J. Dunlosky, & A. Graesser (Eds.), *Handbook of metacognition in education* (pp. 131–153). Mahwah, NJ: Erlbaum.

Harris, K. R., Graham, S., Chambers, A., & Houston, J. (2014). Turning broccoli into ice cream sundaes: Self-regulated strategy development for persuasive writing using informational text. In Gansky, K. (Ed.), *Write now! Empowering writers in today's K–6 classrooms* (pp. 87–111). Newark, DE: International Reading Association. Reprinted as e-book, New York: Teachers College Press, *www.tcpress.com/write-now-9780807775899.*

Harris, K. R., Graham, S., MacArthur, C., Reid, R., & Mason, L. (2011). Self-regulated learning processes and children's writing. In B. Zimmerman & D. H. Schunk (Eds.), *Handbook of self-regulation of learning and performance* (pp. 187–202). London: Routledge.

Harris, K. R., Graham, S., & Mason, L. H. (2006). Self-regulated strategy development for 2nd-grade students who struggle with writing. *American Educational Research Journal, 43*(2), 295–340.

Harris, K. R., Graham, S., Mason, L., & Friedlander, B. (2008). *Powerful writing strategies for all students.* Baltimore: Brookes.

Harris, K. R., Graham, S., Mason, L., McKeown, D., & Olinghouse, N. (2018). Self-regulated strategy development in writing: A classroom example of developing executive function processes and future directions. In L. Meltzer (Ed.), *Executive functioning in education: From theory to practice* (2nd ed., pp. 326–356). New York: Guilford Press.

Harris, K. R., Kim, Y.-S., Yim, S., Camping, A., & Graham, S. (2022). *Yes, they can: Developing transcription skills and oral language in tandem with SRSD instruction on close reading of science text to write informative essays at Grades 1 and 2.* Manuscript submitted for publication.

Harris, K. R., Lane, K. L., Driscoll, S., Graham, S., Wilson, K., Sandmel, K., . . . Schatschneider, C. (2012a). Tier 1, teacher-implemented self-regulated strategy development for students with and without behavioral challenges. *Elementary School Journal, 113,* 160–191.

Harris, K. R., Lane, K. L., Graham, S., Driscoll, S., Sandmel, K., Brindle, M., & Schatschneider, C. (2012b). Practice-based professional development for self-regulated strategies development in writing: A randomized controlled study. *Journal of Teacher Education, 63*(2), 103–119.

Harris, K. R., Ray, A., Graham, S., & Houston, J. (2019). Answering the challenge: SRSD instruction for close reading of text to write to persuade with 4th and 5th grade students experiencing writing difficulties. *Reading and Writing: An Interdisciplinary Journal, 32*(6), 1345–1357.

Jones, B., Chang, S., Heritage, M., Tobiason, G., & Herman, J. (2015). *Supporting students in close reading.* Los Angeles: National Center for Research on Evaluation, Standards, and Student Testing (CRESST). Retrieved from *https://cresst.org/wp-content/uploads/SupportingStudents_CloseReading.pdf.*

Mason, L. H. (2004). Explicit self-regulated strategy development versus reciprocal questioning: Effects on expository reading comprehension among struggling readers. *Journal of Educational Psychology, 96*(2), 283–296.

Mason, L. H., & Basile, J. (in press). Building writing skills for summaries and quick writes. In X. Liu, M. Hebert, & R. A. Alves (Eds.), *The hitchhiker's guide to writing research: A festschrift for Steve Graham.* New York: Springer.

Mason, L. H., Benedek-Wood, E., & Valasa, L. (2009). Quick writing for students who struggle with writing. *Journal of Adolescent and Adult Literacy, 53*(4), 313–322.

Mason, L. H., Dunn Davison, M., Hammer, C. S., Miller, C. A., & Glutting, J. (2013a). Knowledge, writing, and language outcomes for a reading comprehension and writing intervention. *Reading and Writing: An Interdisciplinary Journal, 26*(7), 1135–1158.

Mason, L. H., & Graham, S. (2008). Writing instruction for adolescents with learning disabilities: Programs of intervention research. *Learning Disabilities Research & Practice, 23*(2), 103–112.

Mason, L. H., Kubina, R. M., Kostewicz, D. E., Cramer, A. M., & Datchuk, S. (2013b). Improving quick writing performance of middle-school struggling learners. *Contemporary Educational Psychology, 38*(3), 236–246.

Mason, L. H., Kubina, R., & Taft, R. (2011). Developing quick writing skills of middle school students with disabilities. *Journal of Special Education, 44*(4), 205–220.

Mason, L. H., Reid, R., & Hagaman, J. (2012). *Building comprehension in adolescents: Powerful strategies for improving reading and writing in content areas.* Baltimore: Brookes.

Mason, L. H., & Zheng, S. (2018). Writing from text in eight middle school learning support classrooms: Ascertaining aspects of intensive intervention. *Learning Disabilities: A Multi-Disciplinary Journal, 23*(2), 87–101.

National Governors Association Center for Best Practices & Council of Chief State School Officers. (2010). *Common Core State Standards.* Washington, DC: Authors.

Salas, N., Birello, M., & Ribas, T. (2020). Effectiveness of an SRSD writing intervention for low- and high-SES children. *Reading & Writing, 34*(2), 1–28.

Schunk, D. H., & Zimmerman, B. J. (2003). Self-regulation and learning. In W. M. Reynolds & G. E. Miller (Eds.), *Handbook of psychology* (Vol. 7, pp. 59–78). Hoboken, NJ: Wiley.

Vygotsky, L. (1986). *Thought and language.* Cambridge, MA: MIT Press.

CHAPTER 9

Writing and Reading Connections
in the Digital World

Allison N. Sonia
Laura K. Allen
Scott A. Crossley

Writing and reading are interrelated tasks that draw on a shared set of knowledge and skills to complete successfully (Allen, Snow, Crossley, Jackson, & McNamara, 2014; Shanahan, 1988). With an increased reliance on the Internet for many literacy-based tasks, the lines between reading and writing have become even more blurred as technology has changed the way we interact with written text. For example, the majority of writing tasks that take place in classrooms require students' use of multiple sources. Thus, students must be able to search for, process, and integrate the texts they have read in order to generate a coherent piece of writing on a specific topic.

The development of search engines, text-to-speech technology, and digital sharing and storing capabilities has made a wider variety of texts available and accessible to more people (Graham, 2021). More tools have been developed to communicate and share ideas, ranging from speech-to-text technology as a way of generating text, platforms for sharing and presenting multimodal information (e.g., images, video, slides, gifs) that presume advanced literacy skills, tools that enable reading and writing collaborations with peers (e.g., social media, cloud-based documents), techniques to automatically subtitle face-to-face meetings and videos, and systems that deliver personalized instruction and feedback to users on reading and writing tasks (e.g., spelling and grammar check, automatic tutoring systems; Graham, 2021). Given these significant changes to literacy practices, it is important to understand how the inherent connections between reading and writing skills have been altered in this new *digital literacy* age.

The purpose of this chapter is to provide a broad overview of writing and reading connections in the digital world. We specifically place an emphasis on source evaluation/selection and peer collaboration as they relate to reading and writing processes. While these elements have historically been factors in literacy teaching and learning, technology has advanced their importance by allowing for greater opportunities to both find and evaluate supporting texts and to collaborate. Additionally, we discuss how educational technologies that focus on literacy instruction can be used to support the development of reading and writing skills. Consider the following questions in your reading:

GUIDING QUESTIONS

- How have reading and writing skills been altered in the Internet era?
- How can students' strategies impact their processing of digital information? What unique strategies provide the best learning outcomes in digital reading and writing tasks?
- What types of digital tools can be implemented to help students learn more effectively and to evaluate the quality of their reading comprehension and writing outcomes?
- How can instructors' structure online reading and writing tasks to maximize learning outcomes and promote effective digital literacy skills?

The Emergence of Digital Literacies

Research on reading and writing has often occurred across separate disciplines, in line with classroom practices that have largely focused on distinct instruction and assessment of either reading or writing. With the emergence of digital technologies and more complex, online social contexts, however, reading and writing skills have become more difficult to disentangle. Critically, Internet-based reading and writing almost always take place in parallel. For example, developing and communicating an opinion or argument online simultaneously involve the ability to read and learn from multiple sources of information (Braasch, Bråten, & McCrudden, 2018) as well as the ability to synthesize this information into coherent discourse for a particular audience (Allen et al., 2021). To be effective, online reading and writing activities require the development of new skills and strategies. Thus, researchers have begun to examine the skills and processes that are necessary to be considered *digitally literate*—that is, the skills that are necessary to successfully read and write in a digital context.

Digital literacy (sometimes referred to as "media literacy" or "Internet literacy") can be defined as "the ability to properly use and evaluate digital resources, tools and services, and apply it to lifelong learning processes" (Gilster, 1997, p. 220). It has often been assumed that younger students will be naturally proficient in digital literacy skills because they have spent their entire lives surrounded by and immersed within technology and the Internet (Seely-Brown, 2008). Known as *digital natives* (i.e., students typically born after 1980), they have been reported to have an innate confidence and proficiency using new technology such as the Internet and mobile technologies (Prensky, 2001a, 2001b; Selwyn, 2009). Some researchers argue that this access to technology has created a generation of students who learn differently from past generations that did not grow up with the same technology (Selwyn, 2009). Assumptions about the proficiencies of digital natives (e.g., that that they are better at multitasking, more open to collaboration, have a greater working memory capacity, and are more proficient active learners as compared to students of previous generations) are often forwarded but still lack in evidence (Selwyn, 2009). Adults born before 1980, who spent some of their lives in a predigital world, are seen as needing to adapt to the online world and therefore less fluent or capable with technology than digital natives (Prensky, 2005; Long, 2005). Many argue that the differences between digital natives and older adults are so great that educational practices need to be changed drastically to accommodate the learning styles of the newer generation (Prensky, 2001a).

Despite these arguments, others have argued that there is a lack of empirical evidence that such large-scale changes to our educational practices are needed (Bennett, Maton, & Kervin, 2008). One reason why changes may not be warranted is because students typically do not engage with the Internet and digital media in learning environments like schools or online learning platforms in the same way that they do at home (McWilliam, 2002; Selwyn, 2009). Surveys indicate that, at home, students typically use technology for video-gaming, texting, and viewing online content (e.g., videos and images), rather than for learning or information gathering (Livingstone, 2009). Furthermore, students' proficiency with technology has also been strongly linked to individual differences in gender, socioeconomic status, geography, and home technology access (Golding, 2000; Kennedy, Krause, Judd, Churchward, & Gray, 2008); therefore, treating all students as if they are naturally digitally literate could leave many low-access students at a disadvantage. As an example, Nasah et al. (2010) found that age, gender, and socioeconomic status together accounted for 30% of the variance in digital proficiency scores, while age alone accounted for only 15% of the variance. This finding indicates that age is clearly not the sole factor determining digital literacy.

From a literacy perspective, there is considerable evidence that today's students struggle with using the Internet to find, understand, and integrate information into their writing (Bennett et al., 2008; Coiro, Knobel, Lankshear, & Liu, 2008; Nasah et al., 2010; Selwyn, 2009; Greene, Yu, & Copeland, 2014). In addition, students are highly susceptible to accepting misinformation found online (Eysenbach, Powell, Kuss, & Sa, 2002; Greene et al., 2014). Thus, researchers in digital literacy have focused efforts on identifying the complex set of cognitive and affective processes common in receiving and using computer-based, multimodal information (Goldman et al., 2010; Mayer, 2005; Schnotz, 2005; Sweller, 2005).

This work has resulted in the identification of basic cognitive principles that likely guide learning in multimedia contexts (Mayer, 2005). For instance, Mayer's (2005) cognitive theory of multimedia learning describes the dual channel whereby humans have two separate channels for processing incoming information: one for information presented visually (e.g., pictures, animations, video, on-screen text) and one for information presented auditorily (e.g., narration, background noise). While information may initially be processed through one channel, it can also be converted for processing in the other channel. For example, an image displayed on a screen may be processed visually at first but then mentally converted into words. Alternatively, the narration of a story may be processed first as auditory input but then used to form mental images that are processed in the visual channel. Of course, there is a limit to how much information a person can process at one time, and students can easily become overwhelmed by the amount of information available to them on the Internet. Thus, when students actively engage in cognitive processes such as attending to and organizing incoming information (the active processing assumption), they need to be taught strategies that will help them engage with the abundance of information that they are exposed to online. For example, researchers have found that instructing students on how to critically select and evaluate sources leads to better outcomes on source-based writing tasks (Coiro, Coscarelli, Maykel, & Forzani, 2015; Cho & Afflerbach, 2017; Bråten, Brante, & Strømsø, 2019).

Overall, digital literacy in an educational setting thus involves both searching for information (i.e., using a Google search to find primary source articles) as well as integrating that information and keeping track of progress to the learning goal (Bråten, Britt, Strømsø, & Rouet, 2011). To be successful in this, students must be able to self-regulate their learning and have strong epistemic cognition skills (i.e., be able to monitor their own beliefs and skills related to the learning process). The Internet and digital tools have the potential to greatly enhance educational outcomes, especially in students' reading comprehension and writing skills. With the proper guidance and instruction on how to find, evaluate, and use information, students can gain the digital literacy skills necessary to succeed not only in the classroom but also in an increasingly digitized world (Castek, Gwinn, Dagen, & Bean, 2020).

Evaluating Sources during Writing and Reading

Given the importance of assessing the reliability of source information for documents on the Internet, research has placed substantial emphasis on students' ability to engage in sourcing behavior (Braasch et al., 2018). One of the major changes to reading and writing tasks in the age of the Internet is how writers search for and analyze sources (Cho, Afflerbauch, & Han, 2018). Cho et al. (2018) proposed that when conducting an inquiry task (i.e., reading multiple sources with the goal of answering a question or forming an argument/opinion), the reader must not only construct a mental model of the ideas in a single source or text (i.e., a situation model) and the ideas across multiple texts (i.e., an intertextual model), but they must also create a "reading path" model of the series of steps that the reader takes while gathering information in an online space.

The New Literacies Framework (Kinzer & Leu, 2017; Leu, Kinzer, Coiro, Castek, & Henry, 2013) provides a model of a typical online inquiry task. The first step in this framework is for the student to identify a specific question or problem that they need to address, such as a classroom assignment that asks a student to write an essay about the causes of global warming. In the second step, the student locates sources and gathers information that might help address the question or problem (e.g., developing a set of search terms or scanning information from various websites). In the third step, the reader engages in *sourcing*—in other words, they evaluate which information is reliable using relevant information. Finally, the fourth step involves synthesizing the information that they have found in a coherent way (Leu et al., 2013).

The ever-growing quantity of sources available on the Internet and the speed at which they can be accessed make the process of accurate online information gathering especially difficult. A simple Internet search can return thousands of sources, substantially more than a learner needs for a task or even has the ability to process (Eliopoulos & Gotlieb, 2003; Braasch et al., 2009). If a student lacks the strategies necessary to select and evaluate sources, they are likely to become overwhelmed and experience cognitive overload (Brandt, 1997; Graesser et al., 2007; Nachmais & Gilad, 2002). Therefore, to make sense of a diverse array of sources (that may or may not contain conflicting information), students need the skills to organize, evaluate, compare–contrast, and integrate information from multiple sources (Britt & Rouet, 2012; Goldman, Lawless, & Manning, 2013). However, many studies have shown that students often have difficulty in these types of online tasks, particularly in monitoring and regulating the search process (Kuiper, Volman, & Terwel, 2005; Zhang & Quintana, 2012), engaging critically with the material (Coiro et al., 2015; Stanford History Education Group, 2016), and making connections across sources (Barzilai & Zohar, 2012). Evidence shows that students tend to assume that information on the Internet is correct, but that with the proper instruction they can conduct inquiry tasks more critically (Kuiper et al., 2005; Walraven, Grand-Bruwel, & Boshuizen, 2008).

Gathering information from multiple sources online requires the learner to engage in *sourcing*. Sourcing refers to the evaluation of source information such as reliability, the author's credentials, the type of publication (e.g., a peer-reviewed journal article vs. an opinion piece), or the date of publication (Bråten, Strømsø, & Britt, 2009; Britt & Aglinskas, 2002; Rouet & Britt, 2011; Wiley et al., 2009; Wineburg, 1991). Despite the importance of sourcing to online multiple source comprehension, research suggests that students are not often sensitive to source information under natural reading circumstances (Britt & Aglinskas, 2002; Claassen, 2012; Wineburg, 1991). Additionally, multiple source comprehension often requires readers to navigate through multilevel text structures. Online sources often include hyperlinks (i.e., built-in links to other sources), and this structure can cause additional confusion or frustration among learners (Cho & Afflerbach, 2017).

Braasch et al. (2009) conducted a study to investigate students' sourcing abilities and strategies. They looked specifically at middle school students' evaluations of source quality and usefulness. Students were presented with sources that varied based on their usefulness and were asked to rate the sources' usefulness based on the title, author, venue, type/date of publication, and a short summary of the text. The students who did a better job at differentiating useful sources from less useful ones tended to rely more on content indicators such as the title and summary. Students who did a poorer job of differentiating tended to rely more on surface indicators such as the author and venue of publication. Similar research has shown that inexperienced readers tend to focus on surface-level source information that is found easily (such as the Web address or copyright date; e.g., Coiro et al., 2015). Experienced readers consider more source markers (such as the author and text content) and are more likely to actively seek out more information to determine if a source is reliable.

Similarly, Goldman et al. (2012) collected readers' self-explanations as they navigated a researcher-generated search engine containing multiple websites. They found that more skilled readers were more likely to make judgments about the quality, reliability, and usefulness of a source, while poorer readers were less likely to make these types of judgments and more likely to easily accept what they had read as accurate. In addition, better learners spent more time on reliable sites, while poorer learners spent more time on unreliable sites.

Sourcing Strategies and Interventions

Because of the large volume of sources that an online search can produce, students need to develop skills that allow them to critically evaluate the results of their searches and pick out the most relevant sources (Coiro, 2005; Kuiper et al., 2005; Leu, 2002; Zhang, Duke, & Jiménez, 2011). Interventions to increase students' reading comprehension typically focus on increasing their attention to source information through source evaluation training (Bråten et al., 2019). Bråten et al. (2019) conducted a study on a 6-week intervention that focused on teaching students how to critically select, evaluate, and use multiple sources to complete a writing task. Students in the intervention group spent more time during the selection process justifying their sources. They also spent more time reading their sources and included more mentions of source features in their final writing products. The authors note that this intervention was particularly successful because it focused on sourcing not simply for selecting texts to read, but also to help guide writing and understanding of the topic. The intervention was also integrated into a traditional classroom experience such that the writing task the students completed had an impact on their grades in the class, which is believed to increase motivation (Paul, Macedo-Rouet, Rouet, & Stadtler, 2017).

One potential method of instruction could involve teachers giving students sources that vary widely in their relevance and trustworthiness and asking students to practice evaluating their usefulness as they would in a traditional search process (McCrudden, Stenseth, Bråten, & Strømsø, 2016). Practice doing this would increase students' metacognitive skills and help them develop the skills necessary to perform good searches. McCrudden et al. (2016) found that, when students were evaluating sources for task relevance, they tended to disregard important source information when the topic was more familiar to them. This may require that instructors give more explicit instruction about evaluating source features, especially for topics with which the students feel familiar.

Goldman et al. (2012) used a self-explanation paradigm to explore how readers make judgments about the quality and reliability of sources. Self-explanation involves explaining aspects of the text to yourself while reading as well as monitoring your level of understanding (McNamara, 2004). Self-explanation can be a useful tool in understanding how readers are selecting sources and evaluating them. Instructing students to engage in self-explanation while they conduct a search task can help the instructor understand what approaches the student is currently using in order to tailor further instruction. Self-explanation, when used in conjunction with comprehension monitoring, may also help the student become more self-aware of their search process, which evidence suggests improves reading comprehension (Griffin, Wiley, & Thiede, 2008; McNamara & Magliano, 2009).

Directing students' attention to source information and guiding their evaluations of it are crucial to improving their sourcing skills. One way this can be done is by providing students with questions that they can use to guide their source evaluation while reading. Some important questions for students to ask themselves while sourcing include: "What do I want to get out of this source?" "Is the information in this source useful?" "How would I use this information to complete my task?" "What should I read first, next, and then . . . ?" (Cho & Afflerbach, 2017). In an investigation of how instructors can encourage students to practice good evaluation during an online inquiry task, Coiro et al. (2015) identified five main techniques: (1) encourage students to use information about the author and their affiliations when determining source trustworthiness, (2) explicitly instruct students on how to describe and elaborate on the author's level of expertise, (3) help students understand how the author's point of view (e.g., their personal biases or motive) influences the information they present, (4) model how students should approach dealing with conflicting sources, and (5) show students how to use multiple indicators when judging the reliability of sources.

Peer Collaboration in Online Inquiry

Another major change to the reading and writing landscape in the Internet age has been the emergence of online inquiry as a social process. The Internet allows for more direct collaboration between learners and writers with the advent of tools that allow multiple people to create, share, and edit documents across multiple devices simultaneously. Access to these types of tools in the Internet age has turned online inquiry and generative projects like writing into more of a social practice, rather than an individual one (Kiili, Laurinen, Marttunen, & Leu, 2012; Leu et al., 2013; Graham, 2021). Many workspaces require high levels of collaboration on reading and writing tasks, and therefore it is important that students learn not only how to use digital tools effectively but also how to use them in collaboration with others.

Laal and Laal (2012) describe collaborative learning as "an educational approach to teaching and learning that involves groups of learners working together to solve a problem, complete a task, or create a project" (p. 491). Peer collaboration has been shown to increase students' understanding of a topic and help them work through the challenges of online inquiry tasks (Duschl & Osborne, 2002; Liu & Hmelo-Silver, 2010). Previous research suggests that students who do online reading tasks in pairs learn and use more strategies than those who work independently and have better comprehension outcomes (Foster, 2009; Coiro, Castek, & Guzniczak, 2011).

Peer collaboration can also cause additional challenges due to the social nature of the task (Chung, Lee, & Liu, 2013; Kreijns, Kirschner, & Jochems, 2003). In an investigation of collaborative essay writing with 16- to 18-year-old students, Kiili et al. (2012) found a variety of different dyad styles varying in their level of active collaboration and communication. They determined that many students showed a preference for working individually and that those who were more individually oriented spent only 7–8% of their work time actively working together with their partner. Other groups spent up to 83% of their time actively working together. This drastic difference in styles indicates that simply asking students to work in pairs is not enough for them to collaborate productively; some students may need more instruction and guidance. Furthermore, the teachers in this study reported that, in general, students' essays were better when they worked collaboratively rather than individually.

There are generally two approaches students use during collaborative Web inquiry tasks. The first is a shared approach in which each student shares one computer (this could be on a single device or via screen sharing across multiple devices), while the second is a parallel approach where each student has their own computer. There is some evidence that students who work on their own computers in a group task are typically unaware of what their fellow students are doing, and this lack of group awareness can be detrimental to collaborative learning (Liu & Kao, 2007). However, some research has indicated that students who use a shared approach tend to engage in more information exchange, which can lead to better group communication (Chung et al., 2013).

Research has demonstrated that during group projects certain forms of communication improve collaboration. Evidence shows that engaging in active discussion and asking questions can help foster positive interactions during collaborative reading (Mercer & Littleton, 2007; King, 2007; Volet, Summers, & Thurman, 2009). King and Rosenshine (1993) investigated an intervention in which they trained pairs of students to ask elaborative questions (e.g., "Why is _____ important?" "What would happen if _____?")

during a collaborative task. Students trained on this type of communication performed better on all measures of comprehension compared to control pairs that were given no guidance. This suggests that giving students guiding questions can help improve communication during collaborative work.

Digital Technologies for Literacy Instruction

Throughout this chapter, we have focused on digital literacy and how our notions of literacy have changed in the Internet age. As a final point, we want to briefly discuss one additional way in which literacy education has been altered in the digital age—that is, the development of educational technologies for reading and writing (Crossley & McNamara, 2016). Given the increasing importance of reading and writing skills, a number of technologies have been developed to provide students with personalized instruction, practice, and feedback on literacy skills. Importantly, these systems are not intended to replace teachers; rather, they are designed to provide supplementary instruction and opportunities for deliberate practice. As such, many of these technologies are adaptive; they model students' strengths and weaknesses over time and adapt instruction and practice based on students' greatest needs (Chryasfiadi & Virvou, 2013; Woolf, 2009).

For example, iSTART (Levinstein, Boonthum, Pillarisetti, Bell, & McNamara, 2007; McNamara, Levinstein, & Boonthum, 2004) is an intelligent tutoring system (ITS) that was developed to help high school, college, and adult literacy students learn about and receive targeted practice with comprehension strategies. Specifically, iSTART includes ways for students to learn about how to effectively self-explain while learning from text using comprehension strategies: comprehension monitoring, paraphrasing, prediction, bridging, and elaboration. The system provides short lessons on how to use the strategies as well as game-based practice to engage with these strategies in a more targeted way (Jackson & McNamara, 2013). Students' use of these strategies has been linked to their enhanced comprehension of expository texts. iSTART has been shown to improve the quality of students' self-explanations, as well as their comprehension of the texts themselves (Magliano et al., 2005; McCarthy, Kopp, Allen, & McNamara, 2018; McNamara et al., 2007). These benefits have been shown to be particularly beneficial for low-knowledge and less skilled readers.

iSTART provides an example of an educational technology that targets traditional reading skills. More recently, educational technologies have begun to incorporate features that can better address some of the issues most relevant to digital literacy. For example, Peerceptiv (formally known as SWoRD; Cho & Schunn, 2007; Patchan, Schunn, & Clark, 2018) is an online peer-reviewing system that is used by students in high schools and colleges throughout the world. This system allows students to engage in iterative writing and revision processes based on feedback from their peers. Specifically, students write essays in response to assignments from their teachers; their essays are then randomly and anonymously assigned to multiple peer reviewers who can then provide formative and summative feedback on these essays. The feedback rubrics include analytic rating forms as well as options for providing open-ended comments and feedback. By assigning multiple students to serve as peer reviewers, the system can provide the student writers with a more reliable assessment of their performance based on the highest correlated peer ratings. Importantly, Peerceptiv and iSTART are only two examples of a number of educational technologies currently being developed to better aid students in their development of digital literacy skills. As technology continues to improve, these systems will likely become increasingly common in the literacy classroom.

Conclusion

In this chapter, we have described the ways that reading and writing have shifted in today's digital world. The emergence of the Internet and digital tools have shifted how we interact, learn, and communicate online, all of which have implications for the ways in which we teach literacy. When it comes to information gathering and processing, individuals now have access to a practically unlimited number of sources of information at the click of a button (Braasch et al., 2009). Despite the popular assumption that today's young students are naturally gifted at navigating the technological landscape, evidence shows that students still struggle to organize, evaluate, and integrate information from multiple online sources (Kuiper et al., 2005; Bennett et al., 2008; Zhang & Quintana, 2012; Barzilai & Zohar, 2012; Coiro et al., 2015; Stanford History Group, 2016). To be successful in online inquiry tasks, students need guidance in developing the skills to critically evaluate source information for accuracy, trustworthiness, and usefulness (Bråten et al., 2019).

Students would also benefit greatly from the development of social collaboration skills. With the Internet allowing for more direct forms of collaboration, online reading and writing tasks are becoming more social, both within a classroom setting and in the modern workspace (Kiili et al., 2012; Leu et al., 2013). Students of all ages need guidance in performing collaborative tasks effectively. Good collaboration involves active listening and engagement as well as asking elaborative questions to push inquiry further (King & Rosenshine, 1993; Chung et al., 2013).

The ever-changing digital landscape of reading and writing will continue to provide new challenges for educators who are dedicated to giving students the skills and strategies they need to succeed. However, it also provides many new opportunities for those who are willing to be flexible and open to technological advancement in the classroom.

Finally, we provide questions for educators to consider when dealing with issues surrounding reading and writing in the digital age. These include the following:

- How can the connections between reading and writing be leveraged to teach students about the importance of evaluating sources as they learn online?
- How do digital technologies shape how we conceptualize the reading and writing processes?
- What interventions should be implemented in the classroom to aid students in their development of digital literacy skills in the Internet age?

REFERENCES

Allen, L. K., Magliano, J. P., McCarthy, K. S., Sonia, A. N., Creer, S. D., & McNamara, D. S. (2021). Coherence-building in multiple document comprehension. *Proceedings of the Annual Meeting of The Cognitive Science Society, 43.* Retrieved from *https://escholarship.org/uc/item/4qs6j38d.*

Allen, L. K., Snow, E. L., Crossley, S. A., Jackson, G. T., & McNamara, D. S. (2014). Reading comprehension components and their relation to the writing process. *L'année Psychologique: Topics in Cognitive Psychology, 114,* 663–691.

Barzilai, S., & Zohar, A. (2012). Epistemic thinking in action: Evaluating and integrating online sources. *Cognition and Instruction, 30*(1), 39–85.

Bennett, S., Maton, K., & Kervin, L. (2008). The "digital natives" debate: A critical review of the evidence. *British Journal of Educational Technology, 39*(5), 775–786.

Braasch, J. L. G., Bråten, I., & McCrudden, M. T. (Eds.). (2018). *Handbook of multiple source use.* London: Routledge.

Braasch, J. L. G., Lawless, K. A., Goldman, S. R., Manning, F. H., Gomez, K. W., & Macleod, S. M. (2009). Evaluating search results: An empirical analysis of middle school students' use of source attributes to select useful sources. *Journal of Educational Computing Research, 41*(1), 63–82.

Brandt, S. D. (1997). Constructivism: Teaching for understanding on the Internet. *Communications of the ACM, 40*(10), 112–117.

Bråten, I., Brante, E. W., & Strømsø, H. I. (2019). Teaching sourcing in upper secondary school: A comprehensive sourcing intervention with follow-up data. *Reading Research Quarterly, 54*(4), 481–505.

Bråten, I., Britt, M. A., Strømsø, H. I., & Rouet, J.-F. (2011). The role of epistemic beliefs in the comprehension of multiple expository texts: Toward an integrated model. *Educational Psychologist, 46*(1), 48–70.

Bråten, I., Strømsø, H. I., & Britt, M. A. (2009). Trust matters: Examining the role of source evaluation in students' construction of meaning within and across multiple texts. *Reading Research Quarterly, 44*(1), 6–28.

Britt, M. A., & Aglinskas, C. (2002). Improving students' ability to identify and use source information. *Cognition and Instruction, 20*(4), 485–522.

Britt, M. A., & Rouet, J. F. (2012). Learning with multiple documents: Component skills and their acquisition. In M. J. Lawson & J. R. Kirby (Eds.), *Enhancing the quality of learning: Dispositions, instruction, and learning processes* (pp. 276–314). New York: Cambridge University Press.

Castek, J., Gwinn, C. B., Dagen, A. S., & Bean, R. M. (2020). Literacy and leadership in the digital age. In A. S. Dagen & R. M. Bean (Eds.), *Best practices of literacy leaders: Keys to school improvement* (2nd ed., pp. 258–278). New York: Guilford Press.

Cho, B.-Y., & Afflerbach, P. (2017). An evolving perspective of constructively responsive reading comprehension strategies in multilayered digital text environments. In S. E. Israel (Ed.), *Handbook of research on reading comprehension* (2nd ed., pp. 109–134). New York: Guilford Press.

Cho, B.-Y., Afflerbauch, P., & Han, H. (2018). Strategic processing in accessing, comprehending, and using multiple sources online. In J. L. G. Braasch, I. Bråten, & M. T. McCrudden (Eds.), *Handbook of multiple source use* (pp. 133–150). New York: Routledge.

Cho, K., & Schunn, C. D. (2007). Scaffolded writing and rewriting in the discipline: A web-based reciprocal peer review system. *Computers and Education, 48*(3), 409–426.

Chryasfiadi, K., & Virvou, M. (2013). Student modeling approaches: A literature review for the last decade. *Expert Systems with Applications, 40*(11), 4715–4729.

Chung, C.-W., Lee, C.-C., & Liu, C.-C. (2013). Investigating face-to-face peer interaction patterns in a collaborative Web discovery task: The benefits of a shared display. *Journal of Computer Assisted Learning, 29*(2), 188–206.

Claassen, E. (2012). *Author representation in literary reading.* Amsterdam: John Benjamins.

Coiro, J. (2005). Making sense of online text. *Educational Leadership, 63*(2), 30–35.

Coiro, J., Castek, J., & Guzniczak, L. (2011). Uncovering online reading comprehension processes: Two adolescents reading independently and collaboratively on the internet. In R. Jimenez, V. Risko, M. Hundley, & D. W. Rowe (Eds.), *Sixtieth yearbook of the Literacy Research Association* (pp. 354–369). Oak Creek, WI: National Reading Conference.

Coiro, J., Coscarelli, C., Maykel, C., & Forzani, E. (2015). Investigating criteria that seventh graders use to evaluate the quality of online information. *Journal of Adolescent & Adult Literacy, 59*(3), 287–297.

Coiro, J., Knobel, M., Lankshear, C., & Leu, D. J. (Eds.). (2008). *Handbook of research on new literacies.* Mahwah, NJ: Erlbaum.

Crossley, S. A., & McNamara, D. S. (Eds.). (2016). *Adaptive educational technologies for literacy instruction.* New York: Taylor & Francis, Routledge.

Duschl, R. A., & Osborne, J. (2002). Supporting and promoting argumentation discourse in science education. *Studies in Science Education, 38*(1), 39–72.

Eliopoulos, D., & Gotlieb, C. (2003). Evaluating web search results rankings. *Online, 27*(2), 42–48.

Eysenbach, G., Powell, J., Kuss, O., & Sa, E. R. (2002). Empirical studies assessing the quality of health information for consumers on the World Wide Web: A systematic review. *Journal of the American Medical Association, 20*, 2691–2700.

Foster, J. (2009). Understanding interaction in information seeking and use as a discourse: A dialogic approach. *Journal of Documentation, 65*(1), 83–105.

Gilster, P. (1997). *Digital literacy.* Hoboken, NJ: Wiley.

Golding, P. (2000). Forthcoming features: Information and communications technologies and the sociology of the future. *Sociology, 34*(1), 165–184.

Goldman, S. R., Braasch, J. L. G., Wiley, J., Graesser, A. C., & Brodowinska, K. (2012). Comprehending and learning from internet sources: Processing patterns of better and poorer learners. *Reading Research Quarterly, 47*(4), 356–381.

Goldman, S. R., Lawless, K. A., Gomez, K. W., Braasch, J. L., McLeod, S., & Manning, F. (2010). Literacy in the digital world: Comprehending and learning from multiple sources. In M. G. McKeown & L. Kucan (Eds.), *Bringing reading research to life* (pp. 257–284). New York: Guilford Press.

Goldman, S. R., Lawless, K., & Manning, F. (2013). Research and development of multiple source comprehension assessment. In M. A. Britt, S. R. Goldman, & J. F. Rouet (Eds.), *Reading from words to multiple texts* (pp. 180–199). New York: Routledge.

Graesser, A. C., Wiley, J., Goldman, S. R., O'Reilly, T., Jeon, M., & McDaniel, B. (2007). SEEK Web Tutor: Fostering a critical stance while exploring the causes of volcanic eruption. *Metacognition and Learning, 2*, 89–105.

Graham, S. (2021). A walk through the landscape of writing: Insights from a program of writing research. *Educational Psychologist* (online).

Greene, J. A., Yu, S. B., & Copeland, D. Z. (2014). Measuring critical components of digital literacy and their relationships with learning. *Computers & Education, 76*, 55–69.

Griffin, T. D., Wiley, J., & Thiede, K. W. (2008). Individual differences, rereading, and self-explanation: Concurrent processing and cue validity as constraints on metacomprehension accuracy. *Memory & Cognition, 36*(1), 93–103.

Jackson, G. T., & McNamara, D. S. (2013). Motivation and performance in a game-based intelligent tutoring system. *Journal of Educational Psychology, 105*(4), 1036–1049.

Kennedy, G., Krause, K.-L., Judd, T., Churchward, A., & Gray, K. (2008). First year students' experiences with technology: Are they really digital natives? *Australasian Journal of Educational Technology, 24*(1), 108–122.

Kiili, C., Laurinen, L., Marttunen, M., & Leu, D. J. (2012). Working on understanding during collaborative online reading. *Journal of Literacy Research, 44*(4), 448–483.

King, A. (2007). Beyond literal comprehension: A strategy to promote deep understanding of text. In D. S. McNamara (Ed.), *Reading comprehension strategies: Theories, interventions and technologies* (pp. 267–290). Mahwah, NJ: Erlbaum.

King, A., & Rosenshine, B. (1993). Effects of guided cooperative questioning on children's knowledge construction. *The Journal of Experimental Education, 61*(2), 127–148.

Kinzer, C. K., & Leu, D. J. (2017). New literacies and new literacies within changing digital environments. In M. A. Peters (Ed.), *Encyclopedia of educational philosophy and theory* (pp. 20–31). New York: Springer.

Kreijns, K., Kirschner, P. A., & Jochems, W. (2003). Identifying the pitfalls for social interaction in computer-supported collaborative learning environments: A review of the research. *Computers in Human Behavior, 19*(3), 335–353.

Kuiper, E., Volman, M., & Terwel, J. (2005). The web as an information resource in K–12 education: Strategies for supporting students in searching and processing information. *Review of Educational Research, 75*(3), 285–328.

Laal, M., & Laal, M. (2012). Collaborative learning: What is it? *Procedia—Social and Behavioral Sciences, 31*, 491–495.

Leu, D. J. (2002). The new literacies: Research on reading instruction with the internet. In A. E. Farstrup & S. J. Samuels (Eds.), *What research has to say about reading instruction* (3rd ed., pp. 310–336). Newark, DE: International Reading Association.

Leu, D. J., Kinzer, C., Coiro, J., Castek, J., & Henry, L. (2013). New literacies: A dual-level theory of the changing nature of literacy, instruction, and assessment. In N. Unrau (Ed.), *Theoretical models and processes of reading* (6th ed., pp. 1150–1181). Newark, DE: International Reading Association.

Levinstein, I. B., Boonthum, C., Pillarisetti, S. P., Bell, C., McNamara, D. S. (2007). iSTART 2: Improvements for efficiency and effectiveness. *Behavior Research Methods, 39*, 224–232.

Liu, C.-C., & Kao, L. C. (2007). Do mobile devices facilitate face-to-face collaboration? Mobile devices with large shared display groupware to facilitate group interactions. *Journal of Computer Assisted Learning, 23*, 285–299.

Liu, L., & Hmelo-Silver, C. E. (2010). Conceptual representation embodied in hypermedia: An approach to promoting knowledge co-construction. In M. S. Khine & I. M. Saleh (Eds.), *New science of learning: Cognition, computers and collaboration in education* (pp. 341–356). New York: Springer.

Livingstone, S. (2009). *Children and the internet.* Cambridge, UK: Polity.

Long, S. (2005). Digital natives: If you aren't one, get to know one. *New Library World, 106*(3/4), 187–189.

Magliano, J. P., Todaro, S., Millis, K., Wiemer-Hastings, K., Kim, H. J., & McNamara, D. S. (2005). Changes in reading strategies as a function of reading training: A comparison of live and computerized training. *Journal of Educational Computing Research, 32*(2), 185–208.

Mayer, R. E. (2005). Cognitive theory of multimedia learning. In R. E. Mayer (Ed.), *The Cambridge handbook of multimedia learning* (pp. 31–48). New York: Cambridge University Press.

McCarthy, K. S., Kopp, K. K., Allen, L. K., & McNamara, D. S. (2018). Methods of studying text: Memory, comprehension, and learning. In H. Otani & B. L. Schwartz (Eds.), *Handbook of research methods in human memory* (pp. 104–124). New York: Routledge.

McCrudden, M. T., Stenseth, T., Bråten, I., & Strømsø, H. I. (2016). The effects of topic familiarity, author expertise, and content relevance on Norwegian students' document selection: A mixed methods study. *Journal of Educational Psychology, 108*(2), 147–162.

McNamara, D. S. (2004). SERT: Self-explanation reading training. *Discourses Processes, 38*, 1–30.

McNamara, D. S., Boonthum, C., Levinstein, I., & Millis, K. (2007). Evaluating self-explanations in iSTART: Comparing word-based and LSA algorithms. In T. K. Landauer, D. S. McNamara, S. Dennis, & W. Kintsch (Eds.), *Handbook of latent semantic analysis* (pp. 227–241). Mahwah, NJ: Erlbaum.

McNamara, D. S., Levinstein, I. B., & Boonthum, C. (2004). iSTART: Interactive strategy training for active reading and thinking. *Behavior Research Methods, Instruments, & Computers, 36*, 222–233.

McNamara, D. S., & Magliano, J. P. (2009). Self-explanation and metacognition: The dynamics of reading. In J. D. Hacker, J. Dunlosky, & A. C. Graesser (Eds.), *Handbook of metacognition in education* (pp. 60–81). New York: Routledge.

McWilliam, E. L. (2002). Against professional development. *Educational Philosophy and Theory, 34*(3), 289–300.

Mercer, N., & Littleton, K. (2007). *Dialogue and the development of children's thinking: A sociocultural approach.* New York: Routledge.

Nachmais, R., & Gilad, A. (2002). Needle in a hyperstack: Searching for information on the World Wide Web. *Journal of Research on Technology in Education, 34*, 475–486.

Nasah, A., DaCosta, B., Kinsell, C., & Seok, S. (2010). The digital literacy debate: An investigation of digital propensity and information and communication technology. *Education Technology Research Development, 58*, 531–555.

Patchan, M. M., Schunn, C. D., & Clark, R. J. (2018). Accountability in peer assessment: Examining the effects of reviewing grades on peer ratings and peer feedback. *Studies in Higher Education, 43*(12), 2263–2278.

Paul, J., Macedo-Rouet, M., Rouet, J.-F., & Stadtler, M. (2017). Why attend to source information when reading online? The perspective of ninth grade students from two different countries. *Computers & Education, 113*, 339–354.

Prenksy, M. (2001a). Digital natives, digital immigrants. *On the Horizon, 9*(5), 1–6.

Prenksy, M. (2001b). Digital natives, digital immigrants, part II. Do they really think differently? *On the Horizon, 9*(6), 1–6.

Prensky, M. (2005). Listen to the natives. *Educational Leadership, 63*(4), 8–13.

Rouet, J. F., & Britt, M. A. (2011). Relevance processes in multiple document comprehension. In M. T. McCrudden, J. P. Magliano, & G. Schraw (Eds.), *Text relevance and learning from text* (pp. 19–52). Charlotte, NC: Information Age.

Schnotz, W. (2005). An integrated model of text and picture comprehension. In R. Mayer (Ed.), *The Cambridge handbook of multimedia learning* (pp. 49–70). New York: Cambridge University Press.

Seely-Brown, J. (2008). Foreword. In T. Iiyoshi & M. Kumar (Eds.), *Opening up education*. Cambridge, MA: MIT Press.

Selwyn, N. (2009). The digital native—Myth and reality. *Aslib Proceedings, 16*(4), 364–379.

Shanahan, T. (1988). The reading–writing relationship: Seven instructional principles. *The Reading Teacher, 41*(7), 636–647.

Stanford History Education Group. (2016). *Evaluating information: The cornerstone of civic online reasoning*. Retrieved from *https://sheg.stanford.edu/upload/V3LessonPlans/Executive%20Summary%2011.21.16.pdf*.

Sweller, J. (2005). Implications of cognitive load theory for multimedia learning. In R. Mayer (Ed.), *The Cambridge handbook of multimedia learning* (pp. 19–30). New York: Cambridge University Press.

Volet, S., Summers, M., & Thurman, J. (2009). High-level co-regulation in collaborative learning: How does it emerge and how is it sustained? *Learning and Instruction, 19*(2), 128–143.

Walraven, A., Brand-Gruwel, S., & Boshuizen, H. P. A. (2008). Information-problem solving: A review of problems students encounter and instructional solutions. *Computers in Human Behavior, 24*(3), 623–648.

Wiley, J., Goldman, S. R., Graesser, A. C., Sanchez, C. A., Ash, I. K., & Hemmerich, J. A. (2009). Source evaluation, comprehension, and learning in internet science inquiry tasks. *American Educational Research Journal, 46*(4), 1060–1106.

Wineburg, S. S. (1991). Historical problem solving: A study of the cognitive processes used in the evaluation of documentary and pictorial evidence. *Journal of Educational Psychology, 83*(1), 73–87.

Woolf, B. P. (2009). *Building intelligent tutors, student-centered strategies for revolutionizing e-learning*. New York: Elsevier.

Zhang, M., & Quintana, C. (2012). Scaffolding strategies for supporting middle school students' online inquiry processes. *Computers & Education, 58*(1), 181–196.

Zhang, S., Duke, N. K., & Jiménez, L. M. (2011). The WWWDOT approach to improving students' critical evaluation of websites. *The Reading Teacher, 65*(2), 150–158.

PART III

WRITING AND READING
CONNECTIONS IN THE
CONTENT AREAS

CHAPTER 10

Integrating Writing and Reading Instruction in the English Language Arts Classroom

Carol Booth Olson
Jenell Krishnan
Huy Q. Chung

Why Connect Writing and Reading in the English Language Arts Classroom?

Reading and writing traditionally have been thought of and taught as flip sides of a coin—as opposites; "Readers decode or decipher language and writers encoded or produced written text" (Tompkins, Guo, & Justice, 2013, p. 46). However, researchers increasingly have noted the connections between reading and writing, identifying them as complementary processes of meaning construction (Tierney & Pearson, 1983) and have conceptualized the shared knowledge for reading and writing as "two buckets drawing water from a common well" (Graham et al., 2016, p. 32; see also Chapter 1, this volume). According to Fitzgerald and Shanahan (2000), readers and writers share four basic types of knowledge: metaknowledge about the processes of reading and writing; domain knowledge that the reader or writer brings to the text; knowledge about text attributes; and procedural knowledge to negotiate reading and writing. It is precisely because reading and writing access similar cognitive strategies, but to differing degrees, that reading and writing make such a powerful combination when taught in connection with each other. Research suggests that using writing as a learning tool during reading instruction leads to better reading outcomes (Graham & Hebert, 2010). Conversely, using reading as a learning tool for elaborating on ideas leads to better writing outcomes (Tierney & Shanahan, 1991). When students are offered opportunities to practice the cognitive strategies associated with reading and writing, they learn critical thinking skills, as research suggests (Tierney, Soter, O'Flahavan, & McGinley, 1989).

Foundational theoretical models of the reading–writing connection (Berninger & Fayol, 2010; Fitzgerald & Shanahan, 2000) offer helpful lenses for ways that reading and writing instruction can be combined to support students' development. As students become experienced readers, their skills for noticing elements of texts go beyond mere content. They may notice text structures, variations in syntax, and track ideas or themes throughout a text. Reading experience helps readers to develop metacognitive skills needed to understand a writer's intentions. In the classroom, students also engage in writing to promote their retention of information, assess their understanding of new ideas (Graham & Harris, 2006), and communicate for a variety of purposes (Graham et al., 2016). To write effectively, a writer must consider the comprehension needs of their audience.

Despite the clear connection between reading and writing, conversations in research communities often take place in silos. Prominent organizations like the International Society for Reading and the International Literacy Association tend to primarily focus on the study of reading. Other groups, like the National Council of Teachers of English and the National Writing Project, tend to focus more on writing. We assert that stakeholders need to dismantle such silos in favor of interconnected research to improve reading and writing instruction.

Although silos still exist, some researchers have focused on promoting synergy between reading and writing instruction. For instance, in the 2017 What Works Clearinghouse Practice Guide entitled *Teaching Secondary Students to Write Effectively*, a panel of literacy experts offered three evidence-based recommendations for supporting secondary reading and writing development. The panel writes,

> Combining reading and writing together in an activity or assignment helps students learn about important text features. For example, asking students to summarize a text they just read signals that well-written texts have a set of main points, that students should understand main points while they read, and that when students write certain types of compositions they should focus on main points. Reading exemplar texts familiarizes students with important features of writing, which they can then emulate. (p. 31)

In what follows, we unpack the complexities of integrating reading and writing instruction while weaving in teacher vignettes and examples of classroom practices. Readers can also consider these guiding questions as we explain the relationship between the two.

GUIDING QUESTIONS

- How can we motivate students to write about their reading?
- How can we encourage students to read and write about their own and their peers' writing?

- How can we teach students to synthesize multiple texts?
- How can teachers connect reading and writing across the disciplines?
- How do we go beyond standards-based information to promote students' lifelong literacy learning?

How Can We Motivate Students to Write about Their Reading?

The development of strategic reading and writing is linked to motivation (Paris, Wasik, & Turner, 1991). Furthermore, there is a strong correlation between a student's motivation and the degree to which the student (1) expects to perform successfully if they try reasonably hard, and (2) value the available rewards for success (Good & Brophy, 1997). In other words, reading and writing are affective *and* cognitive. In *Readicide* (2009), Kelly Gallagher remarks that "valuable classroom time presents the best opportunity—often the only opportunity—to turn kids on to reading" (p. 2). One way to connect reading and writing and to motivate students to become readers is to invite them to write about their reading. In fact, research indicates that writing about reading improves reading achievement. Research also indicates that strategy instruction is an especially effective way to connect reading and writing (Olson et al., 2015). One vehicle for engaging students in writing about their reading is to use cognitive strategy bookmarks that include sentence stems that expose students to the cognitive strategies experienced readers and writers use when they construct meaning from and with text. The practice of reading and annotating with bookmarks enhances students' critical thinking, promotes self-confidence, and increases their motivation.

Cognitive Strategy Bookmarks

Prior to introducing students to the cognitive strategy bookmarks, the teacher will need to introduce the concept of a cognitive strategy. To make this accessible, the teacher might say:

> We are going to learn about what experienced readers and writers do when they make meaning out of words. They use something called cognitive strategies. "Cognitive" means thinking and "strategies" are tools people use to solve a problem. So, a cognitive strategy is a thinking tool. Inside your head, you have a lot of cognitive strategies or thinking tools that you use to make sense of what you read and write. It's almost like there's a little voice inside your head that talks to you while you're reading and writing. It tells you when you're confused or when you understand something. It helps you to make pictures in your head or to decide to reread something before going forward. (Olson, 2011, p. 22)

The teacher can then pass out the bookmarks in Figure 10.1 for students to use while annotating a text. Note that the sentence starters such as "At first I thought _____, but now I" or "This is relevant to my life because _____" give students a point of departure and invite them to expand on their thinking.

For students in grades 3–4, these bookmarks might be too sophisticated. Look how third-grade teacher Emily McCourtney has adapted these book-marks. McCourtney uses seven steps to introduce cognitive strategy use:

1. Introduce strategies (videos)
2. Model strategies with a read-aloud weekly in class

Cognitive Strategies Sentence Starters

Planning and Goal Setting
★ My purpose is …
★ My top priority is …
★ I will accomplish my goal by …

Tapping Prior Knowledge
★ I already know that …
★ This reminds me of …
★ This relates to …

Asking Questions
★ I wonder why …
★ What if …
★ How come …

Making Predictions
★ I'll bet that …
★ I think …
★ If _____, then …

Visualizing
★ I can picture …
★ In my mind I see …
★ If this were a movie …

Making Connections
★ This reminds me of …
★ I experienced this once when …
★ I can relate to this because …

Summarizing
★ The basic gist is …
★ The key information is …
★ In a nutshell, this says that …

Adopting an Alignment
★ The character I most identify with is…
★ I really got into the story when …
★ I can relate to this author because…

Cognitive Strategies Sentence Starters

Forming Interpretations
★ What this means to me is …
★ I think this represents …
★ The idea I'm getting is …

Monitoring
★ I got lost here because …
★ I need to reread the part where …
★ I know I'm on the right track because …

Clarifying
★ To understand better, I need to know more about …
★ Something that is still not clear is …
★ I'm guessing that this means _____, but I need to …

Revising Meaning
★ At first I thought _____, but now I …
★ My latest thought about this is …
★ I'm getting a different picture here because…

Analyzing the Author's Craft
★ A golden line for me is …
★ This word/phrase stands out for me because…
★ I like how the author uses _____ to show …

Reflecting and Relating
★ So, the big idea is …
★ The conclusion I'm drawing is …
★ This is relevant to my life because ….

Evaluating
★ I like/don't like _____ because …
★ My opinion is _____ because …
★ The most important message is _____ because …

FIGURE 10.1. Cognitive strategies bookmark with sentence starters.

3. Introduce using sticky notes to track thinking
4. Students use sticky notes to share thinking on Padlet (weekly)
5. Introduce reading response slides
6. Model slides with read-aloud
7. Students complete slides weekly, set goals and reflect monthly.

After introducing the strategies in Steps 1 and 2, McCourtney shows students how to monitor their thinking processes with sticky notes that include the cognitive strategies. In a mini-lesson, she says, "Readers think a lot while they are reading to make sense of the text. We can use sticky notes, to keep track of those thoughts." Next, she models her own strategy use with sticky notes, and then practices with her class, each week focusing on a new group of the strategies until they've learned them all. Using sticky notes becomes a weekly assignment for students.

Reflecting on the Meaning-Making Process

After practicing the skill of identifying parts of the text that make them stop and think, students are ready to go deeper into explaining their thinking. The next step is to use reading response slides that are similar to the cognitive strategy bookmarks. To help scaffold students' learning, the slides have guiding questions:

- What did you notice? What made you stop and think? (Evidence)
- What strategy did you use? What did it make you stop and think about? (Explain)
- What does that part mean? How does it help you better understand the text? (Interpret/Explain)
- Why is that important to the text? Why did the author include it? (Evaluate)

Figure 10.2a demonstrates Jackson's sticky note for predicting the plot of this last book in the Trapped in a Video Game series. Figure 10.2b illustrates Jackson's process of explaining the thinking behind his sticky note.

Book Clubs

Another way to connect reading and writing, and promote cognitive strategy use is to engage students in reading, discussing, and writing about self-selected fiction and nonfiction material in book clubs. To deepen their understanding of texts, researcher Stephen Krashen (1993) identifies voluntary reading as "one of the most powerful tools" in English language arts (ELA) instruction. He writes:

When children read for pleasure, when they get "hooked on books," they acquire, involuntarily and without conscious effort, nearly all of the so-called "language

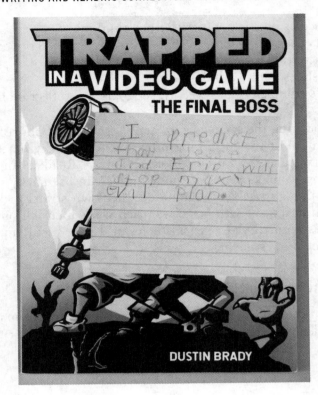

FIGURE 10.2A. Jackson's use of the cognitive strategy of predicting on a sticky note.

skills" many people are so concerned about. They will become adequate readers, acquire a large vocabulary, develop a good writing style, and become good (but not necessarily perfect) spellers. (p. 84)

Engaged readers thrive when a classroom is book-rich. Launching successful book clubs means offering an assortment of texts. In fact, the tangible presence of books in the classroom "is a significant factor in literacy development" (Gambrell, 1996, p. 3). Additionally, students are more motivated to read when they are invited to choose the titles they want to read, and they tend to like books that provide familiar characters, settings, and story lines. Self-selected texts should be at each student's independent reading level and, therefore, span a wide grade of grade levels. Thus, it is important to engage in classroom library audits to ensure that students have access to texts that represent them. Most importantly, students who interact with each other and engage in frequent discussions have higher reading achievement than students who do not interact with others about their reading (Mullis, Campbell, & Farstrup, 1993). A key to this interaction is to have students write and share letters about the fiction and nonfiction texts they are reading to share their experiences and interpretations.

In his seventh-grade classroom, Joey Nargizian was teaching the young adult novel *Freak the Mighty* by Rodman Philbrick. During their reading, the class focused on characterization and the concept of static and dynamic

Name:	Jackson
Date:	1/22/21
Title:	Trapped in a Video Game Robots Revolt
Author:	Justin Brady
Genre:	Fiction

-Cognitive Strategies-

PK TAP PRIOR KNOWLEDGE: I already know that... *because...*

? QUESTION: I wonder... *because...* (Who/what/Where/When/Why)

P PREDICT: I think... will happen *because...*

V VISUALIZE: The text says... which makes me picture... *because...*

CO MAKE A CONNECTION: ... reminds me of... *because...* (text-to-self, text-to-world, text-to-text)

S SUMMARIZE: The important information from this part is... *because...*

AA ADOPT AN ALIGNMENT: I can identify with... *because...*

I INFER: The text says... I know that means... *because...*

RM REVISE MEANING: At first I thought... but now I think... *because...*

AC ANALYZE AUTHOR'S CRAFT: I like the way the author... *because...*

RR REFLECT & RELATE: This is important to me *because...*

E EVALUATE: I think that... is good/ bad *because...*

FI FORM AN INTERPRETATION: To me, this means... *because...*

M MONITOR: I had to reread... *because...*

C CLARIFY: I'm confused about... *because...*

Reminders:

☐ Rate your effort: ☆ ☆ ☆ ☆

Do you have multiple sentences?

strategy

P **Page:** 122 **Paragraph:** 2nd

What did you notice? What made you stop and think? (Evidence)

I noticed in the text that Jesse, Mark and Sam are on a hovercraft as their escape vehicle to get away from a robot dragon. It made me wonder how they are going to use the hovercraft to escape.

What strategy did you use? What did it make you think? Explain.

I used the strategy make a prediction. It made me think that they would be able to use the hovercraft to escape. It made me think that they would be able to escape using the hovercraft because it was rocket powered. I predicted that they would be able to get away from the robot dragon because the hovercraft is super fast.

What does that part mean? How does it help you understand the text?

This part of the story means that they had to be brave because they had to escape from the robot dragon and they had to get out of there fast on the hovercraft. It helped me understand the text better by showing that one of the main themes of the book is that the characters have to be brave and work together to solve problems.

Why is that important to the text? Why did the author include it?

It is important to the text because it shows how dangerous the robots are and how they need to work together to escape them. The author included it because it is an important part of the video game they are trying to escape from.

FIGURE 10.2B. Jackson's reading response reflection.

characters. Nargizian began by focusing on how we, as readers, learn about characters (what they say, do, think, and feel, and what others say about them). After reviewing this, the students examined the evolution of the main charac-ter, Max, and how he evolves over time because of his association with Freak. To do this, students constructed a character evolution timeline and wrote a "lit letter." A character evolution timeline enables a reader to review the sequence of events in a text and to plot it out graphically.

For their timelines, Nargizian's students draw lines longways down a piece of construction paper. For each of their six data points, he asked that students include one symbol to represent Max at that time point, one piece of evidence that revealed an aspect of his character, and an explanation of the symbol and piece of evidence. By completing the six data points, students were: (1) reviewing the novel; (2) culling what they believed to be strong pieces of evidence/important quotes from important scenes; and (3) provid-ing their analysis and understanding of characterization. In terms of cogni-tive strategy instruction, this exercise promotes analyzing author's craft and forming interpretations. See Figure 10.3 for a student's sample of Max's char-acter evolution timeline.

To adapt to the circumstances created by COVID-19, ninth-grade teacher Marianne Stewart derived an adaptation of book clubs by creating virtual book clubs. She writes,

> During this pandemic it has been difficult to ask students to spend more time in front of a screen. Not only are students suffering from "Zoom Fatigue" but many are living through circumstances where they, or family members are sick. And the administration is begging teachers to reduce assignments. Out of those ashes, this idea was born. #BooksAsOutfits keeps a focus on literacy. An actual happy buzz took over the chat while we went over the instructions.

Stewart cultivated the cognitive strategy of visualizing through virtual book clubs with the #BooksAsOutfits activity. After reviewing Molly Bang's *Picture This*, students created an outfit based on a favorite book. They analyzed color symbolism as well as moods created by colors, for example. Then, students created criteria for the assignment and met in weekly, 50-minute book clubs to share their work. Figure 10.4 includes a sample BookAsOutfits and paragraph explanation (contains unedited student work).

Think-Alouds

While book clubs enable students to connect reading and writing and par-ticipate in cognitive strategy use in small groups, the think-aloud strategy is usually demonstrated by the teacher before students practice it independently. According to Kucan and Beck (1997), as a mode of instruction, "thinking aloud was first employed by teachers who modeled their processing during reading, making overt the strategies they were using to comprehend text. Subsequently, instructional approaches were developed to engage the students themselves in

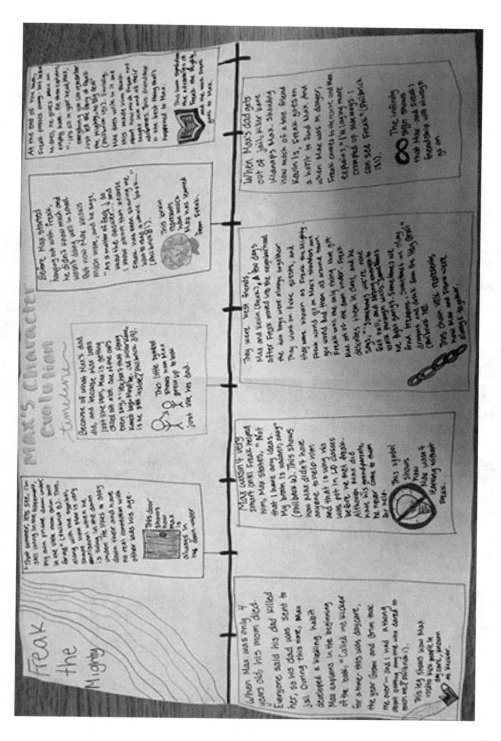

FIGURE 10.3. Max's character evolution timeline.

I wanted to portray the innocent, kind, quiet, teen that reflects off one of the main character that is featured in both the film and novel of "The Help". With the light airy color pallet of pastel pink, yellow, and white; I was able to set a calming tone that not only gives the character an intelligent bookworm persona, but a sense of independence as her connection with nature takes away all her worries. Her world somewhat became her outlet.

Elements of photography:

Using both side and low angles along with the zoom focuses of the props reveals the soft vulnerable mood that the model is creating; verses if the shot was taken from the front thus creating a strong upfront and forward feeling of the characters personality.

FIGURE 10.4. Sample BookAsOutfits submission.

thinking aloud" (p. 1). This line of investigation in reading is paralleled by the use of think-aloud protocols in writing (Flower & Hayes, 1981).

In his book *Improving Comprehension with Think-Aloud Strategies*, Jeff Wilhelm (2001) describes the following procedure for implementing think-alouds in the classroom:

- **Step 1:** Choose an interesting text excerpt that could present some difficulty to students if read independently.
- **Step 2:** Decide on a few strategies to highlight and explain to students what a think-aloud is, why you are modeling, and how these strategies will be helpful to them.
- **Step 3:** State your purpose for reading the excerpt and ask students to pay attention to the strategies you select so they can explain what, why, how, and when you used them.
- **Step 4:** Read the text aloud to students and think aloud as you do so.
- **Step 5:** Have students underline the words and phrases that helped you use a strategy.
- **Step 6:** Ask them to make a list of the strategies you used and the verbal cues that prompted strategy use.

For example, consider the following opening passage from Leonard Pitts's article "Sometimes the Earth is Cruel":

Sometimes, the earth is cruel. That is ultimately the fundamental lesson here, as children wail, families sleep out of doors, and the dead lie unclaimed in the rubble that once was Port-au-Prince, Haiti. Sometimes the rains fall and will not stop. Sometimes the skies turn barren and will not rain. Sometimes the seas rise and smack the shoreline like a fist. Sometimes the wind bullies the land. And sometimes, the land rattles and heaves and splits itself in two. Sometimes, the earth is cruel.

After reading this passage, the teacher might say the following and then model annotating the passage:

Teacher's Think-Aloud

"From reading the passage, I know the article is about Haiti and I have some prior knowledge that there was an earthquake there. When the author talks about children wailing, it reminds me of watching the TV coverage of the disaster. So, I remember that and can make a personal connection. I can really visualize how destructive the earthquake was because of the concrete details the author uses to describe the devastation in the capital city, Port-au-Prince. The author says the earth is cruel, so he's giving it personal emotions. That's called personification. For instance, he says, 'the wind bullies the land,' turning the wind into an enemy and the land into a victim. When he says that 'the seas rise and smack the shoreline like a fist,' I feel like the earth is beating up Haiti. I can really picture the fist and feel the punch because of the simile 'like a fist.' The way the author crafts his language is very powerful. He also repeats the word *sometimes* over and over, and it gives me the feeling that one disaster after another strikes Haiti. I'll bet that the lesson that Pitts refers to will have more to it than just that nature is cruel. But I'll have to keep reading to learn more."

As the teacher thinks aloud, they can annotate the text using the sentence starters such as "I already know that," "I can picture," "I'll bet that," "The idea I'm getting is," and so forth. The annotations can also be labeled with abbreviations such as TPK (tapping prior knowledge) and MC (making connections).

How Can We Encourage Students to Read and Write about Their Own and Their Peers' Writing?

In his recent conceptual writer(s)-within-community model of writing, Graham (2018) reminds us that writing is a social practice. This view of writing is reflected in documents promoting both contemporary learning goals (Battelle for Kids, 2019) and college and career readiness skills (National Governors Association Center for Best Practices & Council of Chief State School Officers [NGA & CCSSO], 2010). Additionally, the What Works Clearinghouse Practice Guide *Teaching Secondary Students to Write Effectively* (2017) notes: "Peer feedback provides a level of support similar to teacher feedback, but it also teaches students how to read a peer's writing and provide meaningful and constructive feedback" (p. 52).

Beyond the theoretical and conceptual reasons for supporting students' reading and writing of their own and their peers' writing, research has shown that it benefits students in a variety of ways. De Smedt, Graham, and Van Keer (2020) found that young students' descriptive writing improved with the support of peer assistance in an explicit writing instruction program. We now focus on responding to this question, "How can we encourage students to read and write about their own and their peers' writing?"

As teachers are considering how to acknowledge and honor the Black Lives Matter (BLM) movement and incorporate anti-racist pedagogy into their classroom, ninth-grade teacher Marianne Stewart thought of Atticus Finch's famous quote "You never really understand a person until you consider things from his point of view. Until you climb inside of his skin and walk around in it." Still, she was uncomfortable with the idea of teaching *To Kill a Mockingbird*. She writes:

> I had a difficult time deciding if I should ask students to read *To Kill a Mockingbird* because it is considered a "white savior text" and it being yet another book in the syllabus that focuses on the struggles of Black Americans over their accomplishments and joy. On the other hand, the book is part of the curriculum at my school—and because the movement to diversify curriculum is still in its starting stages, I didn't want my students to feel excluded from conversations about the

book. So I joined the "Disrupt Texts" movement and carefully layered multiple texts from a variety of points of view. I also thought this activity in experiencing multiple perspectives would be a good opportunity to have my students give and require peer feedback.

The prompt for Stewart's assignment was as follows:

To Kill a Mockingbird: Unheard Voices Project

"In *To Kill a Mockingbird*, Scout, a young White girl, tells the story—but what if we could see the events that take place in Maycomb County from a different point of view? What could we learn from a character with a different perspective? Choose a character from *To Kill a Mockingbird*. Select *one significant event* in the novel to rewrite from that character's point of view. Weave together events from the novel with fictional techniques consistent with the style in the novel and use your best speculative and reflective thinking to bring their point of view to life.

"The most effective papers will:

- Highlight an event that is clearly significant for the character.
- Capture the event as if Harper Lee wrote it, use first-person point of view, and a narrative/descriptive style similar to the author's.
- Weave accurate events derived from the novel together with sensory/ descriptive details about setting, characterization, and plot.
- Reveal the person's thoughts and feelings through such techniques as dialogue; interior monologue; use of showing, not telling description; use of symbolism and other fictional/cinematic techniques, such as flashback.
- Document two or more places in the novel you used for reference in an annotated bibliography."

Stewart scaffolded the steps in writing this narrative account, including helping students select one character whose unheard voice they would like to explore, listing three important events in the novel they would like to write up from that person's point of view, and determining why the event was significant. Then, students created a five senses' cluster to experience what their character saw, felt, heard, smelled, and tasted. With this information, they created a storyboard for their scene. At the draft stage, students completed an unheard voices feedback request form, thinking deeply about what they had written and producing questions for their peers to answer. Each peer in their writing group then read their request and provided feedback. In her unheard voices piece, Pritha aligned with Boo Radley and, in his voice, illustrated his thoughts and feelings as he watched Scout and Jem find the objects he left for them in the tree's knothole. She wanted her group to react to whether she had adequately captured Boo's thoughts. Figure 10.5 features Pritha's feedback request form (contains unedited student work).

Stewart noted that because Pritha and her peers actually requested the

Unheard Voices FEEDBACK REQUEST

In a sentence or two, explain what you were trying to do in your piece.	In a few sentences, describe your character and what you most want your readers to know about him or her.
I was trying to describe what we as readers' think Boo Radley thought about when Scout and Jem found objects in the knot hole of the tree.	Boo or Arthur Radley is a minor character of the story and the author Harper Lee leaves us reader' feeling suspenseful. My goal was to give readers an insight into what I assume occurs in Boo's mind.
How do you want your readers to feel when they read your piece? Or, what do you want your readers to know?	What did this event or experience mean to you?
I want my readers to know that Boo has a unique mind of his own, and that you can never underestimate a character in a book	This experience to me, makes me feel proud of myself because my writing might be displayed as an example.

CRITERIA FOR SUCCESS

As you write your questions, consider:
★ Your writing goals, or
★ The strategy or form you were trying out!

Write two questions below to elicit feedback from your group.
Did I provide good examples of quotations?
Did I create adequate information about Boo Radley's thoughts?

FIGURE 10.5. Pritha's feedback request form.

feedback they most wanted to receive, their peers gave them focused responses that were useful in helping them revise their pieces, rather than simplistic comments like "It was good" or "I liked it." Reading the request form of each group member also enabled students to experience multiple perspectives as well as provide feedback to multiple peers.

How Can We Teach Students to Synthesize Multiple Texts?

The ability to synthesize multiple texts is an important skill for everyone, both for learning in secondary schools, civic engagement, and postsecondary success (see also Chapters 8 and 16, this volume). The importance of this skill is reflected in learning standards across the disciplines. For ELA, students must be able to "synthesize multiple sources on the subject, demonstrating understanding of the subject under investigation" (NGA & CCSSO, 2010). For history and social studies courses, the History Social Science Framework suggests that students' engagement in fruitful academic conversations requires that they "analyze and synthesize a multitude of ideas in various domains" (California Department of Education, 2013, p. 26). In classrooms that engage in the science and engineering practices outlined by the Next Generation Science Standards (NGSS), students must "gather, read, and synthesize information from multiple appropriate sources and assess the credibility, accuracy, and possible bias of each publication" (NGSS, 2013). Thus, synthesizing multiple sources is a valuable skill across disciplines, and this skill has been noted as particularly important for postsecondary success. For instance, the *Framework for Success in Postsecondary Writing* (Council of Writing Program Administrators [CWPA], National Council of Teachers of English [NCTE], and National Writing Project [NWP], 2011) indicates that teachers can help their students develop critical thinking through reading, writing, and research instruction. When compared to other types of writing tasks, writing about multiple texts is particularly complex. For example, writing a summary of one text can be accomplished by adopting the same organizational structure that the focal text used; however, synthesizing several texts requires a sophisticated integration of ideas (Segev-Miller, 2004). Synthesizing texts, despite its value for forming connections between texts (Barzilai, Zohar, & Mor-Hagani, 2018), is less frequently taught to students in secondary schools. So, we ask, "How can we teach students to synthesize multiple texts?"

When tasked with synthesizing multiple texts, students are especially challenged by how to integrate source material. For example, in a recent on-demand writing assessment in a large urban district, students were asked to read "Malala the Powerful" by Kristen Lewis (2012) and "What Is a Role Model: Five Qualities That Matter to Teens" by Dr. Marilyn Price-Mitchell (access at *www.rootsofaction.com/role-model*). Then they were given a prompt asking them to draw from Price-Mitchell's article and select one quality of a role model that was most essential in enabling Malala to successfully promote her mission of obtaining an equitable education for all children. Although over 1,000 grade 7–12 students took this assessment, few cited the "What is a Role Model" source in their essays. One way to teach students to synthesize and incorporate multiple texts in an essay is to teach the concept of *authorizing*. Authorizing is one of the four academic moves writers make ("Harris Moves")—authorizing, illustrating, expanding, and countering—featured in Joseph Harris's book *Rewriting: How to Do Things with Text* (2006). When students authorize, they cite the source and then acknowledge the credibility of the source or author's credentials. Teaching authorizing also involves teaching appositives, as in the following example:

According to _____ [name], _____ [appositive, their credentials], "_____" [quote]
According to Marilyn Price-Mitchell, a developmental psychologist and author of "What Is a Role Model?: Five Qualities That Matter to Teens," a role model is someone who can inspire others to "achieve their potential in life."

After students have become familiar with using the following sentence stems, they can be given alternative phrases for "According to," such as:

In the words of _____ [appositive—credentials], _____ [name], "_____"

As _____ [name], _____ [appositive—credentials], suggests, "_____"

As reported by _____ [name], _____ [appositive—credentials], "_____"

Once students have internalized this concept and learned how to include it in their essays, they are much better able to synthesize multiple sources and use one text to support claims about another, as in the following example:

> "Let us pick up on our books and our pens. They are our most powerful weapons. One child, one teacher, one book, and one pen can change the world."
>
> These words, spoken by Malala Yousafzai in a speech to the United Nations, and reported by Kristen Lewis in her article "Malala the Powerful," highlight the power of education to defeat oppressive regimes who subjugate people, deny them certain rights, silence them, and rule them through brutality. At the age of fifteen, Malala risked her life to speak out against the Taliban when they banned girls over the age of eight from obtaining an education. In doing so, she became a role model, not only for Pakistani girls but also for children and adults around the world who value education and understand its power to transform the world. According to Dr. Marilyn Price-Mitchell, a developmental psychologist and author of "What is a Role Model? Five Qualities That Matter to Teens," a role model is someone who can inspire others to achieve their potential in life. She identifies a number of qualities exhibited by role models that are especially influential. Chief among these, and most essential to Malala's incredible impact, is the ability to overcome obstacles. Her steadfast determination and resilience in confronting and overcoming challenges to obtaining an education have been an inspiration to all.

How Can Teachers Connect Reading and Writing across the Disciplines?

Step onto a high school campus and take a walk down the corridors. As you peek into each classroom, you might see an art teacher engaging students in analyzing images and the application of *chiaroscuro*, or a physics teacher using mirrors and a laser beam to demonstrate how light travels a path, or an ELA teacher describing the symbolism of fire and light in ancient Greek mythology vis-à-vis Prometheus. However, as students transition from one period to the next, are students finding connections across the disciplines as they read texts and write texts? In the same way that reading and writing have been disconnected, the disciplines at the secondary level are in silos (Kilgore & Reynolds, 2010) and collaboration across departments is lacking. How much more powerful would it be if there was a synergy across content areas in what and how students are learning, especially when similar topics cut across them? As the Common Core State Standards remind us, all teachers have a "shared responsibility for students' literacy development" (NGA & CCSSO, 2010, p. 4). If content-area teachers promote reading and writing across the disciplines, this practice will allow students to not only "transfer" learning from one subject to the next, they will also be able to compare and contrast the discipline-specific literacy practices that surface as they engage in comprehending and interpreting texts (Ippolito, Lawrence, & Zaller, 2013; see also Chapters 6, 11, and 15, this volume).

An example of a project that incorporates the combination of ELA's expository skills with social studies or science is called "The Six Things You Should Know About. . . . " It is inspired by ESPN magazine's column with the same name that gives six quick and interesting facts about a sports-related topic. Kelly Gallagher, in his book *In the Best Interest of Students* (2015a), asks students to use this as a model to write about a variety of topics. In Figure 10.6, Mary Widtmann asks her fifth-grade students to use this activity as a way to complete a graphic report about a historical figure or event from the Revolutionary War. They choose a famous person, battle, or event to research and write six interesting facts about their chosen subject and then create an infographic in Google Slides. This can also be used for a variety of other forms of writing. For example, they could use it for character analysis, to summarize a unit in science, or even as a community builder during the beginning of the school year. Students who engage in this activity tap into a number of Common Core–based standards and depth-of-knowledge skills as they *research*, *summarize*, *synthesize*, and *create* such reports.

Widtmann's "The Six Things You Should Know About" activity could be one entry in a multigenre paper. Tom Romano, author of *Blending Genre, Altering Style: Writing Multigenre Papers* (2000), encourages teachers to engage students in inquiry beyond the traditional research paper. Students will still focus on a topic of sustained inquiry, but the demonstration of the learning occurs in the form of a portfolio that includes a variety of different genres through mini-lessons around mentor texts, such as a recipe, lab report, or obituary. Students still include a brief traditional essay in their multigenre paper, but the additional pieces (a diary entry, "Where I'm From Poem . . . ," marriage license) they choose to incorporate and practice with allow them to experiment with writing in different genres while learning about new content, such as the causes of the Revolutionary War in history or how the Mars Rover operates in science.

The identification of different genres of writing and their core components is also fundamental to employing Gretchen Bernabei's kernel essay structures (Bernabei & Reimer, 2013). By discovering the logic and patterns of thought behind different genres of writing, Bernabei creates writing prompts that help structure writing pieces for a variety of disciplines. For example, she identified the underlying text structure and writing moves the Council members of the Indians of the Six Nations used in their response letter to the College of William and Mary inviting them to send their sons to be educated at the college. The Council wrote a reply that recognized the good in their invitation but declined the offer. From this text, Bernabei was able to create a kernel text structure that she transforms into an emulation assignment she calls the "unsent thank-you message." In five kernels or steps, writers draft a thank-you letter that follows this structure:

6 Things You Should Know About The Boston Tea Party

By: Lindsey

1. Taxation Without Representation: Britain was in huge debt after the war causing the British parliament to tax many essential products the colonists used. The stamp act of 1765 taxed every printed piece of paper, this included things like business cards and even legal documents. Then came the Townshend Act of 1767, which taxed products like paint, and tea. The colonists thought the British parliament's taxation was unfair and decided to take action.

2. Boycott the British: The colonists wanted to resist Britain's taxation policies. The men knew they needed the support of women. The political leaders asked the women to stop buying British products. These women became known as the Daughters of Liberty. They organized boycotts and began making their own clothes. They also stopped drinking and purchasing British Tea.

3. Boston Tea Party: In protest of the British Parliament's Tea Act of 1773, Massachusetts colonists disguised themselves as the Mohawks and boarded three British ships that carried tea. After boarding, they dumped about 342 chests of tea into the Boston Harbor. This is known as the Boston Tea Party.

4. After the Party: After the Tea Party, the Coercive Acts, later known as the Intolerable Acts of 1774, were passed. These Acts were meant to punish the Massachusetts colonists. The Acts closed Boston Harbor until the tea was paid for and revoked many of Massachusetts' freedoms. Britain hoped that by passing these acts, a rebellion would be avoided and that the colonists wouldn't come together. The opposite happened. The colonies came together and made a plan to resist Britain's tyranny.

5. The First Continental Congress: Many colonists thought that Britain's actions were unfair, so they decided to elect delegates from each colony to plan how they were going to resist the British policy. Delegates from each of the thirteen colonies, except Georgia, met. This was known as the very first Continental Congress.

6. First Shots Fired: The Revolutionary war began in 1775, when tension continued between Great Britain's 13 colonies. The first shots were fired in Lexington and Concord in April 1775. This led the rebels into a full war for their independence by the summer.

FIGURE 10.6. Lindsey's "6 Things You Should Know About the Boston Tea Party."

1. What the audience to whom you are writing has given to you
2. One way both the letter writer and recipient are alike
3. What the gift has done for the letter writer
4. So . . . thank you (or students have the option to say: "Thanks, but no thanks")
5. What the letter writer hopes to give to the recipient

Bernabei has found other effective text structures that, when broken down for writers, help motivate students. Even the most reluctant of writers can write sentences using this kernel outline, can combine these sentences into a paragraph, and can elaborate on each of these sentences creating multiple paragraphs, an art history critique, lab reports, or argumentative essays.

How Do We Go Beyond Standards-Based Instruction to Promote Students' Lifelong Literacy Learning?

At the beginning of this chapter, we mentioned that reading and writing are not just the result of cognitive skills, but there is also an affective component to be(come)ing readers and writers. According to the Common Core State Standards,

> Being able to read complex text independently and proficiently is essential for high achievement in college and the workplace and important in numerous life tasks. Moreover, current trends suggest that if students cannot read challenging texts with understanding—if they have not developed the skill, concentration, and stamina to read such texts—they will read less in general. (NGA & CCSSO, 2010)

Helping students to read complex texts independently and proficiently is one way teachers can support their students' lifelong literacy learning. Perhaps just as important, however, is the affective (the feeling) side of reading and writing. Research suggests that students need to have positive feelings about reading and writing to build a life of literacy. At times, the types of reading and writing that students enjoy and the types of reading and writing that students are asked to do in ELA classrooms do not intersect. This begs the question "How do we go beyond standards-based instruction to promote students' lifelong literacy learning?"

Because the National Assessment of Educational Progress (Rampey et al., 2009) proposed a distribution of communicative purposes by grade for their writing framework for the 2011 NAEP assessment, which shows a decreasing emphasis on narrative reading and writing as students progress up the grade levels, the Common Core State Standards tend to prioritize argumentative and informative reading and writing, minimizing the importance of narrative. However, we believe narrative texts are central to the development of reading and writing ability and should be given equal, if not more, weight than the other genres in ELA instruction. First of all, narrative reading and writing build on students' existing knowledge of genres and text structures, previous experience, and linguistic resources. All students have ideas for stories that they have gained through their own life experiences and are able to utilize their prior knowledge to understand and to develop narratives. As a number of researchers have pointed out, most students in the United States are already familiar with narratives when they arrive in kindergarten and are able to link real events to stories they have heard (Heath, 1986). By the time they reach adolescence, students have gained a variety of narrative skills from reading, from writing, and from oral discussions and storytelling both in school and in everyday communicative environments (Snow & Beals, 2006). Like monolingual English speakers, English learners are also highly familiar with narratives, since this text type is often presented to them through oral and written stories in their homes, schools, and communities (Schleppegrell, 2009).

Narrative reading and writing also play a pivotal role in building students' confidence. As Ann Mechem Ziergiebel (2013) points out, "Whether stories are read or written in school or out of school, students become engaged and motivated by just a turn of a phrase, a voice, an image, or a character, conflict, setting, or theme" (p. 140). Teenagers, especially, use narratives to explore their own identities, the way they see themselves. Consequently, they are highly motivated to read young adult literature and to write stories about their own lives. Narrative not only motivates students; it is the key to their progress in developing other types of writing, such as persuasive and report writing (Smith, Wilhelm, & Fredricksen, 2012). It helps students develop voice, audience awareness, organizational skills, and the ability to select and use specific concrete details, all of which are essential to reading and writing informative and argumentative texts.

Finally, reading and writing narrative texts benefit students both cognitively and affectively. When students read and write rich narrative texts, they develop a unique kind of thinking that Judith Langer (2013) terms "horizons of possibility thinking" in which the goal is to discover, imagine, gain perspective, ponder, and develop deep understanding. She contrasts this with the kind of "point of reference" thinking that is generated when one reads an expository text and the aim is to come away with specific knowledge about a topic. While both types of knowledge are necessary and useful, this more literary thinking "is an important cognitive piece in the development of deeper thinkers" (Gallagher, 2015, p. 102). Affectively, engaging with narrative texts builds students' capacity for empathy, develops their social skills, and enhances perspective taking. In fact, cognitive psychologist Keith Oatley (2011) points out that the "process of entering imagined worlds of fiction" while it might seem like a solitary act is actually "an exercise in human interaction" that can strengthen one's "social brain" (p. 1). To sum up, we agree with Kelly Gallagher (2015) that reading and writing narrative texts are " not a school skill, [they are] . . . a life skill, and as such, should be given greater, not less, emphasis" (p. 102).

Students need explicit instruction in the elements of narrative texts (Harris, Graham, & Mason, 2006). These elements are plot, setting, character, conflict/

resolution, and theme. Before asking students to create their own narratives, it may be helpful to first guide students in analyzing the model text they are reading. For example, to reinforce plot structure, teachers may want to engage students in creating a book wheel, a pedagogical teaching practice involving a visual that students can use to reconstruct the sequence of events in a narrative and to identify the plot's structural elements. To create a book wheel, students must review the story's plot, determining what key events represent the plot's structural elements and what visual might depict or symbolize each event. Then, students use a pattern to cut out two circles from pieces of card stock or construction paper. The bottom circle should be divided into sections like a pie, with a brief summary, pictures, and key quotes. After the bottom of the book wheel is completed, the students should cut a pie-shaped section out of the top circle to create a window through which one can see the lower circle. Both circles are then connected with a brad fastener. Once completed, students can use their book wheels to present a plot-based book talk to their peers.

Once students are comfortable with identifying the structural elements of plot in classroom literature, they can practice writing a fictional story of their own choosing. One stimulus for such a story is *The Mysteries of Harris Burdick* by Chris Van Allsburg (1996). The book consists of a series of provocative pictures, a title, and a single-sentence caption. For example, one of the pictures, titled "Under the Rug," depicts a frightened-looking man holding a chair above his head, about to strike a suspicious, moving lump rising up from beneath his carpet. At the bottom of the picture is the caption "Two weeks passed and it happened again." *The Mysteries of Harris Burdick* can be purchased in a portfolio edition, where each of the drawings is reproduced in separate poster-sized sheets. Teachers can post these around the room and students can participate in a gallery walk, taking notes and deciding which posters pique their interest. Working in groups, pairs, or independently, students can then create a Freytag pyramid (exposition, rising action, climax, falling action, resolution) to brainstorm the plot points and proceed to write their stories.

While reading and writing fictional narratives is a good way to learn the conventions of the genre, personal narratives are pivotal to creating lifelong learners. Kelly Gallagher and Penny Kittle (2018) like to quote Nobel Prize–winning author Doris Lessing who says, "The storyteller is deep inside everyone of us." They tell their students, "You have stories that no one can tell but you. You have ideas and experiences that can teach all of us" (p. 1). They explain that they want their students to use their ELA class as a place to imagine and create, not just to argue or relay information. Additionally, they suggest that narrative is the most appropriate genre to begin the school year with, as it is the genre most students are reading independently.

In her ninth-grade ELA classroom, Marianne Stewart developed a unit inspired by "The Great Thanksgiving Listen" by Storycorps. This project empowers students to connect with an elder during their break from school and record an interview. Stewart adapted the Storycorps idea into her own Stories Untold Gift Project. She had students select one story from their interview to preserve so that it could be presented back to the elder in a form appropriate to the story told (short story, letter, personal narrative, poem, children's book, digital story, short poem). This narrative would be a gift—not something written for a grade. Thus, Stewart linked it to a reading and analysis of "The Gift of the Magi" by O Henry. The students selected a family member or trusted adult to interview and spent time generating customized questions. After recording the interview, they listened to it, looking for gems or kernels to expand into their written "gift." They also recorded a short speech on flipgrid to explain their project to their peers. Stewart writes, "The presentation step is a big community builder and often leads to teary moments. One year we had so many students share parents immigrating from so many places we spontaneously created a world map marking all the places they or their parents had emigrated from." Figure 10.7 includes Myra's gift speech to share her tribute to her father with the class.

As Gholdy Muhammad reminds us in *Cultivating Genius* (2020),

Through the developmental years, young people are constantly understanding and (re)making a sense of positive self-hood. This is especially important for culturally and linguistically diverse youth who have a history of being negatively

---

1- Tell about the person you interviewed. Why you interviewed them, where and when.

For the Stories Untold Gift I interviewed my dad. I interviewed my dad for the thanksgiving project. I interviewed him at home on November 27, 2020.

2- Tell about an important message you learned from the interview OR share an important story you learned.

I learned about my dad's teenage years and how society impacted his life. I also learned that he was in a band. That surprised me. He would always make a beat by banging on the table and me and my sister would sing to it. I thought he just was really good at it but I found out that he was a drummer in a band. I think an important message I learned would be that time is precious. You should savor it as much as you can or you will lose those memories. Memories of your childhood.

3- Explain the gift you made. How does it relate to the interview? Why did you make it for that person? Why do you think they will like it?

The gift I made for my dad is a Band poster. It relates to my interview because I found out he was in a band. That really shocked me so I thought that it would be fun to make him a poster to remind him of those days. The days when he would go to a party and play an awesome rock and roll song with his band. Crowds cheering. I think he will like it because it will remind him of the days when he would play the drums.

FIGURE 10.7. Myra's gift speech tribute to her father.

represented and marginalized across large public platforms, including media and schools. To combat this, students need opportunities in class to make sense of their lives so that others cannot tell their stories. (p. 50)

In essence, then, narrative writing is a vehicle for student agency, identity development, and authority.

This chapter has been about connecting reading and writing, but the integration of reading and writing leads to many other important connections. In closing, we offer these three action questions:

- What plans can you make to connect cognition and affect to motivate students to become empowered readers and writers who can tell their own stories?
- Where in your curriculum can you connect research and pedagogy by teaching your students strategies they can apply independently to construct meaning from and with texts?
- How might you collaborate with teachers from other content areas to promote a shared responsibility for literacy across the curriculum and cultivate disciplinary literacy in students?

REFERENCES

Abbott, R. D., Berninger, V. W., & Fayol, M. (2010). Longitudinal relationships of levels of language in writing and between writing and reading in grades 1 to 7. *Journal of Educational Psychology, 102*(2), 281.

Barzilai, S., Zohar, A. R., & Mor-Hagani, S. (2018). Promoting integration of multiple texts: A review of instructional approaches and practices. *Educational Psychology Review, 30*(3), 973–999.

Battelle for Kids. (2019). *Framework for 21st century learning definitions*. Hilliard, OH: Partnership for 21st Century Learning.

Bernabei, G. & Reimer, J. (2013). *Fun-size academic writing for serious learning: 101 lessons & mentor texts—Narrative, opinion/argument, informative/explanatory, grades 4–9*. Dallas, TX: Corwin.

California Department of Education. (2013). *History social science framework for California public schools: Kindergarten through grade twelve*. Sacramento: California Department of Education.

Council of Writing Program Administrators, National Council of Teachers of English, and National Writing Project. (2011). *Framework for success in postsecondary writing*. Retrieved from *https://wpacouncil.org/aws/CWPA/asset_manager/get_file/350201?ver=7548*.

De Smedt, F., Graham, S., & Van Keer, H. (2020). "It takes two": The added value of structured peer-assisted writing in explicit writing instruction. *Contemporary Educational Psychology, 60*, Article 101835.

Fitzgerald, J., & Shanahan, T. (2000). Reading and writing relations and their development. *Educational Psychologist, 35*(1), 39–50.

Flower, L., & Hayes, J. R. (1981). A cognitive process theory of writing. *College Composition and Communication, 32*(4), 365–387.

Gallagher, K. (2009). *Readicide: How schools are killing reading and what you can do about it*. Portsmouth, NH: Stenhouse.

Gallagher, K. (2015). Where the Common Core writing standards fall short. In *In the best interest of students: Staying true to what works in the ELA classroom* (p. 102). Portsmouth, NH: Stenhouse.

Gallagher, K., & Kittle P. (2018). *180 Days: Two teachers and the quest to engage and empower adolescents*. Portsmouth, NH: Heinemann.

Gambrell, L. B. (1996). Creating classroom cultures that foster reading motivation. *Reading Teacher, 50,* 14–25.

Good, T. L., & Brophy, J. E. (1997). *Looking in classrooms* (7th ed.). New York: Longman.

Graham, S. (2018). A revised writer (s)-within-community model of writing. *Educational Psychologist, 53*(4), 258–279.

Graham, S., Bruch, J., Fitzgerald, J., Friedrich, L. D., Furgeson, J., Greene, K., . . . Smither Wulsin, C. (2016). *Teaching secondary students to write effectively.* Educator's Practice Guide (NCEE 2017–4002). Washington, DC: What Works Clearinghouse.

Graham, S., & Harris, K. R. (2006). Strategy instruction and the teaching of writing. *Handbook of Writing Research, 5,* 187–207.

Graham, S., & Hebert, M. (2010). *Writing to read: Evidence for how writing can improve reading.* New York: Carnegie Corporation.

Harris, J. (2006). *Rewriting: How to do things with texts*. Logan: Utah State University Press.

Harris, K. R., Graham, S., & Mason, L. H. (2006). Improving the writing, knowledge, and motivation of struggling young writers: Effects of self-regulated strategy development with and without peer support. *American Educational Research Journal, 43*(2), 295–340.

Heath, R. W. (1986). *Summary of program evaluation results: 1986–1986 school year pre-kindergarten educational program.* Washington, DC: Education Resources Information Center.

Kilgore, S. B., & Reynolds, K. J. (2010). *From silos to systems: Reframing schools for success.* Dallas, TX: Corwin.

Krashen, S. D. (1993). The case for free voluntary reading. *Canadian Modern Language Review, 50*(1), 72–82.

Kucan, L., & Beck, I. L. (1997). Thinking aloud and reading comprehension research: Inquiry, instruction, and social interaction. *Review of Educational Research, 67*(3), 271–299.

Langer, J. A. (2013). The role of literature and literary reasoning in English language arts and English classrooms. In K. S. Goodman, R. C. Calfee, & Y. M. Goodman (Eds.), *Whose knowledge counts in government literacy policies* (pp. 161–166). New York: Routledge.

Lewis, K. (2012). *Malala the powerful*. New York: Scholastic.

Muhammad, G. (2020). *Cultivating genius: An equity framework for culturally and historically responsive literacy.* New York: Scholastic.

Mullis, I., Campbell, J., & Farstrup, A. (1993). *NAEP 1992: Reading report card for the nation and the states.* Washington, DC: U.S. Department of Education.

National Governors Association Center for Best Practices & Council of Chief State School Officers. (2010). *Common Core State Standards*. Washington, DC: Authors.

Next Generation Science Standards. (2013). *Next generation science standards: For states, by states.* Washington, DC: The National Academies Press.

Oatley, K. (2011). In the minds of others. *Scientific American Mind, 22*(5), 62–67.

Olson, C. B. (2011). *The reading/writing connection: Strategies for teaching and learning in the secondary classroom* (3rd ed.). London: Pearson.

Olson, C. B., Scarcella, R., & Matuchniak, T. (2015). English learners, writing, and the Common Core. *The Elementary School Journal, 115*(4), 570–592.

Paris, S. G., Wasik, B. A., & Turner, J. C. (1991). The development of strategic readers. In R. Barr, M. Kamil, P. B. Mosenthal, & P. D. Pearson (Eds.), *Handbook of reading research* (Vol. II, pp. 609–640). New York: Longman.

Price-Mitchell, M. (2011). *What is a role model: Five qualities that matter to teens.* Retrieved from *www.rootsofaction.com/role-model.*

Rampey, B. D., Dion, G. S., & Donahue, P. L. (2009) *NAEP 2008 trends in academic progress* (NCES 2009–479). Washington, DC: National Center for Education Statistics, Institute of Education Sciences, U.S. Department of Education.

Romano, T. (2000). *Blending genre, altering style: Writing multigenre papers.* Portsmouth, NH: Boynton/Cook.

Schleppegrell, M. J. (2009). *Language in academic subject areas and classroom instruction: What is academic language and how can we teach it.* Paper presented at Workshop on the Role of Language in School Learning. National Academy of Sciences, Menlo Park, California.

Segev-Miller, R. (2004). Writing from sources: The effect of explicit instruction on college students' processes and products. *L1-Educational Studies in Language and Literature, 4*(1), 5–33.

Smith, M. W., Wilhelm, J. D., & Fredricksen, J. E. (2012). *Oh yeah?! Putting argument to work both in school and out.* Portsmouth, NH: Heinemann.

Snow, C. E., & Beals, D. E. (2006). Mealtime talk that supports literacy development. In R. W. Larson, A. R. Wiley, & K. R. Branscomb (Eds.), *Family mealtime as a context of development and socialization* (pp. 51–66). San Francisco: Jossey-Bass.

Tierney, R. J., & Pearson, P. D. (1983). Toward a composing model of reading. *Language Arts, 60*(5), 568–580.

Tierney, R. J., & Shanahan, T. (1991). *Research on the reading–writing relationship: Interactions, transactions, and outcomes.* Mahwah, NJ: Erlbaum.

Tierney, R. J., Soter, A., O'Flahavan, J. F., & McGinley, W. (1989). The effects of reading and writing upon thinking critically. *Reading Research Quarterly,* 134–173.

Tompkins, V., Guo, Y., & Justice, L. M. (2013). Inference generation, story comprehension, and language skills in the preschool years. *Reading and Writing, 26*(3), 403–429.

Van Allsburg, C. (1996). *The mysteries of Harris Burdick.* Boston: Houghton Mifflin Harcourt.

Wilhelm, J. D. (2001). *Improving comprehension with think-aloud strategies.* New York: Scholastic.

Ziergiebel, A. M. (2013). Digital literacy in practice: Achieving a cosmopolitan orientation. In J. Ippolito, J. F. Lawrence & C. Zaller (Eds.), *Adolescent literacy in the era of the Common Core: From research into practice* (pp. 131–142). Cambridge, MA: Harvard University Press.

CHAPTER 11

Writing, Reading, and Social Studies

Nell K. Duke
Anne-Lise Halvorsen
Abby Reisman

Why Connect Writing, Reading, and Social Studies?

Imagine a political scientist or geographer attempting to carry out their work without the ability to read and write proficiently. That this is so difficult to imagine is testament to the importance of reading and writing to professions that involve social studies (e.g., economists, historians, psychologists, archeologists). Reading and writing are also central to engaging in a variety of citizenship activities, such as community organizing, petitioning, voting, and jury duty.

The purpose of this chapter is to explain how writing, reading, and social studies can be addressed simultaneously, to the mutual benefit of each. Research finds that social studies education can support reading and writing development and that reading and writing development can support social studies learning. We offer examples of elementary and secondary classroom practices that support literacy and social studies and guidelines for lessons and units that integrate writing, reading, and social studies.

GUIDING QUESTIONS

- Why does social studies have a place in a book about writing and reading connections?
- What are some core disciplinary practices in social studies that we should prioritize in our teaching?
- How can you connect writing and reading within social studies lessons?

■ How can you connect reading and writing within social studies units?

■ How can you center justice and equity when connecting writing and reading with social studies in authentic ways?

The Importance of Social Studies

Reading and writing are important to social studies, and social studies is also important to reading and writing. Students need something to read and write *about*. Social studies can offer content that is engaging and culturally consequential for students. We have observed students fascinated as they read and write about ancient Egyptian society, appalled as they learn about the incarceration of Japanese Americans during World War II, and inspired as they write about activists in the Civil Rights Movement. Content knowledge students develop from social studies supports their reading and writing development. In addition, research has found that readers comprehend better when they have content and cultural knowledge relevant to the text (e.g., Hwang & Duke, 2020; Pritchard, 1990). Students who develop more knowledge in history, economics, geography, civics, and other social studies domains will have stronger reading comprehension of a range of texts. Similarly, writing is strengthened when we have knowledge of the topic or subject we're writing about. Thus, the relationship between social studies and literacy is bidirectional—reading and writing support social studies learning and practice; social studies knowledge and skills support literacy reading and writing.

Reading and writing aside, social studies education is crucial to society in its own right. The National Council for the Social Studies (NCSS, 1994) has defined social studies as follows:

> Social studies is the integrated study of the social sciences and humanities to promote civic competence. Within the school program, social studies provides coordinated, systematic study drawing upon such disciplines as anthropology, archaeology, economics, geography, history, law, philosophy, political science, psychology, religion, and sociology, as well as appropriate content from the humanities, mathematics, and natural sciences. The primary purpose of social studies is to help young people develop the ability to make informed and reasoned decisions for the public good as citizens of a culturally diverse, democratic society in an interdependent world.

Articulated in this way, it is difficult to deny the importance of social studies education. Yet, social studies is often marginalized in elementary education, particularly in the primary grades (e.g., Fitchett & Heafner, 2010). Although social studies is far better represented in middle and high school, educators in those settings speak to the long-term consequences of not having built a foundation—or a passion—for social studies in the elementary grades.

In the elementary grades, the abundance of curricular time devoted to reading and writing education outside of social studies (or science) is a major cause of inattention to social studies—the "curricular bully" if you will (Cervetti, Pearson, Bravo, & Barber, 2006). This is ironic given the interrelationship of reading, writing, and social studies described earlier. In any case, teachers and administrators can push back to provide greater attention to social studies. In the article "Outliers: Elementary Teachers Who Actually Teach Social Studies," Anderson (2014) identified teachers who, either on their own or prompted by school or district mandates, did devote a considerable amount of time to social studies education in the elementary grades.

Likely due to the influence of the *Common Core State Standards for English Language Arts and Literacy in History/Social Studies, Science, and the Technical Subjects* (ELA CCSS; National Governors Association Center for Best Practices [NGA] & Council of Chief State School Officers [CCSSO], 2010) and other English language arts (ELA) and literacy standards documents, as well as a growing recognition of the role of content knowledge in reading development, many published ELA curricula, as well as curricula developed by individual educators, have attempted to incorporate social studies into ELA instruction. However, in doing so, they often

- miss key disciplines within social studies (e.g., focusing on history but not economics);
- present inaccuracies or misconceptions via texts that have been vetted from an ELA and not a social studies perspective; and
- do not incorporate disciplinary practices that are central to social studies, such as inquiry and consideration of the source and context of text.

These phenomena would be less concerning if another part of the day was devoted to social studies education. However, as noted earlier, that is often not the case in the elementary years. In this chapter, we suggest that social studies should be at least a co-lead domain, if not the lead domain, in integrated reading, writing, and social studies curriculum. Social studies provides the domain or context, with reading and writing taught as tools in the service of social studies learning and communication. In the next section, we review research on social-studies-led education that integrates reading and writing. We then turn to specific classroom examples and to guidelines for designing your own lessons and units that integrate writing, reading, and social studies.

Scholarship on the Importance of Reading and Writing Connections for Social Studies

Social studies learning naturally engages students' reading, writing, listening, and speaking skills. For example, interpreting a historical document requires skills in close reading and citing textual evidence to analyze and draw inferences from the document. Evaluating a fiscal policy requires writing arguments to support claims with reasons and evidence. Standards state that reading and writing and social studies reinforce each other. The ELA CCSS cited in the previous paragraph have a specific strand for social studies beginning in the sixth grade and suggest the importance of social studies teachers integrating reading, writing, speaking, and listening when teaching content (NGA & CCSSO, 2010). The standards include a focus on reading complex texts, drawing on evidence from texts, and building knowledge through informational text. Similarly, social studies standards argue for the integration of literacy in teaching civics and government, economics, geography, and history. The *College, Career, and Civic Life (C3) Framework for State Social Studies: Guidance for Enhancing the Rigor of K–12 Civics, Economics, Geography, and History* (NCSS, 2013) recognizes its responsibility in literacy learning.

As documented throughout this volume, research shows that reading and writing skills are mutually reinforcing in general as well as in social studies education (De La Paz et al., 2014; Graham & Hebert, 2010). Students' comprehension of texts improves through writing activities, such as writing personal reactions, analyzing and interpreting texts, writing summaries of texts, and answering questions about texts in writing (Graham & Hebert, 2010). Writing helps students understand and retain information they read. Just as writing helps with reading, reading helps with writing (Graham et al., 2018). However, growth can vary widely among students (Nokes, 2017). In this section, we describe the research that supports the importance of integration of reading and writing with social studies at the elementary and secondary levels.

Elementary Level

Integration of social studies and literacy has great potential for improving achievement and increasing opportunities to learn social studies, which, as mentioned earlier, is often neglected at the elementary level. Social studies education offers multiple opportunities for children to "read to learn" through informational texts such as biographies, secondary sources, and historical documents. These texts have features common to specific social studies disciplines, such as maps, graphs, and diagrams. Instructional approaches such as project-based learning lend themselves to integrating domains including literacy and social studies (Duke, 2014) and have promise for increasing achievement in both domains (Duke, Halvorsen, et al., 2021; Halvorsen et al., 2012). However, effective integration requires pedagogical knowledge and planning to ensure that social studies content is not watered down (Alleman & Brophy, 2010; Bennett & Hinde, 2015). Later in this chapter, we will walk through the planning and implementation of an elementary unit that integrates social studies, writing, and reading.

Secondary Level

In grades 6 through 12, as the demands for students' comprehension, reasoning, and knowledge become increasingly complex, generic comprehension strategies are not enough for students to do disciplinary work such as contextualizing, sourcing, and corroboration (Goldman, 2012; Wineburg, 1991). Robust scholarship in disciplinary literacy (Moje, 2008; Shanahan & Shanahan, 2008) provides evidence that effective integration of reading and writing in history improves learning in all three areas. For example, Monte-Sano and De La Paz (2012) found that writing tasks focused on sourcing, corroboration, and causal analysis improved students' historical reasoning skills. However, as at the elementary level, doing this work effectively is difficult (Reisman, 2017).

The multidisciplinary research team of Project READI (Reading, Evidence and Argumentation in Disciplinary Instruction) developed a framework for "reading for understanding" in literature, the sciences, and history to guide instructional interventions (Goldman et al., 2016). Drawing on the scholarship of Wineburg (1991) and others, the team identified sets of core constructs in history that reflect the kinds of knowledge students need to construct historical arguments from reading multiple sources: epistemology; inquiry practices and strategies; overarching frameworks; representational forms; and discourse and language structures. See Table 11.1 for an explanation and examples of these history core constructs. Teaching and learning of these core constructs are sophisticated and challenging, but they equip students to engage in history in much more advanced ways than through traditional history instruction that entails memorization and recall of factual knowledge.

Planning and Enacting a Social
Studies Lesson with Writing and Reading

Considering the complexity of engaging students in reading and writing about social studies, it's no wonder that doing so requires teachers to orchestrate a range of instructional activities. Reading and writing in social studies cannot be achieved as an isolated activity. Rather, we recommend they be situated in an arc of inquiry. Indeed, most existing curricular materials that target reading and writing in social studies (e.g., *sheg.stanford.edu* or *readwritein-quire.umich.edu*) follow a similar arc in which students engage in a sequence of instructional activities that support them in answering a central question. Students are first provided—or prompted to generate—relevant background information. They then engage in careful reading and analysis of relevant texts that shed light on the central question. After reading, students come together to discuss their interpretations of the texts, and this discourse then supports them in composing a written response to the question. This arc of instruction can be extended over many days, but can also fit into a standard 50-minute period, as Reisman (2012) proposed in her discussion of the document-based lesson. For secondary teachers crunched for time, the document-based lesson may offer a way to infuse social studies instruction with high-level literacy.

Each of the instructional activities that comprise the inquiry arc of document-based lessons contributes to students' comprehension and analysis of texts. For example, consider a document-based lesson from the Stanford

TABLE 11.1. Project READI History Core Constructs

Core construct	Explanation	Example
Epistemology	We have incomplete and provisional knowledge about the past.	When new primary sources about a person or event are discovered, they can contribute to, affirm, or contradict previous knowledge.
Inquiry practices and strategies	History entails a range of practices to conduct inquiry including sourcing, corroboration, contextualization, and evaluation of others' arguments.	When reading a historian's account of an event, it is critical to think about whose perspectives are foregrounded and whose are excluded.
Overarching frameworks	Many interpretative frameworks can be used to study events in the past.	Critical race theory is a framework that could be used to study voting rights in the United States.
Representational forms	History involves a range of sources: primary, secondary, and tertiary sources.	Primary sources are those that originated during the time period under investigation. They can be written documents as well as art, music, and video recordings.
Discourse and language structures	Historical information uses particular forms of language and historical arguments are governed by particular forms of discourse.	Historical documents use particular kinds of language to make arguments about causes and effects.

Note. Based on Goldman et al. (2016).

History Education Group's Reading Like a Historian curriculum, in which students are prompted to investigate this question: "Why did the Homestead Strike of 1892 become violent?" The lesson's documents include an excerpt from anarchist Emma Goldman's 1931 autobiography that describes the strikers as "manly" and accuses Homestead manager Henry Frick of hiring "thugs" who opened fire on strikers, as well as an excerpt from an interview with Frick conducted soon after the strike, in which he blames the strikers for the violence. The document-based lesson includes a sequence of activities designed to support students in analyzing and corroborating the documents in order to formulate a reasoned, contextualized response to the central question.

Establishing Background Knowledge

To comprehend, interpret, and synthesize texts, students first need to have some contextual information about the Homestead strike that allows them to situate it in the broader struggles between labor and industry that characterized the late 19th century in the United States. They also should know something about the specific tensions that led the union at Homestead to strike in the first place. Teachers can draw on any number of resources to establish this background knowledge—videos, timelines, texts, slide presentations, and even textbooks. Rather than present history as a closed narrative, as is typical of traditional textbook instruction, the purpose of this segment is to whet students' appetite for inquiry, to offer enough information about the topic while leaving many questions unanswered. Done well, this instructional activity leaves students motivated to learn more.

Supporting Disciplinary Reading

As students turn their attention to the document set, they must be supported with scaffolds that focus their attention on salient features of the text. In this particular lesson, guiding questions would prompt students to attend to the date of Emma Goldman's autobiography, or the purpose of Frick's interview. These questions assist students in evaluating the reliability of each text as a source of information that sheds light on the central question. In designing similar lessons, teachers should attend to selecting texts that represent a range of perspectives on a given matter so that students can see how an author's views and goals manifest in their written accounts. By attending to a document's authorship, perspective, and reliability, students build a toolkit that allows them to become critical consumers of information. Furthermore, they begin to ask questions that challenge dominant narratives, such as: "Whose perspectives are represented here?" "Whose perspectives are missing?" "What additional information do I need to deepen my understanding of this issue?"

Facilitating Disciplinary Discussion

Once students have worked independently or in small groups to analyze the texts, they should engage in whole-class discussions that surface competing interpretations and help students reconcile them. In facilitating such discussions, teachers should engage students as sense-makers and orient students to the texts, to each other, and to the central constructs and practices of the discipline (Reisman et al., 2018). For example, the teacher should probe students' reasoning (e.g., "Why would Frick benefit from that argument?"), prompt students to substantiate claims with evidence in the text (e.g., "What in the text led you to think Goldman felt strongly about this?"), and support students in building on or challenging one another's arguments (e.g., "What do others think of Carlota's argument?"). Ultimately, in a successful and productive discussion, students have an opportunity to articulate and refine a complex answer to the central question.

Supporting Student Historical Writing

The whole-class discussion also serves as an opportunity for students to formulate and defend claims that they later elaborate on in their argumentative writing. Students back these claims with evidence drawn from the lesson's documents and contextualize the evidence in the background knowledge gleaned at the start of the lesson. Following the lesson, students could broaden the audiences for their writing. For example, they could exchange their written arguments, reading their classmates' work at home to deepen their understanding and own analyses. Or, they could use their arguments as a basis on which to develop a presentation for a local historical society or for a letter directed at a publisher regarding their coverage (or lack thereof) of this historical event. All of the instructional activities in the document-based lesson work together to infuse the study of history with instruction in high-level literacy.

Planning an Elementary-Level Social Studies Unit with Writing and Reading

The four steps described with regard to a lesson—establishing background knowledge, supporting reading, facilitating discussion, and supporting student writing—can be applied in an entire unit of study at the elementary level, with some additions. Here, we present a unit targeted at second-grade students that aligns with standards in the C3 Framework (NCSS, 2013) as well as social justice standards (Southern Poverty Law Center, 2018). The unit is on the topic of environmental justice and focuses most on civics and government but is interdisciplinary in nature, drawing on knowledge and skills in economics, geography, and history. The students engage in reading, writing, and social studies through an inquiry arc guided by this question: "What is the government's role in providing clean air to the community, and how can we influence their work?" Reading and writing are naturally integrated into the disciplinary work of this social-studies-led unit; reading is critical to gaining knowledge about the topic and writing is critical to taking action based on the knowledge gained.

Engaging in Unit-Level Planning

Units comprise large amounts of precious instructional time, so they need to be planned especially carefully. When designing units that address social studies, writing, and reading, we recommend considering the following questions.

What Social Studies Standards Do We Want to Address?

It is important that we lead our thinking with social studies standards to avoid some of the pitfalls of ELA- and literacy-dominated curricula. When considering social studies standards, be sure to consider not only content standards (e.g., identifying the branches of the federal government), but also process standards (e.g., analyzing and constructing an argument). Also, be sure to keep your mind open to addressing multiple social studies disciplines at once. For example, you might find that history is the lead social studies discipline for a given unit, but that the fields of geography and economics also have relevance to the unit.

Which Literacy Standards Do We Want to Address?

Consider your major goals for literacy development for this unit. When possible, cluster standards across different modes that are conceptually related and could work synergistically. For example, the following is a possible standards cluster for the fourth grade based on the ELA CCSS:

> Grade 4, Reading Informational Text, Standard 8: Explain how an author uses reasons and evidence to support particular points in a text.
>
> Grade 4, Writing, Standard 1: Write opinion pieces on topics or texts, supporting a point of view with reasons and information.
>
> a. Introduce a topic or text clearly, state an opinion, and create an organizational structure in which related ideas are grouped to support the writer's purpose.
> b. Provide reasons that are supported by facts and details.
> c. Link opinion and reasons using words and phrases (e.g., *for instance*, *in order to*, *in addition*).
> d. Provide a concluding statement or section related to the opinion presented.
>
> Grade 4, Speaking and Listening, Standard 3: Identify the reasons and evidence a speaker provides to support particular points.
>
> Although your state or other jurisdiction may use a different set of standards, there are likely to be possible clusters of standards within your state or other jurisdiction as well.

What Could Be a Driving Question for the Unit?

A driving, compelling, central, or essential question can be a powerful tool for unit design and is a hallmark of many approaches to project-based learning and of C3-aligned social studies (e.g., Grant, Swan, & Lee, 2017). The driving question can provide cohesion and momentum in a unit. Often, an overarching driving question for a unit can give rise to subquestions generated by students. For example, the driving question for the unit we are discussing, "What is the government's role in providing clean air to the community, and how can we influence their work?," could give rise to subquestions such as: "What is the judicial system's role in addressing pollution from businesses? How can mayoral administrations promote citizens' use of environmentally friendly modes of transportation?" And so on.

What Is a Compelling Purpose in Students' Minds for Addressing the Standards?

Research strongly suggests that when students read and write for a compelling purpose and, in the case of writing, audience, their reading and writing development is enhanced (e.g., McBreen & Savage, 2020; Purcell-Gates, Duke, & Martineau, 2007). Once you know the social studies, reading, writing, and other standards that you want to address, it is a good time to think about purposes and audiences for your students' work. For example, for a unit with the driving question—"What is the government's role in providing clean air to the community, and how can we influence their work?"—the purpose might be to develop a persuasive statement arguing for the government to take particular action. That statement could be directed to any number of audiences, such as a community council or a legislator. It could be submitted in writing or read aloud during the public participation period of a council meeting. See Table 11.2 (p. 219) for other ideas with regard to potential audiences for integrated social studies, writing, and reading projects. Research suggests that a project-based learning approach can support both social studies and literacy development (Duke, Halvorsen, et al., 2021).

What Opportunities for Advancing Equity and Criticality Exist in the Unit?

As shown earlier, even individual lessons can provide an opportunity to begin to ask questions that challenge dominant narratives, such as "Whose perspectives are represented here? Whose perspectives are missing? What additional information do I need to deepen my understanding of this issue?" Units provide more extended opportunities for criticality and for engaging with content through an equity lens, which is important not only to planning social studies instruction but also to literacy instruction (Muhammad, 2020).

What Lessons Can Contribute to Students Achieving the Standards and Their Purpose?

At this point in the planning process, you can begin to move to lesson-by-lesson planning. Each lesson should contribute to developing social studies, reading, and/or writing knowledge, skills, and/or dispositions. Lessons should also contribute to addressing the driving question and, if project-based learning is being used, to advancing the project. We suggest at least three components of every lesson:

1. Whole-class time that includes some explicit instruction in and discussion of social studies, reading, and/or writing
2. Small-group, partner, or individual work in which students apply their

developing knowledge and skills toward addressing the driving question and project purpose

3. Whole-class time in which the teacher reviews key points from the instruction at the outset of the lesson and invites students to reflect on their learning, application, and project progress

For further discussion of these three lesson components and examples of project-based units in addition to the one discussed in this chapter, see Halvorsen, Duke, and Strachan (2019) and Revelle, Wise, Duke, and Halvorsen (2019). Now that we have laid out the planning process, we turn to some key moves within a unit.

Establishing Background Knowledge

To be able to engage effectively with a unit's driving question, students need to gain relevant background knowledge on the topic. The unit with the driving question "What is the government's role in providing clean air to the community and how can we influence their work?" might start with students generating questions like these:

- How does air become unclean?
- How do we know whether air is clean?
- What are the responsibilities of the government regarding the natural environment?
- What can individuals do to protect the natural environment?
- Is air quality different in different parts of our community?
- How can we influence causes of unclear air?

These questions can be addressed in part through explicit instruction and presentations. They can also be addressed through student reading and discussion, which are the focus of the following two sections.

Supporting Reading

Students can develop initial background knowledge and engage in ongoing knowledge-building through interactions with a range of informational texts (e.g., books, Internet sites, multimedia resources)—engaging in the practice of "reading to learn." These texts might include informational books on human–environmental interactions, the role of the government, and Indigeneous ways of interacting with the natural environment. Students might also use other sources for knowledge building, such as conducting interviews that also require reading (of notes taken during the interview) as well as writing (of the notes and the interview questions).

When supporting reading over the course of a unit, there are many key considerations. One is using texts that students can access, at least with support if not independently. There are many strategies one can use to help with text accessibility:

- **Building initial background knowledge.** Students understand texts better when they bring to those texts more relevant background knowledge. Therefore, the initial background knowledge building discussed in the previous section can support students' later reading. It can also be helpful to provide some more accessible texts early on so students can work their way up to more difficult texts.

- **Preteaching vocabulary and strategies that will support access to the text.** Some terms are so central to a text or concept that it is important to engage in some preteaching to help students begin to understand these terms and how to decode them. For example, preteaching the meaning and decoding of the terms *judicial*, *legislative*, and *executive* would likely be helpful in the example unit we are discussing. Teaching comprehension strategies that may be useful when students come to difficult parts of the text would also be helpful (Duke, Ward, et al., 2021) (also see Chapter 3, this volume).

- **Providing explicit instruction and discussion of text features and structure.** Students may better access text if taught specific features of a text (e.g., insets, use of specific terms such as *whereas*) or the overall structure or organization of the text (e.g., compare–contrast, problem–solution, cause–effect, sequential/chronological, topical) (Duke, Ward, et al., 2021) (also see Chapter 6, this volume). Williams et al. (2014) compared social studies instruction with or without embedded text structure instruction. Those who experienced the text structure instruction had higher comprehension and learned an equal amount of social studies content.

- **Using graphic organizers.** Graphic organizers (GOs) can reflect the structure of the text and can support conceptual learning in social studies (Thacker, Friedman, Fitchett, Journell, & Lee, 2018). It is important to involve students in filling out GOs and modifying them as needed. Providing precompleted GOs is not likely to work as well.

- **Supporting students in sourcing the texts and contextualizing the sources.** Students benefit from explicit guidance in sourcing: identifying the author, the date of publication, and the publisher, as well as thinking about the text's purpose and the author's perspective. Answers to those questions will help students determine the credibility of the text. Contextualizing the sources entails thinking about what was going on when the source was created and whether those events influenced the content of the text.

- **Chunking the reading tasks to be manageable.** Both primary and secondary texts can be daunting in content and length. With chunking, the teacher breaks the text into manageable sections for students to read. Then, students can write about what they read in their own words, as a summary or reflection, for example. This strategy helps students learn vocabulary, comprehend the main ideas, and synthesize information in the text. See *Facing History and Ourselves* (2021) for more about chunking.

- **Supporting students' emotional responses to texts.** Social studies involves the study of difficult history—traumatic, contested, painful, and/or violent events (Epstein & Peck, 2018). Visual texts can be particularly evocative and can result in emotional responses by students. Teachers can support students' responses by preparing them for what they will read or view, selecting sources that are powerful but not overly graphic, encouraging them to talk about and write about their responses, answering their questions sensitively but candidly, and highlighting the ways in which groups have engaged in resistance, protest, and other means of activism in the face of trauma or oppression.

- **Modifying texts for accessibility.** If other measures are not adequate to render texts accessible for students, it may be necessary to modify the texts. For example, in working with second graders, we created texts about their local community's history that were based on more sophisticated documents but were written to be readable by children of that age (Halvorsen, Duke, Strachan, & Johnson, 2018). Also see Wineburg and Martin (2009) for guidance on adapting primary sources for students.

Supporting Student Writing

Many of the writing instructional practices shared in this volume can be productively applied in the context of social studies education. Rather than repeat all those practices here, we focus on a small set of writing instructional practices that are especially important for writing in the context of social studies.

- **Establishing and reminding students of the purpose and audience for their writing.** Establishing a purpose and audience is important for writing instruction in general (e.g., Graham et al., 2012). However, doing so may be especially important for motivating students to engage in the complex work of grappling with social studies content and communication. There are many potential audiences for writing in social studies, as suggested in Table 11.2. We recommend reminding students regularly of the purpose and audience—and the genre and format appropriate to that purpose and audience—to help sustain engagement.

- **Providing mentor texts that reflect the genre and social studies disciplinary practices you want students to use.** Part of integrating social studies and writing (and reading) is to help students learn how people write in and about social studies. For example, students would benefit from learning about the strategies and processes that children's book author Lesa Cline Ransome uses to write about historical figures—and to study the features of books that result from those strategies and processes. Our recommendation

TABLE 11.2. Possible Audiences for Integrated Social Studies, Reading, and Writing Projects

Civics and government	• Local, state, and federal government personnel • Members of neighborhood and community councils • Political candidates • Personnel at voting rights organizations • Community organizers
Economics	• Local, state, and federal government personnel • Workers at food banks, pantries, and shelters • Local, state, national, and international business owners • Investment bankers • Personnel in endowment offices at universities and nonprofits • Personnel at nongovernmental organizations
Geography	• Children and youth in other countries • Local, state, and federal government personnel • Personnel at local watershed councils, riverfront conservancies, and the like
History	• Extended family members • Libraries and museums • Historical societies • Newspapers • Community spaces

is to seek mentor texts that reflect the genre and disciplinary practices you want students to use, but that are on a topic different than the one on which students will write (Philippakos et al., 2015). That way, students can focus on the way in which the content is being conveyed, rather than the content itself, and use of the mentor text does not undermine the need for the writing students will do on their topic.

• **Incorporating research through the writing process.** A common characterization of the writing process is that it entails brainstorming, planning, drafting, revising, editing, and publishing. However, when writing informational texts, and many persuasive texts as well, researching is an important part of the process (Duke, 2014). Once a purpose for writing is established, research may be needed before it's even possible to engage in brainstorming, and then again in the course of planning the writing. Once one begins actually drafting, further research may be needed to help flesh out portions of the draft. Even the revision process may require returning to sources for information or verification. In social studies (as well as in science), research is a central part of the writing process.

• **Teaching the use of tools to organize information.** With the large amount of information—ideas, facts, figures, different types of sources, and so on—needed for writing in social studies, it is helpful to teach students tools to organize information, such as GOs or digital tools such as Evernote. Students should be explicitly taught ways to organize information from their research, and should be invited to share their strategies with one another as well.

Facilitating Discussion

Throughout the unit, whether when establishing background knowledge, supporting reading, or supporting writing, discussion is a powerful tool for student learning. Discussion provides students with the opportunity to use and refine their speaking and listening skills. Discussion is defined in different ways, but here we draw on Parker's (2003) definition: "a kind of shared inquiry the desired outcomes of which rely on the expression and consideration of diverse views" (p. 129). We recognize the challenges of leading effective discussion (Halvorsen, 2011; Parker & Hess, 2001). To facilitate discussions effectively, key practices include:

- **Creating a physical environment conducive to discussions.** The physical arrangement of a classroom can promote substantive discussion. For example, a circular arrangement (at desks/tables or, for younger children, on a carpet) allows everyone to see each other, ensures that everyone has the same chance of being seen and heard, and doesn't position the teacher apart from the students (Brookfield & Preskill, 1999).

- **Preparing students for discussion.** Effective discussions tend to be inspired by a text that students have read beforehand. Equitable access to materials helps to ensure that students are similarly prepared to engage with the content (Brookfield & Preskill, 1999). Texts that engage students, help them make connections to their worlds beyond school, and offer different perspectives are generative for discussion (Hess, 2004).

- **Scaffolding discussion.** Teachers play a key role in starting, facilitating, and concluding discussions, and there are many research-tested approaches to doing so (Wilkinson & Bourdage, 2022). Students benefit from explicit guidance in entering and participating in discussion. For example, sentence starters, such as "I see your point, but I believe . . . ," can be used to give students the language to frame their contributions (Brookfield & Preskill, 1999).

- **Engaging students with each other in discussion.** In effective discussions, students engage with each other by asking questions and responding directly to others' comments (Harris, 2002). Reisman et al. (2018) developed a framework to support novice teachers in facilitating discussions; one of the framework's four practices is "orienting K–12 students to each other" (p. 280). In this practice, the teacher conveys to students that complex historical work involves "shared knowledge construction" by encouraging students to listen carefully to each other's ideas and consider different perspectives.

- **Centering equity and justice in discussions.** Facilitating discussions that allow for equitable participation is critical but takes effort. Sociocultural identity, personal experiences, and political leanings can shape who participates and the dynamics of discussion (Crocco, Segall, Halvorsen, & Jacobsen, 2018). This is especially relevant for social studies discussions that center on issues of power, trauma, controversy, and disempowerment.

Evidence-Based Recommendations for Writing and Reading in Social Studies

The research reviewed in this chapter and the discussion of how to plan and implement integrated social studies, reading, and writing lessons and units point to many evidence-based practices. We conclude here by identifying some of the themes across these practices. One theme is the need to provide a supportive context for learning. For example, we need to guide students to engage in productive and respectful discussion and to be mindful of strategies to make texts more accessible for students. Another theme is the need to establish compelling and discipline-appropriate purposes for writing and reading within social studies. We are supported in doing so when we think of how writing and reading are authentically used in citizenship and in the work of social scientists.

Another theme is the need to attend to equity and criticality. Although this need exists in any domain—mathematics, physical education, and so on—it is especially acute in social studies, in which we are shaping the future citizenry. Related to this is a theme around supporting students to understand the source and context of the texts they read. Supporting students in *how to* read and *how to* write texts in social studies was also a theme in the chapter. The value of teaching text features and structures and comprehension and writing strategies arose multiple times in the chapter. At the same time, building content knowledge and specific disciplinary literacy practices was also discussed repeatedly. Generic literacy instruction cannot be allowed to replace or even dominate social studies education. Finally, a recurring theme in the chapter was the role that discussion can play as the curricular glue in integrated social studies, writing, and reading. In the social studies field of economics, students learn about investment and return. Learning to engage in productive discussion is an investment with a rich return.

Too often, specific school domains are siloed from one another. In this chapter, we have presented evidence from observations of the practice of social science, analysis of standards documents, and review of research studies that provide considerable support for an integrated approach to teaching social studies, reading, and writing. Improving our ability to develop reading and writing within social studies, and affording far greater time to teaching social studies content and processes, will enable us to develop more effective scholars and citizens in the next generation.

We suggest that you reflect, plan, and act with the following questions in mind:

- How can you make room in your day and year for integrated writing, reading, and social studies education?
- How do you ensure that social studies content and skills do not take a back seat in your literacy instruction?
- How do you prepare for, facilitate, and assess the effectiveness of student discussion of a range of texts in social studies?
- How can you modify texts or provide scaffolds to help make the texts, such as primary sources, accessible to students?
- How do you help students draw on what they learned from class discussion in their writing?
- How do you ensure that your lessons advance equity, justice, and criticality?

REFERENCES

Alleman, J., & Brophy, J. (2010). Effective integration of social studies and literacy. In M. E. McGuire & B. Cole (Eds.), *Making a difference: Revitalizing elementary social studies* (pp. 51–66). Silver Spring, MD: National Council for the Social Studies.

Anderson, D. (2014). Outliers: Elementary teachers who actually teach social studies. *The Social Studies, 105*(2), 91–100.

Bennett. L., & Hinde, E. R. (2015). *Becoming integrated thinkers: Case studies of integrated elementary social studies.* Silver Spring, MD: National Council for the Social Studies.

Brookfield, S. D., & Preskill, S. (1999). *Discussion as a way of teaching: Tools and techniques for university teachers.* London: Society for Research into Higher Education and Open University Press.

Cervetti, G., Pearson, P. D., Bravo, M. A., & Barber, J. (2006). Reading and writing in the service of inquiry-based science. In R. Douglas, M. P. Klentschy, & K. Worth (Eds.), *Linking science and literacy in the K–8 classroom* (pp. 221–244). Alexandria, VA: National Science Teaching Association.

Crocco, M., Segall, A., Halvorsen, A., & Jacobsen (2018). Deliberating public policy issues with adolescents. *Democracy and Education, 26*(1), Article 3. *https:// democracyeducationjournal.org/home/vol26/iss1/3*

De La Paz, S., Felton, M., Monte-Sano, C., Croninger, R., Jackson, C., Deogracias, J. S., & Hoffman, B. P. (2014). Developing historical reading and writing with adolescent readers: Effects on student learning. *Theory and Research in Social Education, 42,* 228–274.

Duke, N. K. (2014). *Information in action: Reading, writing, and researching with informational text.* New York: Scholastic.

Duke, N. K., Halvorsen, A., Strachan, S. L., Kim, J., & Konstantopoulos, S. (2021).

Putting PjBL to the test: The impact of project-based learning on second-graders' social studies and literacy learning and motivation in low-SES school settings. *The American Educational Research Journal, 58*(1), 160–200.

Duke, N. K., Ward, A. E., & Pearson, P. D. (2021). The science of reading comprehension instruction. *The Reading Teacher, 74*(6), 663–672.

Epstein, T., & Peck, C. (Eds.). (2018). *Teaching and learning difficult histories in international contexts: A critical sociocultural approach.* New York: Routledge.

Facing History and Ourselves. (2021). *Chunking.* Retrieved from *www.facinghistory. org/resource-library/teaching-strategies/chunking.*

Fitchett, P. G., & Heafner, T. L. (2010). A national perspective on the effects of high-stakes testing and standardization on elementary social studies marginalization. *Theory and Research in Social Education, 38*(1), 114–130.

Goldman, S. R. (2012). Adolescent literacy: Learning and understanding content. *The Future of Children, 22*(2), 89–116.

Goldman, S. R., Britt, M. A., Brown, W., Cribb, G., George, M., Greenleaf, C., . . . Project READI. (2016). Disciplinary literacies and learning to read for understanding: A conceptual framework for disciplinary literacy. *Educational Psychologist, 51*(2), 219–246.

Graham, S., Bollinger, A., Booth Olson, C., D'Aoust, C., MacArthur, C., McCutchen, D., & Olinghouse, N. (2012). *Teaching elementary school students to be effective writers: A practice guide* (NCEE 2012-4058). Washington, DC: National Center for Education Evaluation and Regional Assistance, Institute of Education Sciences, U.S. Department of Education. Retrieved from *https://ies.ed.gov/ncee/ wwc/PracticeGuide/17.*

Graham, S., & Hebert, M. A. (2010). *Writing to read: Evidence for how writing can improve reading. A Carnegie Corporation Time to Act Report.* Washington, DC: Alliance for Excellent Education.

Graham, S., Liu, X., Bartlett, B., Ng, C., Harris, K. R., Aitken, A., . . . Talukdar, J. (2018). Reading for writing: A meta-analysis of the impact of reading interventions on writing. *Review of Educational Research, 88*(2), 243–284.

Grant, S. G., Swan, K., & Lee, J. (2017). Questions that compel and support. *Social Education, 81*(4), 200–203.

Halvorsen, A. (2011). Facilitating discussions in social studies classrooms. In W. Russell (Ed.), *Contemporary social studies: An essential reader* (pp. 385–398). Charlotte, NC: Information Age.

Halvorsen, A., Duke, N. K., Brugar, K. A., Block, M. K., Strachan, S. L., Berka, M. B., & Brown, J. M. (2012). Narrowing the achievement gap in second-grade social studies and content area literacy: The promise of a project-based approach. *Theory and Research in Social Education, 40*, 198–229.

Halvorsen, A., Duke, N. K., & Strachan, S. L. (2019). Project-based learning in primary-grade social studies. *Social Education, 83*(1), 58–62.

Halvorsen, A., Duke, N. K., Strachan, S. L., & Johnson, C. (2018). Engaging the community with a project-based approach. *Social Education, 82*(1), 24–29.

Harris, D. E. (2002). Classroom assessment of civic discourse. In W. C. Parker (Ed.), *Education for democracy: Contexts, curricula, assessments* (pp. 211–32). Charlotte, NC: Information Age.

Hess, D. E. (2004). Discussion in social studies: Is it worth the trouble? *Social Education, 68*(2), 151–155.

Hwang, H., & Duke, N. K. (2020). Content counts and motivation matters: Reading comprehension in third-grade students who are English learners. *AERA Open,* 6(1), 1–17.

McBreen, M., & Savage, R. (2020). The impact of motivational reading instruction on the reading achievement and motivation of students: A systematic review and meta-analysis. *Educational Psychology Review.*

Moje, E. B. (2008). Foregrounding the disciplines in secondary literacy teaching and learning: A call for change. *Journal of Adolescent and Adult Literacy, 52*(2), 96–107.

Monte-Sano, C., & De La Paz, S. (2012). Using writing tasks to elicit adolescents' historical reasoning. *Journal of Literacy Research, 44*(30), 273–299.

Muhammad, G. (2020). *Cultivating genius: An equity framework for culturally and historically responsive literacy.* New York: Scholastic.

National Council for the Social Studies. (1994). *Expectations of excellence: Curriculum standards for social studies.* Silver Spring, MD: Author.

National Council for the Social Studies. (2013). *The college, career, and civic life (C3) framework for social studies state standards: Guidance for enhancing the rigor of K–12 civics, economics, geography, and history.* Silver Spring, MD: Author. Retrieved from *www.socialstudies.org/standards/c3.*

National Governors Association Center for Best Practices & Council of Chief State School Officers. (2010). *Common Core Standards for English language arts and literacy in history/social studies, science, and technical subjects.* Washington, DC: Author. Retrieved from *www.corestandards.org/ELA-Literacy.*

Nokes, J. D. (2017). Exploring patterns of historical thinking through eighth-grade students' argumentative writing. *Journal of Writing Research, 8*(3), 437–467.

Parker, W. C. (2003). *Teaching democracy: Unity and diversity in public life.* New York: Teachers College Press.

Parker, W. C., & Hess, D. (2001). Teaching with and for discussion. *Teaching and Teacher Education, 17,* 273–289.

Philippakos, Z. A., MacArthur, C. A., & Coker, D. L. (2015). *Developing strategic writers through genre instruction: Resources for grades 3–5.* New York: Guilford Press.

Pritchard, R. (1990). The effects of cultural schemata on reading processing strategies. *Reading Research Quarterly, 25*(4), 273–295.

Purcell-Gates, V., Duke, N. K., & Martineau, J. A. (2007). Learning to read and write genre-specific text: Roles of authentic experience and explicit teaching. *Reading Research Quarterly, 42,* 8–45.

Reisman, A. (2012). The "Document-Based Lesson": Bringing disciplinary inquiry into high school history classrooms with adolescent struggling readers. *Journal of Curriculum Studies, 44*(2), 233–264.

Reisman, A. (2017). Integrating content and literacy in social studies: Assessing instructional materials and student work from a Common Core-aligned intervention. *Theory and Research in Social Education, 45*(4), 517–554.

Reisman, A., Kavanagh S. S., Monte-Sano, C., Fogo, F., McGrew, S. C., Cipparone, P., & Simmons, E. (2018). Facilitating whole-class discussions in history: A framework for preparing teacher candidates. *Journal of Teacher Education, 69*(3), 278–293.

Revelle, K. Z., Wise, C. N., Duke, N. K., & Halvorsen, A. (2019). Realizing the promise of project-based learning. *The Reading Teacher, 73*(6), 697–710.

Shanahan, T., & Shanahan, C. (2008). Teaching disciplinary literacy to adolescents: Rethinking content area literacy. *Harvard Educational Review, 78*(1), 40–61.

Southern Poverty Law Center. (2018). *Social justice standards: The teaching tolerance anti-bias framework*. Retrieved from *www.learningforjustice.org/sites/default/files/2020–09/TT-Social-Justice-Standards-Anti-bias-framework-2020.pdf.*

Thacker, E. S., Friedman, A. M., Fitchett, P. G., Journell, W., & Lee, J. K. (2018). Exploring how an elementary teacher plans and implements social studies inquiry. *The Social Studies, 109*(2), 85–100.

Wilkinson, I. A. G., & Bourdage, K. (2022). *Quality talk about text: Discussion practices for talking and thinking about text*. Portsmouth, NH: Heinemann.

Williams, J. P., Pollini, S., Nubla-Kung, A. M., Snyder, A. E., Garcia, A., Ordynans, J. G., & Atkins, J. G. (2014). An intervention to improve comprehension of cause/effect through expository text structure instruction. *Journal of Educational Psychology, 106*(1), 1–17.

Wineburg, S. S. (1991). Historical problem solving: A study of the cognitive processes used in the evaluation of documentary and pictorial evidence. *Journal of Educational Psychology, 83*, 73–87.

Wineburg, S., & Martin, D. (2009). Tampering with history: Adapting primary sources for struggling readers. *Social Education, 73*(5), 212–216.

CHAPTER 12

Liberation through Literacy in Science

Catherine Lammert
Brian Hand

In this chapter, we draw on our own research, as well as that of others, to show the ways in which connected reading and writing can be used to teach science. We primarily look to two frameworks: the Science Writing Heuristic (SWH; Hand, 2008; Keys, Hand, Prain, & Collins, 1999), which is supported by a robust research base (Hand, Chen, & Suh, 2020) and the Activism in the Curriculum model (Hoffman, Lammert, DeJulio, Tily, & Svrcek, 2020), which is more emergent. As a way of highlighting the possibilities that exist inside of convergent approaches, we intentionally describe one model that is rooted in the field of science, but makes significant use of literacy practices, as well as one model that is rooted in the field of literacy, but has been applied to science teaching.

Then, after describing the theoretical underpinnings of these frameworks, we provide concrete pedagogical examples of shared reading and writing practices for teaching science: (1) reading to help students generate questions for further exploration and plan an investigation, (2) using peer audiences as readers when writing summaries and arguments, and (3) reading using structured frameworks to consult with experts during summary and argument writing. In the sections that follow, we will introduce the design behind each shared reading and writing practice and describe the research base that supports its inclusion in science teaching. We conclude by providing evidence-based recommendations for practice, and we note areas of opportunity for practitioners to continue to innovate.

GUIDING QUESTIONS

■ How can teachers maximize the reciprocal benefits of reading–writing instruction in the context of teaching science?

■ How can writing serve as a tool for knowledge generation in science? How is this similar to and different from the role of reading?

■ How do models such as SWH and Activism in the Curriculum provide pathways for teachers to engage students in liberatory writing and reading in science?

Background

First, we frame the historical and contemporary context of reading and writing connections in science learning environments, and we outline relevant theories and frameworks that connect literacy and science.

Reading and Writing Connections in History

In order to understand the ways reading and writing connections manifest themselves in today's science classrooms, it is helpful to begin by looking backward in time. In her James Russell Wiggins Lecture titled *Reading for the Enslaved, Writing for the Free: Reflections on Liberty and Literacy,* educational historian E. Jennifer Monaghan explained that in the early antebellum South, "Reading was usually viewed as a tool that was entirely compatible with the institution of slavery. Writing, on the other hand, was almost invariably perceived by southern slaveholders as intrinsically dangerous" (2000, p. 309). Monaghan noted that in the United States, legislation initially prohibited the teaching of writing, which could lead to the documentation of injustice, communication with outside parties, and the forging of official documents in the process of escape. However, reading, which was deemed less threatening and necessary for religious education, was initially allowed. Ultimately, trying to prevent readers from learning to write proved nearly impossible. "They who can write hold power" (Monaghan, 2000, p. 321), and so eventually both were prohibited in an attempt at controlling the minds and fates of the enslaved.

Reading and Writing Connections in Contemporary Classrooms

The absurdity of trying to teach reading while banning writing is obvious in hindsight. Furthermore, Monaghan's analysis highlights the distinction between literacy practices that are relatively safe and serve to replicate existing knowledge, and those that are liberatory and generative of new understandings. This distinction is particularly relevant in contemporary science education, which is rapidly shifting toward the view that classrooms must function as knowledge-generation environments (Hand et al., 2020). Knowledge generation environments operate in sharp contrast to traditional constructions of school as a space of knowledge replication, where the purpose of reading and writing is to obtain and accept information (Klein & Yu, 2013). In knowledge-generation environments, learners must negotiate new ideas with their existing ones and decide whether or not to shift their thinking. The negotiation process, which includes both individual and collaborative elements and involves much more than reading and memorizing pieces of information, is primarily achieved through writing to learn (Galbraith, 1999; Graham, Kiuhara, & MacKay, 2020; Hand & Prain, 1996). In defining writing to learn in science, Norton-Meier has described a "border convergence" (2008, p. 13) inside of inquiry and argument practices. The foundational role of language in learning science is well known, although researchers and teachers are still exploring the epistemic value language makes to the learning process and defining particular pedagogies consistent with this approach (Hand, 2017; Norris & Phillips, 2003).

Reading, Writing, and Science Connections

The border convergence of reading and writing in science is disruptive to traditional practices in a variety of ways, since meaningful science investigations offer a context within which children can use literacy for the purpose of knowledge generation. Learning in a context such as this can benefit students' reading comprehension (Guthrie et al., 2004; also see Chapter 5, this volume) and knowledge of genre (Purcell-Gates, Duke, & Martineau, 2007). It can also create a space for young learners to develop the ability to use academic language as speakers and writers, and make sense of academic language as readers, while developing critical language awareness (Moore & Schleppegrell, 2020; also see Chapter 3, this volume). Finally, it can create a space for learners to use their disciplinary knowledge to ask ethical questions and create designs and innovations that better their communities (Wilson-Lopez & Minichiello, 2017), which is an important goal of the Next Generation Science Standards (NGSS; NGSS Lead States, 2013). With this background in mind, we now turn to presenting two models of teaching consistent with these goals.

The Science Writing Heuristic

SWH (Hand, 2008; Keys et al., 1999) is a model of argument-based inquiry rooted in a knowledge-generation approach to teaching science. Features of SWH teaching involve students generating questions, conducting investigations, constructing and critiquing evidence-based claims, and participating in argumentation. Consistent with the NGSS (2013), in SWH, a *Big Idea* such as "Weather impacts our daily lives" anchors students' relationship to what is typically considered the content of science teaching, while dialogue, negotiation, and writing enable learners to develop academic language of science and construct explanations of phenomena. A major element of SWH is that it builds students' understanding that scientists support their claims with evidence. In addition to improving science content learning, this immersive disciplinary literacy approach supports students' agency (Moje, 2007) and interdependence (Lewis, Enciso, & Moje, 2007).

Given the rapidly shifting student demographics in K–12 classrooms today (National Center for Education Statistics [NCES], 2018), it is notable that SWH has the potential to create the conditions under which learners from diverse positions can excel. Many of the inequities faced by students from marginalized racial, cultural, and gender backgrounds are manifested through language. In particular, the academic language of science can become a gate-keeping mechanism for students who view scientific ways of using reading and writing as inaccessible (Rosato, 2007). This is why it is unsurprising that approaches that invite students to grow as readers and writers in science, such as SWH, have been shown to have particularly strong benefits for students from historically underserved communities (Laugerman et al., 2013) including women, students from lower socioeconomic status families, students with dis-abilities, and students of color. SWH teaching provides instruction to students on ways to leverage their everyday language into scientific vocabulary and ways to structure their arguments that give them authority in the sciences, while also honoring students' own agency as learners (Schoerning et al., 2015). The SWH model was designed with science teaching in mind, but it has untapped libera-tory potential to purposefully combine reading and writing practices. Thus, we provide several concrete examples of SWH teaching throughout this chapter. Now, to show the diversity of ways in which literacy and science learning can be brought together, we turn to a complementary model rooted in combined writing–reading practices and that has potential for teaching science.

Activism in the Curriculum

The Activism in the Curriculum model (Hoffman et al., 2020) is rooted in lit-eracy research, where there is increasing recognition of the benefits of teaching reading and writing in disciplinary settings (Moje, 2007; Shanahan, Shanahan, & Misischia, 2011) concurrently and simultaneously (Graham, 2020a; Inter-national Literacy Association [ILA], 2020). Contemporary studies have dem-onstrated that a reciprocal relationship exists; developing reading abilities can contribute to improved writing abilities and developing writing abilities can contribute to improved reading outcomes (Graham & Hebert, 2011). In fur-ther identifying the common sources of knowledge on which readers and writ-ers both draw, Fitzgerald and Shanahan (2000) have noted the role of general knowledge, which includes the content learned through reading; metaknowl-edge, which includes the functions and purposes of text; pragmatic knowledge, which consists of text features, syntax, and knowledge of word usage; and procedural knowledge, which includes how to set goals, question, predict, and summarize. Ongoing research continues to identify the advantages of building these common sources of knowledge, and more importantly for practice, con-tinues to define ways to operationalize these knowledges in teaching (Graham 2020b). One emergent model that draws on these knowledges and has been applied to teaching in science is the Activism in the Curriculum model (Figure 12.1).

At the center of the model is activism, the intended goal, which is defined as any work intended to improve the human condition (Ahmed & Daniels, 2017; Marshall & Anderson, 2009). In this model of curriculum, activism is advanced by (1) students' identification of their own interests, including their

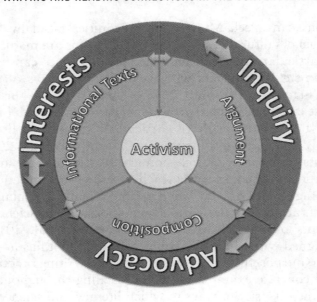

FIGURE 12.1. The Activism in the Curriculum model (Hoffman et al., 2020). Reprinted by permission of the National Council of Teachers of English (NCTE). Copyright © 2020 NCTE.

questions about their communities (i.e., "Why doesn't everyone in my city have access to fresh produce?"); (2) moving from interests into inquiry, where questions are explored through engagement with informational texts, writing, and experiences (i.e., reading about the food supply chain, touring a nearby farm); and (3) advocacy, when students promote attention to the topic by composing arguments and sharing them with audiences outside the classroom (i.e., writing a letter of support to a local food co-op). In these ways, reading and writing are tightly connected as tools for both individual learning and social change, and learning science is framed as "making a difference, or as harnessing the creative and productive power of design to make tangible improvements in the lives of students and their loved ones" (Wilson-Lopez & Minichiello, 2017, p. 13). This framing of science as a tool to improve the lives of marginalized people is consistent with the philosophy of the NGSS authors who have stated that "by solving problems through engineering in local contexts . . . students engage in science in socially relevant and transformative ways" (Rodriguez & Berryman, 2002; NGSS Lead States, 2013, p. 29). Activism in the Curriculum is one framework in which this is possible.

When used in science teaching, this model has been particularly useful for socioscientific teaching (Sadler, 2004) on topics such as climate change that have obvious social and cultural implications that must be understood in relation to scientific evidence. This model also provides a way to center informational texts, which are often absent from early reading instruction (Duke, 2000) in curricula. Although these texts can be used in highly engaging ways, and reading them is central to the development of critical media awareness, two separate, recent studies revealed that just 5% of read-aloud texts in early childhood classrooms were informational (Pentimonti, Zucker, & Justice, 2011; Yopp & Yopp, 2006). In schools with a high percentage of students eligible for free and reduced-price lunch, children are provided with even fewer informational texts (Duke, 2000) and less related instruction than their economically advantaged peers (Wright & Gotwals, 2017). Thus, this model provides a practical way to increase the use of informational texts inside of purposeful investigations, and in ways that support students' composition of argument as they write to inspire change. We provide additional examples of the Activism in the Curriculum model throughout this chapter.

We now turn to examining three different ways in which reading and writing connections exist in the teaching of science. First, we explore the practice of reading to explore, generate questions, and plan investigations.

Practice 1: Reading to Explore, Generate Questions, and Write a Plan for an Investigation

Studies of critical thinking suggest that the inductive phase of an investigation is especially important for student learning (Hwang, 2018). Consistent with notions of teaching as *mining* knowledge rather than *banking* knowledge (Rossato, 2007), in inductive teaching, teachers draw on what children already know about a topic, what questions they have, and they think with them about possibilities for investigation. In teaching reading, we engage children in induction when we hold up a book and ask them questions such as: "Has anyone read this before?" "What do we already know?" "Based on the cover, the title, and the author, can we predict what this book will be about?"

In science education, the NGSS emphasize that an anchoring phenomenon can serve similarly as an opening point for induction and a space to generate questions. After students observe a phenomenon (i.e., watch a video of a dust storm, view photos of plants and animals in different climates), they might want to find more information or conduct an investigation to learn more about how the phenomenon works. This is a perfect space to incorporate informational text reading, annotation, and argument writing.

A Research Example

In their study of literacy teacher preparation, Hoffman et al. (2020) used the Activism in the Curriculum model as they encouraged preservice teachers to conduct inquiry units of study with their students. One preservice teacher, Elizabeth, chose to focus on the topic of the Amazon rainforest. Elizabeth's second-grade class was designated as a special education inclusion classroom, with about 25% of her students carrying various labels of learning disability, so she chose a topic she believed would be exciting enough for her students to become engaged readers and writers. However, when she initially introduced the topic and asked her students what questions they had, their responses were very limited. Puzzled, Elizabeth decided to engage in inductive teaching and engaged her students in three practices that each involved a combination of reading and writing.

First, she created a book flood. She collected a wide range of books on the plants, animals, and people who live in the Amazon, set them around the room, and let her students explore independently. Afterward, she asked them to write their reactions and questions in their journals. A partial listing of the texts she used is included in Table 12.1.

Elizabeth ensured that a range of genres, text features, and text structures were available so that students with different interests, background knowledge, and existing ideas could find connections to the topic. At this stage, she was not concerned with the difficulty level of the texts. Although many of her students experienced challenges as readers, she focused more on ensuring the texts had features that might spark her students' curiosity than on choosing easy reads her students would be able to decode fluently.

Then, she conducted a read-aloud of the book *The Great Kapok Tree* (Cherry, 2000). Elizabeth knew that "the reading of a well-written piece by someone who is familiar with and loves the texts is one of the best advertisements for literacy there is" (Lammert, Long, & Worthy, 2020, p. 195). The next day, she invited students to take on different roles in the text through reader's theater and tableau, a drama-based strategy in which students pose in different ways to represent the characters in a text. Again, she followed this

TABLE 12.1. Texts Used in the Inductive Phase of a Second-Grade Unit on the Amazon Rainforest

Title	Text type	Image type	Text features
50 Simple Things Kids Can Do to Save The Earth (The Earthworks Group, 2009)	Informational	Illustrations	Headings, diagrams, table of contents
Loving the Earth: A Sacred Landscape Book for Children (Lehrman, 1990)	Informational	Photographs and illustrations	Quotations from multiple authors, poetry
Planet Ark: Preserving Earth's Biodiversity (Mason, 2013)	Informational	Illustrations	Headings, diagrams, table of contents, index
The Great Kapok Tree (Cherry, 2000)	Narrative	Illustrations	Characters, plot/problem-driven
Tree of Life: The Incredible Biodiversity of Life on Earth (Strauss, 2013)	Informational	Illustrations	Headings, diagrams, table of contents, index
Extreme! Earth: Level 2 (Kenah, 2013)	Informational	Photographs	Captions, diagrams

activity by asking students to react in writing. Finally, she showed students a brief video clip documenting farming and environmental destruction in the Amazon. After writing in their journals for a third time, the students met as a class to plan an investigation. The difference in student engagement and understanding was palpable. Elizabeth was amazed by how much the depth of their thinking had increased from her first mention of the Amazon to now, even though she felt she had not directly taught them any science content about the rainforest.

Implications and Opportunities for Classroom Application

Reading can be a starting point for science learning, particularly when children have the opportunity to write notes, questions, and wonderings as they look across a wide range of sources. At the inductive stage, it is not essential for children to conventionally read all of the text for them to use reading to generate ideas that can lead to inquiry and advocacy. What is essential is that a wide range of texts are provided so that learners with different experiences and interests can begin to harness what they know and bring it forward into investigations and subsequent writing. This writing does not need to be bound by the four walls of the classroom. In fact, several youth-led grassroots efforts have emerged to attempt to address environmental justice and climate change, including Extinction Rebellion (*https://rebellion.earth*), Zero Hour (*http://thisiszerohour.org*), the Sunrise movement (*www.sunrisemovement.org*), and School Strike Australia (*www.schoolstrike4climate.com*). The popularity of these outlets demonstrates the value of using student activism as one product of investigation that is highly engaging for young learners.

Questions for future exploration remain, though. One opportunity for practitioners is to continue to look toward the ways in which texts, when conceptualized multimodally to include photos, charts, and physical artifacts, can serve as anchoring phenomenon in inductive teaching, particularly in virtual learning environments. Next, we describe a second practice that connects reading and writing in science education: reading arguments and summaries written by peers.

Practice 2: Writing and Reading Arguments and Summaries Written by Peers

In every field of study, members of the discipline construct explanations (Wright & Domke, 2019). A literature critic might analyze the meaning behind an author's use of metaphor, or a historian might explain what motivated the passage of a particular law. In science, the construction of arguments to explain a natural phenomenon is particularly important and tends to rely on specific structures in the presentation of questions, claims, and evidence. Yore et al. (2004) explain as follows:

> Science is a process of inquiry conducted through the use of language that estab-
> lishes knowledge claims based on arguments that draw in the available evidence
> and canonical science. Scientific explanations must be consistent with observa-
> tional evidence about nature, emphasize physical causality, and facilitate accurate
> predictions. (p. 348)

Although researchers are well able to define what written arguments "must be,"
actually teaching children to engage in argumentation has proven persistently
challenging. One national study of fourth-grade student writers indicated that
only 10% were able to demonstrate strong written arguments (NCES, 2012),
and across content areas, students have struggled to support their claims with
evidence effectively (De La Paz, Ferretti, Wissinger, Yee, & MacArthur, 2012).

However, there have been attempts at describing the cognitive processes
that writers engage in as they work, and using what is known about these processes to shape instruction. Klein (1999) argued that writers engage in a process
of forward and backward searching as they compose text. Writers must search
backward to explain concepts and use text structures to their advantage, as
well as forward to decide how to proceed in constructing a new text (also see
Chapter 6). Part of looking forward is to consider the intended audience of the
writing and to consider how to shape ideas in a way that will be most compelling to that audience. Research suggests that when students are asked to write
arguments using questions, claims, and evidence structures, the audience of the
argument is important (Cavagnetto, 2010).

One particularly powerful audience can be students in a different class
or another grade level. For students, having ones' writing viewed as a text
worth sharing can be highly motivating and can validate the feeling of being
an author (Maloch & Hoffman, 2004). In addition, the work of crafting a text
that is able to be understood by someone else is a demanding cognitive task
that can lead to growth in content knowledge in science.

A Research Example

In their study, Chen et al. (2013) invited fourth-grade students to write letters
to 11th-grade students as part of a science unit on force and motion. Three letters were written at the beginning, midpoint, and end of an 8-week unit, and
the letters followed the argument structure promoted by SWH of using questions, claims, and evidence. Chen and colleagues (2013) found that the letter-
writing process encouraged the fourth-grade students to master challenging
content so that they could explain it to their older peers. As the 11th-grade
students asked the fourth-grade students for clarification, the fourth-grade
students learned even more. The researchers also gave the students pretests
and posttests of their conceptual understandings in science and determined
that students who participated in letter writing learned more than those who
did not. The results showed that the benefit of argument writing on learning
was most pronounced for female, special education, low socioeconomic status, and gifted students.

In a similar study, Gunel et al. (2009) invited high school students to write explanations of biological processes for four different audiences: the teacher, younger students, similar-aged students, and their parents. In this study, the high school students also received feedback on their writing from the instructor, as well as from their target audiences. The researchers used a writing prompt and a prompt to structure feedback. In their analysis, they found that students made more gains writing to younger and similar-aged students than they did writing to their parents or to the teacher. An example of a writing and feedback prompt that could be used for different audiences is included in Figure 12.2. The focus (i.e., climate change) and the genre of text (i.e., a textbook definition) can be adapted for other units or topics.

Implications and Opportunities for Classroom Application

There is a clear link between having a sense of belonging, and the connection between writing and reading; students tend to be more motivated to write when someone besides the teacher will read their work, and they tend to be more motivated to read when they feel a connection to the author. In both cases, having the sense that one is part of a *thought community* or discipline of study is supportive of learning in literacy and in science.

In addition, having an audience to write to also helps students learn by requiring them to make decisions about the scientific language and phrasing they want to use in their arguments. We encourage teachers to invite students to write to peers in a different classroom, at a different grade level, or at a different school. Partnerships that invite children to explain natural phenomena to others can provide an authentic space to combine reading and writing and ultimately strengthen student learning.

One area that may continue to be explored is the value of combining the letter-writing and sharing process with discussion across differently aged peers. Clearly, writers benefit, but the impact on the reader of engaging one-on-one with a peer's argument is not well understood. Particularly as dialogue has been demonstrated to be supportive of students' development of argument (Firetto et al., 2019), more models that explore the ways peers can develop in-person relationships as science colleagues, and studies of the impact of these relationships on students' critical thinking, science learning, and writing merit development. We now turn to a third practice that connects reading and writing in science education: consulting with experts.

Practice 3: Reading to Consult with Experts to Support Argument and Summary Writing

There are many reasons why students might engage with published texts and expert viewpoints as they construct explanations in science. This reading can serve at least two functions: first, these texts can serve as mentor texts to help

---

Writing Assignment

Purpose

Your purpose for writing is to explain how human-caused climate change impacts daily life. You will explain all elements of this system, including the different ways humans have impacted climate change, the impact of climate change on weather, air quality, supply chains, and natural resources, and the ways these impacts shape how people live.

Activity

Your job is to write a description of this process. You should model your writing to sound like it would if you were writing a textbook. You should define any key terms in your writing. For example, "climate" and "weather" should be clearly defined and their differences and similarities described. Just like in a real textbook, you can include diagrams, charts, photos, and other visuals to help you make your argument.

Audience

Write your textbook for your peers (3rd/4th graders). Consider that other audiences will read it too, including your teacher and your parents/ guardians.

Process

First, draft your explanation and share it with your teacher. They will give you ideas of things to add, take out, or change as you revise. Then, you will turn in a final copy that reflects the changes you have made based on your peer's responses to the feedback sheet below.

Feedback Sheet

1. Which places in the writing made sense? Why?
2. Which places in the writing made you slow down or reread because they were hard to understand? Why?
3. As someone who has read this paper, what do you understand about the impact of climate change on human life?
4. As someone who has read this paper, what are you still unsure about regarding the impact of climate change on human life?
5. If the paper included visual elements like diagrams, charts, or photos, did they help you understand the author's argument? How?
6. What else do you think the author should know?

FIGURE 12.2. A writing and feedback prompt that could be used for different audiences.

students identify particular features of summary and argument writing that they may want to adopt to make their own explanations more effective, and second, they can serve as a space for students to compare their ideas and explanations of scientific phenomena with those held by actual scientists. However, one of the most persistent challenges in teaching writing is that less experienced writers often engage mostly with published, finalized texts with little conceptualization of the many revisions an author might have gone through to arrive at that product (Bomer, 2011; Murray, 1972). No matter what type of writing a child is working on, when the thinking process authors use is invisible to students, it can leave them feeling unsure how to move from an idea to a finalized piece of writing.

Cognitive load theory (Mayer, 2005) suggests that it can be helpful to provide support to students who are new to the process of reading multiple sources, recalling what ideas each source contained and where they were located in the text, and synthesizing the information they find into their own writing. The organization of these related tasks can feel like a monumental undertaking even to fluent adult readers, but it is especially challenging to emergent readers for whom decoding and making-meaning of text can already be a laborious process (Johnston, 2000).

Some researchers have cautioned against the overuse and ritualization of teacher-provided graphic organizers, which can contribute to an emphasis on a fixed process rather than encouraging students to design their own structures for organizing their thinking (Assaf, Ash, Saunders, & Johnson, 2011). While we agree that it is important for students to have ownership of the process, there are also documented benefits to using structured reading frameworks inside of generative teaching (Wei et al., 2019). Studies have shown that secondary teachers are often prepared to help their students critique a single source at one time, but they are rarely capable of helping students work across multiple sources in discipline-specific ways (Ruiz & Many, 2009). However, the use of structured reading frameworks has been shown to improve the quality of children's summary writing as well as their development of conceptual understandings in science, likely because they encourage and create space for children to engage in deeper critical thinking (Jang, 2013; Jang & Hand, 2017).

Two Research Examples

Hoffman et al. (2020) used the activism in the curriculum model in a socioscientific (Sadler, 2004) language arts simulation focused on the science fiction novel *The Green Book* (Walsh, 1986). In this study, preservice teachers and their bilingual fourth-grade students participated in a guided reading of the story combined with a simulation in which competing parties sent students two types of messages: some claimed the Earth was beyond repair, and they must prepare to leave the planet permanently, while others claimed the Earth could be saved and they should stay. To keep track of competing arguments and positions, the students tracked their ideas using post-it notes on a shared argument chart they co-designed with the preservice teachers and course instructors. Each student read informational texts widely on the topic, then announced their decision whether to stay or leave, and offered the evidence that supported their position. Then, students shared their argument charts with other groups. The charts clearly showed a combination of teacher guidance with student writing, and a progression from making sense of the situation, to gathering evidence, to determining a course of action. The charts also showed that students varied in their understanding of the problem itself, which led to them making different decisions about whether to stay on or leave Earth.

A second example comes from Jang (2013), and Jang and Hand (2017) who developed a Scaffolded Critique Framework (SCF) for reading and embedded it in SWH teaching. Inside of argument-based inquiry teaching, sixth- and seventh-grade students in Jang's study used one of two templates as they conducted an investigation and completed a summary writing task. One template was open-ended. It simply encouraged students to write down information from outside sources on blank paper. The other included specific prompts for the students to attend to as they gathered information, including author, title, and a brief description of how the author's ideas compared to their own. Jang and Hand (2017) found that the students who used the more specific SCF template performed better on the summary writing task. In particular, they tended to avoid confirmation bias (Mercier & Sperber, 2011), whereby a person ignores new information that contradicts their viewpoint and only seeks confirmatory evidence. Instead, they were able to consider other views and construct more coherent explanations. An example of a critique framework is provided in Figure 12.3. This framework can be adapted based on the age/grade level of the students, and the types/sources of information available to them.

Jang and Hand (2017) found that the students who used the more specific SCF template performed better on the summary writing task. In particular, they tended to avoid confirmation bias (Mercier & Sperber, 2011) through which a person ignores new information that contradicts their viewpoint and only seeks confirmatory evidence. Instead, they were able to consider other views and construct more coherent explanations.

Implications and Opportunities for Classroom Applications

While some young writers may feel constrained by the suggestion to use writing templates, and they may not be necessary for all tasks or for all readers, research suggests templates can contribute to the composition of better written products, better understandings of scientific concepts, and deeper engagement in critical thinking. This may be because the introduction of the template takes some of the organizational work off the writer and allows them to engage more fully with the ideas they encounter.

For teachers who are concerned about overusing these structures, one option is to co-construct argument charts with students, either individually, in small groups, or as a class. Another option is to provide students with different options for organizational tables they can choose based on their particular questions and topics. For example, a teacher might have SCF templates, Venn diagrams, and T charts available to students to select from as needed.

Graphic organizers create a valuable bridge between what is read and the writing process. Particularly in more deductive work such as summary writing, the use of graphic organizers can be a valuable source of support. One area of opportunity that still exists is the exploration of digital tools to support children's writing. As school increasingly shifts to virtual environments, the use of templates and organizers that draw on technological tools merits a closer look.

Framework for Critiquing Outside Sources
Record your notes from outside experts here. Use the scaffolds below to help you.
Title of the Source: Type of Source: (e.g., websites, podcasts, news articles, informational books) Author(s) & Illustrators:
Rationale: State why you thought this text would help you with your investigation.
Information: Write what this source tells you that will help with your investigation.
Negotiation-with-self: Does this source fit with what you already thought? How and how not?
Negotiation-with-text: Compare your own claim with the one presented in this text. Are you relying on the same or different evidence?
Next steps: After reading this text, do you still need more information? What information do you need?

FIGURE 12.3. A scaffolded critique framework.

Conclusion

As we wrote this chapter, we considered that one way of viewing the topic of reading and writing connections in science would be through the perspective of *integration*. For example, one might support integrated reading and writing instruction or the integration of literacy learning in science. We see value in the process of layering goals and linking overlapping areas; however, our position is that the work of this type of teaching is actually *uncover* and *reveal* the inherent connections that already exist. While schools often separate content, real-world problems almost always require more than one set of knowledge. In our view, there is no science without language, and literacy always constitutes both reading and writing. With the intention of further uncovering the unified nature of these knowledges and envisioning ways in which their integration can be revealed, we conclude this chapter by exploring Monaghan's proposition that "they who can write hold power" (2000, p. 321). Then, we offer readers some areas in which they might contribute to the field by exploring such ideas in their classrooms.

First, we see the power of connected reading and writing as especially important to extract given the diversifying student demographics in K–12 classrooms today (NCES, 2018). Teachers are often very different racially, culturally, and linguistically from their students, and outcomes in both literacy and science achievement continue to favor higher-income, White, native-born English speakers (Swartz & Stiefel, 2011; Vigor, 2011). Students' development of disciplinary academic language is essential, as is their development of critical awareness of why this type of language exists (Moore & Schleppegrell, 2020). For students who are rarely regarded as having perspectives worth sharing, approaches that emphasize activism (Ahmed & Daniels, 2017) and the use of argument to influence audiences outside the classroom are particularly relevant.

Although writing holds power, unfortunately, there is a concerning but not altogether surprising decline in students' motivation to write as they progress from the elementary to middle and high school grades (Koster, Tribushinina, de Jong, & van den Bergh, 2015). Wright and colleagues (2020) have noted that pressure related to high-stakes standardized assessment is one influence on students' declining interest in writing. We realize that as professionals, teachers have a responsibility to ensure their students' success on these measures; however, when teachers focus exclusively on writing for the purpose of test preparation, and when coursework becomes increasingly departmentalized as children progress through school, it limits the possibility of the literacy-supported investigative science learning that we promote in this chapter. In our work, we have seen high levels of engagement (as well as measurable academic gains), particularly for students with learning differences, English learners, and students from lower socioeconomic status communities (Hoffman et al., 2020; Laugerman et al., 2013).

Finally, we argue that much of the power that literacy provides comes through the use of reading and writing for the purpose of learning. While many children are marginalized due to their racial, cultural, and linguistic positions, we view experiences with science learning that are replicative of existing knowledge, rather than generative, as contributing toward another type of marginalization. Generative learning environments such as those constructed through SWH teaching provide ideal spaces for students to engage in the disciplinary practices of the sciences, to learn to base their arguments on evidence, and to gain an understanding of how the natural world works. This is more important than ever as the global climate crisis looms, and every student with whom we interact has a potential role to play in preserving the environment.

In this chapter, we have shown how SWH and the Activism in the Curriculum model can contribute to equitable learning experiences that draw on reading and writing in the teaching of science. While the SWH has a long and substantial history of contributing to improved academic outcomes and has been extensively studied, Jang and Hand's (2017) work shows that any model can continue to be strengthened. In contrast, the Activism in the Curriculum model is an emergent framework with limited but growing research to support its utility. Thus, we invite preservice teachers, inservice teachers, instructional coaches, and other practitioners to join us in innovating on these ideas as we, together, elevate the liberatory nature of science education.

To conclude, we offer the following action questions:

- How can teachers use language-based tools like dialogue and negotiation to support students' understanding of the big ideas of science? What are ways teachers can prepare for the flexibility and adaptability that this type of teaching requires?
- How can teachers recognize whether their classrooms are functioning as knowledge-replication environments or as knowledge-generation environments? What evidence of learning is needed?
- How can science curriculum invite students to engage with social issues through informational text reading? How can science curriculum invite students to advocate for change through argumentative text writing? What are the barriers and what are the advantages to doing so?
- How can teachers and administrators adopt approaches to curriculum and assessment that uncover the ways writing, reading, and science learning operate together?

REFERENCES

Ahmed, S., & Daniels, H. (2017). Identity, empathy and inquiry. *Literacy Today, 34*(5), 44–45.

Assaf, L. C., Ash, G. E., Saunders, J., & Johnson, J. (2011). Renewing two seminal literacy practices: I-Charts and I-Search papers. *Voices from the Middle, 18*(4), 31–42.

Bomer, R. (2011). *Building adolescent literacy in today's English classrooms.* Portsmouth, NH: Heinemann.

Cavagnetto, A. R. (2010). Argument to foster scientific literacy: A review of argument interventions in K–12 science contexts. *Review of Educational Research, 80*(3), 336–371.

Chen, Y.-C., Hand, B., & McDowell, L. (2013). The effects of writing-to-learn activities on elementary students' conceptual understanding: Learning about force and motion through writing to older peers. *Science Education, 5*, 745–771.

De La Paz, S., Ferretti, R., Wissinger, D., Yee, L., & MacArthur, C. (2012). Adolescents' disciplinary use of evidence, argumentative strategies, and organizational structure in writing about historical controversies. *Written Communication, 29*, 412–454.

Duke, N. K. (2000). 3.6 minutes per day: The scarcity of informational texts in first grade. *Reading Research Quarterly, 35*(2), 202–224.

Firetto, C. M., Murphy, P. K., Greene, J. A., Li, M., Wei, L., Montalbano, C., . . . Croninger, R. M. V. (2019). Bolstering students' written argumentation by refining an effective discourse intervention: Negotiating the fine line between flexibility and fidelity. *Instructional Science, 47*, 181–214.

Fitzgerald, J., & Shanahan, T. (2000). Reading and writing relations and their development. *Educational Psychologist, 35*(1), 39–50.

Galbraith, D. (1999). Writing as a knowledge-constituting process. In D. Galbraith & M. Torrance (Ed.), *Knowing what to write: Conceptual processes in text production* (pp. 139–159). Amsterdam: Amsterdam University Press.

Graham, S. (2020a). The sciences of reading and writing must become more fully integrated. *Reading Research Quarterly, 55*(Supp. 1), 35–44.

Graham, S. (2020b). Reading and writing connections: A commentary. In R. A. Alves, T. Limpo, & R. M. Joshi (Eds.), *Reading–writing connections: Towards integrative literacy science* (pp. 313–317). New York: Springer.

Graham, S., & Hebert M. (2011). Writing to read: A meta-analysis of the impact of reading and writing instruction on reading. *Harvard Educational Review, 81*(4), 710–744.

Graham, S., Kiuhara, S. A., & MacKay, M. (2020). The effects of writing on learning in science, social studies, and mathematics: A meta-analysis. *Review of Educational Research, 90*(2), 179–226.

Gunel, M., Hand, B., & McDermott, M. (2009). Writing for different audiences: Effects on high-school students' conceptual understanding of biology. *Learning and Instruction, 19*, 354–367.

Guthrie, J. T., Wigfield, A., Barbosa, P., Perencevich, K. C., Taboda, A., & Davis, D. (2004). Increasing reading comprehension and engagement through concept-oriented reading instruction. *Journal of Educational Psychology, 96*(3), 403–423.

Hand, B. (Ed.). (2008). *Science inquiry, argument and language: A case for the science writing heuristic.* Rotterdam, the Netherlands: Sense.

Hand, B. (2017). Exploring the role of writing in science: A 25-year journey. *Literacy Learning: The Middle Years, 25*(3), 16–23.

Hand, B., Chen, Y.-C., & Suh, J. K. (2020). Does a knowledge generation approach to learning benefit students? A systematic review of research on the science writing heuristic approach. *Educational Psychology Review, 33*, 535–577.

Hand, B., & Prain, V. (1996). Writing for learning in science: A model for use within classrooms. *Australian Science Teachers Journal, 42*(3), 23–27.

Hoffman, J. V., Lammert, C., DeJulio, S., Tily, S., & Svrcek, N., (2020). Preservice teachers engaging elementary students in an activist curriculum. *Research in the Teaching of English, 55*(1), 9–31.

Hwang, J. (2018). *Bridge the gap between cognitive attributes and mathematics achievement: Which cognitive attributes for mathematical modeling contributed to better learning in mathematics?* PhD dissertation, University of Iowa.

International Literacy Association. (2020). *Teaching writing to improve reading skills* [Research advisory]. Newark, DE: Author.

Jang, J.-Y., & Hand, B. (2017). Examining the value of a Scaffolded Critique Framework to promote argumentative and explanatory writings within an argument-based inquiry approach. *Research in Science Education, 47*, 1213–1231.

Jang, K. H. (2013). *(The) effect of argumentation-based negotiation in the Science Writing Heuristic (SWH) approach on students' question and claim-evidence.* PhD dissertation, Pusan National University, Busan, South Korea.

Johnston, F. R. (2000). Word learning in predictable text. *Journal of Educational Psychology, 92*(2), 248.

Keys, C. W., Hand, B., Prain, V., & Collins, S. (1999). Using the science writing heuristic as a tool for learning from laboratory investigations in secondary science. *Journal of Research in Science Teaching, 36*(10), 1065–1084.

Klein, P. (1999). Reopening inquiry into cognitive processes in writing to learn. *Educational Psychology Review, 11*, 203–270.

Klein, P. D., & Yu, A. M. (2013). Best practices in writing to learn. In S. Graham, C. A. MacArthur, & J. Fitzgerald (Eds.), *Best practices in writing instruction* (pp. 166–189). New York: Guilford Press.

Koster, M., Tribushinina, E., de Jong, P. F., & van den Bergh, H. (2015). Teaching children to write: A meta-analysis of writing intervention research. *Journal of Writing Research, 7*(2), 249–274.

Lammert, C., Long, S. L., & Worthy, J. (2020). Amplifying diverse voices with read alouds in elementary, middle, and high school classrooms. In M. R. Kuhn & M. J. Dreher (Eds.), *Developing conceptual knowledge through oral and written language* (pp. 188–210). New York: Guilford Press.

Laugerman, M., Fostvedt, L., Shelley, M., Baenziger, J., Gonwa-Reeves, C., Hand, B., et al. (2013, March 7–9). *Structural equation modeling of knowledge content improvement using inquiry-based instruction.* Interactive poster presentation at the Spring 2013 Conference of the Society for Research on Educational Effectiveness, Washington, DC.

Lewis, C., Enciso, P., & Moje, E. B. (2007). *Reframing sociocultural research on literacy: Identity, agency, and power.* Mahwah, NJ: Erlbaum.

Maloch, B., & Hoffman, J. V. (2004). Local texts: Reading and writing "of the classroom." In J. Hoffman & D. Schallert (Eds.), *The texts in elementary classrooms* (pp. 145–156). Ann Arbor, MI: Center for the Improvement of Early Reading Achievement.

Marshall, C., & Anderson, A. L. (2009). *Activist educators: Breaking past limits.* New York: Routledge.

Mayer, R. E. (2005). Cognitive theory of multimedia learning. In R. E. Mayer (Ed.), *The Cambridge handbook of multimedia learning* (pp. 31–48). New York: Cambridge University Press.

Mercier, H., & Sperber, D. (2011). Why do humans reason? Arguments for an argumentative theory. *Behavioral and Brain Sciences, 34*(2), 57–74.

Moje, E. (2007). Developing socially just subject-matter instruction: A review of the literature on disciplinary literacy teaching. *Review of Education Research, 31*, 1–44.

Monaghan, E. J. (2000). Reading for the enslaved, writing for the free: Reflections on liberty and literacy. In *The history of the book in American culture* (pp. 309–341). Worcester, MA: American Antiquarian Society. Retrieved from *www.americanantiquarian.org/proceedings/44525153.pdf.*

Moore, J., & Schleppegrell, M. (2020). A focus on disciplinary language: Bringing critical perspectives to reading and writing in science. *Theory into Practice, 59*(1), 99–108.

Murray, D. (1972). Teach writing as a process not product. *The Leaflet*, 11–14.

National Center for Education Statistics. (2012). *The nation's report card: Writing 2011* (NCES 2012-470). Washington, DC: Institute of Education Sciences, U.S. Department of Education. Retrieved from *https://nces.ed.gov/nationsreportcard/pdf/main2011/2012470.pdf.*

National Center for Education Statistics. (2018). *Adult training and education survey* [Data file]. Retrieved from *https://nces.ed.gov/nhes/pdf/ates/2016_ates.pdf.*

NGSS Lead States. (2013). *Next generation science standards: For states, by states.* Washington, DC: The National Academies Press.

Norris, S., & Phillips, L. (2003). How literacy in its fundamental sense is central to science literacy. *Science Education, 87*, 224–240.

Norton-Meier, L. (2008). Creating border convergence between science and literacy: A case for the Science Writing Heuristic. In B. Hand (Ed.), *Science inquiry, argument and language: A case for the Science Writing Heuristic* (pp. 13–24). Rotterdam, the Netherlands: Sense.

Pentimonti, J. M., Zucker, T. A., & Justice, L. M. (2011). What are preschool teachers reading in their classrooms? *Reading Psychology, 32*(3), 197–236.

Purcell-Gates, V., Duke, N. K., & Martineau, J. A. (2007). Learning to read and write genre-specific text: Roles of authentic experience and explicit teaching. *Reading Research Quarterly, 42*(1), 8–45.

Rossato, C. A. (2007). *Engaging Paulo Freire's pedagogy of possibility: From blind to transformative optimism.* Lanham, MD: Rowman & Littlefield.

Ruiz, A. M., & Many, J. E. (2009). Are they ready to teach students how to do research? An examination of secondary teacher education programs. In K. M. Leander, D. W. Rowe, D. K. Dickinson, M. K. Hundley, R. T. Jiménez, & V. J. Risko (Eds.), *58th Yearbook of the National Reading Conference* (pp. 144–155). LaGrange, GA: Literacy Research Association.

Sadler, T. D. (2004). Informal reasoning regarding socioscientific issues: A critical review of research. *Journal of Research in Science Teaching, 41*(5), 513–536.

Schoerning, E., Hand, B., Shelley, M., & Therrien, W. (2015). Language, access, and power in the elementary science classroom. *Science Education, 99*(2), 238–259.

Shanahan, C., Shanahan, T., & Misischia, C. (2011). Analysis of expert readers in three disciplines: History, mathematics, and chemistry. *Journal of Literacy Research, 43*(4), 393–429.

Swartz, A., & Stiefel, L. (2011). Immigrants and inequality in public schools. In G. Duncan & R. Murnane (Eds.), *Whither opportunity? Rising inequality, schools, and children's life chances* (pp. 419–442). New York: Russell Sage Foundation.

Vigor, J. (2011). School desegregation and the black–white test score gap. In G. Duncan & R. Murnane (Eds.), *Whither opportunity? Rising inequality, schools, and children's life chances* (pp. 443–464). New York: Russell Sage Foundation.

Wei, L., Firetto, C. M., Murphy, P. K., Li, M., Greene, J. A., & Croninger, R. M. V. (2019). Facilitating fourth-grade students' written argumentation: The use of an argumentation graphic organizer. *The Journal of Education Research, 112*(5), 627–639.

Wilson-Lopez, A., & Minichiello, A. (2017). Disciplinary literacy in engineering. *Journal of Adolescent & Adult Literacy, 61*(1), 7–14.

Wright, K. L., Hodges, T. S., Dismuke, S., & Boedeker, P. (2020). Writing motivation and middle school: An examination of changes in students' motivation for writing. *Literacy Research and Instruction, 59*(2), 148–168.

Wright, T. S., & Domke, L. M. (2019). The role of language and literacy in K–5 science and social studies standards. *Journal of Literacy Research, 51*(1), 5–29.

Wright, T. S., & Gotwals, A. W. (2017). Supporting kindergarteners' science talk in the context of an integrated science and disciplinary literacy curriculum. *The Elementary School Journal, 117*(3), 513–537.

Yopp, R. H., & Yopp, H. K. (2006). Informational texts as read-alouds at school and home. *Journal of Literacy Research, 38*(1), 37–51.

Yore, L. D., Hand, B., Goldman, S. R., Hildebrand, G. M., Osborne, J. F., Treagust, D. F., & Wallace, C. S. (2004). New directions in language and science education research. *Reading Research Quarterly, 39*(3), 347–352.

CHILDREN'S LITERATURE

Cherry, L. (2000). *The great kapok tree: A tale of the Amazon rainforest.* Boston: Houghton Mifflin Harcourt.

The Earthworks Group. (2009). *50 simple things kids can do to save the Earth.* Kansas City, MO: Andrews McMeel.

Kenah, K. (2013). *Extreme! Earth: Level 2.* Spectrum Readers. Greensboro, NC: Carson Dellosa Education.

Lehrman, F. (1990). *Loving the Earth: A sacred landscape book for children.* (L. Tune, Illus.). San Mateo, CA: Celestial Arts.

Mason, A. (2013). *Planet ark: Preserving Earth's biodiversity* (M. Thompson, Illus.). Toronto: Kids Can Press.

Strauss, R. (2013). *Tree of life: The incredible biodiversity of life on Earth* (M. Thompson, Illus.). Toronto: Kids Can Press.

Walsh, J. P. (1986). *The green book.* New York: Macmillan.

CHAPTER 13

Thinking Beyond Symbols
Writing and Reading in Mathematics

Sarah R. Powell
Michael A. Hebert

When you think of *mathematics*, what comes to mind? Maybe you think about counting or numbers? Perhaps you think about multiplying or fractions? Maybe you think about your high school algebra course or taking the mathematics section of a college entrance exam? When most people think about mathematics, they think about numbers and symbols. Mathematics, however, involves reading and understanding vocabulary as well as formulating and sharing ideas, often through conversation or writing.

As defined by Kilpatrick et al. (2001), mathematical proficiency includes conceptual understanding (i.e., knowledge of concepts, operations, and relations); procedural fluency (i.e., skill with using mathematical procedures efficiently and flexibly); strategic competence (i.e., representing and solving problems); adaptive reasoning (i.e., using thought, reflection, explanation, and justification); and productive disposition (i.e., seeing mathematics as useful and worthwhile). The learning of these proficiencies occurs through reading, listening, speaking, and writing. Therefore, understanding the language of mathematics is essential for developing full proficiency in mathematics.

In this chapter, we focus on reading and writing in mathematics. We focus on two important reading skills in mathematics—understanding mathematical vocabulary and solving word problems. Then, we describe mathematical writing and focus on mathematical writing assessments and instruction in the mathematics classroom. You may use these guiding questions to comment and reflect on your reading:

GUIDING QUESTIONS

- When you hear the word *mathematics*, what comes to mind?
- What's the role of understanding mathematical vocabulary for mathematical proficiency?
- How can you support students in the setting up and solving of word problems?
- What are ways to assess the mathematical writing of students?
- How can you support students' mathematical writing?

Reading in Mathematics

Reading and reading comprehension are an important part of mathematics. Students read textbooks and other mathematical material (e.g., workbooks, storybooks) to learn new concepts. When watching a video about mathematics, students may read text on the screen. On many formal and informal assessments, students read mathematical problems and answer prompts. When students experience difficulty reading within mathematics, they will likely have greater difficulty with mathematics.

Figure 13.1 features several examples of mathematical problems similar to those from high-stakes tests (Powell, Namkung, & Lin, 2022). The first problem is a routine word problem in which a student has to read the prompt and answer the question about boxes for the tomatoes. To answer this problem, a student has to read 25 words and 2 numbers; interpret that 504 tomatoes will be placed into groups of 24; and solve to determine that Lando needs 21 boxes. Both the second and third problems are directive word problems in which a student is directed to do something (e.g., measure an angle). In these problems, understanding mathematical vocabulary is essential. A student would not likely answer either question correctly without knowledge of the terms *measure*, *angle*, *nearest*, and *degree* or *expressions* and *equivalent*. The fourth problem is a nonroutine word problem in which the student can answer the question in several different ways. This problem, with 38 words and 4 numbers, requires a student to read the prompt and understand they need to determine three different ways to spend $120 on frames.

Reading in mathematics requires an understanding of general English and its conventions, such as sentences and paragraphs as well as punctuation and grammar. Reading in mathematics also involves understanding of mathematical vocabulary terms, some of which a student may have seen or heard outside of the mathematical environment and some of which are brand-new terms. In the next section, we focus on mathematical vocabulary.

Mathematical Vocabulary

We define mathematical vocabulary as terms necessary for understanding mathematical concepts (e.g., *trapezoid* or *zero pairs*) and procedures (e.g., *multiply*

1 Lando has 504 tomatoes to put into boxes for the farmer's market. Each box holds 24 tomatoes. How many boxes does Lando need for all the tomatoes?

2.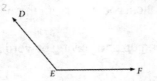

What is the measure of angle DEF to the nearest degree?

3 Which two expressions are equivalent?

a.	$7 + (3x)$	$x(7 + 3)$
b.	$(24 \div y) + 5$	$5 + (y \div 24)$
c.	$15 - (x2)$	$15 - (2x)$
d.	$(12 - 4) \div y$	$12 - (4 \div y)$

4 At the frame shop, small frames cost $16, medium frames cost $32, and large frames cost $40. If Alec wants to spend $120 on frames, which type and how many frames can Alec buy? Determine three ways that Alec can buy frames.

FIGURE 13.1. Examples of mathematical problems.

or *regroup*), as well as terms that would allow for full participation in mathematics activities (e.g., *measure* or *combine*). In an analysis of the mathematical vocabulary terms in mathematics textbooks, Powell, Bos, and Lin (2021) identified over 1,200 distinct mathematical vocabulary terms across kindergarten through grade 8. In the early elementary grades, glossaries contained 120 to 150 distinct terms. This number jumped in third grade to over 300. By middle school, the number of terms wavered between 400 and 500. Interestingly, some mathematical vocabulary terms, once introduced, continued across grade levels, whereas some were used at only one or two grade levels. There is a tremendous amount of mathematical vocabulary students need to understand and use (Barnes & Stephens, 2019).

Why Is Mathematical Vocabulary Difficult?

On assessments of mathematical vocabulary, student scores vary greatly with many students performing below grade-level expectations (Hughes, Powell, & Lee, 2020; Powell, Driver, Roberts, & Fall, 2017; Powell & Nelson, 2017). Mathematical vocabulary may be difficult for some students because of the complexities of the terms. Rubenstein and Thompson (2002) outlined different reasons students may struggle with mathematical vocabulary. Some of these reasons included: (1) Some mathematical terms have meanings in mathematics and English but with different meanings (e.g., an *expression* like 2 + 3 vs. a facial *expression*); (2) some mathematical terms have meanings in mathematics and English with a more precise mathematical meaning (e.g., 5 is the *difference* between 9 and 4 vs. determining the *difference* between restaurants); (3) some mathematical terms have more than one meaning in mathematics (e.g., a *square* root vs. a *square* shape); (4) some mathematical terms are homophones (e.g., *eight* vs. *ate*); and (5) some mathematical terms can be confused because they are related but have distinct meanings (e.g., *factor* and *multiple*). Furthermore, many mathematical terms are not found outside of mathematics, therefore limiting prior knowledge (e.g., *numerator, commutative property, rhombus*; Schleppegrell, 2007).

How Do You Teach Mathematical Vocabulary?

While the research base related to instruction on mathematical vocabulary is in the emergent phase, there are several suggestions for helping students increase their knowledge of mathematical vocabulary (Riccomini, Smith, Hughes, & Fries, 2015). First and foremost, teachers need to understand the formal language of mathematics (e.g., *numerator* and *denominator* instead of *top number* and *bottom number*) and use such language consistently (Hughes, Powell, & Stevens, 2016). Teachers sometimes use informal mathematical terms (e.g., *box* or *reduce*) to help students understand mathematics, but eventually students also have to learn the formal mathematical terms (e.g., *square* or *simplify*). Imagine a student who participates in mathematics intervention with one teacher who describes *borrowing* when solving a subtraction problem. This student then goes to their general education classroom, where another teacher uses the term *regrouping*. By teaching the informal term (e.g., *borrowing*), teachers may force students to learn a greater number of vocabulary terms. Also, informal terms at one grade level may not transfer to what a student learns in subsequent grade levels. For example, talking about the equal sign as "railroad tracks" in the first grade is not going to transfer to formal conversations about the *equal sign* meaning *balance* or *same* in grade 2 and beyond. Teachers also need to be precise with their mathematical language (e.g., understanding and stressing the difference between *coefficient, term, variable,* and *constant*; Powell, Stevens, & Hughes, 2019). Students often confuse terms used within the same mathematical content, so explicit discussion about the similarities and differences among terms is essential.

Teachers should explicitly teach students mathematical terms (Nelson, Pfannenstiel, & Zumeta Edmonds, 2020). When starting a new unit, preview mathematical terms by sharing the terms and student-friendly definitions. Students should speak and write terms and receive multiple opportunities to hear and use the terms. Teachers could create word walls of mathematical terms or have students create their own glossaries or journals of mathematical terms. Teachers could also play games with mathematical vocabulary (e.g., *Jeopardy!*), do crosswords or seek-and-finds with mathematical terms, or use one of many technology-based programs that review mathematical vocabulary. There are many ways to emphasize mathematical vocabulary to help students access the language of mathematics.

Word-Problem Solving

We define word-problem solving as the act of setting up and solving mathematical word problems. Here is an example fourth-grade word problem: *Alexa had a total of 36 bottles of water. She drank half of the bottles of water last week. Alexa will drink the remaining water bottles during the next 6 days. If she drinks the same number of bottles each day, how many bottles will Alexa drink per day?* (State of Texas, 2019). Word-problem solving is important because problem solving relates to real-life mathematics. Problem solving allows students to develop reasoning skills in mathematics. It is also important because students have to solve word problems in textbooks, on chapter tests, on unit tests, and on high-stakes standardized tests to demonstrate their mathematical proficiency. Often, students' mathematics scores are determined by their performance on word-problem tasks—just look at any state or country's high-stakes mathematics test.

Why Is Word-Problem Solving Difficult?

There are many reasons students experience difficulty with the solving of word problems. Reading a word problem, with its many words, can be difficult for students, as can be the interpretation of vocabulary terms (Shaftel, Belton-Kocher, Glasnapp, & Pollio, 2006; Walkington, Clinton, Ritter, & Nathan, 2015). Students may have difficulty interpreting the information in the problem (Pongsakdi et al., 2020), especially if the problem contains irrelevant information (Wang, Fuchs, & Fuchs, 2016). Identifying the schema (or conceptual structure) of the word problem is often tricky (Scheibling-Sève, Pasquinelli, & Sander, 2020), as is determining which operation(s) to use for solving the problem (Kingsdorf & Krawec, 2014). Students experience greater difficulty solving word problems with a missing addend, minuend, or subtrahend rather than a sum or difference (Powell, Fuchs, Fuchs, Cirino, & Fletcher, 2009). The same is true for multiplication and division. Word problems with an unknown product or quotient are easier to solve than those with an unknown factor, dividend, or divisor. Furthermore, single-step word problems are easier for students than multistep word problems (Fuchs & Fuchs, 2002).

How Do You Teach Word-Problem Solving?

As described earlier in this chapter, word-problem solving occurs through three types of problems: routine, directive, and nonroutine (see Figure 13.1). Students solve nonroutine problems infrequently or not at all (Powell et al., 2022). Directive word problems involve following directions to answer questions about a variety of mathematical content. It is routine word problems that cause much difficulty for many students (Fuchs et al., 2021; Peltier, Sinclair, Pulos, & Suk, 2020); therefore, we provide information about how to help students set up and solve routine word problems. This information would also help students with the solving of directive and nonroutine word problems.

First, let us focus on ineffective word-problem strategies. A common word-problem strategy is locating a keyword (or key term) in a word problem and connecting that keyword with an operation. For example, a student might think *total* means to add or *share* means to divide. This is an ineffective strategy. In fact, keywords matched to a specific operation led to a correct word-problem answer less than 50% of the time for single-step word problems and less than 10% of the time for multistep word problems (Powell et al., 2022). Many teachers will have keywords posters in their classrooms in which students match a keyword to an operation without any consideration of the meaning of the word problem (Karp, Bush, & Daugherty, 2019).

So, how should students learn to set up and solve word problems? There are several evidence-based strategies that contribute to gains in word-problem knowledge, such as cognitive strategies (Krawec, Huang, Montague, Kressler, & Melia de Alba, 2012), use of diagrams (van Garderen & Scheuermann, 2015), and use of explicit instruction (Swanson, Moran, Lussier, & Fung, 2014). We will focus on the use of two strategies that have a rich evidence base—use of an attack strategy and a focus on word-problem schemas (Fuchs et al., 2021; Griffin, Gagnon, Jossi, Ulrich, & Myers, 2018; Peltier et al., 2020; Powell, Berry, et al., 2021). These strategies are often combined, giving them greater utility and effectiveness.

An attack strategy is a metacognitive strategy that walks students through the general process for solving a problem. There are many different attack strategies used in schools, but the general components to look for include reading the problem, making a plan, solving the problem, and checking the work (Pólya, 1945). For example, Freeman-Green et al. (2015) used the SOLVE attack strategy: Study the problem (by reading it), Organize the facts, Line up a plan, Verify your plan, and Evaluate your answer. In Figure 13.2, we present the attack strategy of UPSCheck. With this attack strategy, students aim to Understand the problem by reading it and explaining what the problem is about. Next, they make a Plan about how they will solve the problem. Then, Solve the problem by doing computation. And finally, they do a Check of the work to ensure the answer makes sense. The attack strategy should be modeled by the teacher every time the teacher teaches about word-problem solving, and it should be used by students every time they solve mathematical word problems. At some point, the attack strategy should become an internalized process for attacking any word problem.

In combination with an attack strategy, teachers should help students understand several general schemas that appear in word problems across grade levels (Cook, Collins, Morin, & Riccomini, 2020; Jitendra et al., 2015). A schema refers to the underlying structure of the word problem and allows for students to recognize similar word problems as falling into a category in which the student can apply a common solution strategy (Marshall, 1995). Across the elementary and middle school grades, there are six schemas that students see with regularity (Carpenter, Hiebert, & Moser, 1981; Van de Walle, Karp, & Ray-Williams, 2019; Willis & Fuson, 1988; Xin & Zhang, 2009).

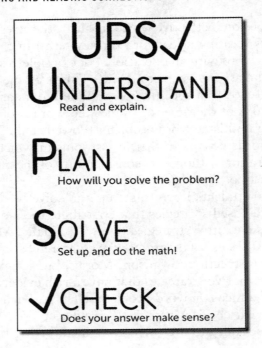

FIGURE 13.2. Word-problem attack strategy.

There are three schemas in which students may add and subtract within the schema (Powell & Fuchs, 2018). With *total* or *combine* problems, students combine two or more parts for a total (e.g., *The movie theater sells 1,130 tickets for movies on Friday, Saturday, and Sunday. If the theater sells 456 tickets on Friday and 540 tickets on Saturday, how many tickets did the theater sell on Sunday?*). With *difference* or *compare* problems, students compare two amounts for a difference (e.g., *Gena walked 32 miles in October. Jessica walked 49 miles. How many fewer miles did Gena walk than Jessica?*). With *change* problems, students have an amount that increases (i.e., *joins*) or decreases (i.e., *separates*) from an existing set (e.g., *Xin made 65 bookmarks and then sold some of them at the book fair. Now, she has 17 bookmarks. How many bookmarks did Xin sell?*).

Similarly, there are three schemas in which students may multiply or divide within the schema (Powell & Fuchs, 2018). With *equal groups* problems, students have groups with an equal number in each group (e.g., *At the school, 65 students showed up for lunch period. If the students sit at tables with 5 students each, how many tables are needed?*). With *comparison* problems, students have to multiply a set a number of times (e.g., *Ashli read her book for 15 minutes. Jeni read her book for 3 times as many minutes as Ashli. How many minutes did Jeni read her book?*). With *ratio* or *proportion* problems, students explore the relationships among quantities (e.g., *Corey plants 6 plants in 15 minutes. At this rate, how many plants will Corey plant in 90 minutes?*).

How do students learn about the schemas? Learning occurs through lots of explicit modeling from the teacher with many, many guided and independent practice opportunities (Powell & Fuchs, 2018). Often, teachers use graphic organizers (Jitendra, Star, Dupuis, & Rodriguez, 2013; Xin & Zhang, 2009) or equations (Fuchs et al., 2014; Powell, Berry, et al., 2021) to represent the different schemas. Students can then use the graphic organizer or equation and plug in the information from the word problem to aid with solving the problem. Learning the schemas takes a lot of time, sometimes weeks or months, and students need refreshing on the schemas as they progress through the grade levels and start to see word problems with fractions, decimals, or algebraic notation.

Writing in Mathematics

Similar to reading, writing is an integral part of mathematics. Over the last two decades, practice standards (i.e., how students should engage in mathematics learning) have suggested students should make sense of problems, reason abstractly, construct viable arguments, and critique the reasoning of others, among other practice standards (National Governors Association Center for Best Practices & Council of Chief State School Officers, 2010). To address these practice standards and to determine whether students can follow through on these practices, students have been asked to write about mathematics more and more. In fact, half of states in the United States ask students to write about mathematics on the mathematics portion of the state's high-stakes test. Writing in mathematics can help students learn mathematics (Graham, Kiuhara, & MacKay, 2020), but if students experience difficulty with the structure and grammar of writing, they will likely have greater difficulty with mathematics and demonstrating their mathematics proficiency through writing.

Because of the greater emphasis on mathematical writing, Casa et al. (2016) described four types of mathematical writing. First, students may engage in exploratory writing in which they tease out ideas. Second, students may engage in informative or explanatory writing in order to describe or explain something in mathematics. On high-stakes mathematics tests across the United States, explanatory writing is the most common type of mathematical writing students are asked to do. Third, students may participate in argumentative mathematical writing in which they construct an argument or critique an argument. Fourth, students may write creatively in mathematics to show original ideas or to elaborate on ideas.

As stated, writing in mathematics requires an understanding of general English and conventions in English, such as sentences, paragraphs, punctuation, and grammar. Mathematical writing also involves understanding mathematical vocabulary terms. In a national survey of teachers of mathematics, the majority of teachers suggested they felt underprepared to assess mathematical writing and teach students how to write mathematically (Powell, Hebert, et al., 2021). In the next section, we focus on assessments that can help teachers gauge the mathematical writing of students. Then, we highlight instructional practices to improve mathematical writing.

Mathematical Writing Assessment

We define mathematical writing assessment as asking students to write about mathematics to either assess their mathematical ability or to assess their ability to communicate about mathematics through writing. The difference between these two ideas is not insignificant. When assessing students' mathematical knowledge by having them write, there is an implicit assumption that students have the requisite writing skill to be able to demonstrate their mathematical knowledge (Powell & Hebert, 2016); their mathematical knowledge is the primary focus. On the other hand, when evaluating students' ability to communicate their mathematical knowledge through writing, the focus of the assessment changes to examining the ways in which students present and organize mathematical concepts or procedures; the precision of the mathematical language used; the formal or informal use of mathematical vocabulary; and the use of numbers, symbols, expressions, and equations in writing (Hebert & Powell, 2016).

We advocate for always assessing both students' mathematical knowledge and their ability to communicate their knowledge when using mathematical writing assessments. Although this is often not the purpose of many mathematics assessments involving writing, neglecting to evaluate students' ability to communicate about mathematics in writing may lead teachers to mistake a student's inability to communicate their mathematical knowledge for a lack of mathematical knowledge. Evaluating mathematical writing skills can avoid this misunderstanding and help teachers understand how to provide instruction to improve mathematical writing.

Why Is Assessing Mathematical Writing Difficult?

Mathematical writing includes the integration of mathematics and writing skills. Therefore, difficulty with mathematical writing may stem from difficulty with mathematics, difficulty with writing, or both. Additionally, some students with mathematical writing difficulty may have strong mathematics and writing skills independently, but lack the mathematical vocabulary or mathematical language to combine these skills to effectively communicate about mathematics. When assessing mathematical writing, therefore, it can be difficult to determine the source of a student's difficulty.

Such challenges with mathematical writing assessments can be compounded when assessing mathematical writing involving only a single mathematical skill, as students may have difficulty writing about some mathematical constructs, but not others. For example, Powell and Hebert (2016) identified higher scores on a mathematical writing assessment focused on fractions than one focused on word problems. This suggests that mathematical writing is related across types of mathematical content, but that students' mathematical writing ability is not always consistent across mathematical content.

Despite these challenges, mathematical writing assessments are easy to implement and teachers are capable of scoring mathematical writing accurately. For example, Namkung et al. (2020) taught preservice teachers to score mathematical writing using multiple scoring methods with high reliability. This was true for multiple methods of scoring, including scoring for overall (i.e., holistic) quality, scoring for writing and mathematics separately, and scoring for discrete mathematical concepts. Additionally, on a recent national survey, 56% of teachers agreed or strongly agreed that they know how to assess mathematical writing, and 46% reported assessing mathematical writing in their classrooms, with 30% agreeing or strongly agreeing that assessing mathematical writing is easy (Powell, Hebert, et al., 2021). These results are encouraging and suggest that teachers can overcome any challenges of assessing mathematical writing and use the results to inform instruction if they learn about different ways to assess mathematical writing.

How Do You Assess Mathematical Writing?

When assessing mathematical writing, it is helpful to think about three stages: (1) preparing the assessment, (2) administering the assessment, and (3) scoring the assessment.

When preparing the assessment, teachers need to determine the form of mathematical writing to assess, the topic(s), and whether to have students explain their own work or someone else's. In a comprehensive review of mathematical writing assessments, Powell, Hebert, et al. (2017) learned that, although there are many potential forms of mathematical writing (e.g., explanatory, argumentative, creative), 75% of mathematical writing assessments involved explanatory writing. Explanatory writing was also the only form of mathematical writing found to be assessed by states in the United States that require student to write about mathematics for high-stakes mathematics assessments in the elementary grades (see Figure 13.3 for examples). Therefore, we recommend teachers start by assessing explanatory writing when developing mathematical writing prompts for their classroom. In explanatory mathematical writing, students describe and explain mathematical content or procedures (Colonnese, Amspaugh, LeMay, Evans, & Field, 2018). This can be done for any type of mathematical content. Powell, Hebert, et al. (2017) identified examples of mathematical writing assessments for geometry, measurement, rational numbers, statistics, algebra, and problem solving.

After identifying the form and topic, it is important to identify whether to ask students to write about their own work or about worked examples. Both have advantages. Asking students to write about their own work allows the teacher to assess students' ability to do the mathematics, as well as their ability to explain it in writing. However, if students have difficulty with solving the mathematical problem, it makes assessing their mathematical writing more difficult. On the other hand, worked examples allow students to focus on a problem's conceptual framework (Booth, Lange, Koedinger, & Newton, 2013), reduce cognitive load (Sweller & Chandler, 1991), help students quickly understand the math (Salden, Koedinger, Renkl, Aleven, & McLaren, 2010), and alleviate the pressure to generate a solution (Kapur, 2014). Yet, it does not allow for teachers to identify whether students can do the mathematics. In our

1. You need 120 bottles of water for your school's field trip. Your teacher has 6 packs of water. Each pack has 18 bottles of water. Is this enough bottles of water for the field trip?

   Explain the steps you used to figure this out.

2. Maya plans to use 22 wooden boards to build a border for the area around her dog house.
   - Each board is 1 foot long.
   - The boards will be placed end-to-end.
   - The area around the dog house will be in the shape of a rectangle.
   - The width of the area will be either 3 feet or 4 feet.

   A. Based on the information given, what are the two possible rectangles, Rectangle Q and Rectangle R, that Maya can use to represent the length and width of the area around the dog house?

   B. Which width, 3 feet or 4 feet, will give Maya a dog area with the greater area? Show your work and explain how you got your answer.

3. Wren says that, to subtract fractions with different denominators, you always have to multiply the denominators to find the common unit; for example:

   $$\frac{3}{8} - \frac{1}{6} = \frac{18}{48} - \frac{8}{48}$$

   Use what you know about subtracting fractions to state whether Wren is correct or not. Justify your thinking.

FIGURE 13.3. Examples of mathematical writing from high-stakes tests.

own work, we have asked students to write about multistep worked examples to increase the chances that they will be able to write a response about at least one aspect of the problem (Hebert & Powell, 2016).

After developing the assessment, teachers need to administer it. This is fairly straightforward. Important considerations are providing students with enough time to evaluate or complete the mathematics, time to plan and complete their writing, and whether to provide them with tools for completing the work (e.g., paper for working a problem, calculators, manipulatives). We typically allow for 10 to 15 minutes to respond to one mathematical writing prompt (Hebert & Powell, 2016). This will vary based on the content and goals of the teacher.

After students complete their mathematical writing, teachers will need to decide how to score the assessment. Based on prior research by Namkung et al. (2020), our recommendation is for teachers to use analytic scoring rubrics. Analytic scoring allows teachers to evaluate multiple dimensions of mathematical writing, each on their own scale (e.g., 1 to 5 scores each for *mathematics content, mathematics vocabulary, writing organization, writing grammar*, and *clarity and precision*). In other words, it allows teachers to examine aspects of writing and mathematics together and separately at the same time. Another advantage is that analytic scoring can be applied to any mathematical writing form, topic, or type (i.e., students completed a mathematical problem or responded to a worked example). They can be used to score mathematical writing assessments quickly and reliably. An example of an analytic mathematical writing scoring rubric is provided in Figure 13.4. This rubric can be adapted for different grade-levels or mathematical content, as desired.

Namkung et al. (2020) compared analytic scoring to other scoring methods that may also be considered by teachers. Holistic rubic scoring involves providing a single overall score and can be done even more quickly than analytic rubrics, but does not provide enough information on specific components. Elements scoring provides for even more specificity than analytic rubrics, as teachers can develop a scoring guide for every specific element or procedure for a mathematical problem, but they require that a unique scoring guide be prepared for each individual mathematical writing prompt. Furthermore, teachers can also examine mathematical writing sequences, which is a scoring system

	5	4	3	2	1
Math content	Complete understanding of math concepts and procedures	Adequate understanding of math concepts and procedures	Partial understanding of math concepts and procedures	Limited understanding of math concepts and procedures	No understanding of math concepts and procedures
Math vocabulary	Accurate use of formal math vocabulary	Adequate use of formal math vocabulary	Use of formal and informal math vocabulary	Use of informal math vocabulary only	No use of (or incorrect use of) math vocabulary
Math-writing organization	Clear progression of math ideas and steps including effective transitions between ideas	Adequate progression of math ideas and steps including effective transitions between ideas	Weak progression of math ideas and steps including ineffective transitions between ideas	Limited progression of math ideas and steps including ineffective transitions between ideas	No progression of ideas or steps
Math-writing grammar	Free of grammatical errors that interfere with communication about math concepts and procedures	1 or 2 grammatical errors that may or may not interfere with communication about math concepts and procedures	Several errors that may or may not interfere with communication about math concepts and procedures	Many errors that interfere with communication about math concepts and procedures	Grammatical errors make comprehension impossible
Clarity and precision	Conveys math concepts and procedures clearly and precisely	Conveys math concepts and procedures clearly but not quite precisely	Only some concepts and procedures are conveyed clearly and precisely	Most concepts and procedures conveyed are unclear and imprecise	Completely lacks clarity and precision

FIGURE 13.4. Scoring rubric for mathematical writing.

based on curriculum-based measures of writing that were expanded to include the evaluation of the use of numbers, symbols, expressions, and equations in writing. This can provide teachers with excellent information on their students, but may require more training and time. Therefore, analytic rubrics seem to provide the best blend of speed, reliability, and information for teachers across a range of mathematical writing content.

Finally, we would be remiss if we ended a section on mathematical writing assessment without discussing providing students with feedback. If students are writing about mathematics, it is important to assess their mathematical writing and provide feedback. Students' writing improves when they receive feedback (Graham, Harris, & Hebert, 2011), and this is likely extended to mathematical writing.

Instruction about Mathematical Writing

In a review of instructional practices related to mathematical writing, many opportunities teachers provide for students are informal, such as journal writing (Baxter, Woodward, & Olson, 2005; Tan & Garces-Bascal, 2013) or letter writing (Shield & Galbraith, 1998). Even with the complexity of mathematical writing, as described in the section about mathematical writing assessment, only half of teachers provide explicit instruction about mathematical writing (Powell, Hebert, et al., 2021).

Why Is Instruction on Mathematical Writing Difficult?

Mathematical writing is a complex task. Students often have to read and understand a mathematical writing prompt (see Figure 13.3 for example prompts). Each of these prompts requires multiple steps in order to respond appropriately to the prompt. After reading the prompt, students often have to engage in a mathematical task and solve a mathematical problem. Finally, students have to formulate a written response to the prompt. As noted by Powell and Hebert (2016), there is a strong positive correlation between mathematical knowledge and mathematical writing as well as writing skill and mathematical knowledge. Therefore, because mathematical writing involves two separate skill sets (i.e., writing skill and mathematical knowledge), teachers need to provide instruction on the art of mathematical writing.

In an examination of mathematical writing in the elementary grades compared to a non-mathematical writing sample (i.e., write about your favorite game and why you like it), Hebert and Powell (2016) noted students wrote fewer introductions and conclusions when writing mathematically. They also noted students used fewer paragraphs and transition words. In fact, the overall word count of words written was less in the mathematical writing than the non-mathematical writing. This indicates that students can produce strong writing samples, but their writing skill (i.e., introductions, conclusions, paragraphs, transitions) does not always transfer to mathematical writing. This is another reason students need to receive instruction on mathematical writing.

How Do You Teach Mathematical Writing?

Of all the things we have written about in this chapter, the research base for instruction on mathematical writing is the weakest, but we can provide several promising practices related to mathematical writing. Hughes et al. (2019) and Hughes and Lee (2020) provided a framework for engaging students in mathematical writing. They taught students the PRISM√ strategy. For the **P**roblem step, students read the problem, identified the question, and gathered important information. For **R**epresentation, students connected a mathematical concept to a visual. For **I** (I do), students wrote equations to reflect the problem. For **S**tate, **S**ay, **S**hare, students restated the questions in writing, connected the representations to procedures using correct mathematical terms, and shared (via writing) why their strategy worked. For **M**y answer, students wrote a concluding sentence that included an answer with a label. For the checkmark, students checked for evidence at each step. Kiuhara et al. (2020) also used self-regulation strategy development to help students build knowledge related to fractions. Here, teachers worked with students to develop background knowledge, discuss, model, memorize, support, and engage in independent practice. In these examples, the teacher explicitly modeled how to write mathematically, and students engaged in a series of steps to solve the mathematical problem and provide a written response to the mathematics.

In another example that did not use self-regulated strategy development, Hebert et al. (2019) taught students about mathematical writing using worked examples and practice opportunities. During each lesson, students viewed a worked example from a pseudo-student that contained a mistake. Students wrote about the mistake. Then, students solved a similar problem to the worked example and wrote about how they solved the problem. Teachers used modeling and guided practice to show students how to write an effective explanation. When students showed some confidence with writing mathematically, the teachers engaged the students in independent practice for their mathematical writing.

Besides responding to mathematical writing prompts typical of those on high-stakes tests (see Figure 13.3), other methods for engaging students in mathematical writing could involve the use of journals (Baxter et al., 2005; Glogger, Schwonke, Holzäpfel, Nückles, & Renkl, 2012) or writing letters (Norton & Rutledge, 2010; Shield & Galbraith, 1998). Regardless of the method for mathematical writing, teachers should model for students how to write mathematically and engage students in guided and independent practice. Teachers should also provide specific instruction related to using symbols to replace written words or how to incorporate equations and drawings into written sentences. Teachers may need to review mathematical vocabulary to ensure students engage in appropriate descriptions of mathematical concepts and procedures. And teachers need to provide these mathematical writing opportunities to students regularly, at least every 1 to 2 weeks (Powell, Hebert, et al., 2021). Students will not develop strong mathematical writing skill if they do not have multiple opportunities to practice and get feedback on their mathematical writing.

Conclusion

In this chapter, we focused on reading and writing in mathematics. Related to reading in mathematics, we emphasized the need to explicitly teach mathematical vocabulary. Teachers also need to help students improve their word-problem solving by modeling and practicing the use of an attack strategy combined with a focus on word-problem schemas. Related to writing, teachers should regularly assess students' mathematical writing and then provide explicit instruction in the areas of mathematical writing in which students experience difficulty. Mathematics is so much more than mathematical symbols. For students to become successful mathematicians, learning to read and write in mathematics is essential.

We invite you to consider the following action questions:

- What is your plan for increasing the mathematical vocabulary knowledge of your students?
- How will you teach word-problem solving to your students?
- How will you engage your students in mathematical writing?

REFERENCES

Barnes, E. M., & Stephens, S. J. (2019). Supporting mathematics vocabulary instruction through mathematics curricula. *The Curriculum Journal, 30*(3), 322–341.

Baxter, J. A., Woodward, J., & Olson, D. (2005). Writing in mathematics: An alternative form of communication for academically low-achieving students. *Learning Disabilities Research and Practice, 20*(2), 119–135.

Booth, J. L., Lange, K. E., Koedinger, K. R., & Newton, K. J. (2013). Using example problems to improve student learning in algebra: Differentiating between correct and incorrect examples. *Learning and Instruction, 25,* 24–34.

Carpenter, T. P., Hiebert, J., & Moser, J. M. (1981). Problem structure and first-grade children's initial solution processes for simple addition and subtraction problems. *Journal for Research in Mathematics Education, 12*(1), 27–39.

Casa, T. M., Firmender, J. M., Cahill, J., Cardetti, F., Choppin, J. M., Cohen, J., . . . Zawodniak, R. (2016). *Types of and purposes for elementary mathematical writing: Task force recommendations.* Storrs: University of Connecticut. Retrieved from *http://mathwriting.education.uconn.edu.*

Colonnese, M. W., Amspaugh, C. M., LeMay, S., Evans, K., & Field, K. (2018). Writing in the disciplines: How math fits into the equation. *The Reading Teacher, 72*(3), 379–387.

Cook, S. C., Collins, L. W., Morin, L. L., & Riccomini, P. J. (2020). Schema-based instruction for mathematical word problem solving: An evidence-based review for students with learning disabilities. *Learning Disability Quarterly, 43*(2), 75–87.

Freeman-Green, S. M., O'Brien, C., Wood, C. L., & Hitt, S. B. (2015). Effects of the SOLVE strategy on the mathematical problem solving skills of secondary students with learning disabilities. *Learning Disabilities Research and Practice, 30*(2), 76–90.

Fuchs, L. S., & Fuchs, D. (2002). Mathematical problem-solving profiles of students with mathematics disabilities with and without comorbid reading disabilities. *Journal of Learning Disabilities, 35*(6), 563–573.

Fuchs, L. S., Powell, S. R., Cirino, P. T., Schumacher, R. F., Marrin, S., Hamlett, C. L., . . . Changas, P. C. (2014). Does calculation or word-problem instruction provide a stronger route to pre-algebraic knowledge? *Journal of Educational Psychology, 106*(4), 990–1006.

Fuchs, L. S., Seethaler, P. M., Sterba, S. K., Craddock, C., Fuchs, D., Compton, D. L., . . . Changas, P. (2021). Closing the word-problem achievement gap in first grade: Schema-based word-problem intervention with embedded language comprehension instruction. *Journal of Educational Psychology, 113*(1), 86–103.

Glogger, I., Schwonke, R., Holzäpfel, L., Nückles, M., & Renkl, A. (2012). Learning strategies assessed by journal writing: Prediction of outcomes by quantity, quality, and combinations of learning. *Journal of Educational Psychology, 104*(2), 452–468.

Graham, S., Harris, K. R., & Hebert, M. (2011). It is more than just the message: Presentation effects in scoring writing. *Focus on Exceptional Children, 44*(4), 1–12.

Graham, S., Kiuhara, S. A., & MacKay, M. (2020). The effects of writing on learning in science, social studies, and mathematics: A meta-analysis. *Review of Educational Research, 90*(2), 179–226.

Griffin, C. C., Gagnon, J. C., Jossi, M. H., Ulrich, T. G., & Myers, J. A. (2018). Priming mathematics word problem structures in a rural elementary classroom. *Rural Special Education Quarterly, 37*(3), 150–163.

Hebert, M. A., & Powell, S. R. (2016). Examining fourth-grade mathematics writing: Features of organization, mathematics vocabulary, and mathematical representations. *Reading and Writing, 29*(7), 1511–1537.

Hebert, M. A., Powell, S. R., Bohaty, J. J., & Roehling, J. (2019). Piloting a mathematics writing intervention with late elementary students at-risk for learning difficulties. *Learning Disabilities Research and Practice, 34*(3), 144–157.

Hughes, E. M., & Lee, J.-Y. (2020). Effects of a mathematical writing intervention on middle school students' performance. *Reading and Writing Quarterly, 36*(2), 176–192.

Hughes, E. M., Lee, J.-Y., Cook, M. J., & Riccomini, P. J. (2019). Exploratory study of a self-regulation mathematical writing strategy: Proof-of-concept. *Learning Disabilities: A Contemporary Journal, 17*(2), 185–203.

Hughes, E. M., Powell, S. R., & Lee, J.-Y. (2020). Development and psychometric report of a middle school mathematics vocabulary measure. *Assessment for Effective Intervention, 45*(3), 226–234.

Hughes, E. M., Powell, S. R., & Stevens, E. A. (2016). Supporting clear and concise mathematics language: Instead of that, say this. *Teaching Exceptional Children, 49*(1), 7–17.

Jitendra, A. K., Petersen-Brown, S., Lein, A. E., Zaslofsky, A. F., Kunkel, A. K., Jung, P.-G., & Egan, A. M. (2015). Teaching mathematical word problem solving: The quality of evidence for strategy instruction priming the problem structure. *Journal of Learning Disabilities, 48*(1), 51–72.

Jitendra, A. K., Star, J. R., Dupuis, D. N., & Rodriguez, M. C. (2013). Effectiveness of schema-based instruction for improving seventh-grade students' proportional reasoning: A randomized experiment. *Journal of Research on Educational Effectiveness, 6*, 114–136.

Kapur, M. (2014). Productive failure in learning math. *Cognitive Science, 38*(5), 1008–1022.

Karp, K. S., Bush, S. B., & Dougherty, B. J. (2019). Avoiding the ineffective keyword strategy. *Teaching Children Mathematics, 25*(7), 428–435.

Kilpatrick, J., Swafford, J., & Findell, B. (2001). *Adding it up: Helping children learn mathematics.* Washington, DC: National Academies Press.

Kingsdorf, S., & Krawec, J. (2014). Error analysis of mathematical word problem solving across students with and without learning disabilities. *Learning Disabilities Research and Practice, 29*(2), 66–74.

Kiuhara, S. A., Rouse, A. G., Dai, T., Witzel, B. S., Morpshy, P., & Unker, B. (2020). Constructing written arguments to develop fraction knowledge. *Journal of Educational Psychology, 112*(3), 584–607.

Krawec, J., Huang, J., Montague, M., Kressler, B., & Melia de Alba, M. (2012). The effects of cognitive strategy instruction on knowledge of math problem-solving processes of middle school students with learning disabilities. *Learning Disability Quarterly, 36*(2), 80–92.

Marshall, S. P. (1995). *Schemas in problem solving.* New York: Cambridge University Press.

Namkung, J. M., Hebert, M. A., Powell, S. R., Hoins, M., Bricko, N., & Torchia, M. (2020). Comparing and validating four methods for scoring mathematics writing. *Reading and Writing Quarterly: Overcoming Learning Difficulties, 36*(2) 157–175.

National Governors Association Center for Best Practices & Council of Chief State School Officers. (2010). *Common Core Standards for English language arts and literacy in history/social studies, science, and technical subjects.* Washington, DC: Authors.

Nelson, G., Pfannenstiel, K. H., & Zumeta Edmonds, R. (2020). Examining the alignment of mathematics instructional practices and mathematics vocabulary between core and intervention materials. *Learning Disabilities Research and Practice, 35*(1), 14–24.

Norton, A., & Rutledge, Z. (2010). Measuring task posing cycles: Mathematical letter writing between algebra students and preservice teachers. *The Mathematics Educator, 19*, 32–45.

Peltier, C., Sinclair, T. E., Pulos, J. M., & Suk, A. (2020). Effects of schema-based instruction on immediate, generalized, and combined structured word problems. *The Journal of Special Education, 54*(2), 101–112.

Pólya, G. (1945). *How to solve it.* Princeton, NJ: Princeton University Press.

Pongsakdi, N., Kajamies, A., Veermans, K., Lertola, K., Vauras, M., & Lehtinen, E. (2020). What makes mathematical word problem solving challenging? Exploring the roles or word problem characteristics, text comprehension, and arithmetic skills. *ZDM Mathematics, 52*, 33–44.

Powell, S. R., Berry, K. A., Fall, A.-M., Roberts, G., Fuchs, L. S., & Barnes, M. A. (2021). Alternative paths to improved word-problem performance: An advantage for embedding pre-algebraic reasoning instruction within word-problem intervention. *Journal of Educational Psychology, 113*(5), 898–910.

Powell, S. R., Bos, S. E, & Lin, X. (2021). *The assessment of mathematics vocabulary in the elementary and middle school grades.* In A. Fritz-Stratmann, E. Gürsoy, & M. Herzog (Eds.), *Spracherwerb und Rechnenlerner im Vor- und Grundshulalter [Diversity dimensions in mathematics and language learning]* (pp. 313–330). Berlin: De Grutyer.

Powell, S. R., Driver, M. K., Roberts, G., & Fall, A.-M. (2017). An analysis of the mathematics vocabulary knowledge of third- and fifth-grade students: Connections to general vocabulary and mathematics computation. *Learning and Individual Differences, 57,* 22–32.

Powell, S. R., & Fuchs, L. S. (2018). Effective word-problem instruction: Using schemas to facilitate mathematical reasoning. *Teaching Exceptional Children, 51*(1), 31–42.

Powell, S. R., Fuchs, L. S., Fuchs, D., Cirino, P. T., & Fletcher, J. M. (2009). Do word-problem features differentially affect problem difficulty as a function of students' mathematics difficulty with and without reading difficulty? *Journal of Learning Disabilities, 42*(2), 99–110.

Powell, S. R., & Hebert, M. A. (2016). Influence of writing ability and computation skill on mathematics writing. *The Elementary School Journal, 117*(2), 310–335.

Powell, S. R., Hebert, M. A., Cohen, J. A., Casa, T. M., & Firmender, J. M. (2017). A synthesis of mathematics writing: Assessments, interventions, and surveys. *Journal of Writing Research, 8*(3), 493–526.

Powell, S. R., Hebert, M. A., & Hughes, E. M. (2021). How educators use mathematics writing in the classroom: A national survey of mathematics educators. *Reading and Writing: An Interdisciplinary Journal, 34*(2), 417–447.

Powell, S. R., Namkung, J. M., & Lin, X. (2022). An investigation of using keywords to solve word problems. *The Elementary School Journal, 122*(3), 452–473.

Powell, S. R., & Nelson, G. (2017). An investigation of the mathematics-vocabulary knowledge of first-grade students. *The Elementary School Journal, 117*(4), 664–686.

Powell, S. R., Stevens, E. A., & Hughes, E. M. (2019). Math language in middle school: Be more specific. *Teaching Exceptional Children, 51*(4), 286–295.

Riccomini, P. J, Smith, G. W., Hughes, E. M., & Fries, K. M. (2015). The language of mathematics: The importance of teaching and learning mathematical vocabulary. *Reading and Writing Quarterly, 31*(3), 235–252.

Rubenstein, R. N., & Thompson, D. R. (2002). Understanding and supporting children's mathematical vocabulary development. *Teaching Children Mathematics, 9,* 107–112.

Salden, R. J. C. M., Koedinger, K. R., Renkl, A., Aleven, V., & McLaren, B. M. (2010). Accounting for beneficial effects of worked examples in tutored problem solving. *Educational Psychology Review, 22*(4), 379–392.

Scheibling-Sève, C., Pasquinelli, E., & Sander, E. (2020). Assessing conceptual knowledge through solving arithmetic word problems. *Educational Studies in Mathematics, 103*(3), 293–311.

Schleppegrell, M. J. (2007). The linguistic challenges of mathematics teaching and learning: A research review. *Reading and Writing Quarterly: Overcoming Learning Difficulties, 23*(2), 139–159.

Shaftel, J., Belton-Kocher, E., & Glasnapp, D., & Poggio, J. (2006). The impact of language characteristics in mathematics test items on the performance on English language learners and students with disabilities. *Educational Assessment, 11*(2), 105–126.

Shield, M., & Galbraith, P. (1998). The analysis of student expository writing in mathematics. *Educational Studies in Mathematics, 36*(1), 29–52.

State of Texas. (2019). *State of Texas assessments of academic readiness: Grade 4 mathematics.* Austin: Texas Education Agency.

Swanson, H. L., Moran, A., Lussier, C., & Fung, W. (2014). The effect of explicit and direct generative strategy training and working memory on word problem-solving accuracy in children at risk for math difficulties. *Learning Disability Quarterly,* *37*(2), 111–123.

Sweller, J., & Chandler, P. (1991). Evidence for cognitive load theory. *Cognition and Instruction, 8*(4), 351–362.

Tan, T., & Garces-Bacsal, R. M. (2013). The effect of journal writing on mathematics achievement among high-ability students in Singapore. *Gifted and Talented International, 28,* 173–184.

Van de Walle, J. A., Karp, K. S., & Bay-Williams, J. M. (2019). *Elementary and middle school mathematics: Teaching developmentally* (10th ed.). Upper Saddle River, NJ: Pearson Education.

van Garderen, D., & Scheuermann, A. M. (2015). Diagramming word problems: A strategic approach for instruction. *Intervention in School and Clinic, 50*(5), 282–290.

Walkington, D., Clinton, V., Ritter, S. N., & Nathan, M. J. (2015). How readability and topic incidence relate to performance on mathematics story problems in computer-based curricula. *Journal of Educational Psychology, 107*(4), 1051–1074.

Wang, A. Y., Fuchs, L. S., & Fuchs, D. (2016). Cognitive and linguistic predictors of mathematical word problems with and without irrelevant information. *Learning and Individual Differences, 52,* 79–87.

Willis, G. B., & Fuson, K. C. (1988). Teaching children to use schematic drawings to solve addition and subtraction word problems. *Journal of Educational Psychology, 80*(2), 192–201.

Xin, Y. P., & Zhang, D. (2009). Exploring a conceptual model-based approach to teaching situated word problems. *The Journal of Educational Research, 102*(6), 427–441.

PART IV

WRITING AND READING CONNECTIONS WITH SPECIFIC GROUPS OF LEARNERS

CHAPTER 14

Writing and Reading with Emergent Bilingual Learners

Alison Boardman
Sandra A. Butvilofsky

Within K–12 schools in the United States, there are over 5 million students who speak more than one language at home (Office of English Language Acquisition, 2021), and of these, over 75% speak Spanish. While there are a variety of programs designed to serve emergent bilingual learners,[1] the majority of students participate in English-only programs. In English-only programs, emergent bilingual students typically spend most or all of their school day in a grade-level general education class. These students often receive some additional language support from an English language development teacher. Within the general education classroom, teachers provide scaffolding to support content learning and language development. Yet, general education teachers are often unsure of how to design instruction that is inclusive of emergent bilingual learners. In this chapter, we explore the reading and writing connection for emergent bilingual learners and provide recommendations that account for the dynamic nature of becoming bilingual. We conclude by examining the importance of connecting reading and writing in the assessment of emergent bilingual learners. As you continue reading, consider the following questions.

GUIDING QUESTIONS

■ In what ways are the challenges that emergent bilingual learners face in connected reading–writing instruction similar to and different from those of native English speakers?

■ Consider the reading–writing practices you already use in your classroom and those you have read about so far in this book. Identify shifts in

---

[1] *English learner* is the federal term used for students identified as having a home language other than English. For the purposes of this chapter, we will use the term *emergent bilingual* to provide a more asset-based orientation to the variability in language proficiency for these students.

instruction you can make to support emergent bilingual learners in your school or classroom.

- How might you incorporate your students' home languages as part of your reading and writing practices within your classroom?
- How can students' writing provide insight into their reading development? How might you use writing to inform reading instruction for emergent bilingual learners?

Literacy learning for emergent bilingual learners is different from literacy learning for monolingual English speakers (Bernhardt, 2003). One of the many differences in literacy acquisition between these groups is the dual task emergent bilingual learners in English-only learning programs confront in needing to learn how to read and write when they are still acquiring English language proficiency. Regardless of the language of instruction, it is important to recognize that emergent bilingual learners draw on their full linguistic, cultural, and experiential knowledge when engaging in reading and writing. This means influences of students' home language in the expressive domains of language should be interpreted as language interaction, an asset-based orientation. Whereas many people falsely believe that learning in two languages will somehow disrupt or interfere with learning in English, research has repeatedly demonstrated the benefits of becoming bilingual in terms of maintaining a student's home language and culture, supporting cognitive development, and developing English proficiency (for a review, see García & Kleifgen, 2018). Unfortunately, most literacy programs and assessments used with emergent bilingual learners were designed for monolingual English speakers and do not take into consideration the ways in which their languages interact to process information as they decode for comprehension and encode to communicate their ideas. It is incumbent on teachers to design and enact effective instruction and language supports for emergent bilingual students that are responsive to their multilingual language development.

It is also worth noting that emergent bilingual learners, like their monolingual peers, are a diverse group. Not only do emergent bilingual learners vary in their English language proficiency, they also vary in their background and culture, their access to high-quality instructional experiences in their home language and in English, and in their interests and motivations. Furthermore, emergent bilingual learners often differ across language domains as they develop English proficiency, and these variations could influence the ways they use reading to support writing and vice versa. Therefore, we draw on research to offer guidelines that should be used flexibly and adapted to the specific needs of individual students.

Research on Reading and Writing Practices for Emergent Bilingual Learners

It may not be surprising that standards across grade levels include expectations for reading–writing connections. For instance, starting in the early elementary grades, the Common Core State Standards (CCSS) require students to engage in analytic writing using textual evidence to support their opinions, arguments, and claims (National Governors Association Center for Best Practices & Council of Chief State School Officers, 2010). As an added complexity, reading–writing activities for emergent bilingual learners should also attend to language development by including objectives (and instruction and supports) that build requisite English language skills (e.g., Kim et al., 2011).

Despite these lofty aspirations for what students need to accomplish, students learning English as a new language tend to receive isolated instruction in reading *or* writing with a much greater emphasis on reading instruction (e.g., Harklau, 2002; Hirvela, 2004), a finding that is similar to research reported in this book on native English speakers. Thus, emergent bilingual students often have limited opportunities to learn and practice integrating reading and writing through activities such as summarizing and synthesizing what they read, writing research reports, or using writing to improve reading (Grabe & Zhang, 2013). Furthermore, cultural and language experiences present themselves in particular ways for emergent bilingual students. For instance, variations may be present in perspectives on audience and author, preferences for organizing texts, ways to use texts as learning resources, and conceptions about the purposes and uses of writing (Grabe, 2003). Integrating reading and writing activities facilitates the processing and application of newly learned content, creating a reciprocal benefit for emergent bilingual students who are developing English and learning content at the same time (Baker et al., 2014; Hirvela, 2004).

The recommendations in this chapter are drawn from the small amount of existing research on effective instruction for emergent bilingual learners along with suggestions made by a panel of researchers assembled to explore and report on research related to teaching academic content literacy to emergent bilingual learners in elementary and middle school (e.g., Baker et al., 2014; Grabe & Zhang, 2013; Hirvela, 2007).

We first share an illustration of a text-based writing activity that attends meaningfully to the reading, writing, and language development of emergent bilingual learners and then highlight several key instructional elements. This type of activity would be appropriate in different forms in upper elementary school through high school.

Students are provided with a relatable dilemma. They are asked to decide whether or not to allow a new superstore to be built on the outskirts of their city. Students read two short articles formatted to look like newspaper articles, one that offers the potential benefits of a superstore (e.g., cheaper prices, convenience of one-stop shopping) and a second article that highlights the downsides (e.g., threat to small businesses, increased traffic). Students begin by summarizing in writing the key ideas in each article. Next, they use their summaries to discuss the pros and cons presented in the texts in small collaborative groups and complete a graphic organizer (GO). After the discussion, students write individual letters to a city council member, stating their position and including evidence from the text and their own experiences to back up their argument. Within the letter, students are required to include three target terms from a list of vocabulary words they have learned in class (e.g., *impact*, *options*, *benefit*, *consequence*). Finally, students are paired with a classmate with an opposing position. They read their letters to one another and discuss the strengths of their arguments. They also provide feedback to one another to make their letters stronger. Finally, students revise their letters and reflect on what they learned.

While just one of many examples, this sort of rich reading–writing experience can support emergent bilingual learners to build content knowledge and language skills at the same time as it develops reading and writing outcomes. And as educators know, reading–writing activities are also complex, and require instruction that attends to a variety of elements, over time.

Instructional Considerations

The style, format, and steps to accomplishing integrated reading and writing activities are unfamiliar to many students and may be even more so to students who are in the process of developing English, new to U.S. schooling, and/or who are learning about local norms and culture. In the superstore text-based argument writing task, students must take individual skills and strategies and apply them in a larger project. As just one example, consider the component of the assignment above that asks students to summarize the texts they read to gather evidence for their argumentative writing. Summary writing is an important activity for emergent bilingual learners to develop both reading and writing skills and is essential for content learning (Grabe & Zhang, 2013; Newell, 2006). There are multiple components involved in this seemingly straightforward activity:

- Understand the particular expectations of summary writing for a given teacher, class, or purpose.
- Distinguish summary writing from other writing tasks such as retelling or argument writing.
- Understand the text genre and its connection to summary writing (summarizing a section of a textbook is different than summarizing a chapter in a novel; some texts cannot be summarized, such as poems or texts containing only lists of facts).
- Comprehend the text (including composite comprehension skills, background knowledge of the content, and vocabulary).
- Distinguish key ideas and important information from examples and extraneous details.
- Synthesize multiple examples into overarching statements.
- Employ vocabulary knowledge and writing conventions to communicate ideas effectively.

Not only are reading–writing activities complex, but the individual component steps are also multifaceted and need to be explicitly taught. We outline the following features of effective reading–writing instruction for emergent bilingual learners that can be included as mini-lessons and in larger projects such as the superstore reading–writing activity above:

1. Use explicit instruction to teach integrated reading–writing skills and strategies.
2. Provide language supports.
3. Facilitate student collaboration.
4. Encourage writing and reading in more than one language.
5. Use genre-based pedagogy.

Use Explicit Instruction

We begin the discussion of best practices with a reminder about the importance of explicit instruction, the practice of teaching skills and strategies directly to students. It is more common for teachers to hint at or make a request for students to enact the necessary components of literacy activities than to teach them explicitly (Pressley & Allington, 2014). Studies of writing instruction with emergent bilingual students that did not include explicit instruction have failed to increase writing outcomes (Genesee & Riches, 2006), and in a review of culturally responsive literacy practices for emergent bilingual learners, 22 studies provided evidence for using explicit instruction (Piazza, Rao, & Protacia, 2015). More than simply learning procedures to perform a skill, explicit instruction includes developing metacognitive awareness, flexibility in application, and thinking critically about content. Piazza and colleagues caution that "even though explicit instruction in the basics is often recommended in the research for diverse learners, long-term reading achievement is most influenced by rich language experiences, critical thinking skills, and making connections to texts" (2015, p. 12). These kinds of experiences can include explicit instruction at the same time as they thoughtfully integrate reading and writing for a greater purpose.

The following format can be used to structure explicit mini-lessons for emergent bilingual learners (see Archer & Hughes, 2011, for further reading):

1. Focus on critical skills that students need and will continue to use.
2. Break down complex skills and strategies into smaller chunks that can be taught in skill-specific mini-lessons.
3. Define the target skill with a brief explanation of the objective for the mini-lesson. Be sure to include why the skill is important and when you would use the skill at school and in life.
4. Model the skill and demonstrate how it fits into a larger process of reading and writing. This might include a step-by-step demonstration, while thinking out loud the thought processes behind each step.

5. Have students interact with the content and with each other during the mini-lesson.

6. Use comprehensible input (clear and concise language, with multiple modalities).

7. Provide language supports (e.g., list of steps, word bank, sentence frames, collaboration with peers).

8. Create many opportunities to practice with feedback.

9. Encourage flexible use of the skill by expanding application (e.g., applying summary writing with different text genres).

Provide Language Supports

As Pauline Gibbons (2015) reminds us, "At no stage are learners expected to carry out alone a task with which they are not familiar, yet at the same time they are constantly being 'stretched' in their language development and expected to take responsibility for those tasks they are capable of doing alone" (p. 125). Language supports or scaffolds provide access to cognitively demanding and engaging learning experiences by building pathways to reading and writing that wouldn't be possible without them. It is essential that teachers provide both language supports and instruction in specific skills and strategies—it is not an either–or scenario. With language supports, students at various stages of learning English can work toward similar outcomes, but utilize different amounts and types of support to reach those shared outcomes. These accessibility tools are also helpful for many native English speakers as they develop literacy skills. The following writing supports can be used by students when they are writing as part of reading–writing activities:

- **Utilize word banks that are specific to the writing genre.** For instance, in the superstore argument activity, students will need to make a case for their claim. The word bank might include transition words and phrases (e.g., *however, therefore, in addition to, consequently*) relevant to argument writing.

- **Offer word banks specific to the content.** Text-specific vocabulary lists can include important words and terms that have been taught and are key to text understanding and content standards (e.g., *consumerism, independently owned business, big box store*).

- **Make translation tools available.** Offer or co-create with students' bilingual dictionaries and allow use of technology tools such as Google Translate (see more on technology below).

- **Create task-specific GOs that help students organize important ideas and information.**

- **Have writing models available and use texts as writing models.** Students know they can utilize examples either published or created by the class as they consider how to structure and format their own writing.

- **Use sentence starters or writing outlines.** These writing frameworks model the sentence structure and formatting of a particular writing genre. While outlines provide a great deal of structure for students who are emerging in their writing skills, sentence starters offer more flexibility and choice for the writer as students can choose which sentence starters to use. Students can even use sentence starters to get an idea of how they might structure their own prose. See the difference in the two formats below.

Outline Example

Students compose their writing by "filling in" the sections that are outlined.

Introduction

I believe that the superstore [should/should not] be allowed in our city because _____. There are several reasons why I believe this.
First, _____
Next, _____
Finally, _____

Sentence-Starter Examples

Students select from a variety of genre-specific sentence starters or use the sentence starters as models for their own writing. These sentence starters have been adapted from Kim and colleagues (2011).

Making Claims

The superstore [should/should not] be allowed in our city because _____.
I believe that _____ because _____

Using Evidence

In the text, the author states that _____
According to _____ [author name]
Based on what I read in _____ [text name]

Forming Interpretations

What this means to me is _____.
This represents _____ because _____.
Based on my identity as a _____, I feel _____.

Facilitate Student Collaboration

Language is a mediational tool that students use to negotiate, process, and express their understanding of procedures, content, and ideas. Students do this work of meaning-making by interacting with texts, by composing messages for and receiving messages from others, and by interacting with peers and adults. Collaboration among students is a recommended practice to increase reading and writing outcomes for emergent bilingual learners (Baker et al., 2014; Piazza et al., 2015). When students are in small groups, they have more opportunities to discuss with one another what they are learning. They take more turns, ask more questions, have more chances to clarify understanding, and without the teacher to provide all the information, they spend more time figuring things out together. Emergent bilingual learners also benefit from collaborative spaces where "words are repeated, ideas are rephrased, problems are restated, and meanings are refined" (Gibbons, 2015, p. 40). In addition, emergent bilingual students benefit from models of language provided by students with greater English proficiency, and they can also provide and receive support from peers who share the same home language. The following examples are just a few ways that students can support each other during reading–writing activities (Baker et al., 2014). Students can:

- Work together to brainstorm and organize ideas prior to writing or when trying to figure out the meaning of a text.
- Complete a shared GO.
- Discuss a text and respond together in writing to questions that require comprehension of the text.
- Connect reading and writing to larger ideas or work together to come to consensus (e.g., take a stand about an issue).
- Discuss and answer each other's questions in the language of their choice.
- Share writing with one another and give and receive feedback, prior to revising (see Table 14.1).

Collaboration can be structured and include protocols that guide students to participate and work together, such as in the feedback protocol. These sorts of structures specify how to use time and how to participate; they can include roles in which different students take responsibility for different parts of an activity; and they can involve protocols that are repeated over time with different content (feedback protocol, using text-based discussion roles). Collaboration can also be more informal, where students learn to use each other as resources in a just-in-time manner (e.g., "John, what is another way to say 'very much'?" "Marianna, can you look at my ending and see if it makes sense?"). Regardless of the nature of the activity, students benefit from knowing the *goals* for collaboration ("Why are we working together?") and the *expectations* (e.g., "Does everyone turn in their own graphic organizer, or do we create one together?").

While collaboration among students can provide language supports and more informal communication opportunities for emergent bilingual students to negotiate language and understanding, productive collaboration does not usually happen automatically. Collaboration should be viewed as a skill that students develop, just like other literacy skills they learn. Therefore, teachers

TABLE 14.1. Feedback Protocol with Sentence Starters

Feedback protocol

1. Each student comes to the revision meeting with a question about their writing.
2. Set timer (7 minutes per person).
3. Partner 1: Share writing and ask for feedback in one specific area.
4. Partner 2: (a) Answer Partner 1's question. (b) Share one aspect of the writing you like. (c) Offer one specific suggestion or ask a clarifying question.
5. Partner 1 takes notes.
6. Repeat.

Ask for feedback

- I would like your help on _____ because _____.
- I am stuck on _____. I tried _____. What ideas do you have?
- _____ is my favorite part. What did you think about it?
- What would you add to _____?

Ask clarifying questions and give feedback

- What did you mean by _____?
- I was confused by _____.
- I like when you wrote _____. Here is an idea to expand that part.
- One suggestion I have is _____.

need to provide instruction so that peers can benefit from their interactions and dialogue, and so that every student becomes a valued and contributing member of the group. Furthermore, as teachers know, there is a risk that student group dynamics will mirror unjust social norms that are not productive, such as giving higher-status students more airtime or valuing the ideas of some students more than others (Cohen & Lotan, 2014). Providing instruction in collaboration skills, facilitating, and providing feedback during and after group work, and creating a welcoming classroom environment that values the contributions of all learners set the table for the kinds of dialogue and supportive interactions in which every student can thrive.

Encourage Writing and Reading in More Than One Language

"The outdated argument that a first language is a bridge to English must be abandoned to make room for a broader conceptualization of all languages contributing to a whole that is greater than the sum of its parts" (Hopewell, 2011, p. 616). Regardless of the program model emergent bilingual learners may be participating in, they should have opportunities to use their full linguistic repertoire within the classroom. This fluid and flexible use of language is referred to as translanguaging (García, 2009), in which bilingual individuals use multiple discursive strategies to make sense of their world (García & Wei, 2014). In 1994, Cen Williams, a Welsh scholar, coined the concept of *translanguaging*. Translanguaging, in its origin, involved the pedagogical practice of providing bilingual students with opportunities to alternate languages for productive or receptive purposes (Menken & Sánchez, 2019). More recently, García and Wei have expanded the term to promote the dynamic process by which bilinguals strategically draw on features from one linguistic system to communicate effectively. While teachers would benefit from learning more about translanguaging through professional development or professional reading (see, especially, García, Johnson, Seltzer, & Valdés, 2017), we provide some tips for incorporating students' home language into the classroom when engaging in reading and writing (Menken & Sánchez, 2019).

1. Encourage translanguaging in small-group discussions purposefully. When working on comprehension skills or negotiating written texts, teachers may want to group students who share a home language. As with all groupings, they should be organized flexibly and purposefully to promote linguistic and literacy competencies.

2. Incorporate multilingual reading texts. Seek out and include texts in the languages represented from the emergent bilingual learners in the classroom. Find translations of books/texts being read in English or books with similar content information. The inclusion of such texts promotes comprehension and expands students' content knowledge.

3. Encourage translanguaging in writing. While final written products may be required to be written in English, students can be encouraged to plan, draft, and revise using their full linguistic repertoires. To produce published pieces in English, provide additional supports such as bilingual dictionaries, translation apps, or assistance from bilingual peers.

4. Provide opportunities for emergent bilingual students to share bilingual writing with authentic audiences. For instance, students can create a bilingual introduction for parents at a school event, a bilingual poetry book to share with families, or bilingual autobiographies that are published on a class website.

Use Genre-Based Pedagogy

While there are a variety of routines that attend to the practices outlined in this chapter, we highlight genre pedagogy, a framework that supports elementary-aged emergent bilingual learners to deepen their understanding of text and writing (see more in Brisk, 2014; also see Chapter 6). Genre-based pedagogy has been effective at shifting instruction in elementary classrooms to foster a language rich environment that honors and mobilizes students' bilingualism, even in English medium classrooms. "The writing practices of a culture are characterized by recurrent forms of texts used for specific purposes with specific discourse organization and language features" (Brisk & Parra, 2018, p. 128). Because genres vary across cultures—for example, persuasive writing in China, is indirect, while in the United States, persuasive writing is direct—it is important to provide explicit instruction on the unique structure of specified genres. Through reading texts, the text can be deconstructed to emphasize the structure and the language used. Emergent bilingual learners should also be invited to share ways in which genres from their own culture are similar or different. For instance, students might learn about the genre of argument in which they explore the text structures and language choices writers use to meet the purpose of persuasion. Genres can also be studied in relation to purposes specific to a content area, such as science or social studies, and should have real-world applications whenever possible, such as writing an autobiography, a research report, or a blog post. In genre-based pedagogy, models of writing are used as mentor texts to apprentice students into writing in particular genres. These texts are studied and analyzed as students read like writers and then compose their own texts. Educators use a teaching and learning cycle that includes the elements of evidence-based instruction described in this chapter:

1. Teacher introduces a particular genre (e.g., autobiography, writing a research report), providing content and background information about the genre, its purpose, when to use the genre, and why it is important.

2. Class deconstructs and analyzes mentor texts to explore how and why the authors wrote in the target genre. Language choices are also examined. Students additionally develop metalanguage to talk about writing.

3. Class engages in the shared writing of a text in the target genre, going through the different stages of writing (planning, drafting, revising, and editing). The teacher writes on chart paper, or another means that is visible to students. The teacher asks for input from students in areas where students need to develop their writing (e.g., word choice, sentence expansion, attention to audience). The teacher thinks out loud, and the class discusses various choices as they co-create a model text.

4. Students practice writing in the target genre, with support and feedback from peers. Students can write in collaborative groups, in partners, or independently depending on their readiness level.

Genre-based pedagogy has been effective at shifting instruction in elementary classrooms to foster a language-rich environment that honors and mobilizes students' bilingualism, even in English medium classrooms. There are many opportunities for students to experience language with mentor texts, to learn more about the choices authors make when composing, to play with language as they compose together with their peers and the teacher, and then to apply what they are learning in individualized ways. Brisk (2014) also reminds us that students develop metalanguage that enables them to hone their use of specific and precise language in their analysis of mentor texts and in their own writing. So for instance, in the superstore example, students might examine various letters to the city council that include claims and reasons. In their analysis, they discuss if it would be more persuasive and appropriate in that genre to use the personal pronoun "I" or the more formal "they." These deep explorations support students to increase their knowledge about language, writing, and reading, and to gain confidence in themselves as writers and readers.

Incorporate Technology

Technology is commonplace in many classrooms, with almost unbounded limits on the ways that both teachers and students can leverage digital tools to deliver content, interact with ideas and people, compose, and share work. For emergent bilingual learners, technology can also provide instant access to translations of words or texts, facilitate collaboration, and allow students to look up information, find explanations in multiple formats (e.g., text, videos), multiple languages, and more. If there is anything that educators are learning about technology, it is that youth will be leading the way in its creative use and application for learning and communicating in and out of the classroom.

In a recent visit to a high school English language development classroom in which the activity was to answer comprehension questions about a class novel, Alison, one of the authors, was struck by the incorporation of technology into everyday activities. The teacher pushed the assignment to students through Google Classroom. She could also observe students composing and could provide feedback by entering the shared documents in real time. Students had their print novels open. Most students also had their phones in use for multiple purposes. One student was typing his responses to the questions in Spanish and then translating them to English. He checked the translation and typed his English responses into the computer. Another student was using the camera feature of Google Translate, pointing her phone at the computer to translate the questions into Arabic. She then referred to the English text and formulated her responses in English. Still another student was using a thesaurus feature to find the right word for one of her responses. The vibe was active and vibrant. Students were conversing and sharing their ideas with one another in multiple languages. The responses to the teacher's activity were in English.

Much of the technology in use was new to the teacher. What she provided to students was a flexible learning environment, with enough structure in place to allow for these varied but appropriate uses of technology. Phones for a translation app were okay, but to play games or go onto social media during class was not okay. Similarly, the teacher and students talked openly about translanguaging and how using multiple languages with digital tools could support their language development. As with any instructional tool, it's important that teachers are aware of how digital tools are used and of both the affordances and potential limitations they present, particularly for aspects that are automated. For instance, Google Translate can give a student the sense of a word or phrase that is unclear, but the translations lack context and nuance for language use so they need to be checked. Similarly, Newsela is a helpful resource that adjusts the reading level of text to make it accessible to students reading at various levels. However, teachers need to preview the adjusted versions (e.g., a sixth-grade text on osmosis that has been automatically adjusted for a fourth-grade level) to be sure they make sense. Sometimes important information is lost in the simplified version.

Teachers might find Puentedura's SAMR (substitution, augmentation, modification, redefinition) model useful in considering the shifts, and even transformations, that can come with technology integration (Parris, Estrada, & Honigsfeld, 2016). Initially, teachers may use technology to enhance their instruction, substituting a paper-and-pencil task with a digital one. An example of a "substitution" task is to create digital flashcards to remember key ideas (e.g., using a platform such as Quizlet). Alternatively, writing an essay on a computer rather than by hand has affordances and falls in the "augmentation" phase. This version of the assignment is a functional improvement over a paper-and-pencil task because of spell check, a thesaurus, translation options, and the ease of sharing with others for feedback, but the task and what is produced are essentially the same. More substantive shifts come when technology is used to redesign a task in the "modification" phase and to create new activities that wouldn't be possible without digital tools in the "redefinition" phase.

A promising practice for emergent bilingual learners that falls in the redefinition phase combines digital tools with multiple modalities to leverage students' linguistic and academic strengths (Smith, Pacheco, & Khorosheva, 2020). Multiple modalities refer to the way that students can combine text, with visuals, sound, and movement, across modes (e.g., print, video, audio). In a recent review of research on adolescent EBs using multiple modalities with digital tools, studies found that classrooms were transformed to be more inclusive of students' identities and language use. Students were provided opportunities to learn about and use a variety of linguistic resources and they became multimodal designers, engaging in authentic tasks that were focused on the "unique communicative affordances of multiple modes when conveying meaning for distinct purposes and audiences" (Smith et al., 2020, p. 42). Young children can also compose and interact in multimodal activities.

To provide an example of how multiple modalities can be integrated into classroom instruction, imagine again a unit focused on argument writing standards in which students begin by reading and annotating a variety of digital and print resources to conduct research (see the Changing the Conversation project at *http://sprocket.lucasedresearch.org/ela9*). Their final assignment is to create a multimodal argument product that includes at least three modes. One student creates a poster making an argument for why teens should be afforded a later start to their school day, with the goal of convincing the school administration to make the desired change. The student might include a QR code (a visual barcode that links to additional resources through a phone's camera) on the poster that takes the audience to the other modes, such as a letter to the school board and a short public service announcement (PSA) video. The QR code could also include a translation of the poster, or the poster could be created bilingually. Writing for authentic purposes (e.g., to convince the school administration to make an important change) and writing with authentic modalities that include technology (e.g., creating a PSA, writing blogs, creating websites, posting to social media) are motivating and creative ways for students to learn and practice important reading and writing skills. Incorporating the use of technology into teaching and learning not only increases access but also broadens the range of learning opportunities for all students and for emergent bilinguals in particular. And remember, it is okay to start small and to let students co-create the possibilities.

Assessment Practices

Up to this point, we have focused on reading–writing connections in instruction. Now, we turn to the potential writing assessment has in providing an authentic understanding of reading and writing. This is especially important for emergent bilingual learners because through their writing, they demonstrate knowledge through their full linguistic repertoire.

Changing Perceptions of Bilingual Learners' Writing Abilities

Emergent bilingual learners' writing abilities are most often evaluated using monolingual norms, and as a result, interpretations of their abilities are viewed from a deficit perspective. These deficit orientations underestimate emergent bilingual learners' potential and often limit their learning opportunities (Butvilofsky, Escamilla, Gumina, & Silva Diaz, 2021). Furthermore, it is quite uncommon to view writing as a means to understand literacy development, despite evidence that assessing writing provides a more nuanced understanding of literacy development alongside the assessment of reading skills (Clay, 1975, 1991; Vernon & Ferreiro, 1999). In this section, we provide a framework to examine emergent bilingual student writing that is strength-based (Escamilla et al., 2014; Hopewell & Butvilofsky, 2016) and incorporates Shanahan's (2006) research on the common knowledge that is shared between reading and writing.

In a study with 29 emergent bilingual second graders, Butvilofsky and colleagues (2021) used reading–writing research and a biliterate writing rubric (Escamilla et al., 2014) to examine emergent bilingual learners' literacy development through biliterate writing samples. They found that the use of such a formative evaluation framework provided more relevant information related to emergent bilingual learners' biliteracy development than the more commonly used reading assessment measures, Dynamic Indicators of Basic Early Literacy Skills (DIBELS; Good & Kaminski, 2002) or Indicadores Dinámicos del Éxito en la Lectura (IDEL, the Spanish version of the DIBELS assessment; Baker, Good, Knutson, & Watson, 2006). In fact, students in this study did not demonstrate growth in their literacy development across time as measured by the DIBELS and IDEL instruments. However, through the use of the expanded writing framework, the authors demonstrated how students progressed in the related reading–writing aspects of the alphabetic principle, organization of text, and punctuation use. In what follows, we explain the framework used, alongside the analysis of a first-grade emergent bilingual student's writing sample, to illustrate how formative writing assessment can provide information related to reading development.

The Literacy Squared Biliterate Writing Rubric (Escamilla et al., 2014) was created to evaluate elementary-aged emergent bilingual students' biliterate writing in both Spanish and English across time, as well as to capture the ways in which bilingual students make use of their full linguistic repertoire as writers. A unique aspect of this writing rubric involves viewing emergent bilingual learners' writing development using a holistic bilingual lens (Gort, 2006; Grosjean, 1989), which recognizes that biliterate writers use the totality of their linguistic and literacy skills across languages and cultures. Instead of viewing influences of one language on another as interference or confusion, a holistic bilingual lens accounts for transfer as strategic and developmental in a bilingual learners' biliteracy trajectory.

To make the Literacy Squared Writing Rubric applicable to interpret and connect bilingual learners' writing to reading, we present the three main linguistic aspects of written text that are related to one another (see Table 14.2): discourse, sentence/phrase, and phoneme–grapheme relationships (Butvilofsky et al., 2021; Clay, 1991; Escamilla et al., 2014; Shanahan, 2006).

Discourse. At the discourse level, the overall structure of the text is analyzed encompassing organization, punctuation use, and coherence. The inclusion of a main idea, introduction, supporting details/ideas, and a conclusion

TABLE 14.2. Reading–Writing Text Features for Writing Analysis

Text feature	Descriptors
Discourse	Coherence—Overall structure of the text: • Title • Organization • Main idea/introduction/conclusion • Punctuation use Rhetorical structures (e.g., composition ends with a question)
Sentence/phrase level	Structure of sentences: • Simple, complex, compound, incomplete Syntax—Word order (note cross-language influences): • Noun/verb, adjective/noun agreement • Subject omission • Overgeneralizations
Spelling	• Language-specific approximations (e.g., *becuse/because, nis/nice*) • Approximations with cross-language influence (*mai/my, da/the, jis/his*)

Note. Based on Butvilofsky et al. (2021).

determines a text's organization, as well as coherence, or how ideas are connected to one another using transitional words or phrases. Punctuation use is included within organization because it guides a reader through the text.

Sentence/phrase. Examining how sentences and/or phrases are expressed provides insight into the structure of sentences, such as complex, compound, or simple. Examining syntactical structures such as noun/verb or adjective/noun agreement gives insight into the influences of cross-language structure.

Phoneme–grapheme relationships. It is important to note the ways in which emergent bilingual learners encode words using phoneme–grapheme relationships. Because emergent bilinguals come from diverse linguistic backgrounds, it is important to understand whether substitutions or omissions for English orthography may be influenced from home language orthographies or are based on the absence of phonemes in the home language.

We provide a writing sample written by Julissa, a Spanish-English first grader who was identified as being in the emerging level of English language acquisition. She had received Spanish literacy instruction in kindergarten. Using the framework detailed in Table 14.2, we will illustrate how her writing can provide insight into her reading development.

To begin our analysis, we examine this writing sample at the discourse level (see Figure 14.1 and Table 14.3). Julissa wrote an innovative retell of the nursery rhyme "Jack and Jill." Her retell demonstrates comprehension of the nursery rhyme as well as many organizational features including a title, an introductory sentence, events conveyed in sequential order, and a conclusion. Julissa employs the use of capitalization for proper names and uses periods conventionally. To connect ideas, Julissa begins several sentences with the conjunction *and*. Another important element of literacy development Julissa demonstrates in her writing is the incorporation of dialogue, although it does not include quotation marks: "Mother said, Jack and Jill go to the water fountain and get water" and "okay mother." Despite the lack of punctuation, the inclusion of dialogue in her retell demonstrates her understanding of how narratives are written. At the sentence/phrase level, Julissa begins her retell with a traditional phrase, "once upon a time," that is used to signify the beginning of a narrative of past events. Julissa wrote simple sentences; however, she demonstrates an emerging knowledge of literary language in her writing with the inclusion of "they went up <u>and up</u> the hill" for added emphasis.

While we include an analysis of Julissa's spelling last, many times teachers stop short of acknowledging the strengths in the other aspects of writing because there are so many spelling approximations (Soltero-González, Escamilla, & Hopewell, 2012). Focusing too much on spelling may prevent teachers from interpreting the many other strengths and abilities an emerging bilingual student might be exhibiting. In our analysis, we want to emphasize the strengths and origins of Julissa's spelling approximations. To begin, Julissa

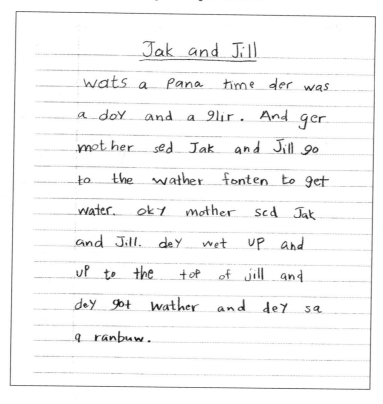

FIGURE 14.1. Julissa's writing sample.

writes many high-frequency words conventionally. such as *and, the, time, get, mother.* Some of her spelling approximations are those that a monolingual English student would make, while others can be attributed to influences from her home language, Spanish. Julissa's spelling of *wats a pana/once upon a,* includes all phonemes except the *n* in *once,* demonstrating her ability to match phonemes with graphemes. Many of the other spelling approximations can be seen as common to monolingual English writers, such as *sed/said, sa/saw, ranbuw/rainbow.* Several of Julissa's approximations can be attributed to the use of Spanish phonetics or cross-language influence. The digraph *th* does not exist in Spanish; thus, her use of the letter *d* in *dere/there* and *dey/they* also reflects her ability to map phonemes to graphemes, using Spanish phonetic knowledge. In Spanish, the letter *h* is silent; thus, her use of the *g* and *j* to represent *ger/her* and *jill/hill* demonstrate her application of Spanish phonetics to English.

Looking at emergent bilingual learners' writing through a holistic bilingual lens can provide valuable information on how students are utilizing their full linguistic and cultural repertoire and give insights into their reading development. Furthermore, the information gleaned from this analysis can be used to guide instruction in both reading and writing.

TABLE 14.3. Analysis of Julissa's Writing Sample

Text feature	Descriptor	Evidence
Discourse	Coherence—Organization: • Title included • Introduction • Conclusion • Sequenced ideas • Punctuation • Rhetorical structures: inclusion of dialogue	• Jak and Jill • Wats a pana time der was a doy and glir. • And dey sa a ranbuw. • Use of and to sequence ideas • Use of periods/ending punctuation • Capitalization of proper names (Jak, Jill) • Mother sed Jack and Jill go to the wather fonten to get water. • Oky mothe sed Jak and Jill.
Sentence/phrase level	• Sentence structures • Syntax	• Many simple sentences • ger/her for their: cross-language influence from Spanish
Spelling	• Language-specific approximations	• wats/once • a pana/upon a • doy/boy: common reversal of b/d • fonten/fountain • mothe/mother • sed/said • wet/went • wather/water • sa/saw • ranbuw/rainbow
	• Cross-language: influence from Spanish phonetics	• der/there • dey/they • jill/hill

Instructional Implications for Considering the Full Linguistic Repertoire in Writing Assessment

While teachers may be inclined to prioritize teaching phonics to improve Julissa's writing, we would be limiting the potential to teach and expand Julissa's literacy knowledge. Using mentor texts, modeled and shared writing experiences, teachers can expand on many of the skills Julissa is exhibiting. For example, Julissa included dialogue in her writing sample, but did not include quotation marks. To teach this skill, several books could be identified to teach the many ways writers use various tools to demarcate dialogue, such as quotation marks or speech bubbles. As students read texts, they can be directed to find more examples and mark them with sticky notes. After making these written elements visible in the reading of texts, it is important to teach this explicitly through modeled or shared writing so that students can see and hear the teacher think through and demonstrate how to use quotation marks or dialogue bubbles in meaningful writing experiences. After several experiences, students can be encouraged to include dialogue in their narrative writing utilizing dialogue bubbles in their illustrations or quotation marks in their writing. In sum, considering a student's bilingualism when evaluating their writing provides much information about their literacy development that more accurately informs next steps for instruction.

Final Thoughts

The previous chapters provided a wealth of information about how teachers can use reading and writing connections to enrich learning experiences for all students. These ideas provide the basis for instruction and assessment that is meaningful and cohesive in classrooms with students from diverse learning and language backgrounds. And still, emergent bilingual learners, students who use and are developing in two (or more) languages, benefit from particular kinds of language support and instruction that should be intentionally integrated into reading—writing plans from the start, as we illustrated with the superstore project. We also provided a writing sample from a first grader to show the importance of using a multilingual and multicultural lens to learn about what students know and can do in writing and in reading. This lens can extend beyond the analysis of writing samples to leverage a curiosity about what students bring to the classroom. As teachers increase their understanding of the ways that academic reading and writing intersect with language and culture, they can expand on and fine-tune instruction that engages their students' unique abilities, experiences, and understandings.

To conclude, we offer the following suggestions and questions to help you connect to your practice:

- In your own school or classroom, reflect on your strengths and areas of growth related to supporting emergent bilingual learners. Is there additional information you need to gather to learn more about the emergent bilingual learners in your school?
- Select one or two key ideas from this chapter that will support you to enhance your instruction for emergent bilingual learners in your school or classroom. Plan to integrate this instruction into your daily classroom activities.
- Speak with at least two of your emergent bilingual learners to learn about their reading and writing abilities in their home language. Learn about their literacy practices in their home and encourage them to draw on those experiences in your classroom by incorporating reading materials and opportunities to write in the home language.
- Collect a writing sample from your emergent bilingual learners and analyze them using the holistic framework provided in this chapter. Analyze at the discourse and sentence/phrase levels and examine phoneme–letter relationships. How can this framework provide information about your students' reading ability and inform your reading and writing instruction?

REFERENCES

Archer, A. L., & Hughes, C. A. (2011). *Explicit instruction: Effective and efficient teaching.* New York: Guilford Press.

Baker, D. L., Good, R. H., Knutson, N., & Watson, J. M. (Eds.). (2006). *Indicadores Dinámicos del Éxito en la Lectura* (7th ed.). Eugene, OR: Dynamic Measurement Group. Retrieved from *https://dibels.uoreg on.edu/assessment.*

Baker, S., Lesaux, N., Jayanthi, M., Dimino, J., Proctor, C. P., Morris, J., . . . Newman-Gonchar, R. (2014). *Teaching academic content and literacy to English learners in elementary and middle school.* Washington, DC: National Center for Education Evaluation and Regional Assistance. Retrieved from *http://ies.ed.gov/ncee/wwc/publications_reviews.aspx.*

Bernhardt, E. (2003). Challenges to reading research from a monolingual world. *Reading Research Quarterly, 38*(1), 112–117.

Brisk, M. E. (2014). *Engaging students in academic literacies: Genre-based pedagogy for K–5 classrooms.* New York: Routledge.

Brisk, M. E., & Parra, M. O. (2018). Mainstream classrooms as engaging spaces for emergent bilinguals: SFL theory, catalyst for change. In R. Harman (Ed.), *Educational linguistics:* Vol. 33. *Bilingual learners and social equity.* Cham, Switzerland: Springer.

Butvilofsky, S. A., Escamilla, K., Gumina, D., & Silva Diaz, E. (2021). Beyond monolingual reading assessments for emerging bilingual learners: Expanding the understanding of biliteracy assessment through writing. *Reading Research Quarterly, 56*(1), 53–70.

Clay, M. M. (1975). *What did I write?* Portsmouth, NH: Heinemann.

Clay, M. M. (1991). *Becoming literate: The construction of inner control.* Portsmouth, NH Heinemann.

Cohen, E. G., & Lotan, R. A. (2014). *Designing groupwork: Strategies for the heterogeneous classroom* (3rd ed.). New York: Teachers College Press.

Escamilla, K., Hopewell, S., Butvilofsky, S., Sparrow, W., Soltero-González, L., Ruiz-Figueroa, O., & Escamilla, M. (2014). *Biliteracy from the start: Literacy Squared in action.* Philadelphia: Caslon.

García, O. (2009). *Bilingual education in the 21st century: A global perspective.* Hoboken, NJ: Wiley-Blackwell.

García, O., Johnson, S. I., Seltzer, K., & Valdés, G. (2017). *The translanguaging classroom: Leveraging student bilingualism for learning.* Philadelphia: Caslon.

García, O., & Kleifgen, J. A. (2018). *Educating emergent bilinguals: Policies, programs, and practices for English learners.* New York: Teachers College Press.

García, O., & Wei, L. (2014). *Translanguaging: Language, bilingualism and education.* London: Palgrave Pivot.

Genesee, F., & Riches, C. (2006). Literacy: Instructional issues. In D. August & T. Shanahan (Eds.), *Developing literacy in second-language learners* (pp. 109–175). Mahwah, NJ: Erlbaum and Washington, DC: Center for Applied Linguistics.

Gibbons, P. (2015). *Scaffolding language, scaffolding learning: Teaching English language learners in the mainstream classroom* (2nd edition). Portsmouth, NH: Heinemann.

Good, R. H., III, & Kaminski, R. A. (Eds.). (2002). *Dynamic indicators of basic early literacy skills* (6th ed.). Eugene, OR: Institute of the Development of Educational Achievement.

Gort, M. (2006). Strategic codeswitching, interliteracy, and other phenomena of emergent bilingual writing: Lessons from first-grade dual language classrooms. *Journal of Early Childhood Literacy, 6*(3), 323–354.

Grabe, W. (2003). Reading and writing relations: Second language perspectives on research and practice. In B. Kroll (Ed.), *Exploring the dynamics of second language writing* (pp. 242–262). New York: Cambridge University Press.

Grabe, W., & Zhang, C. (2013). Reading and writing together: A critical component of English for academic purposes teaching and learning. *TESOL Journal, 4*(1), 9–24.

Grosjean, F. (1989). Neurolinguists, beware! The bilingual is not two monolinguals in one person. *Brain and Language, 36*(1), 3–15.

Harklau, L. (2002). The role of writing in classroom second language acquisition. *Journal of Second Language Writing, 11*(4), 329–350.

Hirvela, A. (2004). *Connecting reading & writing in second language writing instruction.* Ann Arbor: University of Michigan Press.

Hopewell, S. (2011). Leveraging bilingualism to accelerate English reading comprehension. *International Journal of Bilingual Education and Bilingualism, 14*(5), 603–620.

Hopewell, S., & Butvilofsky, S. (2016). Privileging bilingualism: Using biliterate writing outcomes to understand emerging bilingual learners' literacy achievement. *Bilingual Research Journal, 39*(3–4), 324–338.

Kim, J., Olson, C. B., Scarcella, R., Kramer, J., Pearson, M., van Dyk, D., . . . Land, R. E. (2011). A randomized experiment of a cognitive strategies approach to text-based analytical writing for mainstreamed Latino English language learners in grades 6 to 12. *Journal of Research on Educational Effectiveness, 4*(3), 231–263.

Menken, K., & Sánchez, M. T. (2019). Translanguaging in English-only schools: From pedagogy to stance in the disruption of monolingual policies and practices. *TESOL Quarterly, 53*(3), 741–767.

National Governors Association Center for Best Practices & Council of Chief State School Officers. (2010). *Common Core Standards for English language arts and literacy in history/social studies, science, and technical subjects.* Washington, DC: Authors.

Newell, G. E. (2006). Writing to learn: How alternative theories of school writing account for student performance. In C. A. MacArthur, S. Graham, & J. Fitzgerald (Eds.), *Handbook of writing research* (pp. 235–247). New York: Guilford Press.

Office of English Language Acquisition. (2021, January). *Fast facts: Profiles of English learners in the United States.* Retrieved from *https://ncela.ed.gov/sites/default/files/fast_facts/DEL4.4_ELProfile_508_1.4.2021_OELA.pdf.*

Parris, H., Estrada, L., & Honigsfeld, A. (2016). *ELL frontiers: Using technology to enhance instruction for English learners.* Thousand Oaks, CA: Corwin Press.

Piazza, S. V., Rao, S., & Protacia, M. S. (2015). Converging evidence for culturally responsive literacy practices: Students with learning disabilities, English language learners, and socioculturally diverse learners. *International Journal of Multicultural Education, 17*(3), 1–20.

Pressley, M., & Allington, R. L. (2014). *Reading instruction that works: The case for balanced teaching.* New York: Guilford Press.

Shanahan, T. (2006). Relations among oral language, reading, and writing development. In C. A. MacArthur, S. Graham, & J. Fitzgerald (Eds.), *Handbook of writing research* (pp. 171–183). New York: Guilford Press.

Smith, B. E., Pacheco, M. B., & Khorosheva, M. (2020). Emergent bilingual students and digital multimodal composition: A systematic review of research in secondary classrooms. *Reading Research Quarterly, 56*(1), 33–52.

Soltero-González, L., Escamilla, K., & Hopewell, S. (2012). Changing teachers' perceptions about the writing abilities of emerging bilingual students: Towards a holistic bilingual perspective on writing assessment. *International Journal of Bilingual Education and Bilingualism, 15*(1), 71–94.

Vernon, S., & Ferreiro, E. (1999). Writing development: A neglected variable in the consideration of phonological awareness. *Harvard Educational Review, 69*(4), 395–416.

CHAPTER 15

Addressing the Needs of Students Who Struggle with Literacy

Michael A. Hebert
Pamela Shanahan Bazis
Tanya Santangelo

Students with reading difficulties often have difficulty with writing skills (Graham et al., 2021; Hebert, Kearns, Baker Hayes, Bazis, & Cooper, 2018). Similarly, students with specific writing difficulties, such as spelling and handwriting, have been shown to have difficulty with word reading (Berninger et al., 2002). Although this may seem obvious due to the reciprocal nature of reading and writing, some important questions to consider are these: "What are the specific underlying processes that might be impacting writing–reading connections? Do all students who struggle with writing–reading connections struggle for the same reasons?"

The purpose of this chapter is to describe why students who struggle with literacy often have difficulties with writing–reading connections and to offer recommendations for how teachers can help them. Throughout the chapter, we use the phrase *students who struggle with literacy* to refer to students—with and without disabilities—who experience challenges with writing, reading, and/or literacy more broadly.

Within this chapter, we synthesize trustworthy research findings so that teachers can focus their attention on implementing effective instruction. We attempted to distill the research for teachers and provide clear recommendations to save teachers valuable time. We systematically searched scholarly databases for relevant reviews of research published between 1980 and 2020. Then, we identified the instructional practices that were consistently cited as being effective for students who struggle with literacy. The chapter is organized to address the following questions:

GUIDING QUESTIONS

- Do students with reading difficulties also have writing difficulties, and vice versa?
- Why do students who struggle with literacy have difficulties with writing–reading connections?
- How can teachers help students who struggle with literacy build stronger writing–reading connections?

Do Students Who Struggle with Reading Also Struggle with Writing, and Vice Versa?

Before teachers can address the difficulties experienced by students who struggle with literacy, it is important to identify what specific challenge(s) an individual student is experiencing—and why. Indeed, not all students who struggle with literacy have trouble with the same reading and/or writing skill(s)—or for the same reason(s). Thus, a critical first step is for teachers to assess each student's areas of strength and need, so they can design instruction that builds on the former and bolsters the latter (see also Chapter 7, this volume, on assessment). That said, we describe some of the challenges students with literacy difficulties frequently experience, vis-à-vis writing–reading connections, and we discuss some of the common reasons for these difficulties.

First, students with reading difficulties often struggle with writing. In a meta-analysis of 87 studies comparing students with reading difficulties to typically developing peers matched on age, Graham and colleagues (2021) found that students in K–12 with reading difficulties scored well below their same-age peers on overall measures of writing. They also scored lower on many specific measures of writing, including writing output (e.g., total number of words written), organization, sentence skills, vocabulary, syntax, handwriting, and writing quality, with the largest differences found for spelling. Another alarming finding from this research is that students who struggled with reading also performed lower in writing than younger peers who were matched for reading ability level. In other words, the *younger readers* scored higher than the older struggling readers on writing outcomes, despite having the *same reading ability*. This suggests that students who struggle with reading fall behind even further in writing than they do in reading.

Similar findings have been found for students identified with learning disabilities broadly (not just those specifically with reading disabilities, per se). For example, in a meta-analysis of 53 studies, students with learning disabilities in grades K–12 scored lower than their typically developing peers on output, organization, sentence skills, vocabulary, syntax, handwriting, spelling, and writing quality (Graham, Collins, & Rigby-Wills, 2017). Additionally, the authors found that students with learning disabilities also scored lower than their peers on measures of genre elements, and, importantly, on motivation for writing.

It is also true that students with specific writing difficulties sometimes have difficulty with reading. In an examination of the relationships between reading and writing, Berninger and colleagues (2002) identified that handwriting and spelling skills predicted reading skills in early grade levels, and that writing fluency significantly predicted reading comprehension in later elementary grades. Additionally, difficulties with specific writing skills may help indicate which reading skills kids may have difficulty with at specific grade levels. In other words, identifying the specific skills students are struggling with may help teachers understand why they might be having difficulties with writing–reading connections.

Why Do Students Who Struggle with Literacy Have Difficulties with Writing and Reading Connections?

There are two primary reasons why students who struggle with literacy might have difficulties with connections between writing and reading: (1) Deficits in one skill might impact how students use the other skill, and (2) both skills might be impacted by a common underlying process.

First, many students have difficulty with writing–reading connections due to how difficulties in one skill might impact students' ability to use the other. For example, a student with reading difficulties may have difficulty reading and evaluating their own writing to make revisions. According to Hayes (1996), accurate reading skill is necessary to correct grammatical as well as meaning errors in writing. In other words, students with poor reading skills may not be able to identify their own writing errors. On the other hand, students with poor writing skills may not be able to effectively use writing as a tool to organize their ideas when recording information from reading, such as when note taking or summarizing.

Second, it is sometimes the case that both difficulties are due to a similar underlying cause. Reading and writing are not exactly the same, but have been described as "two buckets drawing water from a common well or two buildings built on a common foundation" (Shanahan, 2016, p. 195; see also Chapters 1 and 5, this volume). In other words, difficulties in writing–reading connections may be related to difficulties in common underlying processes (Graham & Hebert, 2010, 2011), such as orthographic awareness. If a student has difficulty with orthographic awareness (e.g., understanding letter patterns that are used to represent specific sounds, and sometimes multiple sounds), the difficulty may affect their ability to read words with those letter patterns (e.g., *though*, *through*), and also to spell those words.

These interrelationships between reading and writing are also the central idea in the interactive dynamic literacy model proposed by Kim (2020; see also Chapter 2, this volume), which illustrates that reading and writing are interconnected and that difficulties in the skills may co-occur due to difficulties in:

- Shared component skills (word reading, spelling, handwriting)
- Foundational literacy skills (orthography, morphology, phonology)
- Oral language skills
- Executive function skills and general cognition (e.g., working memory)
- Higher-order cognition (e.g., goal setting, monitoring, perspective taking)
- Content or discourse knowledge (e.g., the type of language to use when talking about history or social studies)
- Social-emotional skills (beliefs, attitudes, self-concept)

Another area, procedural knowledge, or understanding the steps or procedure required for a specific strategy, has also been identified as a possible area of shared knowledge (Graham et al., 2017). In the next section, we provide specific examples related to foundational skills, oral language, content knowledge, and other difficulties to better illustrate the skill-based and process-based challenges students may face and how they inhibit their writing–reading performance.

Foundational Literacy Skills Example

One example of a common foundational skill is phonological awareness. Phonological information needed for decoding words when reading is also needed for encoding when spelling. Therefore, a learner who has difficulty sounding out words due to a weakness in phonological awareness is also likely to have difficulty spelling words (Hebert et al., 2018; see also Chapter 2, this volume). This would look like a difficulty in blending sounds when reading, whereas it might look like a difficulty segmenting individual sounds when spelling. Because of the difference in how the phonological information is used, not all students who have difficulty with blending sounds also have difficulty with segmenting sounds. However, if a student has difficulty with underlying phonological awareness, this difficulty could manifest as a difficulty in both skills.

Oral Language Skills Example

In many cases, it may be that students struggling with literacy have challenges with similar skills due to relationships with underlying oral language difficulties (see also Chapter 4, this volume). In a meta-analysis of 39 studies comparing students with language difficulties to age-matched peers, Graham and colleagues (2021) found that students with language difficulties scored lower on measures of writing quality, writing output, grammar, written vocabulary, and spelling. The differences were smaller, but still substantial, when students with language difficulties were compared to younger peers with similar language skills. These findings suggest that underlying language difficulties may be a potential reason for writing difficulties. For example, students with smaller oral vocabularies may have difficulty identifying words to more accurately convey their ideas in writing. Similarly, students with reading difficulties have also been found to have significant deficits in oral language skills such as nonword repetition, receptive vocabulary, receptive grammar, recalling sentences, and past-tense production, when compared to students without reading problems (Duff, Hayiou-Thomas, & Hulme, 2012). Consequently, students may not be able to comprehend text that includes many unfamiliar vocabulary words, even if they decode them accurately.

Content or Discourse Knowledge Example

Difficulties with content or discourse knowledge might also cause difficulties with writing–reading connections. Some students who struggle with literacy may have specific difficulties with informational text due to lack of exposure (see Duke, 2000; Moss & Newton, 2002; Bogaerds-Hazenberg, Evers-Vermuel, & van den Bergh, 2021). Without sufficient exposure to informational text, students who struggle with literacy may not develop an understanding of the purposes or goals of informational text writing communities (Graham, 2018), organizational structures used for presenting information (Hebert et al., 2018), or signal words and transition words commonly used (Meyer, 1985; Williams & Pao, 2011; Wijekumar, Meyer, & Lei, 2012; see also Chapter 6, this volume). Additionally, they may lack domain-specific background knowledge and vocabulary needed when reading or writing about specific informational content (Hebert, Bazis, Bohaty, Roehling, & Nelson, 2021; see also Chapter 3, this volume). These deficits may impact students when they read informational text, as well as when they write it.

Procedural Knowledge Example

Students who struggle with literacy may also have difficulty with procedural knowledge related to how or when to use reading comprehension strategies. For instance, they may have trouble making inferences based on information provided across a text (which might involve connecting information in the beginning of the text with additional information provided later), making appropriate predictions, or summarizing information. This type of difficulty can lead to similar procedural difficulties for students when writing their own texts. Those challenges may be twofold. First, they will not know how to proceed with the task and what pockets of knowledge to utilize. Second, they will have trouble thinking through processes other readers might need to use in order to make sense of their writing within a given discourse. Specifically, students who struggle with literacy might have difficulty when trying to consider how their audience might interact with their text. This could include difficulties with understanding how to address questions their audience may have, consider predictions their audience might make, use language to help foster visualization, or provide their audience with a short summary that might help them.

Other Difficulties

In addition to the areas we have provided examples for thus far, some students who struggle with literacy may face challenges with executive function skills, beliefs and attitudes, self-regulation, and so on. We don't have space to go into depth on all of the reasons students may have difficulty with writing–reading connections, so our recommendation for teachers is to consider that children may have difficulty connecting writing and reading skills for one or more underlying reasons. In some cases, students may be having difficulty learning for a combination of reasons. Therefore, it is important to consider those reasons for each of our students, and let that drive the instruction, intervention, and accommodations teachers and specialists might make.

How Can Teachers Help Students Who Struggle with Literacy to Build Writing and Reading Connections?

The ways in which writing, reading, and foundational literacy skills interact is complex. To understand how these complex skills may overload students at time, it is useful to think of component reading and writing skills as multiple devices plugged into a single electrical outlet. Although it is often convenient and efficient to use one nearby outlet to plug in many devices, this practice can sometimes draw too much power, overload the circuit, and result in a blown fuse or tripped circuit breaker. Once this happens, no device can work and all will remain offline until you get to the fuse box.

The electrical outlet is analogous to the cognitive resources young readers and writer have available to them and need to draw from when they engage in writing and reading tasks. Those resources include the foundational literacy skills students need to use at any given moment, including word identification, phonological awareness, decoding/encoding, orthographic knowledge, ideation, and the like. If students have to allocate a lot of attention and working memory resources to one skill, then the cognitive resources (or energy) available to put toward other skills may be impacted. For instance, if a student needs to put a lot of effort into decoding individual words, they may not have as many cognitive resources to apply to comprehension (LaBerge & Samuels, 1974). In other words, when asking students to complete reading and writing tasks together in the same activity, we may overload their cognitive "circuit." Much like the outlet in our example, kids might become frustrated and shut down in some cases.

To avoid overloading students, teachers can learn from the strategies we use to keep ourselves from overloading a circuit in our homes. In some cases, we reduce the load on the circuit by intentionally using fewer devices in a single electrical outlet at once (i.e., don't run the hair dryer and microwave at the same time). Other times, we find alternate power sources when we need to use many devices at once (e.g., using outlets on a different circuit). We may also try to use more efficient devices that draw less power.

Similarly, it may be helpful for teachers to consider instructional strategies for building writing–reading connections as relying on three principles:

1. **Isolate skills (use fewer devices at once).** Effective instructional strategies can reduce cognitive load on students by isolating and working on a specific skill or set of skills, one at a time.

2. **Provide supports or accommodations (use alternate power sources).** Supports or accommodations can reduce cognitive load by assisting students when they may need to draw on multiple skills at once.

3. **Strengthen connections among skills (to improve efficiency).** Strengthening students' writing–reading connections, and helping them use one skill to support the other, can make reading and writing more efficient.

These principles can help teachers contemplate how instruction may impact the cognitive burden placed on students who struggle with literacy during writing and reading activities.

In our next sections, we provide more specific instructional recommendations for teachers to improve writing–reading connections. We organize our recommendations in terms of the writing–reading connections teachers can foster by: (1) using writing to support reading; (2) teaching reading to support writing; and (3) providing interventions that integrate reading and writing skills to support the development of both skills. In each section, we provide general instructional recommendations based on our reviews of the literature, and then highlight instructional principles that should be followed when implementing the recommendations. Finally, we include two in-depth examples for each section (one example for younger students and one example for older students).

Teaching Writing Skills to Improve Reading

Research has shown that writing can be effective for improving reading (Graham & Hebert, 2010, 2011; Hebert, Gillespie, & Graham, 2013). For example, having students write about text can improve reading comprehension. Research also indicates that these effects may actually be stronger for students who struggle with literacy. However, one caveat is that such students may not benefit from writing about reading unless instruction is also provided, whereas students who do not struggle may benefit from simply being asked to write. Therefore, our recommendations are centered on providing instruction when using these approaches.

Recommendations for Teaching Writing to Improve Reading

Our first recommendation is to teach students to write about text they read. Effective writing tasks include summary writing, taking notes, writing questions, writing answers to questions, and writing extended responses to text (Graham & Hebert, 2010, 2011). When having students who struggle with literacy write about the text they are reading, teaching them to employ a specific writing strategy or process may increase their understanding of the text. For example, having students take structured notes results in larger effect sizes than having students take notes without an organizational structure. Similarly, having students use a specific summary strategy (e.g., writing a one-sentence summary after each paragraph, teaching summarization rules) has been found to be effective for poor readers. Teaching students these types of strategies is akin to providing supports when using these skills together.

Our second recommendation is to teach students foundational writing skills (such as spelling and sentence writing) that relate to corresponding reading skills (such as word reading and sentence reading fluency). This can be thought of in terms of the principle of isolating specific skills. Isolating and teaching specific writing skills can improve the corresponding reading skills, even if reading is not specifically taught during the instruction. For example, teaching spelling skills was shown to improve phonological awareness and word reading skills in a meta-analysis involving 53 studies, 12 of which included students with significant learning disabilities (Graham & Santangelo, 2014). Squires and Wolter (2016) found that teaching orthographic patterns during spelling instruction also improved the orthographic knowledge of students with specific reading disabilities, which is a foundational component of reading. Additionally, instruction in spelling and sentence writing skills has been effective for improving reading fluency and reading comprehension (Graham & Hebert, 2010, 2011). While many of the studies examined by Graham and Hebert did not specifically involve students who struggle with literacy, the studies that included such students also led to positive gains in reading comprehension, word reading, and reading fluency.

Although isolating specific writing skills during instruction can be effective for improving reading skill, it may also help to follow up such instruction by making the connections between writing and reading explicit for students who struggle with literacy. For example, when teaching students to write different types of sentences, it may be beneficial to show students how authors have used similar sentence types in their reading material. This can provide students with authentic examples. Similarly, when teaching students to spell words with specific spelling patterns, having them find those words in their reading material can reinforce the connections between writing and reading. Such strategies rely on the principle of strengthening connections among skills.

A third recommendation is to teach multicomponent writing interventions (Graham & Hebert, 2011). These include writing interventions combining activities like process writing and skills instruction. This recommendation is based on a limited number of studies and resulted in smaller impacts for students, perhaps because the instruction was somewhat less targeted, or that generalization to reading was not specifically taught. However, it does suggest that multicomponent writing interventions may lead to gains in reading even when reading outcomes are not the specific focus.

Instructional Tips for Using Writing to Support Reading

In addition to the three recommendations for using writing to support reading, students who struggle with literacy may benefit from specific types of instruction or supports. For example, explicit instruction and specific strategies enhance the benefits of this instruction. Additionally, peer-assisted learning, small-group instruction, and progress monitoring all enhance academic interventions for students with learning difficulties (Dietrichson et al., 2020). Therefore, we also recommend incorporating these instructional practices when using writing to support reading for students who struggle with literacy.

Example Activity for Younger Students: Sentence Combining

Many strategies that are effective for younger students may also be effective for older students who are far behind their peers. That said, isolating and working on foundational skills may have the highest utility with younger students. One effective strategy for teaching writing skills that improve reading skills is sentence combining (Saddler, 2006). Sentence combining can be used to help students understand how to write and read sentences with a variety of grammatical features (such as adjectives or compound subjects), or it can be used to teach different sentence types (such as compound or complex sentences). Sentence combining involves combining two or more kernel sentences to create a more complex sentence. Here is an example with adjectives that might be used with third- or fourth-grade students who struggle with literacy:

Kernel 1: *Crocodiles use their jaws to catch prey.*
Kernel 2: *Their jaws are powerful.*
Combined Kernels: *Crocodile use their powerful jaws to catch prey.*

We recommend applying the following steps from Goodrich, Hebert, Saviano, and Andress (2020) using the crocodile example as a guide (see Figure 15.1 for the illustrated example):

1. Introduce the skill. In the example, read the two kernels aloud and discuss how both kernel sentences tell us something about the jaws of a crocodile, so the information could go together into a single sentence.

2. Model the skill.
   a. Perhaps identify the word *jaws* in both sentences, then circle the adjective used to describe crocodiles' jaws.

b.   Next, draw arrows from the adjective to the space before the word *jaws*, while explaining that we use adjectives before the word they describe.

c.   Read the adjective aloud before the word: "powerful jaws." This will help show the connection between oral language and writing.

d.   Next, rewrite the sentence with the adjective before the noun and point out that the adjective goes before the noun.

3. Teach students to reread the sentence aloud after they have written it. This will reinforce the connection between writing and reading. Also have the students read their written sentences with peers to give and receive feedback to reinforce the writing concepts.

4. Provide a lot of practice opportunities to help students become efficient at sentence writing and avoid overloading students' "circuits."

   This example illustrates how to utilize explicit instruction with microstrategies (circling and drawing arrows), and combining those with small-group work, peer assistance, and progress monitoring. The instructional focus is writing, but this practice will reinforce reading skills and has been shown to improve reading fluency. The same instructional approach can be used for any type of sentence-combining exercise.

Example for Older Students: Summarization Strategies

One example of a strategy that can be used with older learners is summarization. When teaching students who struggle with literacy to summarize multiparagraph texts, it can be helpful to teach them to first write a one-sentence summary for each paragraph, and then use the sentences to put together the summary (e.g., Doctrow et al., 1978). To teach this strategy, use the following steps:

1. Talk to students about how breaking longer texts into smaller parts can help with comprehension. Help them comprehend that paragraphs are an easy way to identify places to stop and summarize.

2. Explain that you are going to show them a trick for stopping to write a short summary after each paragraph to help yourself remember the entire passage.

3. Model.
    a.   Read paragraph 1 aloud. Stop to think aloud about the most important person or thing in the paragraph, and what was important about it.
    b.   Model writing your summary sentence.
    c.   Repeat Steps a and b with additional paragraphs.

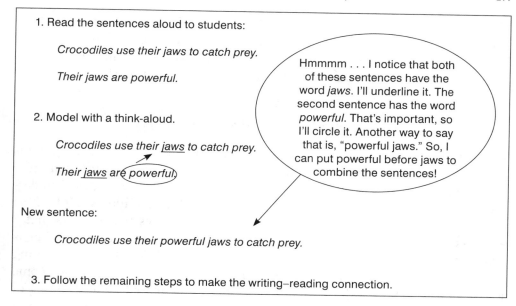

1. Read the sentences aloud to students:

    Crocodiles use their jaws to catch prey.

    Their jaws are powerful.

2. Model with a think-aloud.

    Crocodiles use their <u>jaws</u> to catch prey.

    Their <u>jaws</u> are powerful.

    Hmmmm . . . I notice that both of these sentences have the word *jaws*. I'll underline it. The second sentence has the word *powerful*. That's important, so I'll circle it. Another way to say that is, "powerful jaws." So, I can put powerful before jaws to combine the sentences!

New sentence:

    Crocodiles use their powerful jaws to catch prey.

3. Follow the remaining steps to make the writing–reading connection.

FIGURE 15.1. Model of sentence combining with think-aloud and visual supports.

d. When you've completed the summary statements for each paragraph, model reading all of your summary statements aloud, in succession.

e. Add transition words or phrases that might help to connect the statements and make them more cohesive.

f. Discuss whether your summary captures the important information from the passage. Connect this to self-evaluation of writing.

Doctrow et al. (1978) found that older students who struggle with literacy benefited even more from this approach when they were provided with one or two important words from the passage to help them with their summary of each paragraph. We recommend using that approach as an initial scaffold, and then fading the scaffold as the students get more proficient with the strategy.

Teaching Reading Skills to Improve Writing

Reading instruction has also been shown to enhance writing skills (Graham et al., 2018). More specifically, foundational literacy skills instruction (e.g., phonological awareness, phonics) is effective in improving students' spelling skills (Ehri, 2000; Graham et al., 2021; Share, 1995). Reading comprehension strategies also help students access crucial information and strategies necessary for writing (Graham et al., 2018; Suggate, 2016). Finally, having students read the writing of others, provide feedback on the writing of their peers, and observe other readers as they discuss material also impact writing outcomes

(Graham et al., 2011; Graham et al., 2018; Philippakos & MacArthur, 2016). When teaching specific reading skills to improve writing, it is important to keep in mind the principles of isolating skills and strengthening connections among skills to improve efficiency and to avoid "overloading the circuit."

Recommendations for Teaching Reading to Improve Writing

Our first recommendation is to provide foundational skills for reading (Graham et al., 2018) by isolating specific skills. Providing explicit reading instruction in phonemic awareness and phonics skills can improve students' understanding of how the words work (Ehri, Nunes, Stahl, & Willows, 2001; Ehri et al., 2001). For example, instruction in phonics teaches the students that a sound corresponds with a specific letter or group of letters. This knowledge is crucial for reading and spelling unknown words. Additionally, by providing reading instruction, students will have strategies to draw on when they come across an unknown word. When students have an increased understanding of alphabetic principles and strategies, they can make connections to read and spell unknown words with less effort.

Second, increase the amount of time students spend reading words (Graham et al., 2018). This can improve students' spelling and writing quality. Furthermore, repeated practice with manageable chunks can increase automaticity (Kubina & Morrison, 2000; Logan, 1997). Connecting back to our overcrowded outlet analogy again, we can reduce the amount of power needed by increasing students' automaticity and efficiency.

Our third recommendation is to read the writing of others. This can include opportunities for peer conferencing and for offering feedback to peers (Graham et al., 2018). Asking students to read the writing of others and provide feedback has been shown to improve the writing outcomes of the student giving the feedback (Graham, Harris, & Hebert, 2011; Philippakos & MacArthur, 2016). Students also benefit from watching other readers discuss text (Graham et al., 2018; Moore & MacArthur, 2012). The reader providing feedback has the opportunity to think about the effectiveness of ideas being presented and understand writing from the reader's perspective. These activities rely on the principle of strengthening the connections among writing and reading skills by giving students who struggle with literacy insights into how to become a more effective writer.

Instructional Tips for Using Reading to Support Writing

Whereas writing instruction involves the creation of a tangible written product, comprehension and thinking that occur during reading are a bit more covert. Teachers need to keep this in mind when providing reading support for students who struggle with literacy. Providing think-alouds, modeling, and rich discussion opportunities can help make the comprehension processes more concrete (Pressley et al., 1992).

Reading strategies for improving writing may also be enhanced by including instruction on related foundational skills. Younger students improved their writing skills (i.e., spelling), when provided with reading instruction in phonemic awareness, phonics (Graham et al., 2018), and orthographic patterns (Squires & Wolter, 2016). Additionally, alphabet knowledge (i.e., letter naming, letter sound, letter–sound fluency, letter writing) combined with phonological awareness instruction improved letter–sound outcomes (Piasta & Wagner, 2010).

Example for Younger Students: Phoneme Segmentation with Letter Supports

One foundational skill that has been found necessary for decoding is phonemic awareness (National Reading Panel, 2000). A specific strategy that can be used to help students who struggle with literacy increase phonemic awareness skills to improve their writing is *phoneme segmentation with letter supports*. Phoneme segmentation can be used to help students understand that words may be broken up into individual units of sound or phonemes, and by adding such letter supports, the students are able to associate individual sounds with the corresponding letter. Therefore, a strategy that includes both phoneme segmentation and graphemes (letter or letters representing a phoneme) provides an opportunity for students to manipulate phonemes and graphemes (Foorman et al., 2016; Kerstholt, van Bon, & Schreuder, 1994; Swanson & Hoskyn, 1998). Here is one way to use this strategy:

1. Introduce the letter–sound correspondences between the phoneme and 5 to 10 target letters. Provide each student with a three-dimensional plastic letter or tile of each of the target letters.

2. Provide repeated practice by first saying the phoneme, next have the student repeat the phoneme, and then slide the corresponding letter or letter tile forward. Continue repeated practice until students demonstrate an understanding of the letter–sound associations.

3. Model segmenting the phonemes in high-frequency words. Begin with two-phoneme words and increase the number of phonemes as student knowledge increases.
   a. Place 5 to 10 letters on a magnetic whiteboard (be sure they can be seen by all students).
   b. Next, draw two adjacent, horizontal boxes on the board.
   c. State the first word aloud and model segmenting the word, one phoneme at a time, by pushing the corresponding letters into the boxes.

For example, for the target word *so*, you would push the letter *s* into the first box while making the /s/ sound, followed by sliding the letter *o* into the second box while saying the long /o/ sound. This will help show the connection between the phoneme and grapheme.

    d. Write the word on the board below the boxes and then read the word aloud.

4. Next, direct the students to repeat the word and then segment each phoneme while sliding the corresponding grapheme into the correct box on their own whiteboard. Then, the students will write the word under the boxes. Finally, the students will read the word aloud.

5. Use guided practice techniques to provide repeated practice with additional two-phoneme words.

Example for Older Students: Reading to Understand the Audience Perspective

Some reading activities can be cleverly designed to help students who struggle with literacy develop audience awareness. This can help them anticipate the needs of their audience when writing. One way to do this is with texts describing two or more similar (but not the same) pictures or objects (adapted from Roehling-Flanigan, 2021; see Figure 15.2).

1. Show the students an array of similar pictures. Explain that they will need to identify the correct picture after reading a description.

2. Have the students read a paragraph that does not have enough information to clearly determine the target picture.

3. Next, ask students to discuss which picture might be the image that the author was trying to describe. The teacher and students should focus on identifying features that are well described and those that are not described (or not described in enough detail).

4. Have students choose which image they think is the target picture. Then, reveal the picture the author was actually writing about.

5. Discuss what the author could have included in their description to make it clearer.

    There is some evidence for this strategy, and we believe that it can be effective for older students with support provided. Teachers may want to scaffold by modeling and providing think-alouds, reading text aloud for students, and guiding the discussion carefully.

Read the paragraph below and identify the picture that the writer is describing.

In this picture there is a small house with a picket fence. The house has a rectangular-shaped door in the front. The front of the house also has a square-shaped window. Outside the house is a large oak tree. It is a beautiful day with the summer sun shining and puffy clouds cover the sky above the house.

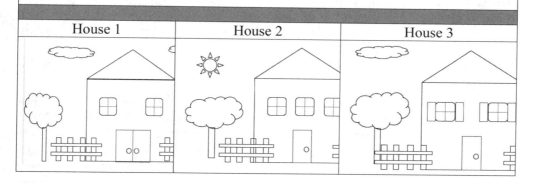

House 1	House 2	House 3

FIGURE 15.2. Example of an audience awareness task with an unclear paragraph.

Teaching Reading and Writing Together

Integrating reading and writing instruction is also effective for enhancing reading and writing for students who struggle with literacy. This is based on the principle of strengthening the connections among skills. In a meta-analysis comparing interventions in which writing and reading instruction were balanced (no more than 60% devoted to either), researchers found improvements for decoding, reading vocabulary, and reading comprehension, as well as for writing quality, writing mechanics, and writing output (Graham et al., 2018). Many of the studies involved students who had reading or writing difficulties, and the authors also found specific effects for remedial reading programs (Graham et al., 2018). Based on the findings of this and other reviews, we have several recommendations. At this point, we remind readers again about being careful not to "overloaded the circuit." When we are integrating reading and writing together, it may be like plugging multiple devices into an outlet, and it could lead to cognitive overload for students. Combining instruction for multiple skills is efficient for getting things done and increasing opportunities for learning, but we may be drawing more cognitive power. Therefore, we recommend being ready to provide scaffolds and supports for students who struggle with literacy when implementing these recommendations.

Recommendations for Integrating Writing and Reading Instruction

First, teach encoding (spelling) and decoding (phonics) together, and include instruction for other foundational literacy skills (see Chapter 2, this volume). In some cases, pairing spelling instruction with phonological awareness instruction, orthography instruction, and word-reading instruction have been found to be effective for improving spelling, word reading, and foundational skill outcomes (Graham et al., 2018; Wanzek et al., 2006; Weiser & Mathes, 2011; Williams, Walker, Vaughn, & Wanzek, 2017). The evidence suggests that teaching these skills together can have impacts for older learners as well as younger learners (Weiser & Mathes, 2011). Teaching these foundational reading skills together can help students understand the relationships between sounds, letters, word reading, and spelling, and may be more efficient than teaching the skills in isolation.

Second, teach complementary cognitive strategies for reading and writing. Results from two research reviews suggest that pairing a reading comprehension strategy with a writing strategy was effective for improving writing outcomes (Kang, McKenna, Arden, & Ciullo, 2015; Mason & Graham, 2008). In one strategy example, a reading strategy named TWA (Think before you read, think While you read, think After you read) was paired with a writing strategy called PLANS (Pick goals, List ways to meet goals, And make Notes, and Sequence notes). Both strategies were taught utilizing Self-Regulated Strategy Development (SRSD; see Chapter 8, this volume) and helped students use the strategies for meeting active reading comprehension and writing goals. The studies also support the use of mnemonics, goal setting, self-monitoring, and scaffolded instruction, and the results suggest that large gains can be made on reading and writing measures by pairing complementary cognitive strategies in this way (Kang et al., 2015).

Third, graphic organizers (GOs) can be used to integrate writing and reading for students who struggle with literacy. GOs can help students organize information, display concepts, and visualize relationships within the content presented (see Chapter 5, this volume). They can similarly be used when planning to write, and can capitalize on shared process knowledge. Swanson and Hoskyn (1998) found that older learners benefited from reading interventions that integrated social studies content while using GOs. Additionally, Ciullo and Reutebuch (2013) found promising results utilizing computer-based GOs (e.g., Inspiration) for students with learning disabilities.

Finally, teach informational text structures using reading and writing activities together to students who struggle with literacy (see also Chapter 6, this volume). Hebert and colleagues (2016) found that teaching text structures was effective for improving reading across 45 studies, especially when paired with writing instruction (29 studies). Five text structures are generally used by authors of informational text, including description, sequence of events, compare–contrast, problem–solution, and cause–effect. Students are less likely to have experience with informational text in early grades (Duke, 2000); this makes it more likely that difficulties with writing–reading connections will be exacerbated when reading or writing informational text. Additionally, students can be taught signal words to identify text structures and help with reading comprehension, as well as to include in their writing. Integrating reading and writing instruction around informational text structures may also lead to improvements in content knowledge.

Instructional Tips for Integrating Writing and Reading Instruction

As with our other recommendations, providing explicit instruction and strategy instruction is important. As we stated earlier, these recommendations do not isolate skills one skill at a time, so we need to provide students with supports. It is important to provide strong modeling, scaffolds, and guided practice opportunities. Progress monitoring and providing regular and consistent feedback can help teachers understand when to spend more time on specific writing–reading tasks and when to challenge students.

Example for Younger Students: Teach Spelling and Decoding Together

Deliberately teaching students to spell and read words simultaneously is simple, and it can make instruction more efficient. We recommend focusing on a specific word feature, such as specifics vowel patterns, blends, diagraphs, and so on.

1. Introduce the letter combination you will focus on (i.e., the orthographic pattern).
2. Introduce the sound or sounds that the letter combination represents.
3. Read words with the pattern and provide immediate corrective feedback or praise.
4. Ask students to spell words with the pattern (also providing immediate corrective feedback or praise).
5. Challenge students to find words with the orthographic pattern in context and use words with the orthographic pattern in their writing (set goals or turn the exercise into a game and track student progress).

Example for Older Students: Text Structure Instruction

When teaching text structures, it is helpful to teach students the features that are unique to each structure and can be used to enhance writing and reading (see Chapter 6, this volume).

1. Discuss the fact that authors of informational text often have one of five purposes: (a) to describe something, (b) to show a sequence of events or stages, (c) to compare and contrast two or more things or ideas, (d) to show problem–solution relationships, and (e) to show a cause–effect relationship.

2. Show students clear example texts for each text structure. It is also helpful to use GOs or charts to explicitly illustrate how the ideas are connected.
3. Introduce signal words associated with each text structure.
4. Model identifying text structures in novel texts and provide guided practice.
5. To reinforce comprehension, pair with taking notes or summarizing information based on the text structure (see Figure 15.3 for an example).
6. Have students write their own informational texts (using text structures and appropriate signal words).
7. Have students read their peers' writing and provide feedback to further support writing–reading connections.

Conclusion

By now, you may have noticed a theme across our recommendations. In each of the examples provided, the instructional approach utilizes both reading and writing skills to enhance the connection between them. Although reading can

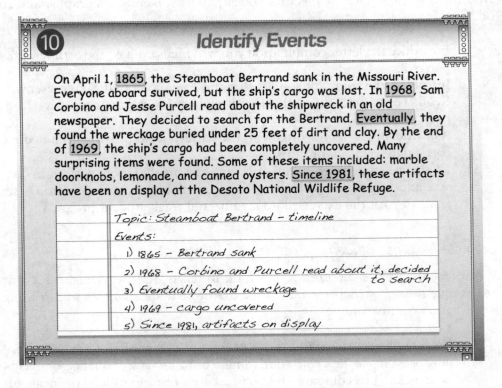

FIGURE 15.3. Example of note taking based on sequence text structure (with signal words).

be separated from writing, it may not be possible to completely separate writing from reading; Readers will intuitively read back what they wrote in many cases. Therefore, you may ask why we do not classify all of these strategies as "integrated writing and reading" instruction. Essentially, we agreed that the separation of strategies by the focus of instruction is useful to help teachers think about the objectives of their lessons. Thus, we separated the sections based on whether writing is the primary focus of instruction, reading is the primary focus of instruction, or there is more of a balance between writing and reading instruction [no more than 60% of instruction focused on either skill—Graham et al. (2018)].

We hope that our chapter has helped teachers to understand:

- that students who have difficulty in writing often also have difficulty with specific reading skills (and vice versa),
- the reasons why students who struggle with literacy might have difficulty with both reading and writing skills (such as shared underlying processes, lack of oral language skills, lack of domain knowledge, or lack of procedural knowledge), and
- specific ways to teach writing to improve reading; reading to improve writing; and integrating writing and reading to improve writing–reading connections for students who struggle with literacy.

In order to help students who struggle with literacy build writing–reading connections, we may be able to more effectively teach them by: focusing on a single skill; providing supports when they use multiple skills to reduce cognitive demands; and ultimately helping students strengthen connections among their skills so that they can use them more efficiently. By helping teachers choose strategies based on how they would like to use instruction of each skill to enhance the other (e.g., writing to support reading; reading to support writing), we hope this will help them consider why and how these writing–reading connections can be fostered effectively when working with students struggling with literacy.

To conclude, we invite you to consider the following action questions:

- Which instructional practices will you try out in your classroom?
- What resources will you need to teach the strategies and specific skills for reading and/or writing?
- How will you scaffold learning, add supports, or isolate skills during instruction to avoid "overloading the circuit"?

REFERENCES

Berninger, V. W., Abbott, R. D., Abbott, S. P., Graham, S., & Richards, T. (2002). Writing and reading: Connections between language by hand and language by eye. *Journal of Learning Disabilities, 35*(1), 39–56.

Bogaerds-Hazenberg, S. T., Evers-Vermeul, J., & van den Bergh, H. (2021). A meta-analysis on the effects of text structure instruction on reading comprehension in the upper elementary grades. *Reading Research Quarterly, 56*(3), 435–462.

Ciullo, S. P., & Reutebuch, C. (2013). Computer-based graphic organizers for students with LD: A systematic review of literature. *Learning Disabilities Research & Practice, 28*(4), 196–210.

Dietrichson, J., Filges, T., Klokker, R. H., Viinholt, B. C. A., Bøg, M., & Jensen, U. H. (2020). Targeted school-based interventions for improving reading and mathematics for students with, or at risk of, academic difficulties in grades 7–12: A systematic review. *Campbell Systematic Reviews, 16,* Article e1081.

Doctorow, M., Wittrock, M. C., & Marks, C. (1978). Generative processes in reading comprehension. *Journal of Educational Psychology, 70*(2), 109.

Duff, F. J., Hayiou-Thomas, M. E., & Hulme, C. (2012). Evaluating the effectiveness of a phonologically based reading intervention for struggling readers with varying language profiles. *Reading and Writing, 25*(3), 621–640.

Duke, N. K. (2000). 3.6 minutes per day: The scarcity of informational texts in first grade. *Reading Research Quarterly, 35*(2), 202–224.

Ehri, L. C. (2000). Learning to read and learning to spell: Two sides of a coin. *Topics in Language Disorders, 20*(3), 19–36.

Ehri, L. C., Nunes, S. R., Stahl, S. A., & Willows, D. M. (2001). Systematic phonics instruction helps students learn to read: Evidence from the National Reading Panel's meta-analysis. *Review of Educational Research, 71,* 393–447.

Ehri, L. C., Nunes, S. R., Willows D. M., Schuster B. V., Yaghoub-Zadeh, Z., & Shanahan, T. (2001). Phonemic awareness instruction helps children learn to read: Evidence from the National Reading Panel's meta-analysis. *Reading Research Quarterly, 36,* 250–287.

Foorman, B., Beyler, N., Borradaile, K., Coyne, M., Denton, C. A., Dimino, J., . . . Wissel, S. (2016). *Foundational skills to support reading for understanding in kindergarten through 3rd grade* (NCEE 2016–4008). Washington, DC: National Center for Education Evaluation and Regional Assistance, Institute of Education Sciences, U.S. Department of Education. Retrieved from *http://whatworks.ed.gov.*

Goodrich, J. M., Hebert, M., Saviano, M., & Andress, T. (2020). Effects of sentence-combining instruction for Spanish-speaking language-minority students: Evidence from two single-case experiments. *Elementary School Journal, 120.*

Graham, S. (2018). A revised writer (s)-within-community model of writing. *Educational Psychologist, 53*(4), 258–279.

Graham, S., Aitken, A., Hebert, M., Camping, A., Santangelo, T., Harris, K. R., . . . Ng, C. (2021). Do children with reading difficulties experience writing difficulties? A meta-analysis. *Journal of Educational Psychology, 113*(8), 1481–1506.

Graham, S., Collins, A. A., & Rigby-Wills, H. (2017). Writing characteristics of students with learning disabilities and typically achieving peers: A meta-analysis. *Exceptional Children, 83*(2), 199–218.

Graham, S., Harris, K., & Hebert, M. (2011). *Informing writing: The benefits of formative assessment.* Washington, DC: Alliance for Excellent Education.

Graham, S., & Hebert, M. (2010). *Writing to read: Evidence for how writing can improve reading.* A Carnegie Corporation Time to Act Report. Washington, DC: Alliance for Excellent Education. Retrieved from *www.carnegie.org/publications/writing-to-read-evidence-for-how-writing-can-improve-reading.*

Graham, S., & Hebert, M. (2011). Writing to read: A meta-analysis of the impact of writing and writing instruction on reading. *Harvard Educational Review, 81*(4), 710–744.

Graham, S., Liu, X., Aitken, A., Ng, C., Bartlett, B., Harris, K. R., & Holzapfel, J. (2018). Effectiveness of literacy programs balancing reading and writing instruction: A meta-analysis. *Reading Research Quarterly, 53*(3), 279–304.

Graham, S., Liu, X., Bartlett, B., Ng, C., Harris, K. R., Aitken, A., . . . Talukdar, J. (2018). Reading for writing: A meta-analysis of the impact of reading interventions on writing. *Review of Educational Research, 88*(2), 243–284.

Graham, S., & Santangelo, T. (2014). Does spelling instruction make students better spellers, readers, and writers? A meta-analytic review. *Reading and Writing, 27*(9), 1703–1743.

Hayes, J. R. (1996). A new framework for understanding cognition and affect in writing. In C. M. Levy & S. Ransdell (Eds.), *The science of writing: Theories, methods, individual differences and applications* (pp. 1–27). Mahwah, NJ: Erlbaum.

Hebert, M., Bazis, P., Bohaty, J. J., Roehling, J., & Nelson, J. R. (2021). Examining the impacts of the structures writing intervention for teaching fourth-grade students to write informational text. *Reading and Writing, 34*, 1711–1740.

Hebert, M., Bohaty, J. J., Nelson, J. R., & Brown, J. A. (2016). The effects of text structure instruction on expository reading comprehension: A meta-analysis. *Journal of Educational Psychology, 108*, 609–629.

Hebert, M., Gillespie, A., & Graham, S. (2013). Comparing effects of different writing activities on reading comprehension: A meta-analysis. *Reading and Writing, 26*(1), 111–138.

Hebert, M., Kearns, D. M., Baker Hayes, J., Bazis, P., & Cooper, S. (2018). Why children with dyslexia struggle with writing and how to help them. *Language, Speech, and Hearing Services in Schools, 49*(4), 843–863.

Kang, E. Y., McKenna, J. W., Arden, S., & Ciullo, S. (2015). Integrating reading and writing interventions for students with learning disabilities: A review of the literature. *Learning Disabilities Research & Practice, 31*(1), 22–33.

Kersholt, M. T., van Bon, W. H., & Schreuder, R. (1994). Training in phonemic segmentation: The effects of visual support. *Reading and Writing, 6*(4), 361–385.

Kim, Y.-S. G. (2020). Interactive dynamic literacy model: An integrative theoretical framework for reading and writing relations. In R. Alves, T. Limpo, & M. Joshi (Eds.), *Reading–writing connections: Towards integrative literacy science* (pp. 11–34). New York: Springer.

Kubina, R. M., Jr., & Morrison, R. S. (2000). Fluency in education. *Behavior and Social Issues, 10*(0), 83–99.

LaBerge, D., & Samuels, S. J. (1974). Toward a theory of automatic information processing in reading. *Cognitive Psychology, 6*(2), 293–323.

Logan, G. D. (1997). Automaticity and reading: Perspectives from the instance theory of automatization. *Reading & Writing Quarterly, 13*(2), 123–146.

Mason, L. H., & Graham, S. (2008). Writing instruction for adolescents with learning disabilities: Programs of intervention research. *Learning Disabilities Research & Practice, 23*(2), 103–112.

Meyer, B. J. F. (1985). Prose analysis: Purposes, procedures, and problems. In B. K. Britton & J. Black (Eds.), *Understanding expository text: A theoretical and practical handbook for analyzing explanatory text* (pp. 269–304). Mahwah, NJ: Erlbaum.

Moore, N. S., & MacArthur, C. A. (2012). The effects of being a reader and of observing readers on fifth-grade students' argumentative writing and revising. *Reading and Writing: An Interdisciplinary Journal, 25*(6), 1449–1478.

Moss, B., & Newton, E. (2002). An examination of the informational text genre in basal readers. *Reading Psychology, 23*(1), 1–13.

National Reading Panel. (2000). *Report of the National Reading Panel—Teaching children to read: An evidence-based assessment of the scientific research literature on reading and its implications for reading instruction.* Washington, DC: National Institute of Child Health and Human Development.

Philippakos, Z. A., & MacArthur, C. A. (2016). The effects of giving feedback on the persuasive writing of fourth- and fifth-grade students. *Reading Research Quarterly, 51*(4), 419–433.

Piasta, S. B., & Wagner, R. K. (2010). Developing early literacy skills: A meta-analysis of alphabet learning and instruction. *Reading Research Quarterly, 45*(1), 8–38.

Pressley, M., El-Dinary, P. B., Gaskins, I., Schuder, T., Bergman, J. L., Almasi, J., & Brown, R. (1992). Beyond direct explanation: Transactional instruction of reading comprehension strategies. *The Elementary School Journal, 92*(5), 513–555.

Roehling-Flanigan, J. (2021). *Evaluating the effects of a reader perspective-taking instructional strategy on the descriptive writing performance of children with a specific learning disability* (Publication No. 28650448) PhD dissertation, University of Nebraska—Lincoln. Available through ProQuest.

Saddler, B. (2006). Improving sentences via sentence combining instruction. *Language and Literacy Spectrum, 16*, 27–32.

Shanahan, T. (2016). Relationships between reading and writing development. In C. A. MacArthur, S. Graham, & J. Fitzgerald (Eds.), *Handbook of writing research* (2nd ed., pp. 194–207). New York: Guilford Press.

Share, D. L. (1995). Phonological recoding and self-teaching: Sine qua non of reading acquisition. *Cognition, 55*, 151–218.

Squires, K. E., & Wolter, J. A. (2016). The effects of orthographic pattern intervention on spelling performance of students with reading disabilities: A best evidence synthesis. *Remedial and Special Education, 37*(6), 357–369.

Suggate, S. P. (2016). A meta-analysis of the long-term effects of phonemic awareness, phonics, fluency, and reading comprehension interventions. *Journal of Learning Disabilities, 49*(1), 77–96.

Swanson, H. L., & Hoskyn, M. (1998). Experimental intervention research on students with learning disabilities: A meta-analysis of treatment outcomes. *Review of Educational Research, 68*(3), 277–321.

Wanzek, J., Vaughn, S., Wexler, J., Swanson, E. A., Edmonds, M., & Kim, A.-H. (2006). A synthesis of spelling and reading interventions and their effects on the spelling outcomes of students with LD. *Journal of Learning Disabilities, 39*(6), 528–543.

Weiser, B., & Mathes, P. (2011). Using encoding instruction to improve the reading and spelling performances of elementary students at risk for literacy difficulties: A best-evidence synthesis. *Review of Educational Research, 81*(2), 170–200.

Wijekumar, K. K., Meyer, B. J., & Lei, P. (2012). Large-scale randomized controlled trial with 4th graders using intelligent tutoring of the structure strategy to improve nonfiction reading comprehension. *Educational Technology Research and Development, 60*(6), 987–1013.

Williams, J. P., & Pao, L. S. (2011). Teaching narrative and expository text structure to improve comprehension. In R. E. O'Connor & P. F. Vadasy (Eds.), *Handbook of reading interventions* (pp. 254–278). New York: Guilford Press.

Williams, K. J., Walker, M. A., Vaughn, S., & Wanzek, J. (2017). A synthesis of reading and spelling interventions and their effects on spelling outcomes for students with learning disabilities. *Journal of Learning Disabilities, 50*(3), 286–297.

CHAPTER 16

Integrated Writing and Reading Instruction in College

Charles A. MacArthur

My eighth-grade English teacher assigned an essay a week, giving us a question or quote to consider and expecting a classically organized essay with a thesis at the end of the first paragraph, supporting paragraphs with topic sentences, and a conclusion. Because he took off a point for each error, I finally learned the rules for comma placement. I would be critical of the practice today, but I did learn to write fluently, and I ended the year with confidence that I could produce clearly organized, coherent text. Compared to the lack of instruction in writing from my other teachers, that experience was pretty good. I also remember writing a research paper for history class in 11th grade, though I don't recall the topic. A few days before it was due, I hit the library and took notes from a couple of encyclopedias and a few other available books, then wrote the paper the night before the deadline. I recall these assignments partly because I was asked to do so little writing in high school. Not surprisingly, I was unprepared for the demands of college writing. In my first college English class, I was expected to write literary analyses of short stories. In sociology, we read a book a week and wrote a three-page reaction paper every third week. I had no idea how to go about either of these tasks, though in both cases I figured it out more or less by the end of the semester.

As illustrated in my personal anecdote, college students are expected to read critically and integrate ideas from readings and class notes with their own ideas to produce original texts. In this chapter, I will focus on two areas of research on integrated reading and writing in college. First, I will discuss research on teaching students to read source materials critically and synthesize information from sources in their own compositions. Second, I will focus on students who are underprepared for college writing and reading and recent efforts to provide integrated reading and writing courses to prepare them for the challenges of college writing. As part of this second topic, I will discuss some research on instruction in developmental writing by my colleagues and myself.

GUIDING QUESTIONS

- ■ What knowledge and skills are needed for critical reading and writing tasks in college?
- ■ What strategies can help in the difficult process of synthesizing information across sources?
- ■ In this age of the Internet, how can we help students learn to evaluate the credibility of sources?
- ■ Which aspects of writing with sources do you think are most challenging for new college students, especially underprepared students?

Writing Using Sources

One central feature of academic writing is that it is based on reading the ideas of others in the field. This is true even for writing about single sources, such as answering questions about reading and writing summaries, both types of writing that have been shown to enhance content learning (Graham, Kiuhara, & MacKay, 2020) and reading comprehension (Hebert, Gillespie, & Graham, 2013). However, writing using multiple sources is more complex, requiring writers to synthesize the ideas from sources and their own thinking to produce a novel text with a new purpose, such as learning and demonstrating understanding, critiquing ideas, or formulating an argument.

A standards document from the Council of Writing Program Administrators (CWPA, 2014) explains four sets of knowledge and skills needed for these critical reading and writing tasks: rhetorical knowledge, critical thinking, strategies, and knowledge of conventions. Students need to develop rhetorical knowledge to analyze audience, author, and purpose and to apply that knowledge in critical reading and composing in varied genres across disciplines. They need to develop critical thinking to analyze, interpret, and evaluate sources, with evaluation of claims and evidence being especially important. To produce their own compositions, they then need to integrate ideas across sources and their own thinking. Students also need to develop a repertoire of strategies for planning, drafting, evaluating, and revising, as well as learning to work collaboratively. Finally, they need to develop their knowledge of conventions and how they vary across disciplines.

Flower (1994) described writing from sources as a sociocognitive task requiring integration of reading, writing, and rhetorical thinking. When reading to write, one needs to consider the rhetorical purposes of the source texts as well as one's own rhetorical purposes. For example, in reading a source for an argumentative essay, one must consider whether the author is trying to persuade readers to take a position or to explain both sides of an issue. Bereiter and Scardamalia (1987) developed a theoretical model of the development from knowledge-telling to knowledge-transforming approaches to writing during adolescence. Young writers tend to see writing as a process of writing down what they know or have read, or knowledge telling. As they develop, they begin to consider their rhetorical purposes and try to select and organize information to communicate their ideas to readers. The process of thinking about whether their audience will understand their content or agree with their ideas can lead students to question and clarify their content understanding and, thus, develop their knowledge through writing. Writing from sources is challenging, but also offers substantial opportunities for knowledge development and transformation. The demand for synthesis promotes learning as readers are pushed to consider how sources agree and disagree and why, as well as to integrate source information with their own understandings.

One influential theoretical framework (Spivey, 1990) includes three processes involved in synthesis writing: organizing, selecting, and connecting. These processes are highly recursive. Comprehension of sources involves construction of an organized set of main ideas, or gist; it also involves making connections to prior knowledge to create a coherent model of the content (Kintsch, 2004). Writers select ideas and information from sources that may be useful based on the purposes of their own writing. They may use organizational schemes and strategies to help in making connections across sources. As writers plan the organization of their own paper, they select content needed to achieve their own purposes and make the connections explicit in their writing. Imagine students writing arguments about a controversial public issue. The students need to be aware of arguments and counterarguments in the source texts and integrate them with their own thinking; if informative sources are used, they will read them looking for possible arguments and evidence. To synthesize the information, they may organize the arguments in a table or outline to look for connections, points of agreement and disagreement. To write their own arguments, they will select appropriate arguments and evidence to use and decide how to organize them to meet their own purposes. As this brief description shows, the three processes are used recursively throughout the reading and writing activities involved in producing a synthesis paper.

Another important aspect of writing using sources is analysis of the sources for author, publication, and context. Analysis of sources is necessary to evaluate credibility when deciding whether to use a source and also to consider authors' perspectives and potential biases when integrating sources. Wineburg (1991) analyzed the thought processes of historians as they use primary sources and found three key processes: sourcing, contextualization, and corroboration. They pay attention to who wrote and/or published the document, consider the historical context, and seek corroboration in other documents. Several research groups (e.g., De La Paz & Wissinger, 2017; Nokes, Dole, & Hacker, 2007) have taught such strategies for source analysis to high school students and have found positive effects on their ability to write historical accounts and arguments. Wineburg and McGrew (2017) have applied their interest in source evaluation to the challenges of judging the credibility of sources on the Internet.

They found that even undergraduates from prestigious universities were unable to accurately judge the reliability of online sources. Based on comparison with the strategies used by professional fact checkers, they realized that such judgment requires checking the author and organization using other websites.

Instruction in Writing Using Sources

Because of the central importance of synthesis to academic writing and its potential to support learning, a number of instructional studies have focused on how to synthesize source material when writing. In a broad review of research on writing from sources, Cumming et al. (2016) concluded that students have difficulty integrating source material effectively in their compositions and that proficiency varies by prior experience, by writing in their first language (L1) or second language (L2), and by the demands of varied text types. The review included 16 studies of instruction in synthesis writing, including 11 with college students. Study quality was mixed; however, all studies did find positive effects on writing quality or the writing process.

A review of research on instruction in learning to write source-based synthesis compositions (van Ockenberg, van Weijen, & Rijlaarsdam, 2019) aimed to identify specific writing activities that helped students to select, organize, and connect ideas from sources. They selected 16 experimental or quasi-experimental instructional studies from middle school to college and analyzed the learning activities used in the six studies with the largest effect sizes. They identified eight learning activities that in various ways supported the processes of selection, organization, and connection. Some studies used tables and graphic displays to provide visual support for comparing sources, selecting main ideas, and organizing their own writing. Other activities involved answering questions on the main ideas of each source. In one study, students analyzed synthesis texts of varying quality to see how they were organized. The next three sections provide specific activities and strategies for note taking and synthesis emphasizing findings from studies with college students.

Text Structure and Genre

A common instructional activity was teaching students about text structures appropriate to the genres of writing involved. Often the text structure was accompanied by a graphic organizer (GO) representing the key elements of the structure. For example, a text structure for argumentative writing might be represented in a GO with places for the issue, position, reasons and evidence, counterarguments and rebuttals, and conclusion. Learning about text structures has been shown to enhance reading comprehension (Hebert, Bohaty, Nelson, & Brown, 2016) and writing (Englert, Raphael, Anderson, Anthony, & Stevens, 1991) (see also Chapter 6, this volume). Text structure or genre organization is also a common feature of most strategy instruction in writing. I will discuss two studies, one focused on the structure of arguments and the other on problem–solution essays.

Nussbaum and Schraw (2007) taught college students to integrate arguments on both sides of controversial issues to formulate their own positions and support them. Students learned to use an *argument vee diagram* (AVD), a concept map in an inverted V with a final conclusion or position at the top, supported by arguments and counterarguments, each supported by reasons. Students learned three ways to integrate conflicting arguments: refuting opposing arguments, weighing arguments to find the stronger side, and synthesizing arguments to generate a new alternative position. Students worked collaboratively to complete the AVDs. In addition to this text structure, instructors taught evaluation criteria for an argument with integration using sample papers and utilized a rubric with those criteria to give feedback. In a two-factor design, the researchers studied the separate and combined effects of the AVD and evaluation criteria. All treatment groups did better than controls; students using the AVD wrote essays with more refutations of counterarguments, while those learning evaluation criteria received higher scores for integration.

Zhang (2013), in a full semester study with L2 college students, taught students to write problem–solution and informative essays using sources from the Internet. Instruction included discussion of text structure, exercises making connections across sources, and peer review and teacher feedback based on an analytic rubric. Students had guiding questions to use as they read the sources, and class discussions focused on text structure and the main ideas of the sources. Connection exercises focused on finding common ideas for informative texts, but on connecting problems and solutions for the other genre. The analytic rubric included criteria for text structure, rhetorical patterns, use of sources, and language. The overall quality of problem–solution writing improved significantly more for treatment students than control students who received a comparable amount of reading and writing instruction not focused on problem–solution.

Both of these studies taught text structure as a central feature but using different methods. Nussbaum and Schraw (2007) used a graphic concept map to emphasize the importance of integrating arguments and counterarguments and actively considering the possibility of finding an integrated position. Zhang (2013) taught text structures for informative and problem–solution essays through class discussion of source texts, class exercises for making connections, and guided discussion of organizing their own papers. In both studies, students worked collaboratively to organize information for their essays; Zhang (2013) also included peer review. Both studies also included instruction in evaluation criteria for essays that included an emphasis on integration of source ideas. We will return to learning self-evaluation later, but first we need to turn to strategy instruction approaches.

Strategy Instruction

Strategy instruction in writing is based on the straightforward idea that students can learn to use cognitive and metacognitive strategies based on the strategies of proficient writers. Most strategy instruction in writing includes strategies for planning based on text structures or genres (Englert et al., 1991; MacArthur, 2011). Strategies for evaluation and revision are also included in some studies. In addition to specific writing strategies, since the goal of strategy instruction is for students to use the strategies independently, instruction often includes metacognitive strategies for self-regulation, as in the Self-Regulated Strategy Development (SRSD) model (Harris & Graham, 2009). Extensive research on strategy instruction has provided knowledge about pedagogical methods for teaching strategies, including explicit explanation, modeling with think-aloud procedures to make the processes visible, guided and collaborative practice, and gradual release of responsibility. Extensive research has demonstrated the positive effects of strategy instruction on the quality of writing (Graham, Harris, & Chambers, 2016).

In a study by Mateos and colleagues (2018), college students learned a strategy for writing an argumentative essay based on two texts presenting opposing positions on an issue. As in Nussbaum and Schraw (2007), the goal was to integrate opposing perspectives to generate an alternative position. Students learned a basic text structure for an argument—position, arguments, evidence, counterarguments. They also learned a strategy with four stages: (1) exploring and identifying the arguments from both positions, (2) contrasting positions, (3) drawing an integrative conclusion, and (4) organizing and revising the final draft. A written strategy guide provided a worksheet with a graphic organizer (GO) and questions to answer. For example, phase A had questions about the position and arguments on both sides, and a GO with space for reasons and evidence and evaluation arguments on both sides. Phase B included questions about how each side would refute the other; students were directed to draw arrows to connect arguments on both sides. The study compared a control group that used the written guide with a treatment group that received full strategy instruction, including the written explanation and modeling using a video of writers working collaboratively. Both groups worked collaboratively on two essays. The treatment group wrote essays that included more arguments and better integration of conflicting information.

The study by Mateos et al. (2018) was followed by a study (Granado-Peinado, Mateos, Martin, & Cuevas, 2019) that added one instructional component: explicit explanation and modeling of strategies focused on the collaboration processes. Thus, students in the full treatment condition received a written explanation of strategies, video modeling of both the writing strategies and collaboration in thinking about the arguments, and collaborative practice. The two conditions from Mateos et al. (2018) were included plus a control group that collaborated but received no instruction. Adding instruction in strategies for collaboration led to better performance on integration of conflicting information; as in the earlier study, both strategy + video modeling groups did better than other groups on both integration and argument inclusion.

A study by Raedts and colleagues (2017) also used video modeling of a strategy, but it asked a different question about what is needed to learn a strategy. Raedts et al. (2017) offered video modeling of the strategy to all students, but only the treatment group received explicit explanations of the strategy steps. In a psychology class, students wrote a literature review based on sets of notes about three studies with conflicting results. The strategy included locating the topic, comparing results of the studies, generating arguments for contradictory results, outlining the paper, drafting, and evaluating the draft. The video modeling seen by all students showed the work in progress and audio of the writer thinking aloud. In the explicit instruction treatment condition, slides were added that briefly explained the steps of the strategy. The treatment condition had positive effects on students' knowledge of the writing task and the quality of writing.

Taken together, the three studies (Granado-Peinado et al., 2019; Mateos et al., 2018; Raedts et al., 2017) show that explicit explanation of the writing strategies, collaboration with instruction in how to collaborate, and think-aloud modeling all contribute to better learning.

Learning Evaluation Criteria

In this section, I discuss two studies that emphasized discussion of sample texts, including student and published texts, and learning evaluation criteria and applying them to their own writing.

Boscolo et al. (2007) taught synthesis writing in a 12-session workshop connected to an undergraduate psychology course in an Italian university. At pretest and posttest, students wrote synthesis papers about contrasting theories of psychological constructs (e.g., motivation, creativity) and completed a questionnaire about writing beliefs. Instruction included discussion of the features of a good synthesis paper (i.e., evaluation criteria), analysis of good and weak samples of student papers, revision of students' own pretests, analysis of good published synthesis articles, writing about a topic covered in their psychology class, receiving teacher feedback, and revising their paper. Students' synthesis papers improved from pretest to posttest on organization, cohesion, and use of source information, though not on a measure of source integration. Beliefs about writing did not change.

In her own teacher-education course, Segev-Miller (2004) taught students to write literature reviews of research on reading and writing instruction. Instruction included discussion of published literature reviews and reviews written by students. The teacher and students collaboratively developed evaluation criteria including features such as organizational structure, content, interpretation and integration, citations. These evaluation criteria were used for self-evaluation, and students kept process logs (journals) about their reading and writing processes and products. Instruction also included strategies for selecting, organizing, and integrating content from sources. Students wrote literature reviews at the beginning and end of the semester. To make the task authentic, students were given multiple published research articles and had 3 weeks to write their reviews at both times. The reviews were evaluated by the instructor and an independent researcher; posttests were substantially better. Qualitative content analysis of students' process logs and self-assessments found improvements in discourse synthesis strategies and in accurate self-assessments.

Though these two studies did not use experimental methods, the overall finding of the value of teaching self-evaluation is supported by a significant body of research on writing instruction (see meta-analyses by Graham, Hebert, & Harris, 2015; Hillocks, 1984). Research on peer review with instruction in evaluation (Cho & MacArthur, 2011; MacArthur, 2016; Philippakos & MacArthur, 2016) provides further support. The two studies in this section (i.e., Boscolo et al., 2007; Segev-Miller, 2004) offer more detailed information on ways to use analysis of sample synthesis papers, discussion of strategies, and application of evaluation criteria for revision over an extended period to improve knowledge and performance.

Summary

Several instructional approaches have been found effective in teaching students to write using sources. Learning about the text structures of genres of writing supports students in generating and organizing content as they plan. The effects of instruction in text structure can be enhanced by combining it with the instructional methods of strategy instruction, including explicit explanation of strategies, think-aloud modeling, collaborative practice, and gradual release of responsibility. Strategy instruction is more effective if it includes strategies for metacognitive self-regulation. Collaboration in the process of writing, including discussion of ideas during planning and peer review for revision, can further enhance strategy instruction. Finally, learning evaluation criteria through analysis of sample synthesis papers and applying those criteria when revising also helps students to learn how to write more effective papers.

Writing synthesis papers is challenging for most college students, and the research reviewed here has involved typical college students. In the next section, I discuss research on integrating reading and writing instruction for a different population of college students, those who are underprepared for college work and participating in programs variously called basic writing, developmental writing, or even remedial.

Integrated Reading and Writing in Developmental Education

In the United States, 2-year community colleges with open admissions and low tuition offer college opportunities for many students who could not afford or meet entrance criteria for more competitive colleges. Based on entrance assessments, many students are found to be underprepared and placed in developmental courses in reading, writing, or math. Statistics vary by study, but approximately 30% of students are placed in developmental writing and/or reading (Bailey, Jeong, & Cho, 2010; Chen, 2016); about 60% take developmental math. Many are required to take multiple development courses before qualifying for first-year composition (FYC). Although students who complete the sequence of developmental courses do as well as other students in FYC and future progress in college (Bailey et al., 2010; Chen, 2016), many students drop out before then.

In response to poor outcomes for developmental students, community colleges and state agencies have tried a range of new policies and practices (Hodges et al., 2020). Colleges increasingly have supplemented placement tests with other measures, usually high school grade-point average, to reduce overplacement in developmental education. Some colleges have adopted corequisite courses, in which students take FYC in combination with a support course. Other reforms have restructured courses to accelerate progress through developmental education by combining courses, often by integrating separate developmental reading and writing courses. The rationale for such combined courses has included the logic for integration of reading and writing (supported throughout this book), as well as the opportunity to reduce the number of required developmental courses. A recent national survey (Rutschow, Cormier, Dukes, & Cruz Zamora, 2019) found that 67% of community colleges continue to offer separate reading and writing courses, while 64% offer integrated reading and writing. In what follows, I discuss what research has found about how well such courses work and what it takes to make them work.

Comparing Integrated Reading and Writing to Separate Reading and Writing Courses

Two studies found different results for integrated reading and writing (IRW) courses, and the contrast is informative. One study (Edgecombe, Jaggars, Xu, & Barragan, 2014) investigated a program at Chabot College, a community college with an established program that offered students the option of taking separate developmental reading and writing courses or an integrated course. Looking at transcripts over 12 years and using statistical methods to control for differences between students who chose between the two options, they found that students in the IRW course were more likely to pass FYC (60 vs. 40%) and to graduate (25% vs. 18% after 5 years). Based on qualitative analysis of interviews with faculty, administrators, and students and classroom observations, the researchers concluded that the positive effect was due to careful planning of the course to align it with the demands of FYC.

The contrasting study (Paulson & Van Overschelde, 2019) investigated changes over time when Texas implemented a policy requiring all colleges to offer IRW developmental courses. Based on transcripts from multiple colleges before and after the new policy, they compared students who took separate reading and writing, just reading, or just writing, with those taking IRW courses. Controlling for differences in student factors (demographics, tests, GPA), they found that students taking the separate courses were more likely to pass FYC or other reading-intensive courses. The researchers attributed the results to the fact that students in the IRW course had fewer credit hours. However, the same was true in the Chabot College study. Another explanation is that faculty were mandated to integrate courses with limited planning time, rather than being engaged in long-term planning motivated by a belief in the value of such integration.

This interpretation is supported by a qualitative study (Bickerstaff & Raufman, 2017) of faculty efforts to design IRW courses in response to state reform efforts in two states. They contrasted faculty groups taking "additive" versus "integrative" approaches to course design. In the additive approach, faculty attempted to include learning activities from the separate courses, which had been taught by different instructors. The faculty reported that there was not enough time for all the content and worried that they were not teaching all the skills necessary for college. Faculty groups that took a more integrative approach focused more on preparation for FYC and writing in other courses. They emphasized text-based writing and embedded skills and strategies within these larger tasks. This qualitative study and the comparative success of the program at Chabot reinforce the importance of high-quality instruction. Structural reform in course offerings is not sufficient.

Although the studies of IRW courses just discussed provide valuable information on the importance of careful planning and alignment with the demands of FYC, they did not study specific instructional methods. Few studies have systematically evaluated the effects of instructional methods on student outcomes. A review of research on instruction for developmental reading and writing (Perin & Holschuh, 2019) found 30 studies, but only two were experimental studies with control groups; the rest were descriptions of teaching methods or pretest–posttest only studies. Both of the experimental studies involved IRW. One of the experimental studies (Perin, Bork, Peverly, & Mason, 2013) evaluated the effects of supplementary materials completed outside of the developmental class and designed to improve IRW skills. The materials guided students through a series of 12 activities for reading an expository text, writing a summary, and writing an opinion essay on the topic. The study found small to moderate effects on two measures of students' summaries: inclusion of main ideas and accuracy of those ideas. The other experimental study was from work by my colleagues and myself on strategy instruction, the Supporting Strategic Writers (SSW) project (MacArthur, Philippakos, & Ianetta, 2015; Traga Philippakos & MacArthur, 2020) that I now turn to in the next section.

Supporting Strategic Writers

For the past 10 years, the SSW project has been working with developmental writing programs to design and evaluate instructional approaches based on strategy instruction with self-regulation (Harris & Graham, 2009; MacArthur, 2011) and practices common in college composition. The early years of the project focused on teaching students to write essays in multiple genres (e.g., argument, personal narrative, causal explanation, comparison) based on their own background knowledge but without using sources. In two experimental studies (MacArthur et al., 2015; MacArthur, Traga-Philippakos, May, & Compello, 2022), we found very large effects on the quality of writing. We also found positive effects on motivation, particularly on self-efficacy or confidence in one's writing ability. Since 2017, we have extended our instructional approaches to encompass the goal of writing using sources, which requires the integration of reading and writing. For success in college, students need to read source materials critically and synthesize information across sources to write their own compositions in multiple disciplines. An experimental study (MacArthur, Traga-Philippakos, & May, 2021) with 23 instructors and 243 students at two community colleges found a moderate to strong effect on the quality of argumentative essays using two source articles. However, no effects were found on self-efficacy. A more recent study (Nefferdorf, 2020) evaluated a version of the curriculum adapted for a compressed developmental course that met 4 days a week for 4 weeks; instruction had a large effect on quality of argumentative essays with sources.

The goals of the SSW approach are consistent with standards for college writing (Council of Writing Program Administrators, 2014)—that students will develop knowledge of academic genres, strategies for critical reading and writing, and motivational beliefs that support continued learning. The instructional methods include many of the components discussed in the current chapter and supported by research on writing from sources. First, the strategies for critical reading and for writing are based on genres and text structure; students learn about the purposes and text structures of genres and use that knowledge to plan and organize ideas for writing and to identify main ideas when reading. Second, SSW follows the pedagogical principles of strategy instruction, including explanation and modeling of strategies, guided and collaborative practice, and gradual release of responsibility. Metacognitive self-regulation is promoted using a set of Strategies for Academic Success (SAS), including goal setting, task management, progress monitoring, and reflection. Finally, students also learn to evaluate their own writing using genre-specific rubrics for peer review and self-evaluation. In the next few paragraphs, I provide more explanation of the components and reflect on how each component contributes to the overall success of the curriculum.

The reading and writing strategies are based on rhetorical knowledge of genres (Rose & Martin, 2012) and the cognitive processes of proficient writers (Flower, 1994; Hayes, 1996). More specifically, they are based on research on text-structure strategies for expository writing (Englert et al., 1991) and reading comprehension (Hebert et al., 2016). The rhetorical purposes and organizational elements of genres guide both reading and writing processes. For planning, students analyze the rhetorical situation—topic, audience, and purpose—choose an appropriate genre, and use knowledge of the organizational elements of that genre to generate and organize ideas using graphic organizers (GO). Evaluation for revision is guided by rubrics based on the elements of the genre. The critical reading strategies similarly involve rhetorical analysis followed by identification of main ideas based on the genre elements. Notes are taken on a GO in students' own words and used to write summary–response papers, which prepare them to integrate sources in their own essays.

Consider the example of argumentative writing. Arguments can be used to persuade or to analyze problems and generate solutions. Either way, they have some common elements: a controversial issue, the author's position with reasons and evidence in support, an alternative position with reasons and evidence, refutation of alternative reasons, and a conclusion.

Students begin by analyzing the writing task and generating their own ideas on the topic before reading. The SSW writing strategy leads students to analyze the rhetorical situation—topic, audience, purpose, and organization. For an argument, students would then generate reasons and evidence on both sides using a simple T-chart based on their own knowledge. They would proceed to use a GO with spaces for all the elements of an argument; the GO guides them in selecting and organizing appropriate content. If writing without sources, they would go on to draft the essay following the plan on the GO.

The writing task becomes more complex when using sources. Critical reading is supported by a strategy for writing a summary–response essay. We chose summary–response for SSW for several reasons. First, summary writing has been shown to enhance reading comprehension (Hebert et al., 2013). Second, adding a response requires students to critically evaluate the ideas in the source and connect them to their own ideas. Finally, summary–response tasks are common in college courses. Like the writing strategy, the summary–response strategy begins with rhetorical analysis. Students preview the source and note the topic, author and publisher, audience, purpose, and organization (same as for planning plus author). For the topic, they ask themselves what they already know about it, if they have not already done so in preparing for the writing task. Students then read closely, stopping frequently to monitor their understanding. Assuming the source is itself an argument, then students would look for the argument elements, annotating the text and taking notes in their own words on an argument GO (see Figure 16.1). The GO has spaces for a position and alternative position, reasons and evidence presented on each side, any refutations. For each reason/evidence section, there is also a space for students' critical comments, which might be about the strength of the evidence or the students' own ideas. The structure focuses the note taking on the most important ideas—ideas that the student might later use in writing. Taking notes in one's own words also helps to avoid plagiarism. After the reading and note taking, students use the notes to write a summary paragraph. The curriculum includes a structure as well as sentence frames to assist in this summary writing. For example, the first sentence should give the author's name and article title and the overall thesis. When writing the response paragraph, students can use the notes on their reactions from the GO. Note that it is not necessary for students to write summary–response papers every time they write an essay with sources. We think that learning to write such papers enhances students' ability to read deeply and evaluate sources critically in light of their own views. But only the notes on the GO are needed to integrate ideas when writing their own essays.

After reading multiple sources, students return to the writing strategy. They complete the rhetorical analysis and brainstorm their own ideas if they have not already done so. The process of integrating ideas across sources and their own ideas involves comparison of the notes on the GOs. Students look for agreement and disagreement across the source articles and their own thoughts.

TAAPO and Graphic Organizer

Taking Notes to Write a Summary Response Paper

Analyze using TAAPO:

Topic:

Author and source:

Audience:

Purpose:

Organization (elements):

Citation:

Issue/Problem:

Author's position (or central idea)

Reasons (or main points)	Key evidence (or supporting details)	Comments for response

Opposing position (if present)

Opposing reasons	Support/evidence	Rebuttal	Comments for response

FIGURE 16.1. Graphic organizer for the summary–response strategy.

They formulate their own position and an alternative position and use the argument-writing GO to select reasons and evidence on both sides and refutations of opposing arguments; they add a code for which source (or their own knowledge) was used for each idea. This GO is then followed when drafting. Students are encouraged to elaborate as they write and even to change their minds if writing produces new thoughts.

As noted earlier, the SSW methods include an emphasis on learning self-evaluation. The process of learning to evaluate begins early in each unit of instruction. As a new genre is introduced, the first activity is a discussion of the purpose of the genre and examples of when and why it might be used. In the same class period, the class discusses a well-written example, that is, a well-developed student paper, beginning with the open question about what makes it good and proceeding to examine it using the genre-specific rubric. Then the rubric is applied to evaluate a weaker example and to consider how it might be improved. Later in the unit after students have written their own papers, they learn how to engage in peer review through collaborative evaluation with the instructor of essays by unknown peers. Research shows that giving feedback to peers, even without receiving any, can improve students' writing (Cho & MacArthur, 2011; Philippakos & MacArthur, 2016). When students give feedback and make suggestions for improvement, they are doing exactly what they need to do to self-evaluate their own writing (Philippakos, 2017). This same process of peer review is used to evaluate both essays and summary–response papers.

I noted earlier that SSW also includes a set of Strategies for Academic Success (SAS). These are metacognitive self-regulation strategies using terminology common to college support services. SAS include four strategies that make sense if applied across the process of each writing assignment: goal setting, task management, progress monitoring, and reflection. Students set goals for the next writing task, manage when and where to work and what strategies to use, monitor their use of strategies, and once the task is done and evaluated, reflect on their progress and set new goals. As is common in strategy instruction, instructors include these strategies in think-aloud modeling (Harris & Graham, 2009). In addition, in the college context, we support self-regulation by having students write about these issues in journals. For example, students might write about their goals for the course, how a particular strategy is working for them, or what they have done to get tasks done on time. The class then discusses the issue, which provides group support as students learn how to regulate challenging tasks.

Finally, in SSW, the pedagogical methods of strategy instruction are critical to success. Teaching writing strategies is not a new idea in college writing; most textbooks include some suggestions about strategies for planning and revising. However, in our experience, it is rare to see college instructors use think-aloud modeling to show students how to use strategies. One problem for strategy instruction is that the cognitive processes involved are invisible. Showing students how to take notes without revealing the thought processes is not as effective as using think-aloud modeling. It is challenging for teachers to stand in front of the class and think aloud while generating ideas and drafting text, but it is worthwhile. It is fine to get stuck and make mistakes; in fact, research shows that students learn more from models who get stuck and cope with problems than from experts who demonstrate a process without error (Traga-Philippakos, 2021). Collaborative writing is another way to make the cognitive processes visible, while engaging students actively and guiding their use of the strategies. In SSW, after instructor modeling, the teacher and students work collaboratively on the reading and writing tasks, with the students providing content while the instructor scribes, guides the process, and provides supportive feedback.

Concluding Comments

Academic writing almost always involves integrating ideas from reading. Learning to write compositions using ideas from multiple sources is a challenging but essential task in college. In every academic discipline, whether political science, psychology, literature, or physics, written texts are a primary part of the conversation that advances knowledge in the field. Students enter these conversations as novices, as I did in attempting literacy analysis in my first English class and responding to texts about social issues in sociology. Writing about what they are reading advances students' knowledge of the content of the field, its epistemological methods, and the genres used for communication.

Research on instructional methods for writing using sources at the college level is still relatively limited. More research is needed with beginning college students, particularly those placed in developmental classes. Many of these students need to develop both their reading and writing skills. Learning to write essays based on sources is a meaningful way to integrate reading and writing. Research on strategy instruction with self-regulation has shown promise, but more research is needed.

In addition, more research is needed to develop and evaluate instructional methods for teaching writing in the disciplines. The use of genre and text structure has clear relevance for disciplinary writing, as shown in the study on writing literature reviews in psychology (Segev-Miller, 2004). Disciplines have developed written genres to meet their rhetorical and epistemological purposes, and students must learn those genres to read papers in a field, write about them, or produce them.

Finally, although this chapter has maintained a focus on college writing, research with secondary students is equally relevant to the needs of many college students, and the instructional research with college students should be applied at the secondary level.

The research reviewed in this chapter supports instructional approaches that are somewhat more explicit than is common in college composition classes. As you are getting started with new approaches to teaching critical reading and note taking and synthesizing information from sources, consider the following action steps:

- What practices do you currently use? How can you incorporate think-aloud modeling and gradual release of responsibility to support students' learning?
- How do you currently help students learn to synthesize information from sources with their own ideas? I recommend reading some of the articles in the first section of the chapter, especially the one by van Ockenberg et al. (2019). For strategies for critical reading and note taking, you might visit the SSW website: *supportingstrategicwriters.org*. How can you use those resources to address critical reading, summarization, and synthesis?

ACKNOWLEDGMENTS

The research reported here was supported by the Institute of Education Sciences, U.S. Department of Education, through Grant No. R305A160242 to the University of Delaware. The opinions expressed are those of the author and do not represent views of the Institute or the U.S. Department of Education.

REFERENCES

Bailey, T., Jeong, D. W., & Cho, S.-W. (2010). Referral, enrollment, and completion in developmental education sequences in community colleges. *Economics of Education Review, 29,* 255–270.

Bereiter, C., & Scardamalia, M. (1987). *The psychology of written composition.* Hillsdale, NJ: Erlbaum.

Bickerstaff, S., & Raufman, J. (2017). *From "additive" to "integrative": Experiences of faculty teaching developmental integrated reading and writing courses* (CCRC Working Paper No. 96). New York: Community College Research Center. Retrieved from *https://eric.ed.gov/?id=ED577008.*

Boscolo, P., Arfè, B., & Quarisa, M. (2007). Improving the quality of students' academic writing: An intervention study. *Studies in Higher Education, 32,* 419–438.

Chen, X. (2016, September). *Remedial coursetaking at U.S. public 2- and 4-year institutions: Scope, experiences, and outcomes* (NCES 2001-405). Washington, DC: National Center for Education Statistics. Retrieved from *https://eric.ed.gov/?id=ED568682.*

Cho, K., & MacArthur, C. (2011). Learning by reviewing. *Journal of Educational Psychology, 103,* 73–84.

Council of Writing Program Administrators. (2014). WPA outcomes statement for first-year composition (v3.0). *Journal of the Council of Writing Program Administrators, 38*(1), 144–148.

Cumming, A., Lai, C., & Cho, H. (2016). Students' writing from sources for academic purposes: A synthesis of recent research. *Journal of English for Academic Purposes, 23,* 47–58.

De La Paz, S., & Wissinger, D. (2017). Improving the historical knowledge and writing of students with or at risk for LD. *Journal of Learning Disabilities, 50*(6), 658–671.

Edgecombe, N., Jaggars, S. S., Xu, D., & Barragan, M. (2014). *Accelerating the integrated instruction of developmental reading and writing at Chabot College* (CCRC Working Paper No. 71). New York: Community College Research Center. Retrieved from *https://academiccommons.columbia.edu/doi/10.7916/D8CZ359B*.

Englert, C. S., Raphael, T. E., Anderson, L. M., Anthony, H. M., & Stevens, D. D. (1991). Making writing strategies and self-talk visible: Cognitive strategy instruction in writing in regular and special education classrooms. *American Educational Research Journal, 28*, 337–372.

Flower, L. (1994). *The construction of negotiated meaning: A social cognitive theory of writing.* Carbondale: Southern Illinois University Press.

Graham, S., Harris, K., & Chambers, A. B. (2016). Evidence-based practice and writing instruction: A review of reviews. In C. MacArthur, S. Graham, & J. Fitzgerald (Eds.), *Handbook of writing research* (2nd ed., pp. 211–226). New York: Guilford Press.

Graham, S., Hebert, M., & Harris, K. R. (2015). Formative assessment and writing: A meta-analysis. *The Elementary School Journal, 115*, 523–547.

Graham, S., Kiuhara, S., & MacKay, M. (2020). The effects of writing on learning in science, social studies, and mathematics: A meta-analysis. *Review of Educational Research, 90*(2), 179–226.

Granado-Peinado, M., Mateos, M., Martin, E., & Cuevas, I. (2019). Teaching to write collaborative argumentative syntheses in higher education. *Reading & Writing, 32*, 2037–2058.

Harris, K. R., & Graham, S. (2009). Self-regulated strategy development in writing: Premises, evolution, and the future. *British Journal of Educational Psychology Monograph Series II, 6*, 113–135.

Hayes, J. R. (1996). A new framework for understanding cognition and affect in writing. In C. M. Levy & S. Ransdell (Eds.), *The science of writing* (pp. 1–27). Mahwah, NJ: Erlbaum.

Hebert, M., Bohaty, J. J., Nelson, J. R., & Brown, J. (2016). The effects of text structure instruction on expository reading comprehension: A meta-analysis. *Journal of Educational Psychology, 108*(5), 609–629.

Hebert, M., Gillespie, A., & Graham, S. (2013). Comparing effects of different writing activities on reading comprehension: A meta-analysis. *Reading & Writing, 26*, 111–138.

Hillocks, G. (1984). What works in teaching composition: A meta-analysis of experimental treatment studies. *American Journal of Education, 93*, 133–170.

Hodges, R., McConnell, M. C., Lollar, J., Guckert, D. A., Owens, S., Gonzales, C., . . . Shinn, H. B. (2020). Developmental education policy and reforms: A 50-state snapshot. *Journal of Developmental Education, 44*(1), 2–17.

Kintsch, W. (2004). The construction–integration model of text comprehension and its implications for instruction. In R. B. Ruddell & N. J. Unrau (Eds.), *Theoretical models and processes of reading* (5th ed., pp. 1270–1328). Newark, DE: International Reading Association.

MacArthur, C. A. (2011). Strategies instruction. In K. R. Harris, S. Graham, & T. Urdan (Eds.), *Educational psychology handbook*: Vol. 3. *Application to learning and teaching* (pp. 379–401). Washington, DC: American Psychological Association.

MacArthur, C. A. (2016). Instruction in evaluation and revision. In C. A. MacArthur,

S. Graham, & J. Fitzgerald (Eds.), *Handbook of writing research* (2nd ed., pp. 272–287). New York: Guilford Press.

MacArthur, C. A., Philippakos, Z. A., & Ianetta, M. (2015). Self-regulated strategy instruction in college developmental writing. *Journal of Educational Psychology, 107,* 855–867.

MacArthur, C. A., Traga Philippakos, Z. A., & May, H. (2021, March). *Basic writers and the challenges of writing from sources: Experimental study of a strategy instruction approach.* Paper presented at the Triannual Conference of Writing Research Across Borders, Xi'an, China.

MacArthur, C. A., Traga-Philippakos, Z. A., May, H., & Compello, J. (2022). Strategy instruction with self-regulation in college developmental writing courses: Results from a randomized experiment. *Journal of Educational Psychology.*

Mateos, M., Martín, E., Cuevas, I., Villalón, R., Martínez, I., & González-Lamas, J. (2018). Improving written argumentative synthesis by teaching the integration of conflicting information from multiple sources. *Cognition and Instruction, 36,* 119–138.

Nefferdorf, E. (2020). *Design, implementation and outcomes of a condensed curriculum for an accelerated developmental education English course.* Unpublished doctoral dissertation, University of Delaware.

Nokes, J. D., Dole, J. A., & Hacker, D. J. (2007). Teaching high school students to use heuristics while reading historical texts. *Journal of Educational Psychology, 99*(3), 492–504.

Nussbaum, E. M., & Schraw, G. (2007). Promoting argument–counterargument integration in students' writing. *Journal of Experimental Education, 76,* 59–92.

Paulson, E. J., & Van Overschelde, J. P. (2019). Accelerated integrated reading and writing: A statewide natural experiment. *Community College Journal of Research and Practice, 45*(1), 13–30.

Perin, D., Bork, R. H., Peverly, S. T., & Mason, L. H. (2013). A contextualized curricular supplement for developmental reading and writing. *Journal of College Reading and Learning, 43,* 8–38.

Perin, D., & Holschuh, J. P. (2019). Teaching academically underprepared postsecondary students. *Review of Research in Education, 43,* 363–393.

Philippakos, Z. A. (2017). Giving feedback: Preparing students for peer review and self-evaluation. *Reading Teacher, 71,* 13–22.

Philippakos, Z. A., & MacArthur, C. A. (2016). The effects of giving feedback on the persuasive writing of fourth and fifth-grade students. *Reading Research Quarterly, 51,* 419–433.

Raedts, M., Van Steendam, E., De Grez, L., Hendrickx, J., & Masui, C. (2017). The effect of different types of video modelling on undergraduate students' motivation and learning in an academic writing course. *Journal of Writing Research, 8,* 399–435.

Rose, D., & Martin, J. R. (2012). *Learning to write, reading to learn: Genre, knowledge, and pedagogy in the Sydney School.* Bristol, CT: Equinox.

Rutschow, E. Z., Cormier, M. S., Dukes, D., & Cruz Zamora, D. (2019, November). *The changing landscape of developmental education practices: Findings from a national survey and interviews with postsecondary institutions.* New York: Center for Analysis of Postsecondary Readiness. Retrieved from *https://eric.ed.gov/?id=ED600433.*

Segev-Miller, R. (2004). Writing from sources: The effect of explicit instruction on college students' processes and products. *Educational Studies in Language and Literature, 4*, 5–33.

Spivey, N. N. (1990). Transforming texts: Constructive processes in reading and writing. *Written Communication, 7,* 256–287.

Traga Philippakos, Z. A. (2021). Think aloud modeling: Expert and coping models in writing instruction and literacy pedagogy. *The Language and Literacy Spectrum, 31*(1), Article 1.

Traga Philippakos, Z. A., & MacArthur, C. (2020). Writing strategy instruction for low-skilled postsecondary students. In D. Perin (Ed.), *The Wiley handbook of adult literacy* (pp. 495–516). Hoboken, NJ: Wiley.

van Ockenburg, L., van Weijen, D., & Rijlaarsdam, G. (2019). Learning to write synthesis texts: A review of intervention studies *Journal of Writing Research, 10,* 401–428.

Wineburg, S. S. (1991). On the reading of historical texts: Notes on the breach between the school and the academy. *American Educational Research Journal, 28,* 495–519.

Wineburg, S., & McGrew, S. (2017). *Lateral reading: Reading less and learning more when evaluating digital information* (Working Paper No. 2017-A1). Stanford, CA: Stanford University.

Zhang, C. (2013). Effect of instruction on ESL students' synthesis writing. *Journal of Second Language Writing, 22*(1), 51–67.

Index

Note. f or t following a page number indicates a figure or table.

Academic English, 49

Activism, science literacy and, 229–231, 230f

Activism in the Curriculum model, 229–231, 230f, 240–241

African American Vernacular English (AAVE), 33, 132

Amazon rainforest, science literacy and, 231–233, 232t

Argument skills instruction, 62

Argument vee diagram (AVD), 315

Argumentation; *see also* Student discourse instruction

  developing skills in, 72–73

Argumentative writing

  college-level, 314–315

  scenario-based assessment of, 134

  Supporting Strategic Writers Project and, 321–323

Art of Teaching Writing, The (Calkins), 15

Ashton-Warner, Sylvia, 12

Assessment, 121–142

  formative, 122–127

  guiding questions, 121 (*see also* Diagnostic assessment)

  purposes for, 121–135

  questions about, 135

  summative and interim, 132–135

Audience

  analysis of, 312–313

  awareness of, 50, 107, 200, 215, 218, 234, 235

  emergent bilingual learners and, 269, 276, 279

  identifying, 150

  influencing, 240

  intended audience, 85, 234

  needs/reactions of, 85, 86, 182

  peer, 226

  science projects and, 218, 219t

  SRSD and, 145, 158

  SSW and, 322

  struggling students and, 293–294, 302, 303f

  variable, 235

Authorizing concept, 195

B

Bang, Molly, 188, 190f

Bay Area Writing Project, 14

Bernabei, Gretchen, 197, 199

Berninger, Virginia, 17

Black Lives Matter (BLM) movement, honoring, 192–193

Blending Genre, Altering Style: Writing Multigenre Papers (Romano), 197

Bloom, Becky, 59–60

BME structure, genres and, 110–111, 112t, 113

Book clubs, student motivation and, 185–186, 188

BookAsOutfits, 188, 190f

Brainstorm of words, 56–57

Building Our Best Future (Kuhn), 71

Burrows, Alvina Treut, 10, 12

C

California, whole language English language arts framework and, 15–16

Calkins, Lucy, 15

Chall, Jeanne S., 13

Checklists, in formative assessment, 123–124

Chunking instruction, 36–38

  in social studies, 217–218